31   75

Bad
Education

A series edited
by Lauren Berlant,
Lee Edelman,
Benjamin Kahan,
and Christina Sharpe

Bad
Education

Lee
Edelman

Why Queer Theory Teaches Us Nothing

DUKE UNIVERSITY PRESS Durham and London 2022

© 2022 Duke University Press
All rights reserved
Printed in the United States of America
on acid-free paper ∞
Designed by Aimee C. Harrison
Typeset in Garamond Premier Pro
and Century Schoolbook
by Westchester Publishing Services

LIBRARY OF CONGRESS
CATALOGING-IN-PUBLICATION DATA
Names: Edelman, Lee, [date] author.
Title: Bad education : why queer theory
teaches us nothing / Lee Edelman.
Other titles: Why queer theory teaches
us nothing | Theory Q.
Description: Durham : Duke University
Press, 2022. | Series: Theory Q | Includes
bibliographical references and index.
Identifiers: LCCN 2022002026 (print)
LCCN 2022002027 (ebook)
ISBN 9781478015970 (hardcover)
ISBN 9781478018629 (paperback)
ISBN 9781478023227 (ebook)
Subjects: LCSH: Queer theory. | Homo-
sexuality—Philosophy. | Homosexual-
ity—Social aspects. | BISAC: LITERARY
CRITICISM / Semiotics & Theory |
SOCIAL SCIENCE / LGBTQ Studies /
General
Classification: LCC HQ76.25 .E34 2022
(print) | LCC HQ76.25 (ebook) |
DDC 306.7601—dc23/eng/20220613
LC record available at https://lccn.loc.
gov/2022002026
LC ebook record available at https://lccn.
loc.gov/2022002027

Cover art: Mr. Chips. Photograph by the
author.

For Joe,
Always

And in memory of Lauren Berlant,
my coeditor on Theory Q,
my collaborator on *Sex, or the Unbearable*,
and, above all, my beloved friend

Contents:

We all love to instruct, though we can teach only what is not worth knowing.

—ELIZABETH BENNET in Jane Austen, *Pride and Prejudice*

We place no trust in altruistic feeling, we who lay bare the aggressivity that underlies the activity of the philanthropist, the idealist, the pedagogue, and even the reformer.

—JACQUES LACAN, "The Mirror Stage as Formative of the *I* Function as Revealed in Psychoanalytic Experience"

It is better to fail in teaching what should not be taught than to succeed in teaching what is not true.

—PAUL DE MAN, "The Resistance to Theory"

To impose the same "Evil Spirits" on the white man and on the black man is a major error in education. If one is willing to understand the "Evil Spirit" in the sense of an attempt to personify the *id*, the point of view will be understood.

—FRANTZ FANON, *Black Skin, White Masks*

Preface:

As I prepare to send this book off to press in the last week of June 2020, two recent events in the United States compel me to add this brief preface. That fact might seem surprising insofar as *Bad Education* argues for a structural understanding of queerness and not, like much current work in the field, a primarily historical or ethnographic one. Without minimizing the value of scholarship that traces the cultural, political, legal, medical, erotic, affective, and communal experiences of those whom contemporary discursive regimes increasingly describe as *queer*, this book, like my earlier work in queer theory, reads queerness in the context of Lacanian psychoanalysis and de Manian rhetorical theory. While revising those two conceptual frameworks through a sustained encounter with queerness, it also puts them in dialogue with recent theorists of Afropessimism who draw on, extend, or respond to those psychic and linguistic inflections of the social. Notwithstanding their many profound and consequential differences, these critical perspectives share a common approach to political and ethical questions that centers, mutatis mutandis, on the subject's Symbolic determination. To that extent, though never divorced from the pressures of current events, they conceive those events as effects of a structure that demands an account as rigorous as those that engage its local expressions. Each produces a distinctive take on the "human" as linguistically determined, but both affirm an indissoluble link between politics and ontology, where the latter, which interrogates the order of being, follows from the subject's linguistic formation and the former contests the ontology of the "human" to define and control a community.

Given this book's commitment to thinking queerness in such a context, how could contingent historical events have generated this preface? To answer that question, let me sketch those events and suggest their relation to each other. Insistently, through the early weeks of June, protesters, first in the United States and then around the world, took to the streets in anger over the killing of George Floyd, an African American man accused of passing a fraudulent $20 bill and murdered on May 25, 2020, while being taken into police custody. Despite his urgent calls for assistance (like so many Black Americans before him, his appeal—"I can't breathe"—was in vain), Floyd died of cardiopulmonary arrest induced by the force of a policeman's knee pressing into on his neck for an unendurable eight minutes and forty-six seconds, an act of brutality that continued not only after Floyd lost consciousness but also for almost a minute and a half after the paramedics arrived on the scene.[1] The depraved indifference of those who killed him rekindled already smoldering rage over the deaths of Ahmaud Arbery, Sandra Bland, Michael Brown, Philando Castile, Dominque Fells, Eric Garner, Balantine Mbegbu, Elijah McClain, Tony McDade, Riah Milton, Tamir Rice, Breonna Taylor, and hundreds upon thousands of other Black persons killed in acts of anti-Black violence either sponsored or tolerated by the state.

By mid-June, despite warnings against large-scale gatherings during the COVID-19 pandemic, the demonstrations, now stretching from coast to coast, had drawn crowds that were angry, diverse, and large, as well as largely peaceful. Responding to looting and property destruction on the fringes of the protests, however, government officials responded with force: the National Guard and law enforcement at the state and federal levels were mobilized to reassert control; President Donald Trump and Attorney General William Barr initiated and sanctioned violence against protesters gathered lawfully in Washington's Lafayette Park; and more than ten thousand protesters were arrested, while perhaps two dozen others were killed.

Amid all this, on June 15, the Supreme Court announced its decision in *Bostock v. Clayton County*. It determined, by a vote of six to three, that the Civil Rights Act of 1964, passed in response to earlier demonstrations against anti-Black terror and police brutality, made firing "an individual merely for being gay or transgender" unlawful because Title VII prohibits employers from discriminating on the basis of "sex."[2] Both the majority and the dissenting opinions invoked the "ordinary meaning" of *sex*: the former to assert that animus against lesbian, gay, and transgender individuals presupposes that certain "traits or actions" befit only a given sex, and the latter to claim a categorical difference between *sex* and *sexual orientation*.[3] Notwithstanding

Justice Samuel Alito's dissent, obtuse in its heterosexist gloss on dictionary definitions of *sex*, arguments about the meaning of that word did not determine the court's decision. The majority opinion asserted, instead, that however conservative one's definition of *sex* (and Alito's could hardly be more so: "the division of living things into two groups, male and female, based on biology"), discrimination on the basis of transgender status or sexual orientation necessarily rests on normative expectations about how sex should be expressed.[4] As such, it violates Title VII's prohibition on using gender stereotypes to discriminate in employment as determined by the court's decision in *Price Waterhouse v. Hopkins* (1989).

Articulating a widely held sentiment about this victory for gay rights, an analysis in the *New York Times* declared, "In many ways, the decision is the strongest evidence yet of how fundamentally, rapidly and, to some degree, unpredictably American views about gay and transgender people have changed across the ideological spectrum in less than 20 years."[5] Reinforcing this narrative of progress, the authors describe the decision as "the latest in a swift series of legal and political advances for gay Americans after several decades where gains came in fits and starts after the uprising at the Stonewall Inn in Greenwich Village helped usher in the modern gay rights movement."[6] Seventy years after the Mattachine Society was established to counter state-enforced animus against so-called sexual deviants; fifty-nine years after the Supreme Court refused Frank Kameny's request for certiorari after his firing by the Army Map Service on the basis of his homosexuality; fifty-six years after the Civil Rights Act was signed into law by Lyndon Johnson; and fifty-one years after the Stonewall rioters rose up against police abuse, the extension of employment discrimination protections to lesbians, gay men, and transsexuals could be greeted as proof of a "fundamental" change in America's social attitudes. At the same moment, however, and providing a different take on the linear progress of "change," Black Americans, more than half a century *after* they had won those same legal rights, were pushing the country, yet again, to confront its anti-Blackness.

In fact, the most "fundamental" change apparent in the wake of George Floyd's death has been the growth in the number of non-Black Americans beginning to see anti-Blackness as inherent in systems, not just individuals, including in the US political, legal, penal, and educational systems. The concept of structural racism has entered the popular conversation, but without any clear consensus on the nature of the structure to which it refers. A vast distance, for example, separates the "structured racism" articulated by Bobby Seale and other activists in the 1960s and 1970s from the discussions of structural racism by theorists like Frank B. Wilderson III today. For those in the tradition of Black liberation, the "structure" in "structured racism" refers to control of the various institutions through which political power operates. Not only is Black liberation possible by changing who controls those institutions, but so, too, is multiracial cooperation in an anticapitalist context. In a 1988 interview, Seale reflects on that hope as expressed in the sometime alliance between the Black Panther Party and young, white opponents of the Vietnam War:

> The young Whites who did really get out in the streets demonstrated against structured racism. We saw that as a resource. . . . [A]nother aspect of our analysis was that we're talking about power to the people. We made a new analysis of what nationalism was about, Black nationalism. That, whatever Black unity we had, it was really a sort of a catalyst to help humanize the world and we were that catalyst here in Afro-America or Africa, that's what it was about. And that the world was composed of more than just Black folks, you know. So, the coalition aspect to us being what one defined as a minority United States of America, if the White community showed some split, then we should side with that aspect of the group that seemed to be or would act as friends to us.[7]

As remote from Seale's politics as it is from his moment, Ibram X. Kendi's *How to Be an Antiracist* shares, nonetheless, his liberationist hope. Kendi writes that while he "still occasionally use[s] the terms 'institutional racism' and 'systemic racism' and 'structural racism,'" he prefers "the term 'institutionally racist policies'" because he sees it as "more concrete."[8] Even more important than its concreteness, though, the phrase holds on to the possibility of "humaniz[ing] the world," as Seale expressed it, since policies are, by definition, more malleable than structures. This faith, which derives from what Kendi calls "our underlying humanity," constitutes the core of his argument: "We must believe. Believe all is not lost for you and me and our society. Believe in the possibility that we can strive to be antiracist from this day forward. Believe in the possibility that we can transform our societies to be antiracist from this day forward. Racist power is not godly. Racist policies are not indestructible. Racial inequities are not inevitable. Racist ideas are not natural to the human mind."[9] For those who might question this attachment to the "human" and its openness to transformation, Kendi has this to say: "The conviction that racist policymakers can be overtaken, and racist policies can be changed, and the racist minds of their victims can be changed, is disputed only by those invested in preserving racist policymakers, policies, and habits of thinking."[10]

Nothing could be further from the theoretical argument that Wilderson presents. Emphasizing an insight central to Afropessimist thought as a whole, he declares, *"Blacks are not Human subjects, but are structurally inert props, implements for the execution of White and non-Black fantasies and sado-masochistic pleasures."*[11] By recognizing Blackness as external to the ontological framework of the human, Wilderson, building on earlier work by theorists like Ronald Judy, can identify anti-Blackness as inherent in the constitution of (human) being. It follows from this that politics can never escape the anti-Blackness that structures the human in the first place. Both Seale and Kendi, like Angela Davis, push discussions of racism beyond the trap of intentionality and individual guilt, leading to difficult questions about structural determination that remind us, in Davis's words, that "if we don't take seriously the ways in which racism is embedded in structures of institutions, if we assume that there must be an identifiable racist . . . who is the perpetrator, then we won't ever succeed in eradicating racism."[12] But in doing so they also insist that those structures, because they manifest themselves in human institutions, are therefore subject to change *by humans*. For Wilderson and others constructing the intellectual framework of Afropessimism, that very embeddedness in the human makes structural change impossible. Thus, Wilderson rejects the prospect of "coherent liberation campaigns" for Black subjects; Afropessimism, he writes, "describe[s] a structural problem but offer[s] no structural solution."[13] From within the precepts of Afropessimism such a solution cannot exist.

The meaning of *structure* has shifted here from the contingent power to shape and control particular institutions to an ontological imperative bound up with social organization as such. That imperative, as *Bad Education* maintains, grounds being in being meaningful, in conforming to the logic of thinkability that organizes human community. As the introduction argues by attending closely to a passage from *L'Étourdit*, the Symbolic's ontology arises, according to the psychoanalyst Jacques Lacan, through the exclusion of what he calls *ab-sens*, the nonrelation to meaning. Only this enabling subtraction of what, in itself, is subtracted from sense (even before there is a sense from which it could be subtracted), only this negation of a primal negativity, allows the ontology of the human through the language that differentiates culture from nature. To the extent that ab-sens, according to Lacan, is also what "designates . . . sex," its ontology-producing exclusion makes sex external to meaning and being, simultaneously incomprehensible and ontologically impossible.[14] Unlike the sex whose definition Justice Alito can blithely cite, sex for Lacan pertains to the Real, to the beyond of signification where definition does not obtain.

As discussed in *Bad Education*, then, the sex that ab-sens would designate, a priori absented from being, gives way to sex as the difference that governs the Symbolic as *sens-absexe*, Lacan's term for the ontological order linking sexual difference to meaning. Sens-absexe permits signification precisely by absenting sex as ab-sens. It creates, with that negative gesture, the world that swells into being through words. Because sex as ab-sens is exorbitant to the logic of difference and meaning, however, it can have no name of its own. Only through catachresis can it indicate the state of nondifferentiation made unthinkable by sens-absexe, which consigns it to the void of nonbeing that enables being to be. To that extent, the sex foreclosed with the subtraction of ab-sens coincides with incest in psychoanalysis, where incest is seen as impossible either to cognize or to enact, constituting as it does, in Lacanian terms, the impossible Real of sex. Inconceivable in its radical nondifferentiation, incest figures, like sex and ab-sens, the exclusion that structures the Symbolic (as the order of language, ontology, and the human) and permits it to function as the reality procured by sens-absexe.

With this we may seem to have wandered far from the murder of George Floyd, but *Bad Education* argues, to the contrary, that this is the immutable structure to which "structural racism" finally refers. While acknowledging historical differences in lived experience, socioeconomic mobility, degree of precarity, access to power, and positioning in the cultural imaginary among those read as Black, queer, woman, trans*, or any other category of social (non)"being" collectively delegitimated as other than human, this book maintains that the stigma attached to such posited identities corresponds to their inflection (in particular communities and at particular historical moments) as embodiments of a negativity inassimilable to being, reflecting their figural status as personifications of ab-sens or of sex in its Lacanian (non)sense.

This claim may appear to privilege sex over other conceptual frameworks, like race, but only insofar as one confuses sex with the literalizations that (mis)represent it. *Sex*, in this context, does not refer to a conceptual formation at all but instead to what conceptual formation necessarily excludes. Lacan, to be sure, invites this confusion by naming as sex the nondifferentiation he attributes to ab-sens. But the movement from sex as negativity, as the nonbeing associated with the Real, to sex as the sexual difference on which the Symbolic seems to rest conforms to the logic of fantasy so rigorously theorized in Lacanian thought—a logic that attempts to make sex make sense, to positivize its negativity, through the promise of sexual relation. Put otherwise: sexual difference, sexual relation, and the primal prohibition of incest make sex as ab-sens impossible, compelling it always to "mean" in the terms prescribed by sens-absexe. Those terms efface sex as the negativity of the primal nondifferentiation negated and replaced by sexual meaningfulness, which is what sexual difference "means": the libidinized constitution of the subject through difference that libidinizes difference as such, making difference always sexual and sexual difference the Symbolic's mandate that difference both "be" and be known.[15] We come, that is, to be beings through language, which extracts us from ab-sens while making ab-sens inconceivable in the topology of sens-absexe. Sex as determined by ab-sens, therefore, though catachrestically naming *non*being, will seem to signify, nonetheless, the ontological order that *means* and that thereby makes sex as ab-sens unthinkable. Though referring to the nondifferentiation pertaining to incest and ab-sens alike, the psychoanalytic notion of sex, as understood by Lacan, will always be confused with sex as the name for what, in fact, absents it: the differential structure of positive differences.

But sex is far from singular as a catachresis of nonbeing. This book insists on the myriad names by which sex as ab-sens can go, including, but never limited to, *queerness, Blackness, woman,* and *trans**. Like *sex*, these terms never wholly escape their connections to the substantive identities that appear to flesh them out: *the* queer, *the* Black, *the* woman, *the* trans person, *the* genderqueer individual. But they exceed these literalizations to name, or misname, that which "is" not. As the introduction explains more fully, there are two main reasons this book elaborates ab-sens through the figure of queerness . The first is its relatively loose association with any specific identity. Primarily applied to something perceived as "strange, odd, peculiar, eccentric," according to the *Oxford English Dictionary, queer* can refer to anything that thwarts, contradicts, or departs from a norm.[16] Even where its fluidity of reference, its resistance to taxonomic specificity, allows it to serve as a general rubric for nonnormative sexualities, *queer* so relentlessly challenges the boundaries of sexuality and normativity that no one can ever definitively succeed in escaping its connotative reach. Similarly, no one can fully secure it as a proper identity, either, insofar as it signifies diacritically in relation to a norm. What gets taunted as queer in a high school gym class in rural Louisiana may well look heteronormative at an academic conference in New York. By rejecting the positivity of *queerness*, or the prospect of owning it as an identity, I keep faith with its lexical history and its various social applications, something less easily argued, perhaps, when prioritizing Blackness or woman, for example, as catachreses of ab-sens. But this book does not shrink from that latter claim; to the contrary, it gratefully acknowledges the feminist, Black, and non-Black scholars whose theoretical boldness sustains it. But given the entanglement of Blackness and woman with histories and identities more clearly defined (to others and themselves alike) than queerness, with its *determining indetermination*, I make my argument about sex and ab-sens by way of it instead. I am mindful of the political value, or strategic necessity, of affirming the specificity of delegitimated identities and of privileging their uniqueness. But the uniqueness of the histories those identities bespeak, and the differences in how they have functioned as embodiments of negativity, does not contradict their shared positioning precisely *as* such embodiments.

This leads to the second main reason for my choice. Queerness, even when transvalued by those who assume it as an identity, implies a disturbance of order, a nonconformity to prevailing logic or law, a glitch in the function of meaning. It retains the pejorative force it confers when it nominates something unusual or out of place: something not meant to appear where it does or not legible in its appearance. The negative associations of queerness speak to the subject's investment in the system of differences that called it into being in the first place and its intolerance of anything that puts its investment in the stability of those differences at risk. Our constitution through the language of sens-absexe conscripts our thought—our conscious thought—to that differential logic and commits us to its preservation in and as that thought. By fracturing the ontological consistency of what "is," queerness refutes the education in being—an inherently *aesthetic* education—that totalizes the empire of sens-absexe as a comprehensive and comprehensible unity. It insists on the outside of signification that make sens-absexe not all. Whatever asserts that incompletion by representing or embodying ab-sens, whatever appears to instantiate queerness in a given order by doing so, will be charged with promoting a bad education: one inimical to the survival and transmission of meaning required by what this book will call the pedag-archival imperative.

Despite the claims advanced in support of liberationist pedagogies, education is inherently conservative. Even in countering a dominant narrative or advancing a progressive position, it enshrines, preserves, and passes on a construction of "what is." Above all, it conjures the subject as an archive of sens-absexe. Whatever the content of an education, the pedag-archival law affirms the ontology of difference, ceaselessly imposing the conjoined imperatives of knowing, meaning, and being. For just that reason, as this book shows, queerness *teaches us nothing* in two distinct senses of that phrase.

On the one hand, queerness adverts us to what ontology leaves out, if only by figuring—*within that ontology*—what that ontology excludes. It confronts us with a representation of what the Symbolic *posits* as nothing, as external to being or sense, lest ab-sens as the absence of differentiation make ontology nothing itself. The events that prompted this preface respond to an anxiety about human ontology induced by those figures whose presence insists that the world as it "is" is not all. After the Supreme Court announced its ruling in the case of *Bostock v. Clayton County*, for example, Archbishop José H. Gomez of Los Angeles, the president of the US Conference of Catholic Bishops, lamented that the court, by altering "the legal meaning of 'sex' in our nation's civil rights law," was "redefining human nature." It did so, as he saw it, "by erasing the beautiful differences and complementary relationship between man and woman," which is to say, by undoing the sexual difference that absents ab-sens to establish meaning and, in the process, "human" being.[17] Similarly, in the wake of George Floyd's murder, when municipalities across the country authorized murals and street art meant to affirm that "Black Lives Matter," white Americans in places as heterogeneous as New York, Cincinnati, and Fresno defaced or attempted to deface them, often justifying their acts, when caught, with the counterclaim that "*all* lives matter."[18] For them, the "mattering" of Blackness seemed to violate "human nature"; they could register ontological totality only through the (literal) erasure of Blackness. Like queerness, that is, the Blackness that asserts a claim to human mattering can never enter the "all" that comes into being by excluding it. That explains why Calvin Warren, with whose thought my own work resonates, notwithstanding our serious differences, can write that "#Blacklivesmatter is *only* factual if it can reunite black life with a *valuable form*, a valuation determined by political calculus. But what if reuniting black life and form is impossible? What if blackness is always already dead, the 'perfection of death' as David Marriott would call it, so black life-form is but a fantasy? Can we think of blackness as incontrovertibly formless?"[19]

If my claim that queerness teaches us nothing gestures toward such a formlessness, toward the nondifferentiation that *incest, sex,* and *ab-sens* attempt to name, then it also acknowledges that queerness can teach us nothing of the sort. The same necessity that condemns us to designate the Real, the beyond of signification, only in catachrestic terms compels us to think nondifferentiation through the Symbolic logic of difference and merely to imagine that we can imagine the nothing that is foreclosed as such from thought. *Bad Education* takes seriously the structural limit of language on thought, a limit that keeps us from thinking nothing, and so from thinking queerness—or, for that matter, Blackness, woman, trans*, incest, "sex," or any of the catachreses of ab-sens—*except* as posited and positivized in those made to embody nothing. To that extent, the beyond of meaning that these catachreses nominate functions in relation to the subject as irony functions in relation to language, undoing the legibility that is responsible for its production and evading every effort either to pin it down or to know it. Queerness can no more *present* us with nothing than the order of meaning can escape it.

By seeking to specify the consequences of that structural inevitability, *Bad Education* questions the recuperative possibility of progressive politics, including the progressive politics that represents itself as queer. By addressing the logic of exclusion inherent in Symbolic organization and the dependence of that organization on literalizations of figural identities, this book shows how queerness, in its status as a catachresis of ab-sens, exerts an ironic force incompatible with the aesthetic idealism that marks progressivism. A central strand of my argument poses such politics, and its philosophical underpinnings, from Plato to Alain Badiou, against the Lacanian psychoanalysis that insists on what politics, like philosophy, can never accommodate: the division of the subject, the Real of enjoyment, the insistence of the drive. These registers of negativity, as *Bad Education* suggests, correspond to the irony that interrupts every totalization of sense and that requires the designation of authorized readers—judges and courts among them—to assert the particular meaning of laws within a general law of meaning. Such readings, as in *Bostock v. Clayton County*, sublimate linguistic indeterminacy by *positing* the meanings they claim to discover—meanings they discover only by nullifying whatever contradicts them.

Thus, queerness, Blackness, woman, trans*, as catachreses of what "is" not, must ironize *Bostock v. Clayton County* as well as both of these formulations: "Black lives matter" and "All lives matter." Despite the "Q" included in the headline that appeared in the *New York Times*—"A Half-Century On, an Unexpected Milestone for L.G.B.T.Q. Rights"—*Bostock v. Clayton County* did not and could not advance "queer" rights. In extending employment protections to persons who are "homosexual or transgender," it merely continued the juridical dissociation of those categories from queerness. As the murder of George Floyd reminds us, though, juridical recognition does not put an end to the communal construction of abjected identities made to literalize nonbeing. In the same way that *Bostock v. Clayton County* said nothing about a right to queerness (whatever that would mean) but could only contribute to the normalization of "homosexual or transgender" persons, so too can "Black lives matter" only be "factual," to borrow Warren's term, by divorcing Black lives from Blackness. In the context of progressive politics, the Black Lives Matter movement exposes how the "human" leaves Black lives out of its count. But it does so precisely to press a claim for inclusion in that count, for comprehension within the all, and so for the realization of what "All lives matter" (only) promises.

"Black lives matter" rightly mobilizes us in our current social reality, but it does so, and this is implicit in Warren's assertion as well, by reinforcing the ontological illusion of reality's comprehensiveness, by perpetuating its unsustainable claim to totalize what "is." No political transformation can alter or reduce the ontological violence in every word of "All lives matter." There can be no "all" without the "not all" inaccessible to thought; no life, no mode of being, without the nonbeing posed against it; and no mattering without the foreclosure of ab-sens, of what the order of meaning casts out. Wherever lives matter—and assuring that mattering is the matter of education—queerness, Blackness, woman, and trans* are always already excluded. And where Black lives, queer lives, women's lives, or trans* lives achieve legitimation, they will have ceased to signify in terms of queerness, Blackness, woman, or trans*. The events of this June exemplify the imperative of affording the shelter of meaningful being to those living negated identities. But they also remind us that meaningful being occasions those negations in the first place. That is the structural lesson that *Bad Education* attempts to unfold: the lesson that, *as* lesson, can only ironize what it teaches.[20]

—Brookline, MA, June 2020

Acknowledgments:

This book, which took many years to write, carries for me the indelible imprint of conversations, arguments, and professional exchanges with numerous interlocutors. No list of names could properly thank the friends and colleagues whose generous acts, provocative questions, and sustaining companionship both enabled and improved it. That their brilliance could make it no better than it is speaks to my limitations, not theirs.

I want to express my gratitude to the Faculty Research Awards Committee, the deans of the School of Arts and Sciences, and the trustees of Tufts University for the generous research support they provided, including funds to underwrite the color images included in this book.

The insight and rigor of the following people helped me to develop the ideas in this book and to hone them on the whetstone of their intelligence; I am grateful to them all: Henry Abelove, Jean Allouch, Matt Bell, Bobby Benedicto, Courtney Berger, Lorenzo Bernini, Jelisaveta Blagojevic, Pearl Brilmyer, Eugenie Brinkema, Kent Britnall, Judith Brown, Judith Butler, Russ Castronovo, Isabelle Châtelet, Anne Cheng, Rey Chow, Claire Colebrook, Joan Copjec, Cathy Davidson, Nick Davis, Penelope Deutscher, Slavco Dimitrov, Carl Fischer, Anne-Lise Francois, Carla Freccero, Diana Fuss, Jane Gallop, Irving Goh, Jonathan Goldberg, Jack Halberstam, Ellis Hanson, Melissa Hardie, Sonia Hofkosh, Lynn Huffer, Britt-Inger Johansson, Donna Jones, Benjy Kahan, Jacques Khalip, Ranjana Khanna, Karen Kopelson, Kate Lilley, Heather Love, Lisa Lowe, Corey McEleney, Todd McGowan, Petar Milat, Michael

Moon, Hilary Neroni, Andrea Nicolini, Francois Noudelmann, Kevin Ohi, Frank Palmieri, Stanimir Panayotov, Jean-Michel Rabaté, Kane Race, Pallavi Rastoggi, Kenneth Reinhard, Marilyn Reizbaum, Frances Restuccia, Valerie Rohy, Ellen Rooney, David Schalkwyk, Heike Schotten, Kathryn Schwartz, Matt Scully, Christina Sharpe, Ashley Shelden, Kathryn Bond Stockton, Mihoko Suzuki, Rei Terada, Gautam Basu Thakur, Filippo Trentin, Henry Turner, Johannes Voelz, Rebecca Walkowitz, Calvin Warren, Elizabeth Weed, Frank Wilderson, Michele Wright, and Xiang Zairong.

Five colleagues, friends, and interlocutors who were crucial to the formation of this book, and to the field of queer studies itself, died while it was being written: Eve Kosofsky Sedgwick and José Esteban Muñoz both raised questions that queer theory and literary studies continue to address. Like those questions, my long-standing relations with Eve and José, as critics and as friends, leave their trace in ways both large and small in the arguments I make here. Barbara Johnson was a much-loved friend and an endlessly dazzling thinker who perfected the art of the critical essay as a form both rigorous and playful, rhetorically focused and politically *consequential*. I would like to think that something of her practice, however pale the imitation, is legible in this book. As *Bad Education* made its way to press, my collaborator, coeditor of Theory Q, and friend of many, many years, Lauren Berlant, died too. Lauren was involved in the progress of *Bad Education* from the start; while writing *Sex, or the Unbearable* together we often spoke about its relation to *On the Inconvenience of Other People*, which she was working on at the time. It is bittersweet that Duke will be publishing both our books this year, sad that we won't get to mark the occasion with another book party together, and unbearable that she isn't here to read my words of enduring gratitude. Finally, while I was reviewing the copyedited pages of this book, I learned that Leo Bersani had died. No one reading this book needs reminding that Leo was a giant in the fields of gay studies and queer theory and that my thinking is indebted to the brilliance of his work on psychoanalysis, sexuality, and aesthetics. For me, the man and his kindness were inseparable from his genius. I'll miss the joy of our talks and our dinners and the living example of his mind.

At Duke University Press, I have had the great fortune to enjoy Ken Wissoker's patience, counsel, and support. His knack for shepherding books from ideas to gorgeously realized objects never fails to impress me. His keen judgement and generous spirit make him an outstanding editor—and also a valued friend. The remarkable group of people at Duke with whom he works so brilliantly have all contributed to bringing out the best of *Bad Education*. I am delighted to acknowledge the invaluable assistance of Lisl Hampton,

Aimee Harrison, Michael McCullough, Kim Miller, Christopher Robinson, Chad Royal, and Joshua Gutterman Tranen.

For their cogent, detailed, and intellectually generative readings of the manuscript, I am deeply indebted to Stephen Best and Elizabeth Wilson. That both are critics and scholars whose work I profoundly admire makes their faith in this book the more precious. I give special thanks to David Marriott for his ongoing engagement with my projects and for the combination of brilliance, sophistication, and fearlessness that inspires me in his work.

I want to add to the names of those cited above these friends and family members whose presence in my life makes living it that much more fun: Anne Bayley, James and Paul Bayley-Linhart, Alan Edelman, Avi Edelman, Erica Edelman, Leah Edelman, Sam Edelman, Samantha Frank, Barbara Glissant, Pierre Linhart, Joni Litvak, Larry Litvak, and Barbara Mellul. In particular, I want to name those friends who have gone the extra mile for many more miles than I can count. David Halperin has contributed not only through his enlivening companionship, vast knowledge, and generous advice but also through his warmth and persistent encouragement and confidence in my work. Madhavi Menon, who has lived through it all and never wavered in her hyperbole, has shared, in equal amounts, the radiance of her spirit and the sharpness of her mind; I am grateful for that and for a closeness before which even continents shrink. D. A. Miller, my near-daily companion in conversation for thirty-odd years, has contributed the gift of his critical acumen, his astonishing erudition, and his loyalty to friendship and honesty at once. For all of that, but far more for his ongoing enlargement of my life and thought, I give full-hearted thanks.

Joe Litvak alone can know what I mean when I say that this book, like everything else that I do, is done for him, with him, and through him. I owe whatever I may be as a critic to all that I've learned from him. You can call that a good education or a bad one, but I couldn't have asked for a better one.

Introduction: **Nothing Ventured:**

Psychoanalysis, Queer Theory, and Afropessimism

According to the *Oxford English Dictionary, to educate* means, in its earliest sense, "to bring up (a child) so as to form his or her manners, behaviour, social and moral practices." Only later does it signify "to teach (a child) a programme of various academic and non-academic subjects, typically at a school; to provide with a formal education. Also: to provide (an adult) with instruction, esp. in a chosen subject or subjects at a college, university, or other institution of higher education."[1] By twice referring to it within parentheses, these definitions remind us that *the child* is the exemplary object of education, lending even adults engaged in "formal" or "higher" education an implicit association with something that is not—or not yet fully—formed. Such formation (*formation* in French names a program of educational training or development) seeks to "elevate" the child, to bring it up, to raise it from animal existence to human subjectivity by bringing it into conformity with the logic of a given world. Jacques Lacan describes this process as "l'apprentissage humain," thus identifying it both as human learning and as learning to be a human.[2] Education reproduces, it passes on, the world of human sense by turning those lacking speech—*infans*—into subjects of the law. It inculcates not only concepts and values but also the language by which sensory impressions—otherwise fleeting, discontinuous, chaotic—congeal into a universe of entities that are formalized through names.

Building on the work of Claude Lévi-Strauss, who focused on the basic or elementary structures affecting human relations, Lacan asserts from early on the key to a recognizable human order: "that the symbolic function intervenes at every moment and in every aspect of its existence."[3] This Symbolic function, with its con-stitution of a signifying order, produces the subject within a world that appears accessible to comprehension.[4] Lacan insists on this point: "If the human subject didn't name things—as Genesis says was done in the earthly Paradise, with the major species first—if it didn't come to an agreement on this mode of recognition, no world of the human subject's, not even a perceptual one, would be sustainable for more than an instant."[5] Even the Lacanian Imaginary, then, though characterized by our attachment to im-ages that afford a first glimpse of coherence and unity, relies on the Symbolic to imbue its perceptions with stability and duration. The shaping, survival, and transmission of a world thus depend on an education that brings us into being as human subjects by bringing us into, then bringing us up in, the order of the Symbolic.

The language that produces the subject within this order of signification, however, also installs an absence at that order's very core.[6] When Jean Hyp-polite, attending one of Lacan's seminars, responded to the latter's account of the Symbolic by asserting, "We can't do without it, and at the same time we can't situate ourselves within it" (nous ne pouvons pas nous en passer, et toutefois nous ne pouvons pas non plus nous y installer), Lacan immedi-ately agreed: "Yes, of course, naturally. It's the presence in absence and the absence in presence" (Oui bien sûr, naturellement. C'est la présence dans l'absence et l'absence dans la présence).[7] By embedding us in a reality given shape and persistence by Symbolic articulation, by names that impose rela-tional systems on inconsistent Imaginary perceptions, language also enables us to generate the notion of something that escapes it, something that re-mains definitionally exterior to systems of meaning or signification. Alenka Zupančič puts this well: "Within reality as it is constituted via what Lacan calls the Imaginary and the Symbolic mechanisms, there is a 'place of the lack of the Image,' which is symbolically designated as such. That is to say that the very mechanism of representation posits its own limits and designates a certain beyond which it refers to as 'unrepresentable.'"[8] Only the Symbolic organization of a world allows something to be missing from it; only Sym-bolic reality creates the place for the lack of the Image, or for the thought of an absence in the system, and so for an encounter with the unnameable that Lacan names, nonetheless, as the Real. By producing the machinery for "symbolically designat[ing]" what escapes Symbolic designation, for concep-tualizing, in other words, the place of something incompatible with the logic of meaning, the Symbolic allows for the thought of "nothing," of what pos-sesses no being in the world, while making that nothing impossible to think except in the form of "something." Education intends precisely that: the foreclosure of the nothing the Symbolic calls forth as its excess or remainder—a foreclosure that effectively makes something of nothing, reproducing the world as sense, while, correlatively, imposing on certain persons the burden of figuring nothing.

But what if education in its second moment, the one that the both the *Oxford English Dictionary* and common usage describe as "higher," insisted on the nothing, on the exclusion, that threatens to derealize the world? Could such an education resist the imperative of affirmation and reproduction? Could it think the insistence of nothing without attempting to redeem it? Philosophical engagements with the zero or the void, psychoanalytic accounts of the force of the Real, and political analyses of the social structures dooming certain lives to nonbeing: all have entered the curricula of the contemporary Western academy. Woman as ontological impossibility, for example, shapes the work of such prominent feminists as Luce Irigaray ("The question 'what is . . . ?' is the question—the metaphysical question—to which the feminine does not allow itself to submit"), Julia Kristeva ("On a deeper level, however, a woman cannot 'be'; it is something which does not even belong to the category of being"), and Catherine Malabou ("This assimilation of 'woman' to 'being nothing' perhaps opens a new path that goes beyond both essentialism and anti-essentialism"). Similarly, the antithesis of Blackness and being has shaped the thought (from Frantz Fanon forward) of many Black intellectuals, including Sylvia Wynter ("Blacks . . . have been socialized to experience ourselves in . . . negative being"), Jared Sexton ("Black lives matter, not in or to the present order of knowledge that determines human being, but only ever against it, outside the limits of the law"), and Fred Moten ("Blackness is prior to ontology . . . it is ontology's anti- and ante-foundation").[9] Meditations on the function of the void or the null set in the presentation of being, moreover, play crucial roles in my own work as well as in that of philosophers and critics such as Paul de Man, Jacques Derrida, Slavoj Žižek, and Alain Badiou.

Yet even as deconstructive, feminist, psychoanalytic, queer, and race-centered theories have entered the university, they've engendered violently negative reactions to their institutionalization, fueling the ongoing culture wars in the United States and abroad.[10] By addressing nothing's (non)place in any constituted order of thought, and thereby seeming to disturb metaphysics and social value alike, these, like the fields that house them (most often the humanities and social sciences), find themselves reduced by their opponents to the figural status of the nothing they engage. Excoriated for debasing reality and truth (a charge leveled by the right-wing Norwegian mass murderer Anders Behring Breivik as well as by the "liberal" American cultural journalist Michiko Kakutani), these discourses refuse the normative paradigm of education as world transmission—as the preservation, mutatis mutandis, of reality as it "is."[11] They focus, instead, on what thought and education register as the unthinkable, as foreign to logic or sense. They promulgate a "bad education" by attesting to what Slavoj Žižek calls, in the course of a reading of Immanuel Kant, "the ontological incompleteness of reality itself."[12]

Lacan attributes that incompleteness to the Symbolic formation of the subject and the structure of the unconscious. In Seminar XI he remarks that "discontinuity . . . is the essential form in which the unconscious appears to us" and then wonders whether the "absolute, inaugural character" of that discontinuity can manifest itself only against "the background of a totality."[13] "Is the *one* anterior to discontinuity?" he asks; is there a unity, in other words, before the negativity that introduces the division, the "discontinuity" that characterizes the unconscious? He follows with this response: "I do not think so, and everything I have taught in recent years has tended to exclude the need for this closed *one*. . . . You will grant me that the *one* that is introduced by the unconscious is the *one* of the split, of the stroke, of rupture."[14] This inaugural rupture, prior to the "being" of the "one" that it would split, presupposes for Lacan no unified "background," no whole that precedes its division. He thus argues that "the first emergence of the unconscious . . . does not lend itself to ontology."[15] Indeed, the unconscious, as he puts it, "is neither being nor non-being" precisely because "what is ontic in [its] function . . . is the split."[16] That split, which makes possible all that appears, can never appear "in itself"; it possesses no "in itself" *to* appear but produces the appearance of the "in itself" through its primal division or negativity. Escaping containment by the either-or logic of "to be, or not to be," it opens an absence that Lacan rewrites as "ab-sens" in *L'Étourdit*. As the absenting of meaning from being, as the insistence of what can never be counted as part of any world, ab-sens has no place in the order of sense that assumes "the background of a totality" wherein being and meaning both depend on each other and prop each other up.[17]

Whatever disrupts that interdependence undoes, along with the world as we know it, the very *possibility* of a world by undoing the totalizing comprehension, the "closed *one*" that a world implies. But this occasions a seeming contradiction: construing the world as unknowable *still* gives the world a knowable shape; the predicate adjective affirms the world in our "knowing" it *as* unknowable. This torsion inheres in any attempt to sidestep the fusion of world and sense and results in the problem that this book discusses as inseparable from "bad education." If the world induces a pedagogy that excludes what subtracts itself from sense—that excludes, therefore, what its structuring *as* a world makes unthinkable—then what sort of teaching could broach ab-sens, the negativity of subtraction, without recurring to the logic of sense and affirming a world once more? What education could ever break from the reproduction of meaning by which the world appears as self-evident and self-evidence appears as truth?

The very effort to think ab-sens, to conceive it as something outside the binary couple of sense and non-sense (where non-sense is always already trapped in the gravitational field of sense), denies its negativity so it can enter the house of sense, though that house that can never be its home. Lodged therein, it functions like any other signifier in the marketplace of meaning despite the fact that it gestures toward what that marketplace excludes. And the same thing happens to the ontological negations implicit in "woman" or in "Blackness." Despite their figural capacity to signal what being and meaning foreclose, both get substantialized as catachrestic names for identities shaped by and legible within the logics of being and meaning. The same necessity inheres in "queerness," which oscillates between its contemporary reference to nonnormative sexualities, sexual acts, or sexual identities and a nonidentitarian reference to any person or thing delegitimated for its association with nonnormativity.[18] All of these terms, and countless others, stand in for a violent break with the governing constructs of a world, a break with its (onto)logic. To that extent we might think of these terms as "nonsynonymous substitutions," the phrase by which Derrida describes the multiple figures to which différance gives rise.[19] Each attempts, like différance, to signal the intolerable rupture, the primal negativity, that permits the "being" of entities only through the cut of differentiation. But each, at the same time, sutures that break by figuring it in the form of an entity conjured *in order to be excluded*. If the knowledge value these terms accrue as names for social positions reinforces the order of sense, the terms themselves are placeholders for what has no place in that order at all: the ab-sens we encounter unawares and always at our own risk.

Such encounters take shape as obtrusions of the Real, temporary breaches in the structure of reality that flood the subject with anxiety.[20] No teaching could ever master this eruption or allow us to comprehend this Real; comprehension, after all, as the word makes clear, conflates the constitutive seizure, containment, or enclosure of a world with an act of understanding, of intellectual domination, that wrests it into shape. Comprehension affirms the enclosure of a world to preclude the threat of ab-sens. The Real—necessarily divided between its status as a concept permitted by language (the concept of something inaccessible to language) and its status as a psychic encounter that undoes conceptual thought (by confronting the subject with the beyond of language that it literally *cannot* conceive)—provokes both the defensive fantasy of intellectual comprehension (which lets us produce a theory of the Real as a subset of theory in general) and the anxiety that voids comprehension, incompletes the world, and makes one "not-all." The ab-sens inseparable from the Real, therefore, partakes of the negativity associated by Guy Le Gaufey with the Lacanian *objet a*, especially in "its incapacity to receive any imposition of unity whatsoever, something in itself heavy with consequences for its being, if only from a Leibnizian point of view where every single being is, in the first place, a *single* being [*one* being]."[21] Ab-sens makes impossible both the oneness of being and the oneness of *any* being by incising in every entity the cut of a subtraction. With castration, primal repression, and the Lacanian formulae of sexuation lurking in the background as figures for this cut that frames being as always not-all, ab-sens leads us back to the confluence of sex and the unbearable, the terms with which Lauren Berlant and I broached negativity and relationality.[22] If embodiments determined by such categories as woman, Blackness, and queerness (among others) threaten to derealize a given order by exposing it as not-all, that not-all is always implicated in the Lacanian interpretation of sex, where *sex*, as in Lacan's well-known formula, "there is no sexual relation," names the radical negativity, the gap, that makes Symbolic comprehension impossible: the site where sex coincides with the primal subtraction of ab-sens.[23]

Lacan takes up this convergence in a crucial passage in *L'Étourdit*: "Freud puts us on the path of that which ab-sens designates as sex; it's through the swelling up [*à la gonfle*: that is, through the inflation or inspiration] of this sens-absexe that a topology spreads out where the word is determining."[24] At the heart of psychoanalysis, then, Lacan situates the entanglement of sex, as it is designated by ab-sens, with the words whose meanings (*sens*) yield worlds through what he refers to as *sens-absexe*. What sense can we make of this sens-absexe? How does the echo of *ab-sens* in *absexe* affect its signification? And why is the topology it unfolds associated with afflatus, inspiration, or engorging (*gonfler*)? By connecting *sens* (sense, meaning, direction) with the portmanteau term *absexe*, *sens-absexe* reaffirms the *sens* that was subtracted by the *ab* of *ab-sens*. It does so, however, only by putting *sex* in the place of subtraction (the place determined by *ab*): sex, that is, as complicit with and designated by *ab-sens*; sex as the pure negativity that enables meaning but has none. With that act of designation (where to designate—*désigne*—already bears the signifier of signification, *signe*, within it), *ab-sens* posits sex as subtracted (*ab*) from the register of meaning (*sens*) at the very moment of inserting it into the signifying chain (by virtue of "designating" it).[25] Sex, understood as the positive difference between male and female beings, thus positivizes the negativity of ab-sens by positing "complementary" identities. So construed, sex nurtures fantasies of wholeness, union, and repair, but it possesses no positivity for Lacan, no sense before the subtraction from sense that constitutes ab-sens, no meaning and no existence from which sense has subsequently been withdrawn. The absenting of sense is originary and prior to sense as such; sex as designated by *ab-sens* quite simply "is" this primal subtraction, this inherent exclusion from being or meaning that libidinizes the mastery implicit in comprehending an order of things. Ab-sens as subtraction, excision, or cut makes possible the *designation* of sex by condensing the division or negativity sex "is" in Lacanian theory with the division that "is" articulation; such designation, however, dooms sex as ab-sens to the realm of the unthinkable at the very moment of making what we think of as sex accessible to thought.

The excluded negativity of ab-sens (as the cut that precedes, determines, and divides "the closed *one*") swells, through this designation of sex, into the topology of sens-absexe, the order of meaning generated by subtracting ab-sens from the sex that it designates. Once designated, that is, sex hardens into a positive identity and vanishes *as* ab-sens; it suffers, one might say, a subtraction from itself once situated in the topological field where, Lacan notes, "the word is determining" (c'est le mot qui tranche). Though "determining" can adequately translate *qui tranche*, a phrase that indicates the authority to decide or determine a situation's outcome, *qui tranche* refers literally to something that cuts or divides. *Sens-absexe* may operate with reference to a swelling up or engorgement (*la gonfle*), recalling the Lacanian phallus's *Aufhebung* when raised to its privileged position as signifier of the Symbolic order of meaning (sens), but it disseminates a topology wherein only the meaningless priority of the cut lets an entity appear as "itself." This cut, like the cut of castration, is what the phallus would positivize or flesh out. Indeed, the cut, one might say, *is* the phallus before its sublation swells out the world with meaning by cutting out or excising sex as ab-sens, as the absence of sense.

Alenka Zupančič reminds us that "the sexual in psychoanalysis is something very different from the sense-making combinatory game—it is precisely something that disrupts the latter and makes it impossible."[26] Sex, in other words, neither conforms to nor underwrites any "sense-making" logic; it registers the ab-sens in being and meaning that follows from Symbolic articulation, and it speaks to an irreducible gap in the signifier/signified relation, a failure of either fully to seize or to comprehend the other. That's why Ellie Ragland can write, "The real . . . is what gives birth to contingency. . . . Indeed, the real appears in language as that which puts it askew, makes it awkward, uncanny. One could describe the presence of the real as the palpability of the unbearable."[27] The impossibility that Lacan refers to by announcing that "there is no sexual relation" corresponds to this Real that "puts [language] askew" and arises (from within the order of the Symbolic) as the ab-sens that the Symbolic can only *think* by turning it into sense.[28]

As Lacan explains in *L'Étourdit*, the *statement* of sexual relation takes the place of that relation itself, and the "two" sexes figure the will-to-meaning by which language calls forth worlds. "It's starting from there," he writes, referring to the fact that humans reproduce themselves first and foremost through speech, "that we have to obtain two universals, two 'alls' sufficiently consistent to separate out among speaking beings, . . . two halves such that they won't get too confused in the midst of intercourse or co-iteration when they get around to it."[29] Shaped by this fantasy of complementarity and its promise of totalization, sexual difference divides human beings into "two halves" or "two universals" (thereby naturalizing "male" and "female"). It thus disavows the Real of ab-sens, the meaningless division that this "difference" fills out with the meaningfulness of sex.[30] Kenneth Reinhard makes this point forcefully: "Lacan's argument . . . is not that there are men and women (but they don't have a relationship), but rather the converse: there is no such thing as a sexual relationship, and, as a response to that impossibility, *there are men and women*."[31] The lack of a sexual relation, that is, does not attest to some positive difference between men and women as living beings; to the contrary, sexual difference expresses the antagonism inherent in being itself—the antagonism that keeps being from ever fully being "being itself."

That antagonism betrays the insistence of the Real, which, like the Lacanian unconscious, pertains neither to being nor to nonbeing. That's why Alain Badiou can remark with reference to *L'Étourdit*, "Sex proposes—nakedly, if I may put it this way—the real as the impossible proper: the impossibility of a relationship. The impossible, hence the real, is thus linked to ab-sense and, in particular, to the absence of any relationship, which means the absence of any sexual meaning."[32] Ab-sens, by "designat[ing]" something as sex, puts it in the field of meaning while establishing that field itself as inseparable from the Real of sex as ab-sens. What we "know" as sex forecloses sex as senseless negativity, as the unknowable cut or division that precedes the (id)entities that cut makes possible. Thus, sex as we "know" it, as sens-absexe, initiates a quest for sexual meaning while dooming that quest to fail. As the differential relations of words swell into the seeming substance of worlds, as the negativity of division and nonrelation yields to positivized sexual difference, the regime of sense establishes the topology of the subject. And it does so precisely by absenting ab-sens, to which, as sens-absexe attests, it nonetheless remains bound. Sens-absexe, after all, bears a quasi-mathematical relation to ab-sens: to the extent that ab-sens is what designates sex, sens-absexe could be read as *sens-ab(ab-sens)*, bringing out in this way not only the entanglement of the two but also, through the chiasmus it generates, the linguistic self-enclosure by which sens-absexe excludes ab-sens. Foreclosed from Symbolic reality and inaccessible to sense, the absented Real of sex as ab-sens still insists in the topology of sens-absexe through incursions of unbearable anxiety or through the experience of jouissance, itself always shadowed by anxiety.

The unbearable thus reflects an encounter with the Real that shakes our sense of reality and short-circuits the totalizing comprehension that solidifies a world. Whatever exposes the order of being's status as not-all ("the woman," "the Black," "the queer"), whatever makes visible the ontological negations a totalized world demands, must assume the identity of negated being, thus embodying at once the Real as ab-sens and its translation, by way of sens-absexe, into figures constructed to "mean" the "nothing" that incompletes and dissolves "what is." As in Julia Kristeva's account of abjection, where the self acquires its identity by continuously expelling what it takes to be foreign to the self it would become, so ab-sens as ontological negation, as the negativity that *woman*, *Blackness*, and *queerness* (among other catachreses) can name, is cast out and rendered unthinkable by the world of sens-absexe.[33]

Our rootedness in that world compels an ongoing investment in its consistency, attaching us to the conjunction of being and meaning that encounters with the Real undo. As Justin Clemens writes, however, "'Being' arises as the consequence of an operation of sense, but founders as it does so, undermined by its own operations. . . . [T]he operation of meaning-making posits being, only to find both meaning and being are undone in and by that very positing."[34] Just as sens-absexe grounds meaning in what has no meaning in itself (the arbitrary and senseless differences of the signifying chain), so the Real makes vivid the aporia of being's having been posited. In the words of Alenka Zupančič, "The Real is not a being, or a substance, but its deadlock. It is inseparable from being, yet it is not being." Calling this aporetic deadlock "the out-of-beingness of being," she explains that the Real "only exists as the inherent contradiction of being. Which is precisely why, for Lacan, the real is the bone in the throat of every ontology: in order to speak of 'being qua being,' one has to amputate something in being that is not being. That is to say, the real is that which the traditional ontology had to cut off to be able to speak of 'being qua being.'"[35] Such a gesture of cutting off, however, reintroduces what it means to excise: the division that precludes the closure of the one, thus making the one a back-formation from this very act of division. The primacy of the cut gets cut off, as it were, and banished from the world of sense. But the negativity of the cut that produces the one inheres in the one "itself." It divides the one both from itself and from its claim to being qua being, binding it to something other than itself and thus making it both a one minus (minus the very cut its being relies on) and a one plus (plus the excess of the cut that articulates it as itself). That cut, the mark of an articulation inseparable from the thing articulated, constitutes the presence of an absence, an incision that must be excised. Joan Copjec astutely frames this coincidence of excess and incompletion: "The fact that the One is paradoxical, always more than itself, is coterminous with the fact that it is less than itself, that is: that something has been subtracted from it. Something always escapes the One."[36] That something is the Lacanian ab-sens cut off and displaced by sens-absexe.

In such a context the experience of the unbearable, as I discussed it in dialogue with Lauren Berlant in *Sex, or the Unbearable*, follows from the blow to ontological stability struck by the "ex-istence" of the Real, where *existence* names the "out-of-beingness of being" excluded from the framework of reality for "being qua being" to be thought. And what ex-ists above all for the subject, bearing the stain of the unbearable within it, is the jouissance we can neither "achieve" nor "get rid of," as Slavoj Žižek observes.[37] Taking us beyond the pleasure principle, jouissance, in Lacanian parlance, makes us headless or acephalic subjects: not the willful agents we think we are but subjects of the drive.[38] If, as viewed from another perspective (that of the subject of the enunciation), this drive partakes of freedom (freedom from the desire that follows from our submission to Symbolic law), that freedom's subjective corollary (for the subject of the statement) is the experience of compulsion or lost agency, of what Lauren Berlant and I explore in *Sex, or the Unbearable* as nonsovereignty. As ab-sens is subtracted from reality to secure the Symbolic's ontological consistency, so jouissance, bound up with the Real as ab-sens, must suffer exclusion as well. It correlates, after all, with the death drive that threatens the subject of the statement, which is also to say, the philosophical subject or the subject of rational thought. Such thought, in pursuing its project of thinking the purity of being, rightly described by Judith Butler as "disembodied . . . self-reflection," expresses a will for abstraction not only from the body but also, and even more urgently, from jouissance, the drive, and the Real.[39] It expresses the subject's desire to "be" without the cut of its own inconsistency, to be free of the negativity excluded as ab-sens but inseparable, therefore, from the subject produced by this very act of exclusion.

The alternative to this subtraction of ab-sens (and what it designates as sex), the alternative to the thought that philosophy privileges—and that all of us, as subjects of the statement, are fated to privilege as well—is not, from a psychoanalytic perspective, some embodied or materialized "sex." Such a positivized material presence would merely return us to the fantasy of the thing itself, to the Lacanian "closed one." Instead, psychoanalytic materialism emerges as antagonistic through and through. As Zupančič persuasively puts it, "This is . . . what 'the materialism of the signifier' amounts to. Not simply to the fact that the signifier can have material consequences, but rather that the materialist position needs to do more than to pronounce matter the original principle. It has to account for a split or contradiction that *is* the matter."[40]

To think the split as material—as the nonpositivizable matter from which ontology splits into being—and to explore how its negativity matters for the sexual (non)relation requires a willingness to encounter what ontology rejects: the libidinization of this splitting as expressed in the oscillations of the unconscious. This temporal rhythm enacts for Lacan the "*pulsative* function" of the unconscious, "the need to disappear that seems to be in some sense inherent in it."[41] This, of course, is also where he locates sexuality, which "is represented in the psyche by a relation of the subject that is deduced from something other than sexuality itself. Sexuality is established in the field of the subject by a way that is that of lack."[42] We might consider both the materiality and the materialization of this lack by returning to some figures of being's incompletion—"the woman," "the Black," "the queer"—whose exposure of a given world as not-all compels them to bear the unbearable weight of anxiety and enjoyment at once: let us call it the *enjiety* of ab-sens as encountered in the world of sens-absexe.

Consider, in this light, the place of "women" in the feminist rethinking of philosophy proposed by Catherine Malabou. Despite attending to plasticity as the potential in being that enables change, Malabou maintains that philosophy "cannot welcome the fugitive essence of women."[43] Drawing on the work of Luce Irigaray (but responding as well to Hélène Cixous and Julia Kristeva), Malabou associates women with an "excessive materiality" that "transgress[es] the limits of ontology."[44] Women, to that extent, *have* an essence, but more than merely being fugitive, that essence *is fugitivity*. This leads Malabou to reject the prospect of imagining a feminist philosophy, arguing instead that "an ontology of the feminine would no doubt bear all the symptoms of the traditional ontology—that is, an exclusion of the feminine itself. As we know, the discourse of and on property, propriety or subjectivity is precisely the discourse which has excluded women from the domain of Being (and perhaps even of beings). I will refer to Irigaray again on this point: 'Woman neither is nor has an essence.'"[45] This fugitivity essential to woman that prevents her from having or being an essence recalls Lacan's pronouncement in Seminar XX, "There is no such thing as 'the woman,' where the definite article indicates universality."[46] He makes this point earlier in *L'Étourdit* when he refers to his graphs of sexuation to designate woman as not-all and so as a figure for ontological incompletion and the cut of division as such.[47] To the extent that woman, in Malabou's reading, succeeds in slipping ontology's net, she can function as a name for the split that separates ontology from itself. In contrast, were woman to claim a *particular* ontological definition, she would thereby repeat the "exclusion of the feminine," separating herself from her "fugitive essence," which ontology fails to capture.

But this "fugitive essence" also characterizes being, as Malabou notes while discussing Martin Heidegger: "Being is nothing . . . but its mutability, and . . . ontology is therefore the name of an originary migratory and metamorphic tendency, the aptitude to give change . . . whose strange economy we have . . . been attempting to characterize."[48] This strange economy of being—Malabou translates *befremdlich,* the adjective Heidegger attaches to being, as both "astonishing" and "queer"—proves unbearable for the tradition of philosophical thought insofar as it rejects the self-sameness on which identity depends.[49] "The whole question," as Malabou writes, "is of knowing if philosophy can at the end of the day cease evading what it has nevertheless never ceased to teach itself—the originary metamorphic and migratory condition. Even [Friedrich] Nietzsche, who came very close to this teaching, recoiled when faced with the radicality of ontological convertibility."[50] Malabou will repeat this claim when she tries to formulate the question to which her own thinking must respond: *"that of knowing if and in that case how it would be possible to grasp and endure, all the way and without the slightest compromise, the immense question of ontological transformability."*[51] The question is at once epistemological ("how . . . to grasp" or comprehend) and affective ("how . . . [to] endure" what the economy of presence *cannot* comprehend). If this strange economy is unendurable, if even Nietzsche recoils before it, is it not because its "originary metamorphic and migratory condition" expresses the ontic discontinuity binding being to the gap within it, to the not-all propelling being through the pulsions of the drive? Or, to put this somewhat differently, is it not the acephalic subject whose emergence proves unbearable insofar as it supplants the subject of meaning responsive to the law of desire? Philosophy recoils from confronting ab-sens and the negativity of the drive insofar as they require it to confront its own relation to jouissance.

On the one hand, Malabou rejects the possibility of a feminine ontology even while resignifying ontology by linking it to the essential fugitivity of woman: "The feminine or woman (we can use the terms interchangeably now) remains one of the unavoidable modes of ontological change."[52] On the other hand, she recoils from the consequences her negativity entails. She celebrates plasticity, for example, in one of its major aspects, as "the annihilation of all forms," as something that, by "erasing the limits of what used to be 'our' bodies, *unbinds* us from the chain of continuation."[53] While this seems to suggest an openness to the disappropriation of selfhood, even to the point of a radical unbinding that implicates plasticity in the death drive, there remains in Malabou nonetheless a point of attachment that refuses the ontological negation such unbinding demands:

> Personally, I have discovered that it is totally impossible for me to give up the schema "woman." I cannot succeed in dissolving it into the schema of gender or "queer multitudes." I continue to see myself as a woman. I know very well that the word is plastic, that it cannot be reconstituted as a separate reality, and that, as I wrote in "The Meaning of the Feminine," "there is no reason to privilege the 'feminine,' or to name the crossroads of ontic-ontological exchange 'feminine,'" I know the feminine is one of the "passing, metabolic points of identity."
>
> Still, I believe that *the word "woman" has a meaning outside the heterosexual matrix.*[54]

Conforming as it does to the logic of the fetish, the formula for which she all but quotes ("I know very well" but "still"), this belief that Malabou cannot renounce, this point of consistency to which she adheres in spite of what she knows, should be recognized not merely as an attachment to the specific identity of "woman" but also (and even more crucially) as an attachment to the coupling of woman and meaning: "I believe that *the word 'woman' has a meaning outside the heterosexual matrix.*"

Although Malabou will write that "it is necessary to imagine the possibility of woman starting from the structural impossibility she experiences of not being violated, in herself and outside, everywhere," she wants, simultaneously, to preserve *this meaning of woman* from violation: "Anti-essentialist violence and deconstructive violence work hand in hand to empty woman of herself, to disembowel her."[55] For Malabou, it seems, this conceptual violence, stripping woman of the fullness of her being, of the specificity of her meaning as essentially open to the possibility of violation, erases woman as such, despite the fact that this very erasure reenacts "the structural impossibility . . . of [her] not being violated." But isn't this also to say that such violence (as Malabou "know[s] very well") subjects woman to the plasticity of being, to the perpetual process of becoming other that inheres in the "empty[ing]" of her selfhood? With her visceral image of "disembowel[ment]," Malabou insists on woman's positivity, on her meaning "outside the heterosexual matrix," even if, by affirming "the structural impossibility . . . of [woman's] not being violated," she designates woman as the site of a perpetual division, as the essentialized form of the cut that itself disembowels every positivity. Her refusal to submit woman's "meaning" to plasticity's unbinding begins when she fixes a limit to her own plasticity as a subject ("Personally, I have discovered that it is totally impossible for me to give up the schema 'woman'"), and it ends with her unyielding declaration of faith in what she acknowledges as a belief ("Still, I believe that *the word 'woman' has a meaning outside the heterosexual matrix*"). This is a belief to which Malabou clings, attempting to preserve an attachment to being that plasticity, like anti-essentialist discourse, puts at unbearable risk, even in the face of Malabou's identification of being *with* plasticity.

A similar resistance to plasticity as an imperative to unbinding arises when Malabou associates the pain of woman's ontological negation with the pain of writing her own dissertation under Jacques Derrida's supervision—a pain she attributes to Derrida's self-presentation as "a feminine or feminist Derrida," as one "determined to stigmatize and relentlessly critique the distressing comments about women and the female condition by traditional philosophers."[56] Indeed, before the publication of *Marine Lover*, Irigaray's reading of Nietzsche to which Malabou refers above ("Woman neither is nor has an essence"), Derrida, in his own book on Nietzsche, had written, "There is no such thing as an essence of woman because woman averts, she is averted of herself."[57] Citing his call in *Choreographies* for a "multiplicity of sexually marked voices," Malabou responds by demanding, "How could I bear for a man, even speaking in the name of women, 'as' a woman, to speak better than they could, for them, stronger and louder than them, their conceptual and political rights? How could I bear for him to recognize with sharper acuity, sometimes with greater critical insight than they, their overexposure to violence?"[58] In this moment of unbearable enjiety, the feminist negation of traditional ontology (Derrida's speaking "as" a woman) entails a negation of woman's essence (the "they" for which he speaks). This, as Malabou's language makes clear, seems impossible for her to survive; it confronts her with the prospect of coming unbound "from the chain of continuation," which is also to say, from the signifying chain in which the subject is bound to meaning. However much the plasticity she champions disturbs the fixity of identities, including the identity of being, Malabou's will to identify woman as an ontological possibility, as the bearer of a meaning that anti-essentialist arguments "disembowel," reflects her attachment to a sense of woman incompatible with woman as ab-sens. "The choice of feminine recognizes precisely the *body* of woman, its morphology, the anatomy of her sex organs," she writes, suggesting that despite her elaboration of woman's "fugitive essence," that fugitivity remains the fixed property of a conservatively recognizable "woman."[59] She refuses, therefore, to "give up" her attachment to the couple formed by woman and meaning—a refusal that ontologizes woman in relation to the "violence [that] . . . confers her being" and that positivizes sexual difference as produced by sens-absexe.[60]

Now place beside this unbearable encounter with woman as (a figure for) ab-sens Ronald Judy's discussion of the "thanatology" that slave narratives enact. In response to Henry Louis Gates Jr.'s claim that "the slave narrative represents the attempt of blacks to *write themselves into being*," Judy maintains that such texts can produce the opposite effect. "With the first slave narrative," Judy asserts, the Negro "no longer is a transcendental abstraction, but has become a material embodiment of that which exceeds the boundaries of our reasonable truth."[61] As a supernumerary element, the African ruptures the coherence of reason by registering reason's subtraction from itself once its outside appears in its frame. By "exceed[ing] the boundaries of our reasonable truth" and gesturing toward ab-sens, the African figures a limit to thought and a threat to the world's consistency. The "Negro" serves to suture this wound, to positivize, by way of slave narratives, the African's unintelligibility. As Judy puts it, "What is really at issue in the writing of African American culture is not the humanity of the Negro . . . but the universal comprehension of reality, of what is and how it functions."[62] Symptomatizing the not-all of the "universal" one, the African in Judy's reading threatens a subtraction of sense from thought; the African, that is, obtrudes as the excess, as the noncoincidence with itself, that reveals *within* the "closed *one*" of reason the antagonism reason abjects in order to *become* itself in the first place. This ontological gap or division, which the abjection of the "Negro" from the social repeats in a futile effort to refute, becomes visible in the irrational violence with which the embodiment of ontological negation is obsessively negated and cast out. Zupančič describes the Real as "that which the traditional ontology had to cut off to be able to speak of 'being qua being'"; Judy offers a parallel formula with regard to the ontology of the enslaved: "Heterogeneity is removed from reality as a flaw, an aberration of the universal and homogeneous totality of truth."[63]

By demonstrating access to Western reason, slave narratives may, as Gates suggests, represent an attempt by the formerly enslaved to write themselves into being; but, for Judy, that entrance into the ontological realm can never, in fact, take place. Referring to Olaudah Equiano's account of his capture, enslavement, and conversion, Judy proposes that in the very affirmation of his identity as a human, which demands above all "unification into oneness" to attain the "the state of being oneself," the African who had been enslaved succumbs to ontological annihilation or to what Judy calls "the negation of the materiality of Africa."[64] Rather than admitting its author into the register of ontology, "the slave narrative," Judy writes, becomes "a *thanatology*, a writing of the annihilation that applies the taxonomies of death in Reason (natural law) to enable the emergence of the self-reflexive consciousness of the Negro."[65] Instead of writing himself into being, Equiano, as this fatal dialectic suggests, writes himself into a fiction of meaning—a fiction of meaning *for the other* that turns ab-sens into sens-absexe: "The humanization . . . achieved in the slave narrative required the conversion of the incomprehensible African into the comprehensible Negro."[66] Only when recast in terms of such comprehensibility or sense can the material excrescence of ontology, the split or subtraction of ab-sens, become accessible to thought. Judy, committed to what he calls "a nonrecuperable negativity," one that "jeopardizes the genealogy of Reason," draws the unsettling conclusion that "to claim black agency is to claim the Negro."[67] In other words, it is to affirm identity through an attachment to intelligibility that requires negating the negativity of Blackness as figured by the "incomprehensible African."

Engaging and extending Judy's work, Frank Wilderson III draws a lesson from it that reinforces this point: "'Black authenticity,' is an oxymoron," he declares, "for it requires the kind of ontological integrity which the Slave cannot claim."[68] For the Black scholar, as Wilderson puts it, this "is menacing and unbearable," as unbearable as the idea of renouncing the meaning of "woman" is for Malabou. It gives rise, therefore, as in Malabou's case, to a form of disavowal: one evinced in narratives, as Judy writes, of "an emerging subjectivity's triumphant struggle to discover its identity."[69] The unbearable

Real of ontological negation, the ab-sens that undoes the oneness, the comprehensible *identity*, of the world, compels us to seek to preserve that world by affirming our oneness within it. Both the anti-anti-essentialist woman and the "comprehensible Negro" defend the world as comprehension from the assault of pure negativity. Wilderson makes vivid in his powerful text "the unbearable hydraulics of Black disavowal," which, he observes, is "triggered by a dread of both being 'discovered,' and of discovering oneself, as ontological incapacity."[70] With lacerating clarity he anatomizes "the unbearable terror of that (non)self-discovery always already awaiting the Black."[71]

This "ontological incapacity," in Wilderson's account, singularly pertains to Blackness, which finds no place in a Symbolic order that rests on it nonetheless. Drawing imaginatively on earlier work by Frantz Fanon and David Marriott, Wilderson observes that insofar as "slaveness . . . has consumed Blackness and Africanness, . . . it [is] impossible to divide slavery from Blackness."[72] Because "the structure by which human beings are recognized and incorporated into a community of human beings is anti-slave," Blackness remains, *and must remain*, excluded from the realm of humanity and the prospect of social being. But Blackness as ontological impossibility produces a specific type of being: "the Black," a sociogenetic identity defined by a specific "grammar of suffering."[73] Extending Fanon's assertion that "ontology . . . does not permit us to understand the being of the black," Wilderson proposes the necessity of differentiating "Black being from Human life."[74] He does so by reifying Blackness in the specificity of "the Black," who is, moreover, a figure of reification from the outset, "an accumulated and fungible object, rather than an exploited and alienated subject."[75] The Black, "who is always already a Slave," never rises to the status of "a subject who has either been alienated in language or alienated from his or her cartographic and temporal capabilities."[76] To the contrary, the Black remains for Wilderson "an object who has been positioned by gratuitous violence[,] . . . a sentient being for whom recognition and incorporation is impossible," insofar as "accumulation and fungibility" are the Black's "ontological foundation."[77] But while Blackness remains definitionally excluded from any Symbolic framing, excluded in its very essence from ontological possibility, only subjects *inhabiting* the Symbolic could posit, abject, or assume it. "The Black," then, pace Wilderson, would always "be" a Symbolic subject, one divided into subjectivity by having entered the linguistic order, but one consigned to figure what the Symbolic is unable to accommodate: the (Real) negativity of Blackness. Those read as materializations of the ontological impossibility of Blackness would share the quality of fungibility that Wilderson (with reference to Saidiya Hartman) associates with Blackness itself. Incapable of ontological manifestation within the order of sense, unbound from the putative stability of Symbolic coefficients, Blackness would name what has no being, no identity, and no place. It would have no fixed phenomenal form but only a social and political one and would vanish in every positivity that substantialized or embodied it.

Wilderson, however, *does* attach a property to Blackness, one that particularizes the Black not only as excluded from subjectivity but also as *uniquely* excluded. That property, as it happens, coincides with Malabou's analysis of woman, for Wilderson reads the Black as distinctively "positioned . . . by the structure of gratuitous violence" and as "openly vulnerable to the whims of the world."[78] Recall in this context Malabou's words: "It is necessary to imagine the possibility of woman starting from the structural impossibility she experiences of not being violated."[79] In each case a specific entity in the world, a speaking subject acknowledged as human, though by no means universally, lays claim to the unique position of foreclosure from the field of human "being." Small wonder, then, that when David Marriott, characterizing Wilderson's work as situating "black suffering . . . [as] beyond analogy," declares that for Wilderson "there is always a desire to have black lived experience named as the worst" because "the black has to embody this abjection without reserve," his words echo Judith Butler's concern about the work of Luce Irigaray on which Malabou's feminism builds: "Is it not the case that there is within any discourse and thus within Irigaray's as well, a set of constitutive exclusions that are inevitably produced by the circumscription of the feminine as that which monopolizes the sphere of exclusion?"[80]

In each case specifying a *type* of being as, in its essence, nonbeing gives rise to similar problems. Wilderson's argument, for example, though more powerful than Marriott suggests, situates Black sentient beings outside the Symbolic order of subjects. It positions them *ontologically* as materializations of Blackness: essentially and foundationally excluded from the human. But Judy offers a more nuanced project, if no less devastating in its consequences: "to expose the catachresis at work in the biological misnomer of race, to read the Negro as a trope, indeed a misapplied metaphor."[81] The result of this tropological maneuver, for Judy, "is the exclusion of the African from the space of Western history, and the marginal inclusion of the Negro as negativity."[82] Two phrases merit attention here: "marginal inclusion" and "*as* negativity." The ontological foreclosure of Blackness produces a Symbolic subject to figure this lack of a proper place or name. Marriott phrases it precisely: "The black has to *embody* this abjection without reserve." Like woman, that is, the Black is a subject whose status *as a subject* is subject to doubt by virtue of figuring *within* the Symbolic the ab-sens excluded *from* it. Wilderson rightly recognizes, then, that the logic of anti-Blackness, which is nothing other than logic itself as the syntactic imperative of making-sense, will persist in any social or political variation of the world. With good reason, therefore, his position calls for "a total end of the world."[83] But Black persons, despite the history that places them inextricably in relation to slavery, are not, in any given world, the singular or exclusive embodiments of ontological exclusion. If the "Negro," for Judy, permits the translation of African unknowability into the register of meaning, then "the Black," as a category of person, similarly functions as a catachrestic misnaming by which ab-sens, the void of meaning, gets raised up as sens-absexe, fleshed out in a positive identity that reinforces sense.

More than just "the Negro," then, must be read as catachrestic. *Queerness, woman, Blackness, trans**: these terms (like countless others that name the null set of a given order) emerge from the division between the negativity that inheres in division as such—the undoing of the world as unity, comprehension, or identity—and that division's positivization in the catachrestic name of a social being.[84] No list could include every figure for the world's dissolution as comprehension; were that possible, the world would emerge again as totalized, comprehensive. However endless the production of contingent figures for the unbearable, all spring from the inextricability of ab-sens and sens-absexe and thus from the insistence of the not-all that makes the sexual relation impossible. All are rooted in the ontological antagonism that structures the logic of sense by which we are divided into being: divided between the subject of desire and of the subject of the drive, where the former consigns the latter to the status of what is not.

For just that reason, and without denying other (mis)namings of exclusion, I primarily refer to queerness as the catachresis of this nothing, of this ontological negation. I say "for just that reason" because queerness, though linked (in contemporary discourse) to nonnormative sexual identities (and I want to insist on the contingency of that link and so on the impossibility of delimiting what queerness would "properly" name), invokes, as I wrote in *No Future*, the insistence of the drive and of jouissance.[85] Infinitely mobile as an epithet for strangeness, out-of-jointedness, and nonnormativity, queerness colors any enjoyment that seems to threaten a world. Such enjoyments, in the libidinal economy of a given culture's fantasy, may follow from *any* attribute, including, among others, race, gender, gender expression, sexuality, ethnicity, caste, class, religion, mental or physical ability, marital status, and educational background; the list could go on forever. In the words of Annamarie Jagose, "As queer is unaligned with any specific identity category, it has the potential to be annexed profitably to any number of discussions."[86] Queerness, in this, shares with sodomy ("that utterly confused category," as Michel Foucault deemed it), a resistance to definition. Foucault describes "the extreme discretion of the texts dealing with sodomy" and the "nearly universal reticence in talking about it."[87] Constructing a valuable link between sodomy as it was understood in the Renaissance and what he then calls "sites of present confusion," Jonathan Goldberg observes in *Sodometries* that sodomy's regulatory efficacy with regard to criminal behavior follows largely from the fact that it "remains incapable of exact definition."[88] Queerness, similarly, refuses limitation to particular persons, objects, or acts. Associated with the power of a drive that subdues the subject's will or agency and invoking an enjoyment in excess of the pleasures associated with the good, queerness figures meaning's collapse and the encounter with ab-sens. It speaks to the place of the nothing fleshed out by those who are made to embody it. But those entities (persons, objects, acts) cannot, in themselves, *be* queer; they lack an ontological relation to ontological impossibility. Rather, they serve as catachreses for the negativity of ab-sens.

This is not to deny that many use *queer* as a positive identity. Even within such contexts, though, its import remains uncertain. For some it merely substitutes for the continuously expanding roster of sexual or sexually stigmatized minorities. For others it indexes a sexual dissidence at odds with identity as such (whether of gender, sex, or sexuality). Still others use it diacritically within the ranks of sexual minorities to separate opponents of assimilation from those who seek normalization. And if some are content to use *queer* interchangeably with *lesbian* or *gay*, or with the various identitarian positions (currently) codified as LGBTQIA+, others, myself included, construe it as the empty marker of a stigmatized otherness to communitarian norms, thus preserving its force as something that thwarts the straightness of intelligibility.

Other catachreses—woman, trans*, or Blackness, to name just a few—do this work as well, but always at the risk of reproducing (for some) the unbearable encounter to which Wilderson and Malabou attest: the unbearable despecification of a positive identity forged from ongoing material histories of social and cultural violence, a despecification that can seem, as it does for Wilderson and Malabou, to redouble that violence when those positive identities are identified as "mere" figures. I catch a glimpse of a kindred spirit, though, in the work of Jared Sexton, especially in his discussion of Afropessimism as "a meditation on a poetics and politics of abjection wherein racial Blackness operates as an asymptotic approximation of that which disturbs every claim or formation of identity and difference as such," an assertion in line with my earlier claim that "queerness can never define an identity, it can only ever disturb one."[89]

My argument might seem to bolster the argument against Lacanian-inflected queer theory by such critics as José Esteban Muñoz, Amber Jamilla Musser, and Chandan Reddy—arguments Musser summarizes straightfor-wardly: "Sexuality as a frame silences race."[90] Reddy, in *Freedom with Violence*, his ambitious reading of race and sexuality at the end of the twentieth century in the United States, explicitly maintains the need to reverse the relation between these two categories: "In our contemporary moment," he writes, "sexuality is an iteration of—and amendment to and of—race."[91] Certainly sexuality, as Reddy construes it, is always already raced; race, after all, belongs to the various historical contingencies we attach to the subject for whom sens-absexe has cut off from thought the primal cut of ab-sens. But sex in psychoanalytic terms is not, as I've argued, reducible to the positivity of sexual difference or to the framework of "sexuality"; it pertains, instead, to the cut itself as the ontological incompletion dissimulated by contingent forms of Symbolic identity . Never one, and thus never just one *more*, among the myriad elements that appear within and constitute social reality, sex, to quote Žižek, "is the way the ontological deadlock, the incompleteness of reality in itself, is inscribed into subjectivity."[92] As such, it merits the characterization proposed by Jean-Claude Milner as "the place of infinite contingency in bodies."[93] Coinciding with primary process thought, and so with a libidinally freighted movement anterior to the logic of meaning, sex as defined by ab-sens elicits the subject from the primal cut and binds that subject, divided from the outset, to the insistence of the drive whose corollary is jouissance as self-subtraction.

Like gender, sexuality, and other differentially articulated social constructs, race both expresses and denies this split that libidinizes the subject from the beginning. As positivized into something determinate, knowable, and sedimented with meaning, race (like gender, sex, or sexuality as conventionally understood) fills the void of ab-sens with the fantasy of a knowable identity. That this fantasy may be collectively shared—and that its consequences can make, quite literally, the difference between life and death—makes it no less fantasmatic in the psychoanalytic sense; all of Symbolic reality depends on a fantasy frame to support it. Neither sexuality (as we think we know it) nor race can claim a privileged relation to the ontologically negated. Sex (in the psychoanalytic sense: as designated by ab-sens) is the indispensable element here, not any culturally and historically contingent category of identity. This is not to uphold, as Reddy suggests, "the subject's unrelenting attachment . . . to the imagined unity and universality of [the Symbolic] order" (the drive, which springs from the *division* of the subject, expresses resistance to that attachment as it incompletes that unity), and it is certainly not to affirm such attachment *at the expense of* "any plural historicity to the implacable logic that the psychoanalytic subject is seen to be in opposition to."[94] To the contrary, that "plural historicity" confirms the Symbolic's "implacable logic," which is the logic of signification subtending history as the making of sense. No doubt, as Reddy rightly notes, "a variety of contradictions" in the world as it is can portend "the dissolution of a liberal order," producing multiple sites for "mount[ing] a politics of nonidentity."[95] Blackness and woman, for example, can both work powerfully toward that end. But as my readings of Wilderson and Malabou suggest, each tends to return to a substantive *identity* as the locus of ontological exclusion, and each finds it similarly unbearable to renounce an attachment to that *form* of being with which (though differently) each associates the Real of what "is" not (even if those forms are similarly defined by openness to violence and violation). Both Wilderson and Malabou, in other words, elaborate ontological exclusions while positivizing the particular category of beings they view as *essentially* excluded. Reddy, confusing the contingency of the social with the structural law of the Symbolic, denies that ontological exclusions betray the latter's inflexible structure: the "social formation is heterogeneous and always in flux," he correctly asserts, before concluding that this variability "trouble[s] and make[s] unavailable the . . . cultural homogeneity of the symbolic."[96] But the structuring law of the Symbolic demands no "cultural homogeneity." To the contrary, the open set of terms that can figure ontological negation makes clear that what the Symbolic ordains, instead, is the absenting of ab-sens to produce the world as sens-absexe. Social formations, precisely *because* they are "heterogeneous and always in flux," will generate different embodiments to flesh out the place of that negation; but however plastic the *expression* of Symbolic law may be, the structural violence of the law itself, the violence of the word that cuts ("qui tranche") to determine the social order, always calls forth catachrestic identities to fill the place of nonbeing. Those identities themselves are contingent, but their structuring logic is not.

Reddy, however, makes a valuable point about theoretical formalization, especially the sort that privileges structural frameworks over social identities: "The formalism of the psychoanalytic argument against the social can never fully dissociate itself from the cultural archive and texts through which it makes its argument, including the cultural text of Lacanian psychoanalysis."[97] This reminds us that accounts of structures can never access the structures they analyze. In trying to think what governs the positivity of what is and in trying to resist the temptation of acceding to the world as it merely appears, they depend on models of reading drawn from the very world they read and immerse themselves in particulars to observe a logic that informs and exceeds them. They work, as Wilderson writes in a passage describing his own methodology, by "pressing the social and performative into analytic service of the structural and positional; not vice versa."[98]

In this, of course, such structural formalisms run the risk of ignoring alternative structures that other texts, other modes of reading, other social or performative data, might allow us to apprehend. Only counterreadings and subsequent debates can keep that risk in check. If no formalism "can . . . fully dissociate itself" from the content that it engages, if it can never forgo the world whose "reality" it reads through a structuring law, it aims to sketch from *within* the world the frame subtracted *from* that world for the world as such to take shape. Much like that frame, then, formalism expresses the excessive element in any world that exposes that world as not-all, the element that Barbara Johnson calls "a kind of unthought remainder that would be functioning nevertheless, even though it wasn't recognized" and that she specifies as "a formal overdetermination" that instantiates the "death instinct."[99] To translate this more explicitly into the argument I'm making here: ab-sens is "knowable" only through its negation by sens-absexe, but sens-absexe contains ab-sens as its own internal limit, the point of impossibility encountered in the failure of sexual relation. What eludes the grasp of ontology, precluding the closure of being as one, appears in the ontological field through catachreses of ab-sens.

Two things follow closely from this: understandings of formal structure are structured by the forms they would understand, and critical attention to such structures can alter our perception of those forms in the world. Rather than confirming Musser's claim that "sexuality . . . silences race," this suggests that a certain formalism determines race and sexuality alike. Woman, queerness, Blackness, brownness: the point is neither to silence nor to absolutize such identities but to assume them instead *as displacements*, as figural (mis)namings of ab-sens. As such they mean (in both senses of the word) to suture the hole (the cut of the Real) in the reality of sens-absexe. As contingent embodiments of the noncontingent pressure of ab-sens, such figures are conjured to materialize the void, the unnamed and uncounted element that structures a given world. They simultaneously express and disavow what could only ever be *thought* as nothing. If saying this seems to "silence" race, sexuality, gender, gender expression, or any of the other catachreses generated by a sociopolitical reality, then it does so in the hope of sounding out the structure such reality silences in order to produce its illusory coherence. Far from being fictions we could hope to see through, get over, or decolonize, catachreses like these, though not necessarily these catachreses in particular, will populate *any* world that has swollen into shape through sens-absexe, which is to say, any world in which the cut of the word is decisive. Undoing the givenness of a specific world by attending to the void within it can never undo the foreclosure of ab-sens, the primal expression of Symbolic law that governs the logic of worlds. But it can expose the figural structure of the social identities those worlds engender by provoking an encounter with the nothing of the cut or division that creates them. This is the work of the death drive but also, as I continue to insist, of queer theory, at least insofar as queer theory takes *queerness* as "incapable of exact definition," as void of any fixed content, and so as a name, though not the only one, for the ab-sens that counts for nothing.

Although Calvin Warren addresses these issues in strikingly similar terms, he sees things rather differently in a dazzling and provocative essay on Symbolic identities and ontological negation. Interpreting Blackness, like Wilderson, as a "structural position of non-ontology" fundamentally distinct from queerness, he describes the "black queer" as doubly erased by what he posits as "onticide."[100] Building not only on Wilderson's analyses but also on Stefano Harney and Fred Moten's work in *The Undercommons*—especially their description of "the containerized" as occupying "the standpoint of no standpoint, everywhere and nowhere, of never and to come, of thing and nothing"—Warren sees a "differential relation to violence" that separates Blackness from queerness, thereby speaking to the "difference between non-ontology and an extreme condition of unfreedom."[101] With this as his predicate, he argues that the queerness of antihumanist queer theory "conceals and preserves the humanity it proclaims to disrupt," producing a figure that may be "at the limit of subjectivity," but a figure that is not, as the Black is, "the object denied symbolic placement" or inclusion in the human.[102] Thus, Warren, like Wilderson, links Blackness as ontological impossibility to the foreclosure from subjectivity of those who embody it catachrestically.[103]

For Ronald Judy, as already noted, the "Negro," as "catachresis" or "misnomer of race," as the comprehensible form that displaces the incomprehensible African, finds "marginal inclusion" in the Symbolic sphere as a *figure* for negativity. I take this as the stronger claim, despite the significant conceptual opening that Warren's work achieves (especially by thinking ontological negation with reference to structural antagonism and the tension between reason and what exceeds it). Judy avoids the problems that arise when Blackness and queerness in Warren's work become attributes of two distinct entities, as they do in the following passage:

> A person understood as "queer" could purchase a black-object from the auction block like his/her hetero-normative counterpart. In those rare instances where the black-as-object was able to participate in this economy and purchase a black-object as well, the black purchaser could, at any moment, become another commodity—if found without freedom papers or validation from a white guardian—the system of fungible blackness made any black interchangeable and substitutional. This movement between object and subject is not a problem for queerness, but is an unresolvable problem for blackness. This is the important difference between the two.[104]

Warren notes the asymmetry that exempted the (implicitly non-Black) "queer" (which presumably refers here to someone identified with nonheteronormative sexual acts) from commodification as a marketable object in the economy of slavery. As important as this is in approaching the historical experiences of what Warren hypostatizes as "the black" and "the queer" in this passage, it does not follow that the "movement between object and subject is not a problem for queerness"—or, indeed, that queerness as ontological negation is not bound to that very movement. While recognizing the epistemic consequences of centuries in which legal and political institutions have reduced Black persons to the status of objects made to circulate in a global economy, we can still trace the logic that enables that reduction to structures that are psychic and social at once, indeed, to the very structures that may govern the "movement between subject and object."

For Lacan, in fact, such a movement inheres in subjectivization itself. As he famously argues in "The Mirror Stage," the infant, by assuming its specular image, precipitates the "primordial form" of the "I" precisely by identifying *with a form* that situates the ego in an irreducibly "fictional direction."[105] This primordial form of the "I" is subsequently "objectified in the dialectic of identification with the other, . . . before language restores to it, in the universal, its function as a subject."[106] But the division of the subject that results from its very constitution *through* division (between the infant and its image, between the proto-subject and the other, between the signifier and the signified) puts the subject at perpetual risk of losing hold of this fictional "I" and returning to the nonidentity of a body reduced to bits and pieces: to disorganized, objectal matter.[107] Lacan, therefore, goes on to note that when the "specular *I* turns into the social *I*" and the mirror stage comes to an end, leaving in its wake a Symbolic subject mediated by "the other's desire," the very "I" itself becomes "an apparatus to which every instinctual pressure constitutes a danger": the danger of the subject's reduction to an object governed by the drive.[108] While acknowledging the specificity of the Black experience of enslavement and the difference between the "the black-as-object" and the proto-subject's anxiety about falling into objecthood, I trace this psychoanalytic logic to differentiate the ontology of the subject from the particular historical experiences to which that ontology gives rise— experiences that derive from failed attempts to resolve through catachrestic figures a structural antagonism in the subject that admits no resolution and no repair. In this context Wilderson recognizes "the aggressivity toward Blackness not as a form of discrimination, but as . . . a form of psychic health and well-being for the rest of the world."[109] Indeed, as he elsewhere describes it, anti-Blackness functions to "regenerate Humans and prevent them from suffering the catastrophe of psychic incoherence."[110]

The "movement between object and subject," then, is indeed "a problem for queerness," especially when queerness, rather than naming nonheteronormative sexualities, refers to the insistence of those unnamed forces, those catachreses of ab-sens, that make a given world not-all. An encounter with such a figure provokes an influx of enjiety that expresses itself as "aggressivity toward" the catachrestic "queer" whose appearance in the space of being seems to dissipate its consistency. Nonheteronormative sexualities, like the visibility of trans* identities, convey that threat in many contexts, and the violence directed against them (including homophobia, transphobia, lesbophobia, and effeminophobia, to name just a few of its forms), the violence qualified by Warren as "a grammar of suffering, which we call queerness," effects the reduction of a (seeming) subject to a libidinally overdetermined object merely *masquerading* as a subject.[111] Instead of approaching queerness, though, through Warren's "grammar of suffering" (a phrase that Wilderson used earlier to describe the experience of the Black and the slave), where that suffering elicits the humanizing pathos of a distinctive type of being, I would argue that queerness is agrammatical and acephalic both.[112] The encounter with whatever counts as "queer" effects an anacoluthon in the rhetoric of reality. Queerness, like anacoluthon (from the Greek *an*, "not," and *akolouthos*, "following"), cuts or interrupts a sequence (grammatical, narrative, or genealogical) by confronting the logic of meaning with the ab-sens from which *nothing* follows.[113]

"Onticide," for all its conceptual power, positions the "black queer" as uniquely the catachresis of this "nothing." Warren supports this claim by noting that the "black queer" doubles "the black's" exclusion from being while also facing exclusion from "the queer's" "incorpor[ation] . . . into the fold of humanity."[114] He develops this argument through Eric Stanley's observation that "the overwhelming numbers of trans/queer people who are murdered in the United States are of color."[115] This prompts him to reflect on the "differential relationship to violence" of "people of color" and "non-people of color" among "those who might identify as 'queer.'"[116] Based on the disproportionate representation of the former among "trans/queer people" killed in the United States, Warren argues that the Blackness of "black queers" denies them "symbolic placement, differentiating flesh, and a grammar of suffering"— all of which remain possibilities, if only marginally, for "queers" not "of color."[117] Construing "the black," through reference to Fanon, as outside "symbolic placement," Warren asserts that "black suffering" is unintelligible in *any* "grammar of suffering" (which he now associates with "queer theory"), precisely to the extent that Black suffering "lacks a proper grammar of enunciation."[118] As heir to "the violence of captivity [that] expelled the African from Difference, or the Symbolic," "the black-as-object," for Warren, "is situated outside of space, time, and the world," which is also to say, outside of the human as "the order of differentiating subjects."[119] Blackness and queerness, in other words, have not only different relations to violence but also, as Warren puts it, "a differential relationship to 'nothingness,' where 'nothingness' is the symbolic designator of the incomprehensible remainder or exclusion. The fact that the overwhelming majority of those murdered are 'of color' and the position of blackness in the antagonism is one of non-ontology (negative existence) is no mere coincidence."[120]

Underlying this analysis, though, is the conflation of ontological impossibility with entities represented as *ontologizing* this very impossibility. If, that is, the overrepresentation of people of color among trans/queer murder victims and the "position of blackness . . . [as] one of non-ontology" is, indeed, "no mere coincidence," then either "the black" must *essentially* coincide with Blackness as nonontology or the "the black" must be understood as *one* of its highly charged catachreses. But what could it mean, and how could we know it, if "the black" were essentially bound to the "blackness" that remains, not *like* but *as* the Real, excluded from representation? Can an experience historically correlated with African captivity in the Atlantic slave trade *uniquely* define "the Real of ontology" that, in Warren's own phrasing, "ruptures and preconditions symbolization"?[121] "The black," no less than "the queer" or "the woman," is subjectified through language, but what Warren rightly characterizes as the "unresolvable problem for blackness"—the fact that it remains "the 'unthought' and the incommunicable," "outside of life and its customary lexis"—leads him, despite his own warning against it, to slide "between identity and structure" by conflating the ontological exclusion that is "blackness" with the social exclusion of Blacks.[122] He thus presents as non-contingent, nonhistorical, and a priori—in other words, as ontological—"the black's" relation to the structural position of ontological impossibility.[123]

Warren himself sounds a warning about the dangers of such a conflation when responding to Zakiyyah Iman Jackson's analysis of David Marriott's *On Black Men*.[124] Jackson, he argues, errs in her effort to "think race and sexuality together":

> It is here that we seem to slide between blackness as a structural position of non-ontology and the sociology of race (as an identity). In this analysis, blackness becomes a "type" much like sexologist [*sic*] created the "homosexual" as a type. Instead of thinking about blackness as the ontological horizon that fractures epistemology, we locate blackness within the Symbolic Order of scientific discourse and sexology. Blackness, then, oscillates between an identity, a marker of the Symbolic order, and an ontological position, the "Real" that ruptures and preconditions symbolization. This sliding between identity and structure is a symptom of what Wilderson would call "the ruse of analogy." Whenever we equate an ontological position with an identity formation, we perform the very violence that sustains the antagonism.[125]

Notwithstanding the care with which he makes these distinctions, Warren himself, I have argued, identifies Blackness (as the ontologically excluded Real) with "the black" (as the sociological identity of particular Symbolic subjects). He reads "the black" not only as a "being fallen off the map of conceivability," as one who "'does not exist' in the world because lacking symbolic placement," but also as a social identity whose visibility enables the statistical analysis of murdered trans/queer persons of color.[126] This conflation seems to spring from his resistance (rooted in solid political ground) to viewing "the black" and "the queer" as equivalent in their social or historical positions—a resistance reinforced by the preponderance of violence against "trans/queer" people of color. But it results in a less sustainable resistance to the "equivalence" of "blackness and queerness."[127] As "ontological position[s]" that gesture toward what the order of being leaves out, Blackness and queerness would name catachrestically the unnameable void in reality and the *enjiety* aroused whenever a subject comes too close to the Real. Though certainly inflected by unconscious motivations and by my own position as a subject, my focus on *queerness* as an organizing term wagers that its indeterminacy of reference (in contrast to the fungible "black-objects" to which Blackness for Warren is *essentially* fixed) might slow, if not prevent, the slide from ontological position to fixed social identity, thus permitting the negativity of queerness to supplement—rather than to supersede—the ongoing historical and political efforts to read "the queer" and "the black."[128] The work of queer theory thus coincides with interrogations of woman, Blackness, or trans* as ontological exclusions, a point reinforced by David Marriott's insight "that blackness has no locatable referent or unequivocal name, but is something that escapes all attributes, including the unity of an ontic-ontological fugitivity or again the hypostatized name of 'absolute dereliction.'"[129]

Interestingly, Jackson's essay, which Warren charges with enacting that "slide between blackness as a structural position of non-ontology and the sociology of race (as an identity)," explicitly works *against* that slide. Indeed, it is precisely toward that end that Jackson thinks Blackness and queerness together. Addressing herself to "black queerness" instead of to the particularity of "the black queer," Jackson suggests that if "we think about queerness as something other than an identity, gender, or even set of sexual practices," then "we might think of black queerness as an existential matter rather than as an attribution that accompanies only some black subjectivities."[130] Queerness, so considered, would pertain to anyone positioned to represent Blackness as ontological impossibility. While avoiding the factitious equivalence of "the black" and "the queer" as social beings—which is also to say, as allegories of histories that overlap for some subjects at certain points while diverging at and for others—Jackson reads Blackness and queerness alike as figures of negativity: "Arguably, one could see queerness as the ontology of blackness in culture while theorizing how gender and sexual identities and experiences are produced within the context and logic of antiblackness."[131] As radicals of negativity, neither Blackness nor queerness would correlate with any particular social attributes or refer to a mode of "being" that any subject could properly claim. Neither would "have" a history but both, instead, would *engender* histories through the contingent designation of certain persons or groups as their catachreses, which is to say, as figures of "nothing."

What occasions Warren's anxiety in the face of Jackson's text is his confusion of these catachrestic histories with the ontological negation from which they spring. He writes, "The 'existential matter' that preoccupies Jackson's inquiry here is one that reduces the ontological position of blackness to the experience of unfreedom, or human suffering—a grammar of suffering, which we call 'queerness.' Queerness, here, assumes a problematic

interchangeability with blackness[.] ... We might ponder the ethical implications of this collapse and the way that the collapse itself serves to distort
the antagonism that, as she insightfully notes is 'the foundation of ethics and
politics, even of modern sociality itself.'"[132] What's at stake comes into focus
here when Warren insists on the "ethical implications" that make the "interchangeability" of queerness and Blackness "problematic" in his view. By
asserting the primacy of "ethical" consequences, he frames the discussion in
social rather than in structural or ontological terms. That framing becomes
more apparent with his claim that Jackson, by enacting and encouraging this
"collapse," "distort[s] the antagonism" that she sees as the "foundation of
ethics" as such. Though Jackson never mentions "antagonism" in her text,
her essay does, as Warren observes, propose that a structuring logic of negation—in other words, a logic of antagonism—underlies and calls into being
ethics, politics, and sociality. She calls that logic "the negation of blackness,"
before proceeding to suggest that queerness be thought as the "ontology of
blackness in culture."[133] Understood as the ontology of the division or cut in
articulations of reality, queerness expresses the radical force of Blackness as
negativity, a negativity that is not the negation of something substantive and
specifiable ("the Black" or "the queer" as types of beings) but the insistence
of what, in a given order, is inimical to being itself.

Warren may evoke as "antagonism" what Jackson describes as "the negation of blackness," but Jackson, for whom that act of negation produces the
ground of ethics, analyzes the negation of Blackness/queerness as the negation of *the negativity inherent in ontological incompletion.* Warren, by contrast, notwithstanding his interest in antagonism as ontological, elaborates
an ethical discrimination among sociocultural identities.[134] Antagonism, as
a structuring principle, may serve to establish the field of ethics, but for just
that reason it remains outside of ethical determination. Warren's concern
about the "ethical implications" of "distort[ing]" this antagonism springs
less from an engagement with the negativity that structures social reality
than from his (justified) anxiety about effacing the differences between two
figures of that negativity: "We might ask how anything could serve as the
ontology of blackness? ... Frank Wilderson insightfully notes that any rider
that we attach to blackness is a conceptual fallacy and results in nothing
more than a 'structural adjustment'—the attempt to incorporate blacks into
the fold of humanity through the grammar of another's suffering. The queer
subject is constructed as degenerate and transgressive, but the fundamental
distinction between the 'degenerate queer' and the 'derelict black-as-object'

is that one possesses a grammar to express unfreedom and the other lacks communicability altogether."[135]

Here queerness and Blackness quickly slide into "constructed" socio-logical entities ("the 'degenerate queer' and the 'derelict black-as-object'"), each with its own proper attributes. Blackness, according to Warren, must be free of "any rider" that would "incorporate blacks" into humanity by way of "another's" suffering (where "the black" is excluded—transculturally and transhistorically—from the access to being enjoyed by "the queer," whose suffering—also, transculturally and transhistorically—is considered recognizably "human"). But "the black" as social identity becomes the "rider" of Blackness here, the ontological realization of Blackness as exclusion from ontology. The positing, which is also the positivizing, of these determinate social identities negates the negativity of Blackness and queerness as Jackson's essay reads them, thus repeating the violence that establishes ethics to mask and master antagonism.[136] Warren's words are worth repeating: "Whenever we equate an ontological position with an identity formation, we perform the very violence that sustains the antagonism."[137] If, in my reading, he fails to heed his own well-founded warning or to acknowledge that the violence he refers to inheres in the notion of antagonism as such, that testifies less to a failure on his part than to the difficulty (structural, psychic, and political) of broaching the "ontic . . . function," as Lacan describes it, of the cut or of trying to conceive ab-sens within the topology of sens-absexe.

At the same time, however, Warren takes the full measure of antagonism when he writes, "One simply cannot rely on 'rational instruments' to resolve an irrational dilemma, especially when these very instruments depend on the destructive kernel of irrationality to sustain them."[138] This insight bears significantly on what this book calls "bad education"; it also resonates with arguments I made earlier in *No Future* and, together with Lauren Berlant, in *Sex, or the Unbearable*. Indeed, my quarrel with Warren's resistance to considering ontological negation as pertaining to Blackness and queerness both (as well as to other catachrestic figures for ontological exclusion) is prompted by the similarity of our engagements with the structuring antagonism of the Symbolic. Though our differences have serious implications, which Warren might qualify as "ethical," they should not obscure what brings us together (with Marriott, Jackson, and Wilderson, too): our common recognition that the insistence of the Real calls forth our social reality. Warren may propose as unique the relation of Blackness to that negativity, while I maintain that within the contingencies of their historical, political, and cultural constructions, innumerable catachreses will be posited to take the Real's impossible place ("the Black," "the queer," "the woman," etc.), but we come together in attending seriously to that place's impossibility and in trying to address its consequences for the figures of "nothing" made to fill it.

My claim for the embodiment of that nothing and the localization of that impossibility in an open set of catachreses—among which I emphasize queerness for its referential indeterminacy (which Marriott, in my view rightly, also associates with Blackness) and for its designation of something strange, unfamiliar, or out of place—finds support in the concept of atopia as it travels across critical traditions.[139] Derived from the Greek for "without a place," atopia informs discussions of Blackness for scholars from Houston Baker ("the blues singer's signatory code is always *atopic*, placeless") to Fred Moten ("blackness is the place that has no place") to Rebecka Rutledge Fisher ("Harlem is . . . an atopia, the no-place or abyss where black being is presumed to fall inexorably into nothingness").[140] It looms equally large in feminist discourse. Julia Kristeva employs it to conceptualize the mother ("the absolute because primeval seat of the impossible—of the excluded, the outside-of-meaning, the abject. Atopia"); Moira Gatens invokes it in discussing the philosophy of Michèle Le Doeuff ("Atopic feminist thought-on-the-move is an ongoing process without a proper place"); and Adriana Cavarero conceives it as structurally inseparable from the condition of women ("Some women . . . have turned their experience of atopia in the patriarchal 'scientific' and academic order, not into a discomfort that can be remedied through assimilation, but into the place of a fertile rooting").[141]

As inherited from classical Greece, however, atopia correlates with no identity; indeed, by definition, it shuns assignment to any place. Referring to what *lacks* a proper place, to whatever is incongruous, odd, or queer, atopia, in the *Dialogues* and *Symposium* of Plato, is used in describing Socrates. After initially translating atopia as "strangeness" in *Socrates: Ironist and Moral Philosopher*, Gregory Vlastos quickly qualifies that decision in a footnote: "The Greek is stronger; 'strangeness' picks it up at the lower end of its intensity-range. At the higher end 'outrageousness' or even 'absurdity' would be required to match its force."[142] Joel Alden Schlosser extends that range by noting that "we cannot place something characterized by atopia—it eludes categorization, formulation, or a set geography. . . . Atopia thus gains definition in contrast to its topoi, the practices endemic to a given place, location, or context."[143] Expanding on Roland Barthes's discussion of atopia in *Fragments d'un discours amoureux* ("the loved being is recognized by the amorous subject as 'atopos' [a qualification given to Socrates by his interlocutors] i.e., unclassifiable, of a ceaselessly unforeseen originality"), Sarah Kofman returns to this notion of classificatory impossibility when she summarizes Søren Kierkegaard's take on Socrates as atopic: "Socrates is irreducible to all definitions and specifications; he is and is not."[144] Recalling Goldberg's description of sodomy as "incapable of exact definition" and Lacan's description of the unconscious as "neither being nor non-being," this phrasing, which pushes atopia's refusal of norms to its extreme, captures its unthinkability within the order of what is, its defiance of the logic that imbues a world with the appearance of consistency.

As Kofman's formulation implies, moreover, and as reports of responses to Socrates by his contemporaries confirm, atopia's "strangeness" can entail so radical a departure from social convention that those to whom it pertains can appear as illegible, monstrous, or diseased. The oddity of Socrates threatens to contaminate the order of sense itself, thus bringing us to the intersection of queerness, atopia, and irony: the place where meaning, like a Möbius strip, folds over on itself. Read as the corollary of atopia (and, to that extent, of queerness), Socratic irony, for Pierre Hadot, effects "a reversal of values and an upending of the guiding norms of life," which, as he adds, "cannot help but lead to conflict with the state."[145] In fact, for the Kierkegaard of *The Concept of Irony with Continual Reference to Socrates*, the world historical importance of Socrates, the singularity that renders him atopos, springs from what Kierkegaard (giving credit to Georg Wilhelm Friedrich Hegel, who in turn gives credit to Karl Wilhelm Ferdinand Solger) calls the "infinite absolute negativity" of his irony, a negativity that dissolves the ground of his relation to the structures of social meaning: "In this way he becomes alien to the whole world to which he belongs (however much he belongs to it in another sense); the contemporary consciousness has no predicate for him— nameless and indefinable, he belongs to another formation. What bears him up is the negativity that still has engendered no positivity."[146]

By virtue of belonging to this "other formation," Socrates, according to Kierkegaard, puts an end to the world he inherited and ushers in a new one, becoming, for Kierkegaard no less than for Hegel, "the founder of morality."[147] By interrupting the sequence of world history, Socrates functions like an anacoluthon or, as Kierkegaard puts it, "like a dash" or "a magnificent pause in the course of history" that induces us to fill its void with "the meaning of his existence," despite the fact that his irony undoes the assurance such "meaning" would offer.[148] For Kierkegaard, who insists on this anacoluthon even as he sutures it, Socrates embodies the emergence of a "universalizing subjectivity" not "confined in the substantial ethic" of a particular time and place, a subjectivity that Socrates instantiates by having "taken himself out of, separated himself from, this immediate relationship" to the world.[149] But isn't this to say that he does so as a figural embodiment of ab-sens? Socrates, that is, subtracts himself from collective social reality by virtue of deploying his irony not merely as an instrument of his teaching but also, and more disturbingly, as the practice of a life that renders "the individual alien to the immediacy in which he had previously lived."[150]

The guardians of that immediacy, of course, have good reason to find this troubling—and every Symbolic subject is such a guardian to some extent. However resistant a particular subject's relation to the world, that subject's investments and its self-identity are bound to the world it resists—even, or perhaps especially, in its militant promotion of another (such "other" worlds are conceived, after all, as "better" versions of this one). The tension between such militancy and the negativity of Socratic irony resonates with Wilderson's discussion of the difference between what he calls "American activists" and those, like himself, who want to preserve the "state of pure analysis . . . about the totality and the totalizing nature of Black oppression." The former, as he puts it, are "trying to build a better world. What are we trying to do? We're trying to destroy the world."[151] Socratic irony, in a similar vein, is as indifferent to pragmatic political reform as it is to revolution; it dismisses the authority of the world as we know it and the framework in which the world makes sense by insisting on the pressure of the nothing, of the impossibility excluded from being, of the ab-sens that necessarily structures every articulation of what is.

In challenging "the actuality of the whole substantial world," Socratic irony, as Kierkegaard views it, unleashes an annihilating energy like Walter Benjamin's "divine violence."[152] In Kierkegaard's words: "Here then we have irony as the infinite absolute negativity. It is negativity, because it only negates; it is infinite, because it does not negate this or that phenomenon; it is absolute, because that by virtue of which it negates is a higher something that still is not. The irony establishes nothing, because that which is to be established lies behind it. It is a divine madness that rages like a Tamerlane and does not leave one stone upon another."[153] To the extent that it establishes nothing while taking aim at every establishment, such irony sets meaning spinning in rhythms of appearance and disappearance, thus opening up in the order of sense the (non)place of atopia where "nothing" is established. Kierkegaard's reference to Tamerlane, by relating this irony to "madness," relates it as well to the jouissance inseparable from the drive and so to the insistent subtraction of the subject from itself.

It's ironic, then, that Plato should morph this irony into philosophy, the enemy of jouissance. If Lacan, in Seminar XVII, views philosophy as the master's theft of the knowledge that is the jouissance of the slave, then Plato, by writing Socrates into his philosophical text (or more simply, by *writing Socrates*), appropriates the only knowledge that Socrates ever claimed: the knowledge that he knew nothing.[154] Claire Colebrook, considering the possibility that "the Socratic ironic legacy would not lead to truth, recognition, or moral education" but only to "absence or negativity," proposes that "in many ways, Socrates typifies the impossibility of philosophy."[155] Socrates had to die, we might say, so Plato could *turn him into philosophy*—or at least into the sort of philosophy that renounces jouissance. Alain Badiou, Plato's foremost contemporary advocate and heir, underscores this renunciation: "I think that we have to share, at least provisionally, the antiphilosophical verdict of psychoanalysis according to which philosophy wants to know nothing about jouissance. In any case philosophy, when put to the test, which I propose for it here, of thinking the contemporary, will not find its point of departure in jouissance. It will turn away from jouissance methodically, always with the hope of being able to get back to it."[156] Badiou, however, tellingly describes the jouissance to which philosophy might "get back" as a "rehabilitate[d] jouissance," one that philosophy will have learned to "think . . . otherwise," which is also to say, one he imagines as capable of being dominated by thought.[157] In this sense Platonic philosophy's relation to the "madness" of Socratic irony is a "rehabilitate[d] jouissance" from the outset. As Plato makes clear in the *Republic*, such philosophy forswears atopia in order to gain the world.

Badiou, when he "translates" the *Republic* into French, may modernize, rewrite, and reimagine it, but he continues Plato's positivization of Socratic negativity, making Socrates an earnest spokesman for "the supreme calmness of rational thought" and having him repudiate "the wild, animal-like agency" associated with the "drives."[158] Badiou's Socrates has little of what Jonathan Lear associates with the Socrates of the *Phaedrus*: an "ironic uncanniness" that Socrates celebrates as a form of "god-sent madness . . . finer . . . than man-made sanity," an uncanniness about which Lear, continuing to lean on quotations from the *Phaedrus*, observes: "Those who are struck in this way '*do not know what has happened to them for lack of clear perception*' (250a–b). They are troubled by 'the strangeness [atopia] of their condition' (251e), but they also show 'contempt for all the accepted standards of propriety and good taste'—that is for the norms of social pretense."[159] *Badiou's* Socrates, in contrast, even while continuing to gesture toward his ostensible lack of knowledge ("Would you think it right . . . for someone to talk about what he doesn't know as if he *did* know?"), puts the philosopher at the center of politics and the social order both, determining and defending the very propriety, the very allocation of proper places, that atopia puts at risk.[160] Not for him the "consistently sustained irony that lets the objective power of the state break up on [its] rock-firm negativity," as Kierkegaard expresses it.[161] While the latter sees Socrates as "the nothing from which the beginning must nevertheless begin," Badiou reads him, like Plato, as the plenitude from which philosophy will have begun.[162]

At the same time, however, Badiou acknowledges that philosophy must take account not only of atopia's subtraction from meaning but also of absens as pure division. He expands on this theme in his long encounter with Lacanian psychoanalysis, especially in the seminar he devoted to Lacan from 1994 to 1995. He responds to the "antiphilosophical" views he attributes to the French psychoanalyst by denying that philosophy yields to what he calls the "temptation of the One." Instead, he avows the inherence of division in philosophical thought, in particular the division between metaphysical unity and the primacy of division itself. If Badiou, on the one hand, admits philosophy's "temptation toward the recollection of meaning," he affirms, on the other, its "thought of the true as a stranger to meaning."[163] Calling the former the religious temptation (where "truth is absorbed in the space of meaning") that philosophy can never escape, he declares, "You could say that religion insists in philosophy, but only if you add that philosophy, constitutively, is a certain system of interrupting that insistence."[164] Insofar as Badiou understands philosophy as both an investigation of this interruption and the nondialectical, nonsynthesizable system of interruption itself, he rejects the charge that philosophy aims to plug the hole in being through a discourse of political idealism such as Plato's in the *Republic*.

Addressing Lacan's distaste for that text, with its vision of a regulated society that Lacan compares to a well-run horse farm, Badiou claims that rather than dismissing Plato as simply totalitarian, Lacan reads the *Republic* as a work of irony in which Plato is pulling our leg. Without explicitly endorsing that position, Badiou points out how persistently the *Republic* challenges philosophy's "religious" temptation to suture the hole in (political) reality (noting, for example, Plato's insistence on the plurality of politics, the hazards of chance, and the precarity of the ideal). If not ironizing philosophy's ambitions, then, the *Republic*, as Badiou conceives it, stresses the structural negativity to which philosophy responds. Approaching that division or gap ("béance") in terms of the political distribution of places (the focus, in the *Republic*, of political philosophy as such), Badiou affirms its irreducibility even in the face of philosophy's will to establish a new mode of thought.[165]

Having said as much, Badiou nonetheless makes clear his profound investment in the positivity of such new establishments in the face of that "béance." They counter the instantaneous and atemporal cut of Lacanian analysis ("la coupure instantanée"), with the temporality of what he identifies as philosophy's "long détour."[166] With this he privileges philosophy's attachment to thought in its duration over the abruptions and divisions of the analytic act that make psychoanalysis a continuous undoing at odds with any establishment. Lacan may once have described himself as Lenin to Freud's Marx, but for Badiou he fails to answer the central question that Lenin posed: What is to be done? ("Que faire?").[167] This, for Lenin and Badiou alike, is the essentially *political* question whose answer is collective struggle to dismantle the world as it is and *establish a new one*.

But Lacan, as Badiou acknowledges, rejects the survival of collectivities or the fixity of doctrinal transmission, refusing to formulate precise regulations for the analytic session or to produce an organization to define when an analytic act takes place. Observing that "the final thought of Lacan is that there is no intrinsic legitimacy to the duration of any collective whatsoever," Badiou refers to Lacan's "Monsieur A," dated March 18, 1980, in which, after dissolving the École freudienne de Paris, Lacan offers his fellow psychoanalysts the following advice: "Stick together for as long as needed in order to do something and then, afterwards, disband in order to do something else."[168]

This imperative of dissolution encapsulates Lacan's position for Badiou. Dissolution, he maintains, becomes the very maxim of Lacanian psychoanalysis ("la maxime veritable") insofar as it is synonymous with the analytic act ("l'acte, c'est l'acte de dissolution").[169] Such a will to undo embodies, for Badiou, the essence of antiphilosophy insofar as it insists on and reenacts the primacy of the cut. Against the performative recurrence of this Lacanian "I dissolve" ("Je dissous"), Badiou poses a counterinclination that he frames as "I establish" ("Je fonde")—an inclination that he recognizes as present in Lacan as well, but that repeatedly, even symptomatically, gives way to dissolution.[170] "I establish" declares philosophy's resistance to the negativity of the act, its will to overthrow "what is" by founding what might be, and it reflects, for Badiou, the shared commitment of politics and philosophy (but not of psychoanalysis) to the construction of new worlds in the "long détour" that leads the present toward the ideal.

Though acknowledging the gap, the "béance," that precludes the realization of a world or a republic where everything would find its proper place,

Badiou takes the part of Plato against Lacan's atopic Socrates. If, as Claire Cole-brook aptly puts it, Socrates "typifies the impossibility of philosophy" (and so, in Badiou's sense, anticipates Lacan as an antiphilosopher), then Badiou per-sists, nonetheless, in making him Plato's specular double. In his seminar on Lacan, Badiou claims, for example, "Socrates did not have the least intention of winning over the sophists. He just wanted to show the young people that he could shut the sophists up and move on to serious things."[171] To the extent that these "serious things" for Badiou include the thinking of the world in relation to its Real by establishing philosophy as the dominance of thought and the disavowal of jouissance, Badiou's account of what Socrates achieves by "shut[ting] up" the sophists parallels Sarah Kofman's description of Pla-to's (re)construction of Socrates: "Plato, bowing to a non-dialectical neces-sity, especially after Socrates' death, congealed Socrates into a master figure, a founding figure of philosophy."[172] At the same time, however, the "serious things" that this Socrates would "move on to" reveal philosophy's constitu-tive investment in, its *anti-ironic* investment in, proceeding as if the hole in reality (acknowledged in the sophists' resistance to any positive claims of truth) were capable of political repair—a repair whose possibility rests, ac-cording to Badiou, on "the glue of meaning" (la colle du sens).[173]

This phrase echoes Lacan's reference to "l'effet de colle," literally "the glu-ing effect," by which he names the inertia that turns a group into a static institution. Punning on "l'effet d'école" (the effect of a school) to suggest the conformity of education and the formalization of schools of thought, Lacan refers to *l'effet de colle* on March 11, 1980, in a text entitled "D'Écolage" (a takeoff, a beginning, and an unschooling), which announces as irreversible his decision to dissolve the École freudienne de Paris.[174] At the same time, he identifies a series of steps by which his fellow workers in the Freudian field can move on from this "unschooling." These steps programmatically oppose the production of permanent collectivities (where the signifier *collectif* is already marked by the trace of *colle*). Instead, Lacan affirms interruption as central to analytic work. Insisting on the cut of division as the defining analytic act (already enshrined in the scansion that determines when the variable-length session ends), Lacan resists "l'effet de colle" and "l'effet d'école" at once, countering philosophy's flirtation with power and the proper distribution of places with the psychoanalytic focus on what has no place and upsets the distribution of power.

Jean Allouch has something similar in mind when he argues that psycho-analysis has "nothing to do with the side of those in power, those who determine how society should function, what rules it sets out and how it treats its members."

He then goes on to specify what a psychoanalytic ethics might mean: "Marguerite Duras gave the best formulation when she expressed the wish, which she herself registered as the maxim of politics as well, 'Let the world go to perdition!' If one does not set up one's camp with the radicality of that, with what Lacan calls 'décharite,' that of a Big Other barred, non-existent, then there's no way to be on the side of those whose symptoms scream it ceaselessly."[175] With his reference to *décharite*, the charitable noncharity of the analyst's positioning as excrescence, waste, or trash, Allouch promotes a psychoanalysis that aligns itself with those made queer by dominant opinion, those consigned to the position of ontological exclusion, negation, or nonbeing. Such a psychoanalysis would manifest a queerness of its own by opposing the order of meaning that rests on the subtraction of ab-sens and insisting, instead, on the atopia of Socratic negativity over and against its translation (by Plato and the philosophy he initiates) into a positive mode of instruction held together by the glue of meaning, by "la colle du sens," that invariably generates "l'effet d'école."

It follows, as Badiou observes, that philosophy and psychoanalysis must differ on the good of education and also, a fortiori, on education in the good, just as they differ in the value they attach to foundation and dissolution, organization and negativity, thought and jouissance:

> Lacan's views, even if they present themselves in the form of a discourse, are clearly quite far from university discourse, but they are even more profoundly distant from any educational ambition. And this, by the way, is characteristic of antiphilosophy. Because one could establish Lacan's belief—a belief one can easily share—that there's an educational drive within philosophy. After all, the Platonic system, considered as foundational, can be understood as an educational system. In stark contrast to this educational underpinning of philosophy, even taking "education" in as noble a sense as possible, psychoanalysis, even in its discourse, breaks with every educational aim. Lacan says as much, with the greatest rigor, in the text that closed the Congress of 1970. He says: What saves me from education is the act.[176]

To the degree that it dissipates meaning by refusing the Symbolic distribution of places, the act opposes education as the defense and "transmission of a knowledge."[177] Thus Lacan, who conceives the hysteric's discourse as questioning both the master signifier and knowledge as the signifier of mastery, can invite us to "recognize in Socrates the figure of hysteria," the person who poses the question of being as inseparable from discourse as such.[178]

Socrates, that is, like the hysteric, as characterized by Bruce Fink, "pushes the master . . . to the point where he . . . can find the master's knowledge lacking. Either the master does not have an explanation for everything, or his or her reasoning does not hold water."[179]

Rather than assuming the transmission of knowledge as providing a stable ground, irony hystericizes knowledge, generating ever-expanding circles of irony instead. As Sarah Kofman observes, "Kierkegaard believes that he is the only one who has been able to grasp the viewpoint of irony, precisely because irony (like Socrates, who is of a piece with his irony) does not allow itself to be grasped."[180] Escaping one's grasp, precluding comprehension: such an irony approaches madness. So, too, does psychoanalysis, according to Lacan, by engaging in an analytic act "all the madder for being unteachable."[181] This leads him to insist on "the antagonism . . . between education and knowledge" and to declare, while dismissing what he calls the "educational underpinning of philosophy," that "knowledge passes through the act."[182] Knowledge passes, in other words, through ab-sens and through the drive, bypassing a philosophy predicated, as Badiou understands it, on the "colle du sens."

Socrates, of course, was sentenced to death for failing to recognize the gods of Athens and for corrupting the young with his teachings. Lacan, who was investigated throughout his career by psychoanalytic organizations, would be expelled from the International Association of Psychoanalysis, denied the right to conduct training analyses by the Société française de psychanalyse, and forced to stop holding his seminars at the École normale supérieure. Like Socrates, he was accused of promulgating bad educational practices by undermining the institutions of meaning and by substituting foreign gods, as it were, for those officially acknowledged (by following his own daimonion and establishing the variable-length session in defiance of institutional authority). Each was denied a place in his world for engaging the atopia within it and for enacting (by means of irony or the analytic cut) the antagonism responsible for the jouissance against which education defends.

Discussing the daimonion of Socrates, for example, the internal "voice" that interrupted him when he sensed he was on a wrong path (and which, according to his accusers, he enshrined as a god above those of the state), Jean-François Balaudé observes that this "'demonic sign' . . . manifests itself only in a negative manner, and it only distracts Socrates from doing such and such a thing, without offering any positive incitement." He then adds, "This sign, which is beyond Socrates, is at the same time what most intimately belongs to him."[183] Balaudé's language recalls Lacan's formulation of something "in you . . . more than you," a phrase he applies to the *objet a*, the object-cause of desire that resists, as Guy Le Gaufey observes, "any imposition of unity."[184] As Žižek describes it in *The Parallax View*, the *objet a* "stands in for the unknown X, the noumenal core of the object beyond appearances, for what is 'in you more than yourself.' . . . [The] *objet petit a* is the very cause of the parallax gap, that unfathomable X which forever eludes the symbolic grasp."[185] Later, in *Less Than Nothing*, he asserts, "There is 'something in you more than yourself,' the elusive *je ne sais quoi* which makes you what you are, which accounts for your 'specific flavor'"; he exemplifies that "something" in one's proper name, which he understands as "a signifier that falls into its signified."[186] Such "a name," Žižek notes, "far from referring to your collection of properties, ultimately refers to that elusive X."[187] In other words, the name is the empty placeholder that seeks to pin down the impossible Real (in this case, the Real of the subject as enjoyment, as attachment to jouissance). It would capture, precisely as "something" capable of articulation in the Symbolic, the nothingness, incapable of appearing as such, that registers, like Blackness and queerness (inter alia), the ontological negation, the exclusion from being, by which reality appears.

Expressing both his radical self-division and "what most intimately belongs to him," the daimonion of Socrates stands in for this "nothing" by designating his access to jouissance through "infinite absolute negativity." It thus functions as complement and counterpart to the Lacanian agalma, the treasure hidden from common view that irradiates a subject with value. Both the agalma and the daimonion constitutes what Žižek glosses as an "extimate kernel" in the subject that would suture the gap in "what is."[188] Paradoxically, however, the daimonion evinces that kernel as the gap or the nothingness itself; rather than referring to something subtracted or cut off from Symbolic reality, it signals the persistence of the rupture or cut, the determining pressure of the Real as ab-sens that inheres in the structure of reality *as* the cutting off of the Real. This is what Žižek gets at when he writes, "In the case of *objet petit a* as the object of the drive, the 'object' is directly loss itself. . . . That is to say: the weird movement called 'drive' is not driven by the 'impossible' quest for the lost object; it is *a push to enact 'loss'—the gap, cut, distance—itself directly.*"[189] While philosophy's "educational underpinning" seeks to mend the hole in reality by applying the "glue of meaning," Socratic irony and the analytic act dissolve that glue and reveal that hole by establishing (the place of) nothing.

Lacan makes this makes this clear in "Monsieur A," his text of dissolution. Having urged the adherents of La cause freudienne to "stick together [*collez-vous ensemble*] for as long as needed in order to do something and then, afterwards, disband in order to do something else," he declares his intention to "establish a propitious turbulence for you."[190] The only alternative to such turbulence is "the certainty of being stuck in sticking together" (la colle assurée). Apparently referring to his puns on *colle* and *école*, he then goes on to remark:

> You see how I put that by small touches. I will let you take your time to understand.
>
> Understand what? I don't pride myself on making sense. Nor on the opposite. Because the real is what opposes itself to that.
>
> I've paid homage to Marx as the inventor of the symptom. This Marx, however, is also the restorer of order, by the sole fact that he breathed back into the proletariat the di-mention [*dit-mention*] of meaning. It was sufficient for that purpose that he speak or name the proletariat as such.
>
> The Church learned a lesson from that, that's what I told you on January 5. Take it from me, religious significance is going to experience a boom you can't imagine. Because religion is the original home of meaning. This is obvious to those at the top of the hierarchy even more than to others.
>
> I try to go counter to that, lest psychoanalysis become a religion, as it tends to do, irresistibly, once we imagine that interpretation only works by way of meaning. I teach that its spring lies elsewhere, namely in the signifier as such.
>
> And that's what those who are panicked by this dissolution are resisting. The hierarchy only sustains itself by virtue of managing meaning.[191]

Lacan would undo the entrenchment (*la colle*) endemic to every school (*école*) by severing interpretation from meaning and disrupting the institutions—religious, educational, and psychoanalytic—designed to control and pass on meaning by refusing the nothing, the negativity of division, that ab-sens designates as sex.

Queerness, irony, and psychoanalysis all conduce to a bad education by insisting on this "nothing" that irrupts in jouissance. Philosophy, still our paradigm for the "good" of education, founds itself on separating jouissance from rational thought, maintaining, in the words of Colette Soler, "that there exist instruments or organs of knowledge that are autonomous with regard to the demands of the libido and that this separation makes possible what one imagines to be a capacity for so-called objective thought, which is to say, thought dissociated from every interest of jouissance."[192] For Lacan, to the contrary, as Soler remarks, "thought is jouissance," and what she wittily labels "joui-pense" pervades the whole of the conceptual field with its destabilizing libidinal charge.[193] This signals the place of sex in thought as the atopia, the nothing and the nowhere, against which reality defends.

If bad education, while insisting on this nothing, offers nothing by way of repair, then what could we ever hope to learn by attending to its teaching? Can it even "teach" at all? The chapters that follow approach this question as central to queer theory's project and suggest that bad education insists on returning us to this nothing—and, therefore, to nothing "good." "Bad" is not transvalued here, nor does queerness *become* a "good," though the pull of such reabsorption into a dialectically redeemed education, an education construed as *positively* "bad" and so as *positively* "queer," inheres in the problematic that this book engages throughout. To forestall that return of the good, each chapter broaches education as inseparable from ideological suture and poses against its redemptive promise a relentlessly queer negativity: queer because it never resolves into sense, establishes an alternative world, or makes a claim on being.[194] At a moment when the profligate use of the term prompts the question, "Is everything queer?" this book has an answer: "No." Insofar as queerness pertains to ab-sens, it argues that nothing "is" queer, while maintaining that *nothing*, the ontological negation figured by queerness, *is*. Put otherwise: *Bad Education* theorizes queerness without positivizing "queers." Like every critical enterprise, it maximizes certain issues while minimizing others. Structuring logics take precedence over sociological or historical analysis, neither of which is in danger of being scanted by other scholars. Literary and cinematic works take precedence over scientific data insofar as they foreground the roots of queerness in the logics of representation. Inevitable though such limitations must be in any work that foreswears the ambition of providing *The Key to All Mythologies*, they can never escape their implication in ongoing conceptual violence. If this risks, to return to Warren's term, complicity with "onticide," or, to return to Musser's charge, the "silencing" of race and sexuality, then it does so as the necessary consequence of following queerness to the very end. For queerness is inseparable from the violence with which it detotalizes a world and the end, the rupture, the cut is precisely where queerness always leads, even to "the end of the world." Insofar as that end invariably evokes the terrorism of the Real, queerness, like all catachrestic misnamings of the primally absented ab-sens, remains foreign to our thought. This book, therefore, like every attempt to think ontological negation, can only aspire to *approach* the nothing that can never afford us freedom, meaning, identity, or anything good: the nothingness of the bad education this book will try, and fail, to imagine.

Learning Nothing:

Pedro Almodóvar's *Bad Education*

Is teaching inseparable from the fantasy-logic of reproductive futurism? Are all who teach, *whatever they teach*, conscripted to its cause? I've been asking myself these questions since the publication of *No Future*, inspired to do so, at least in part, by a sentence from Leo Bersani's generous (but more than *just* generous) blurb. As printed on *No Future*'s back cover, Bersani's remarks conclude as follows: "Edelman's extraordinary text is so powerful that we could perhaps reproach him only for not spelling out the mode in which we might survive our necessary assent to its argument." "Could," "perhaps," and "only" may labor to mitigate its impact, but the word "reproach," performing a significant labor of its own, makes visible a desire to resist the "assent" here characterized as "necessary." By seeming to assent against his will, by bowing, as it were, to necessity, Bersani locates a compulsive force in *No Future*'s analysis of the relations among queerness, negativity, and the death drive. He regrets, however, that the book stops short of teaching us how to *survive* the drive whose insistence it makes us assent to—the death drive ascribed to those read as queer but also animating the vast social logic *No Future* dubs *reproductive futurism*.

He broaches here something bedeviling to teachers from Socrates to Paul de Man: the ethics of teachings or doctrines construed as endangering those who are taught.[1] If one "could perhaps" reproach *No Future* for inducing the necessity of assent to an argument that deprioritizes communal survival, then such a survival, it goes without saying, must be viewed as necessary too. The word *necessary*, that is, as used in the blurb, where it modifies *assent*, also colors, as if by metathesis, the phrase that comes before it: "the mode in which we might survive." This is the context in which Bersani imagines a pedagogical supplement that would forestall such "reproach" by "spelling out" some alternative to the death drive. That supplement would grant us shelter us in the meaningfulness of language ("spelling out," though a conventional formula, names the relation of material letters to comprehensible words) and so play its part in achieving the "good" that education promises. It would teach us to master the Real of the drive through attachment to Symbolic meaning. Such a supplement, in other words, would speak to the Symbolic's generation *of* other words, all of them links in a signifying chain whose movement toward meaning unfolds in time like the logic of reproductive futurism. Absent that world-preserving confidence in the temporal logic of sense, *No Future* and *No Future*'s author, were Bersani taken at *his* word, would merit our "reproach."[2]

But must teaching necessarily affirm and conduce to the good of our survival? Can we imagine an education—what this book will describe as a *bad* education—that would function, instead, as a *leading out* from whatever we think "we" are, even if that leading out is one that "we" cannot survive? In that case *No Future*'s pedagogical supplement might *court* the reproach of pursuing what is pedagogically unbecoming by putting the process of unbecoming at the heart of its bad education. In the light of such unbecoming, the yet-to-come would no longer refer to the fantasy that makes the future "ours" but would signal, instead, the strangeness, the queerness, associated with Jacques Lacan's ab-sens or Jacques Derrida's monstrosity ("the as yet unnamable which is proclaiming itself"), the queerness that futurism abjects by giving even formlessness a form.[3] But such forms, like the catachreses that figure ontological exclusion, are attempts to embody, or even to ontologize, the negativity of queerness, thus revealing how futurism itself remains bound to the negativity it negates.

No Future asserted that social relations, which imagine an end to their structural antagonism in a tomorrow ceaselessly deferred, invoke the future as the guarantee of meaning's realization. Such a future, as a continuous supplement, as an empty placeholder of totalization, works at once to assert and refute the social system's closure, denying its totalization in the present while filling the gap that denial acknowledges with the pledge of the yet-to-come. The Child, as the privileged figure of that pledge—one with no predetermined identity, such that any child, in the proper context and produced for the proper audience, can exemplify its logic (while any child, correlatively, can be posited as its enemy)—compels us take our social value from our various relations to *it* and to make ourselves, in whatever way, the guardians of *its* future.[4] A class of persons must therefore emerge to materialize the *danger* to that future—a class of persons whose failure to invest the Child as the ultimate value pits them not only against the Child but also against social order. I called those persons *sinthomosexuals* to propose a link between the Lacanian sinthome, the knot that determines each subject's distinctive relation to jouissance, and the emergence in the West of homosexuality as a figure for the stigmatized interimplication of jouissance and the death drive.

As homosexuality, in many Western-style democracies, starts to shed its connotations of queerness (in certain ways, for certain persons, and in certain predominantly urban locations), sinthomosexuality, as a signifier, still names the anxiogenic bonds among sex, sexuality, and the subject's sinthome, the link between jouissance and what, in Lacan's expression, ab-sens designates as sex. In the sinthomosexual the social order posits and localizes the enemy of the Child as the paradoxical "object" form of jouissance itself. The hypostatized queer, in other words, "is" the jouissance that undoes the subject, but that jouissance has been positivized as a particular *type* of subject, one whose relation to enjoyment reduces it to the status of an object. Such "antisocial" jouissance may be disavowed by the social order and projected onto those (non)subjects a given order sinthomosexualizes, but it pulses within as the motor force of social organization, repeatedly erupting in violence against those assigned to that stigmatized class. Futurism's investment in the Child, then, as the icon and promise of meaning doesn't alter the fact that futurism, too, embodies sinthomosexuality, enacting in its violence against those it queers the enjoyment it disavows. We are all sinthomosexuals, as I put it in *No Future*, but those who are queered by a given order are figures, historically contingent, for the ab-sens that threatens its sustaining logic by materializing the void that ruptures the imagined consistency of its world.

It follows that queerness, as the figure of such a radical unbecoming, maintains an intensely negative link to the logic of education. Queerness, wherever it shows itself (in the form of a catachresis), effects a *counter*pedagogy that refutes, by its positivization, the reality that grants it no place—or that grants it the place of what nullifies: the nonplace of the null. Like poetry in W. H. Auden's phrase, queerness makes *nothing* happen; it *incises* that nothing in the world as it is with an acid's caustic bite, dissolving the familiar logic of the world that constitutes our reality.[5] From within that logic, the hypostatized "queer," like a falsehood in the land of the Houyhnhnms, gets construed as "*the Thing which is not*": it signifies, that is, a being who intends the negation of being as such.[6] Thus, queerness, from the normative perspective, promotes what I'm calling here *bad education*, the education that teaches us nothing more than the nothing of "*the Thing which is not.*"

Now "*the Thing which is not*" could also refer to what Lacan calls *das Ding*, or the Thing. With this he refers to the primal lost object or, rather, to the radical non–object form of primal loss as such: to the void occasioned by the advent of being and its corollary, desire, in the Symbolic. Expressing the "beyond-of-the-signified," the Lacanian Thing, as "intimate exteriority," as an otherness experienced as alien to, because alienated from, ourselves, remains forever inaccessible within the signifying order.[7] That order, however, tempts us to see the Thing, that ever-present loss effected by subjection to the signifier, as an *object* that—once sublimated through its positivization *as* an object—could be, but for prohibition, an attainable object of desire. If sublimation, as Lacan defines it in *The Ethics of Psychoanalysis*, "raises an object . . . to the dignity of the Thing," then that dignity marks the prophylactic distance that separates the Thing from ourselves—the distance for the preservation of which the law is called into being.[8] Though enforced as prohibition, this distance or barrier, Lacan makes clear, stands in for the *impossibility* of acquiring knowledge of the Thing. For the Thing is not an object, nor is it, properly speaking, forbidden; it figures the loss, the cut, the primal division that shapes us as subjects by attaching us to the otherness of language. Emerging from *within* the Symbolic as what we are cut off from *by* the Symbolic, the Thing reflects the necessary inconsistency of the Symbolic, the void its signification requires. Determined by its status as the excrescence, the inassimilable remainder, of symbolization, the Thing must be kept at a distance lest it vitiate Symbolic reality and the world(s) that reality calls forth.

In this sense the Thing pertains to the drive more fully than to desire. The particular objects idealized and raised to the "dignity" of the Thing are imaginary forms by which, Lacan writes, a particular culture attempts to "delude itself on the subject of *das Ding*, to colonize the field of *das Ding* with imaginary schemes."[9] The register of representation, and with it the subject's relation to desire, is shaped by that delusion too; for even desire comes to function as a sublimation of the drive.[10] Desire, to put this another way, with its endless metonymic movement from one object to another, positivizes the constant and objectless circulation of the drive.[11]

Central to psychoanalysis, of course, is the subject's investment in the mother, who, in her role as the first sublime object elevated to the place of the Thing, establishes "incest as the fundamental desire" and its prohibition as the "primordial law."[12] But the sublimation by which the mother takes the place of the Thing does not keep other objects from assuming its place over time. Lacan, for instance, cites Freud's discussion in *Moses and Monotheism* of the moment when the function of the father emerges as just such a sublimation, and he examines, as well, and in greater detail, the period when the flowering of courtly love took the Lady as its sublime object, twining her in garlands of proscription that served to vivify desire.[13] But for well over two hundred years in the West, though largely unacknowledged, the place of the unrepresentable Thing has been occupied by the Child. Like the Lady idealized in the practice and aesthetic discourse of courtly love, the Child as sublimated object emerges though a cultural eroticization that appears as obsessive anxiety about the Child's potential for violation. The Child—understood, like the Lady, as an ideological construct—thus functions as the luridly imagined object of hystericized sexual prohibition (even as attacks on child labor laws and the outsourcing of capitalist production put actual children at greater risk), betraying the deep connection between incest and pedophilia (including the latter's expression in the form of pedophilo-phobia).[14]

As the blankness of pure potential, the Child's "innocence" bespeaks its sublimation of the nothingness of the Thing—the nothingness embodied otherwise in the Child's inverted twin: "the queer."[15] Like the Child, the queer fills the void or gap that precludes the world's totalization; the Child, though, portends the realization of that totality in the future, while the queer takes shape as the obstacle that impedes it in the present. Those who are queered substantialize the gap in what is, the cut of division, and their contingent historical identities, made to ontologize ontological exclusion, carry the stain of the negativity associated with the Thing. They threaten the Child and the future it heralds with a radical reduction that translates the Child from the privileged object of (a culturally sublimated) desire to the void at the core of the drive.[16]

But what exactly does *innocence* mean, and how does it manage to sublimate the negativity of the void? Jean-Jacques Rousseau, who helped to establish it as the privilege of the Child, reminds us that "innocence" can coincide with a passion for wholesale destruction: "A child wants to upset everything he sees. He smashes, breaks everything he can reach. He grabs a bird as he would grab a stone, and he strangles it without knowing what he does."[17] Seen from this angle, the child can preserve its "natural" state of innocence (its correlation with the ideological Child) only to the extent that it preserves as well its "natural" state of ignorance. While this is no comfort to the strangled bird, the thoughtless child, knowing nothing of death, bears no guilt for its murderous act. It kills with an innocent exuberance, unconscious of what it does. A greater threat to its innocence, though, lies somewhat closer to hand. When the strangling of birds gives way to the greater menace of "choking the chicken," the drives of the child must be made to submit to the rule of parental law. As the psychoanalyst Lucien Israël observes, "From this period interdictions from outside intervene to deter the child from masturbating, from sucking his thumb, from pissing all over the place whenever he wants to do so."[18] The innocent child must be constrained to safeguard the fantasy of innocence that innocence endangers.

Rousseau's *Émile* understands this well and explores the contradictions of an educational program that models itself on "nothing but the march of nature."[19] Specifying the auto-destructive logic on which such an education would rest, Derrida produced his widely influential analysis of the supplement. As he writes in *Of Grammatology*: "According to Rousseau, the negativity of evil will always have the form of supplementarity. Evil is exterior to nature, to what is by nature innocent and good. It supervenes upon nature. But always by way of compensation for what *ought* to lack nothing at all in itself." Does nature, then—does "innocence"—*require* the "negativity of evil"? Derrida suggests that it does: "Yet all education, the keystone of Rousseauist thought, will be described or presented as a system of substitution ... destined to reconstitute Nature's edifice in the most natural way possible."[20] But how "natural" can supplementing nature be if supplementation, by definition, is "exterior to nature" and, accordingly, exterior to all that is recognized as "innocent and good"?

The prime example afforded by Rousseau of this perverse or contradictory logic centers on the child whose innocence effectively occasions its own perversion. Derrida, who carefully traces this logic, situates the child in the place of negativity associated with the cut or the gap of primal "deficiency" for Rousseau: "Childhood is the first manifestation of the deficiency which, in Nature, calls for substitution [*suppléance*]. . . . Without childhood, no supplement would ever appear in Nature. The supplement is here both humanity's good fortune and the origin of its perversion."[21] In its lack of self-sufficiency, in its need for acculturation, the child exposes an absence internal to the fullness of nature itself. The natural, of course, in a perfect world, would need no supplementation since the supplement evinces a "negativity of evil" *un*natural by definition. The child, however, as the "first manifestation of the deficiency . . . in Nature," introduces, through its blankness or innocence, supplementarity as original sin. It opens, that is, the dimension of futurity imagined as *redeeming* the lack to which it endlessly attests.

Consider Eve's punishment in the book of Genesis: "In sorrow shalt thou bring forth children" (Genesis 3:18, King James Version). Is it clear that the penalty lies in the sorrow (or pain) that accompanies childbirth rather than in the sorry necessity of bringing forth children in the first place? Doesn't this punishment repeat, in fact, the transgression it means to penalize: the pursuit of supplementarity? What else was the fruit by which Eve was enticed but a supplement to Eden's "perfection"? As the positive form of a lack that leaves even Eden incomplete, a lack made perceptible by the serpent—the world's first "queer" and its first bad educator—the supplement, as "intimate exteriority," separates paradise from itself. Like the fruit of the tree, the fruit of Eve's loins makes supplementarity infinite, sublimating in the form of futurity the fatal fall into time's abyss. No wonder our culture protects those children perceived in the form of the Child from "premature" knowledge of their origins; by reading as "innocence" the Child's luxurious immersion in nonknowing, we deny our own knowledge that children confirm the *deficiency* in nature. "Perfection . . . cannot have children," Sylvia Plath declares.[22] Produced in response to, and in order to oppose, the "evil" of knowledge as supplement, the "innocence" of the Child is created as a negation of knowledge's own negativity. Framed as the Child's evil double, though, "the queer," negativity's reified form, desublimates the Child by exposing its implication in the pulsions of the drive, much like "the queer" itself.

Rousseau, acknowledging the extent to which children are subordinated to the drive, urges they be granted a *minimal* knowledge to protect against a greater knowledge their innocence could not survive. *Émile* proposes that children receive, where "the organs of the secret pleasures and those of the disgusting needs" are concerned, an education designed to "turn [them] away from a dangerous curiosity."[23] Rousseau advises parents to make sure that "the first fire of imagination is smothered" by associating, in the minds of their children, the sexual organs with excrement, disease, and death, inducing thereby a connection between "coarse words" and "displeasing ideas." The child "is not forbidden to pronounce these words and to have these ideas," according to Rousseau, "but without his being aware of it, he is made to have a repugnance against recalling them."[24] Thus, the armor most certain to protect the child's innocence is a sort of aversive knowledge, one that effects a disinclination to "dangerous curiosity" and that does so surreptitiously, without the child's becoming conscious of the prophylaxis such education intends.

Given his historical importance in sublimating children into the Child, we should hardly be surprised that Rousseau idealizes the innocence he deconstructs. But Lucien Israël sees the child's education from a starkly different perspective, reading the relation of the child to its excrement and its various "disgusting needs" without supposing, like *Émile*, some innate and "innocent" repugnance that would reject them. It is only, as Israël points out, "good housewives and housekeepers, [who] don't like the child's smearing itself with its shit. . . . Education is education against the drive. To lead out of . . . , that's what educate means, to lead out of the universe of the drive."[25] Education, that is, instills and enacts the imperative to sublimation insofar as, for Lacan, "the operations of sublimation are always ethically, culturally, and socially valorized."[26]

Good education serves the *social* good by negating whatever refuses that good and thereby endangers the Child, even if that danger inheres in the very nature of children themselves. Education, like heterosexuality, becomes a compulsory reproduction, procuring the Child for an order of truth that denies the foundational negativity, deficiency, perversion on which it rests. In the aftermath of such education, as Israël concludes, "one no longer knows anything about the universe of the drive, because the only small way to safeguard something of it is in knowing nothing about it." This is the context in which he defines "education as antidrive."[27] Education effectively seals the drive off from the logic of comprehension as if recognizing the drive's expression of ab-sens within the world of sens-absexe. Not reducible to the mere inversion of either knowledge or sens-absexe, ab-sens as negativity *inheres* in the knowledge sens-absexe affords. Insofar as that knowledge requires the subtraction or absenting of sex as ab-sens, it preserves the primal cut of division (the psychoanalytic referent of sex) in the *ab* of subtraction that makes *sens-absexe* the equivalent of *sens-ab(ab-sens)*.

Adorned with innocence as privileged *non*knowledge, the Child perpetuates, through its sublimation, the *enforced* nonknowledge as and in which the "universe of the drive" insists. It reenacts, by way of allegory, the sublimation of the Thing—the creation of something out of nothing—as the dialectical negation of negativity that generates futurity. Allegory, sublimation, and dialectic, then, share a logic with one another, each naming a mode of production that displaces into systematic knowledge a negativity impossible to comprehend and at odds with all totalized forms.[28] It follows that a fourth term, *education*, must take its place beside them: the education that perfectly complements the Child as the promise of coherent totality—the education that is always, in Friedrich Schiller's formulation, an aesthetic education.

For humanity to attain its proper moral state requires, for Schiller, the realization of an aesthetic self-totalization: "Every individual man, it may be said, carries in disposition and determination a pure ideal man within himself, with whose unalterable unity it is the great task of his existence, throughout all his vicissitudes, to harmonize."[29] The process of this harmonization, as effected by the "cultivation of Beauty," constitutes "the education of humanity" and depends on the coordination of life in time (the life of the individual) with the development of moral possibility through and as the State.[30] Schiller writes, "The great consideration, therefore, is that physical society in *time* may not cease for an instant while moral society is being formed in *idea*, that for the sake of human dignity its very existence may not be endangered. When the mechanic has the works of a clock to repair, he lets the wheels run down; but the living clockwork of the State must be repaired while it is still in motion. . . . We must therefore search for some support for the continuation of society."[31] The Schillerian aesthetic, as Paul de Man notes, links sensory content and abstract form—the "sensuous world to a world of ideas," as Schiller writes—for reasons that have everything to do with the future that the Child is meant to secure.[32] "The necessity of this synthesis," de Man remarks, "is made in the name of an empirical concept, which is that of humanity, of the human, which is used then as a principle of closure. The human, the needs of the human, the necessities of the human are absolute and are not open to critical attack."[33]

Needless to say, this "human," whose continued survival the Child guarantees, constitutes a central site of ideological contestation. But insofar as "we are all Schillerians," according to de Man—adherents, whether we admit it or not, of an aesthetic ideology intimately bound up with reproductive futurism—such contestation concerns the definition, not the *value*, of the "human."[34] Though the regime of aesthetic ideology protects that value from "critical attack," *queerness* refers to whatever poses the *threat* of such attack, to whatever opens a wound within the logic of the aesthetic by exposing the negativity from which Schiller and the Schillerian tradition retreat.[35] To confront such negativity would dismantle the foundation supporting the "empirical concept" of "humanity"—the fantasy of self-authorizing sovereignty. As Schiller writes, "The person must therefore be its own ground, for the enduring cannot issue from alteration; and so we have in the first place the idea of absolute being grounded in itself, that is to say of freedom."[36]

To clarify the stake in this aesthetic ideology—and in the sublimation that gives birth to the Child—let us focus briefly on de Man's account of an even more rigorous effort to establish a self-grounding philosophical system. In "Pascal's Allegory of Persuasion," de Man looks at what happens when Blaise Pascal, having noted that geometry refuses to define its principal objects (movement, number, and space), asserts that this "lack of definition is rather a perfection than a fault" (le manque de définition est plutôt une perfection qu'un défaut) and claims that these principal objects have a "necessary and reciprocal relation" (une liaison nécessaire et réciproque) in which he implicates time as well ("le temps même y est aussi compris").[37] To exemplify this reciprocity, he explains the homology among these "first objects" with reference to the "two infinities" of enlargement and contraction. Just as a movement can be made faster or slower, and numbers can be made larger or smaller, so space can always be increased or diminished, and temporal duration extended or reduced. Movement, number, space, and time are thus, for Pascal, always infinitely distant from their radical extremes: nothingness and infinity ("le néant et l'infini").[38]

But the demand that these realms remain perfectly homologous encounters a certain difficulty when Pascal confronts the status of the "one" (which, according to Euclid, is and is not a number) and then tries to correlate the one with something that cannot be included in the realm of space because it is characterized as "indivisible" and therefore as lacking spatial extension. Pascal writes, "The only reason that the one is not included in the ranks of the numbers is that Euclid and the first authors who dealt with arithmetic, having several properties to give it that were common to all the numbers other than one, excluded the one from the meaning of the word number, so as not to have to say all the time *we find such and such a condition in all numbers other than one*."[39] At the same time, however, according to Pascal, Euclid recognizes that the one, insofar as it cannot be conceived as a nothing ("un néant"), belongs to the same "genre" as number. As soon as they are added together, after all, two ones will produce a number. Two indivisible spatial entities, by contrast, each lacking spatial extension, could never yield a spatial expanse by virtue of being combined. In the absence of this homology between the one (in the realm of number) and an indivisible entity (in the realm of space), Pascal, in de Man's analysis, has to "suspend this separation while maintaining it—because the underlying homology of space and number, the ground of the system, should never be fundamentally in question."[40] So Pascal finds a corollary for the indivisible entity by introducing the zero, which, while not a number itself, is presupposed by number and has equivalents in the registers of motion, space, and time: "If you want to find a comparison in the realm of numbers that accurately represents what we are considering in the realm of extension, it would have to be that of zero to numbers. Because zero is not of the same genre as numbers, . . . it's a veritable indivisible of numbers just as the indivisible is a veritable zero of extension."[41] As Ernesto Laclau describes it, "The zero is radically heterogeneous with the order of number" but "crucial if there is going to be an order of number at all." It allows, moreover, "the homology between number, time and motion . . . to be maintained" insofar as it provides "the equivalent of 'instant' or 'stasis' . . . in the order of number."[42] Much as the aesthetic, in de Man's words, restores for Schiller "equilibrium, harmony, on the level of principles," so the zero, for Pascal, as de Man observes, recovers "the homogeneity of the universe."[43]

De Man locates the zero's importance, however, in its allegorical relation to the arbitrariness of linguistic definition—the arbitrariness that lets Euclid exclude the one from definition as a number while defining magnitudes in such a way that it belongs to the "genre" of number. The zero, as de Man expands on its brief appearance in Pascal's text, correlates with geometry's nondefinition of its own initial principles and the lack of any demonstrable ground to undergird its logic; "all these truths," Pascal writes, "are incapable of demonstration, and yet they are the foundation and the principles of geometry."[44] This allows de Man to characterize Pascal's project in these terms:

> The continuous universe . . . is interrupted, disrupted *at all points* by a principle of radical heterogeneity without which it cannot come into being. Moreover, this rupture . . . does not occur on the transcendental level, but on the level of language, in the inability of a theory of language as sign or as name . . . to ground this homogeneity without having recourse to the signifying function . . . that makes the zero of signification the necessary condition for grounded knowledge. The notion of language as sign is dependent on, and derived from, a different notion in which language functions as rudderless signification and transforms what it denominates into the linguistic equivalent of the arithmetical zero. It is as sign that language is capable of engendering the principles of infinity, of genus, species, and homogeneity, which allow for . . . totalizations, but none of these tropes could come about without the systematic effacement of the zero and its reconversion into a name. There can be no *one* without the zero, but the zero always appears in the guise of a *one*, of a (some)thing. The name is the trope of the zero. The zero is always *called* a one, when the zero is actually nameless, "innommable."[45]

The value of this account for my argument lies in its evocation of the zero's "effacement" and its concomitant "reconversion" into, its representation as, a positivized and enumerable entity, which is to say, a "one."[46]

This "systematic" effacement of the zero as the disruptive and heterogeneous principle on which the "continuous universe" depends enacts a logic that underlies the aesthetic for Schiller, the supplement for Derrida, education for Rousseau, and sublimation for Lacan. Not that these terms are interchangeable or that they signify the same thing, but each reinforces the social imperative toward the "marriage" of "mind and world," toward a unified system, a comprehension, that strives to efface its internal rupture, its structural impossibility, through repetitive tropological substitutions that turn the zero into a one—substitutions that make the ontological negations articulated as queerness or Blackness (for example) assume the positivized form of social identities: "the queer" or "the Black."[47] Consonant with such a logic, though, the negativity of this repetition and its underlying drive experience "reconversion" into the "truth" of reproduction, redescribing the stasis of its iterations as a movement toward futurity.[48] This, of course, is the function of the Child and the stake in its education. Could teachings at odds with this logic add up to anything at all, having nothing at all to add but the persistence of nothing in the "guise" of the one—nothing to add but the negative sign that signals a primal subtraction: the negativity added to the sign as such in order to show, as de Man writes above, that "language as sign is dependent on, and derived from, a different notion"?

If sublimation, aesthetics, and logic turn the zero into one, this "different notion" reverses the process by making the one, the referential entity, into something unintelligible: the "linguistic equivalent" of zero. Such a "different notion" may echo what Brian Rotman has in mind when he discusses the insistence of Simon Stevin, a sixteenth-century Flemish mathematician, "on a semiological account of number, . . . which transferred zero's lack of referentiality, its lack of 'positive content,' to *all* numbers."[49] Like queerness as ontological negation, this notion leads to nothing in the social order of meaning: which is to say, to the nothing of the "zero of signification" that always subtends that order. Andrzej Warminski associates this zero with the "stutter of sheerly mechanical enumeration," a phrase that echoes the words of de Man in "Hegel on the Sublime" and so might gloss the zero as well: "Like a stutter, or a broken record, it makes what it keeps repeating worthless and meaningless. . . . Completely devoid of aura or *éclat*, it offers nothing to please anyone."[50]

How could the nothing of the zero, with its machine-like repetitions, ever generate value or make a positive contribution to life? Simply put, it cannot. The very concept of "value" requires the zero's sublimation insofar as it privileges the framework of meaning, the universe of sens-absexe, that requires the absenting of ab-sens to turn a profit on negativity by swelling the world into sense. A teaching that profits no one and that "offers nothing to please": to what could that teaching amount if not a radical threat to the one, to the Child, to the good, and so to the future? In an aesthetic order based on the harmonization of sign and meaning, that teaching could serve as nothing more than the sign of a bad education.

So I turn to the sign of a bad education to frame this another way—or turn, at least, to the sign used to advertise Pedro Almodóvar's *Bad Education* (*La mala educación*, 2004).[51] At the center of the graphic (figure 1.1) stands Ignacio Rodríguez, whose love for his classmate, Enrique, infuriates his professor of literature, Father Manolo, who passionately longs for Ignacio but whose advances have been rebuffed. To shield his friend from the wrath of the priest when he finds them together one night, Ignacio capitulates to Father Manolo in exchange for the latter's apparent agreement not to expel Enrique. *Bad Education* recounts this narrative as part of a film within the film: a film directed by the grown-up Enrique and adapted from *La Visita* (*The Visit*), an autobiographical narrative by the grown-up Ignacio. Enrique gets hold of the story from Juan, Ignacio's younger brother and an aspiring actor, who, with the aid of his former lover, the very same Father Manolo (now calling himself Sr. Berenguer and working as a publisher), murdered Ignacio four years earlier. When he appears in Enrique's office, though, and offers him the story, Juan presents himself as Ignacio (though insisting on being called by his stage named, Angel) in order to (re)kindle the director's affection and win the starring role (as the adult Ignacio, now presenting as Zahara) in the film of *La Visita* that he hopes Enrique will make.

Depicted as a director animated by the spirit of La Movida Madrileña, the countercultural renaissance that took root in Madrid after Francisco Franco's death, Enrique evokes comparison with Almodóvar from the outset; even the latter's credit as *Bad Education*'s writer and director fades into a similar, diegetic card with the name of Enrique Goded. The poster for Almodóvar's film, as if to further this identification, bears an image from a sequence that takes place diegetically in Enrique's film, *La Visita*. That image—a full-length black-and-white shot of Ignacio meeting the camera's gaze, arms folded across his chest—shows Ignacio in the T-shirt, sneakers, and shorts that he wears in *La Visita* when he realizes, after yielding to the priest's desires, that the latter, despite his promise, has expelled Enrique after all. In the film Ignacio chokes back a sob; in the poster he glowers instead, suggesting that the camera, and by extension the viewer, occupies Father Manolo's place.

But Ignacio is only one element in the poster's logo for the film. His image is encircled by a bright red disk that it bisects like a diameter. The

1.1: Original Spanish poster for *Bad Education*.

difference between this colorful sphere and the black-and-white picture of Ignacio (wherein he functions as the Child) contrasts the photograph's naturalism with the abstraction of the nonrepresentational space upon which it is superimposed. This effect produces a relation between the two geometric elements: the circle and the vertical line of the boy, which function here as versions of the zero and the one. The logo puts the Child in a graphic space atopic and noncognizable, condensing the circular image of the void and its sublimation in the "single stroke," the *"einziger Zug,"* which Lacan identifies as the "first signifier."[52] As a signifier of the singleness or unity of an entity (the unity that singularly permits the concept of an "entity" to be thought), this stroke or notch, this one, asserts the coherence of the signifying system in which the "zero of signification," much like the Thing as loss or division, must always appear "in the guise of a *one*" that sublimates its status *as* zero.

By evoking this zero that threatens the human—while also alluding to the "eye" of the camera (Almodóvar's and Enrique's at once)—the field of this circle could easily be seen as swallowing or engulfing the boy, reducing him to a simple geometric form by inscribing him as the single stroke, the material mark of the signifier at risk of sinking into the void. But that circle can also be seen as yielding to Ignacio's embodiment of the Child: as receding before the figure of meaning that positivizes and displaces it. The aesthetic education interrogated by the film (but from which it never breaks), the normative impulse of education toward the (re)production of the good, tempts us to approach the relation between these possibilities dialectically, to resolve it into an allegory so as to sublate its structural antagonism. This is how education repudiates the "stutter" of the zero whose insistence makes "what it keeps repeating worthless and meaningless," to quote de Man. Such education would deny, in other words, what J. Hillis Miller asserts: that while the zero as such is "unknowable," "the one, however, any one, 'generates' a glimpse of the zero that is at the same time its hiding or covering over by a false or fictional name."[53] Such a name, such a catachresis misconstrued as a substantive identity, affirms the aesthetic unity whose ultimate signifier is "the human."[54] Returning to the work of the philosopher most deeply invested in aesthetic education, de Man ventriloquizes the reasoning behind Schiller's insistence on the reconciliation of the sensory and the formal drives: "Because the category of the human is absolute, and because the human would be divided, or would be reduced to nothing if this encounter between the two drives that make it up is not allowed to take place, for that reason a synthesis must be found. It is dictated, it is forced upon us, by the concept of the human itself."[55] Almodóvar's *Bad Education* similarly engages this division of the human, its potential reduction to the "nothing" of the zero that threatens the social order by attacking, just as queerness does, the Child's guarantee of meaning. The confluence of queerness as ontological negation with the zero or void of ab-sens approaches the end of the Child here by approaching the Child through its end. The film addresses the sort of bad rearing that takes hold of the Child from the rear, displacing thereby its human face and teaching us to view it as nothing more than the nothing we *posit* as more. Such is the bad education whose lesson, from the standpoint of aesthetic ideology at least, invariably lessens us all.

We can see this better by approaching the poster in the context of the film. The picture of Ignacio, as I already mentioned, alludes to his discovery, in Enrique's film, that Father Manolo has betrayed him. The import of the poster depends, however, on the formal, visual connection it draws between that scene and the one that precedes it. Earlier in *La Visita*, Enrique, in the wake of his first sexual contact with Ignacio (mutual masturbation while watching Sara Montiel in *Esa mujer*), finds that he, like Ignacio, is unable to sleep and so follows him into the washroom to talk. Their conversation breaks off, however, when Father Manolo enters the dormitory, intending to awaken Ignacio to serve as his acolyte at daybreak mass. Anticipating their teacher's wrath should he find them together in the washroom, the boys lock themselves in a stall. But the priest, now livid with jealousy when he discovers their empty cots, quickly tracks down their place of concealment and demands that they come out. When Enrique reluctantly opens the door, still trying to shield Ignacio, the priest, incensed by their intimacy, throws Enrique to the ground and then orders him back to the dorm with the threat of further punishment later.

Afterward, in the chapel, Ignacio assists at mass absentmindedly, disdainful of Father Manolo but worried about what he might do to Enrique. As the priest recites the words by which he consecrates the wine, "Hic est enim calix sanguinis mei," Ignacio shoots him a withering glance and begins to speak in voice-over: "I think I've just lost my faith at this moment and, lacking faith, I no longer believe in God or in hell. And as I don't believe in hell, I'm now without fear. And without fear, I'm capable of anything."[56] A void has opened for Ignacio where the Other as the locus of meaning once reigned. When the priest, therefore, incapable of staying angry with his favorite for long, absolves him of responsibility for what happened in the washroom but announces his intention to expel Enrique, Ignacio makes a bold calculation and offers the priest a deal: "If you don't expel him, I'll do what you want" (figure 1.2). As he speaks these words, the camera catches his upward gaze at the priest, whose cassocked shoulder obtrudes on the screen as a mass of darkness on the left. A reverse shot shows us the teacher's response. Urging Ignacio to silence, he starts to move forward to embrace him, as the film, cutting back to the previous shot, shows Ignacio's face in eclipse. The priest's black vestment blocks the lens, and the screen itself goes dark (figures 1.2–1.6).

Given the Hitchcockian texture of the film, established in the opening credits with musical and visual citations of *Psycho* and maintained through allusions to *Vertigo*'s meditations on identity, duplicity, and desire, this shot must recall the hallmark of *Rope*, where the camera's cuts are masked four

1.2.–1.6: Ignacio blacked out by Father Manolo. From *Bad Education* (Almodóvar, 2004).

times by a man's back blocking its view.[57] In his indispensable account of that film, D. A. Miller, connecting this strategy with "the very operation of the closet," observes that these blackouts conceal two things, the anus and the cut, and he adds that by doing so imperfectly, these blackouts *call attention* to them as well.[58] By quoting this signature gesture of *Rope*, Almodóvar, though free to show gay male sex, adduces the *form* of the closet without its indicative social function. Or, rather, he *alerts* us to the form of that closeting, which he thereby brings *out* of the closet, so as to closet something else: not gay male sex, nor pedophilia, nor even Ignacio's sodomization (about which the film leaves no doubt), but rather Ignacio's jouissance in this moment of erotic education, the voiding of his subjectivity through his reduction to the anal opening, the hole, that renders him unintelligible, a zero instead of a one, a site of ab-sens at odds with the Child as the promise of social meaning.[59]

Though the opening of and onto that hole is concealed by Father Manolo's back (which covers the *camera's* opening and so completely blacks out the screen), that hole, as the trace of jouissance, asserts itself nonetheless. The screenplay for *Bad Education* suggests that the blackout gives way to a fade-in: "The screen remains black for two or three seconds. Slowly, from within the darkness of the frame, a group of students begins to define itself (twenty or thirty of Ignacio's schoolmates) doing Swedish gymnastics in the soccer field."[60] But Almodóvar (or, alternatively, Enrique, in whose film, *La Visita*, these scenes take place) makes the transition instead through an iris shot, tattooing on Father Manolo's back the hole that the film brings out of the closet through its displacement to the level of form (figure 1.7). As a reference to the camera's mechanical eye, the characteristic dilation of the iris shot evokes the compulsion of the ocular drive while reinforcing the automatism pertaining to the drive as such. The annular form of the shot, in this context, associates the expansion of the ocular iris with the sphinctral relaxation of the anus. The dilation of the camera's eye evokes what the priest's black cassock conceals: Ignacio's opening to Father Manolo, which will enable Father Manolo to enter Ignacio in more ways than one.

I'll explain that more fully in what follows, but for now let me linger on the iris shot, which inscribes a relation between the anus and the eye that returns us to the zero and the one. Those images the eye desires to take in (like Ignacio's picture on the poster) reaffirm the integrity of the object as such, an integrity or coherence that the anus (like the poster's red circle) threatens to void. If *Bad Education* (or *La Visita*) associates the priest's penetration of Ignacio with the blacking out of the screen, and so with seeing nothing, then this eclipse of Ignacio as image, this desublimation of the Child, correlates

*to avoid Enrique
being expelled.*

1.7: The return of the image. From *Bad Education* (Almodóvar, 2004).

the object's negation with the opening of the anus. As the sphinctral trace of *nothing*, which is, in this case, *nothing to see*, the hole of the iris attempts the visualization of zero *as* zero, as the *atopia* of the void, without reconverting the zero into the meaningfulness of a one. That the effort fails, that representation positivizes the zero, putting *something* in *nothing's* place, can be seen by the seeing made possible by the iris shot's ocular insistence. Though the shot itself takes the form of a hole, that hole, while troping the anus conceived as an opening onto nothing, opens a hole in the *nothing to see*, in the blackness of the screen, by means of which images return. Restoring the objects of visual desire and, with them, the reality of the object world as the object of desire itself, these images fill the iris's hole, negating the negative force of the drive (anal and ocular alike) by reconstructing it as desire. The film's attempt to "see" nothing through the figural conjunction of blackness and queerness in this moment of ontological negation (which reduces the Child to a void), gives way to the visualization of objects that *figure* this negation.

While the hole produced by the iris shot, the referent of the poster's red circle, constitutes one such figure, what widens the camera's eye as the iris increases in diameter is an overhead view of rows of boys, like multiples of Ignacio, all offering the camera, which takes them in from a vantage point far above, the image of their asses rising and falling in the course of their morning gymnastics (figures 1.8 and 1.9). Though filmed as a Hitchcockian god's-eye view divorced from any character's perspective, the Olympian distance cannot efface the shot's pederastic import or its conversion of the anus as *nothing to see* into the positivized form of an image, which, as such, would

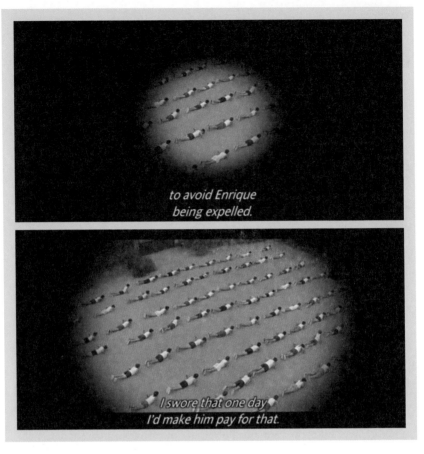

*to avoid Enrique
being expelled.*

*I swore that one day
I'd make him pay for that.*

1.8–1.9: Dilating the iris. From *Bad Education* (Almodóvar, 2004).

guarantee form. The sphinctral inscription of *nothing to see* thus gives way to the visualized object of desire: row after row of Ignacios facing down with their bottoms up.

Perversely, this movement from nothing to number, from zero to multiplications of one, *conceals* the hole of the anus, understood as endangering the Child's integrity, precisely by offering to the viewer's gaze an abundance of young boys' asses. They are glimpsed, like Ignacio by Father Manolo, through a pederastic lens, but that lens, in its function as the lens of desire, *redeems* the *nothing to see* that broaches the void of jouissance, and it does so by affirming desire for the image as desire for the image *of the human.*[61] This echoes de Man's framing of Schiller's compulsion to synthesize sensual reality and pure form: "Because the category of the human is absolute, and because the human would be divided, or would be reduced to nothing if this encounter between the two drives that make it up [the formal and the sensory drives—*Formtrieb* and *sinnlicher Trieb*] is not allowed to take place, for that reason a synthesis has to be found. It is dictated, it is forced upon us, by the concept of the human itself."[62]

In this context, whatever reduces the human to "nothing" performs the Lacanian act that gets figured as "radical evil." It perpetrates a violence against the social order that threatens to strip it of meaning. Alenka Zupančič describes what must follow: "The gap opened by an act (i.e., the unfamiliar, 'out-of-place' effect of an act) is immediately linked in this ideological gesture to an *image*. As a rule this is an image of suffering, which is then displayed to the public alongside this question: *Is this what you want?* And this question already implies the answer: *It would be impossible, inhuman, for you to want this!*"[63] The question, however, in another sense, implies the opposite answer: regardless of whether or not we want what a given image depicts (we might or might not recoil from "an image of suffering," after all), we still want the image *as such*. To negate the image (which signifies, if only dialectically, the image of reality) would be "impossible, inhuman," the work of the death drive projected onto those a given culture sinthomosexualizes.

If pederastic vision in the logo becomes paradigmatic of vision itself, if it instantiates the object fixation of the law (understood as the law of desire) by taking the Child as the object it raises to the dignity of the Thing, then the formless and object-wasting drive that lends its movement to desire takes the form, instead, of the hole evoked by the poster's flaming red circle, the hole by which, as de Man would suggest, the human is "divided, or . . . reduced to nothing."[64] That division expresses the persistence of the zero we can never know as such, the ubiquitous access to jouissance we can never endure as such, and the ceaseless pulse of the death drive we can never master as such.

Rupturing what "is" in response to the constant pressure of what "is not," the negativity of the cut preoccupies Almodóvar's *Bad Education*. From its opening credits, where collages of images evocative of sex, religion, and film get torn or peeled back to disclose something else (encapsulating thereby the logic of montage, which paradigmatically cuts to "something else" to fill the gap it opens: the *atopia* of the cut), the film reads division as inherent in the negativity at once produced and denied by the topology of sens-absexe. If all our institutions hammer home the belief, as Lacan disdainfully voices it, "that interpretation only works by way of meaning," then such belief corresponds to our "being" as subjects, committing us to seeking Imaginary "meanings" in the Symbolic's signifying chain.[65] But Lacan, by aligning the analytic act with the Real inaccessible to sense, leads interpretation back to the signifier's status as pure division. Affirming the fundamental difference between education and the act, he recognizes psychoanalysis as inseparable from what I call "bad education."

The prime referent of "badness" in Almodóvar's film, of course, is Father Manolo, the teacher whose desire for Ignacio leads to the latter's undoing as Child. Expressed in the visual eclipse of Ignacio when he makes his deal with the priest, that undoing is echoed in the voice-over that bridges the transition from the blackout produced by that eclipse to the opening of the iris shot. As embedded in the multiple layers of *Bad Education*'s textuality, the voice that speaks the voice-over belongs to Ignacio, *La Visita*'s narrator. Almodóvar gives us his story through scenes from Enrique's adaptation—scenes presented, for the most part, proleptically within the diegesis of *Bad Education* as Enrique, in the process of reading the tale, seems to imagine the film he will make of it. In a sort of structural reversal, though, the prolepsis of Enrique's movie includes a flashback to Ignacio's childhood as Father Manolo, confronted by his former pupil, reads the text of *La Visita*.[66] Ignacio, now presenting as Zahara, a performer who lip-synchs to Sara Montiel, has cornered the priest in his office, claiming to be the sister of the now-dead Ignacio (in Enrique's film of *La Visita*, Juan/Angel, Ignacio's brother, who had pretended to be Ignacio—by then already dead—when he met Enrique, plays the part of Zahara/Ignacio). In both Ignacio's story and Enrique's film, Zahara presents Father Manolo with the manuscript of *La Visita*, in which, as she tells him, Ignacio exposes their sexual relations. Threatening to arrange for its publication unless the priest can give her enough money for "una vida mejor, y un cuerpo mejor" (a better life and a better body), Zahara encourages him to read it to see how much damage it would do.[67] While Enrique, in Almodóvar's film, reads the text of *La Visita*, we see a scene from his future film, in which the priest is reading it too. Enrique films him "hearing" its words as spoken by Ignacio, before the visual yields to a flashback depicting what Ignacio describes. But if the story depicts Ignacio's recollections as an adult, the voice we hear in the voice-over belongs to Ignacio as a Child. When our view of the screen is blocked by the priest and we encounter the *nothing to see*, it is the voice of the Child Ignacio that declares, "Me vendi por primera vaz en aquella sacristía par evitar la expulsion de Enrique" (I sold myself for the first time in that sacristy to prevent Enrique's expulsion)."[68]

The tension between the voice *as* the voice of the Child and its confession that the *nothing to see* of this blackout was his *first* act of prostitution opens a gap in "Ignacio" much as the hole of the iris shot does on the screen. The boy whom the scenario describes as possessing a voice of the greatest purity ("la voz blanquísima de Ignacio-niño") here uses his voice to qualify this moment as a beginning, not an end. He looks back on what happened less as a rape or a *sexual* violation than as the violation of a binding contract on whose terms the priest reneged: "Me vendi por primera vaz en aquella sacristía par evitar la expulsion de Enrique, *pero el Padre Manolo me engañó*" (I sold myself for the first time in that sacristy to prevent Enrique's expulsion, *but Father Manolo cheated me*).[69] Afterward, Zahara repeatedly enacts that fraudulent transaction in reverse, symptomatically robbing her clients as if to make good on Ignacio's loss. She avenges herself by betraying the men who purchase her body for sex just as the priest betrayed Ignacio. In this way she lends her sexual adventures a supplementary jouissance while funding her access to the jouissance made possible by drugs.

Having sold himself in the interval between the blacked-out screen and the iris shot (an interval meant less to keep something unseen than to try to visualize *nothing*), Ignacio loses his coherence as a Child. Hence, the scene that follows, the one to which the photo on the poster alludes, provides our last glimpse of Ignacio as the Child the film would have us desire (in all the ways such desire at once constructs and destroys the Child). Standing amid the rows of boys revealed as the iris shot widens, Ignacio catches sight of Enrique being taken away from the school; at the moment he registers his betrayal by the priest, his body is racked by a force that morphs him from the Child Ignacio of Enrique's film into the Juan/Angel of Almodóvar's, who has already murdered his brother (figures 1.10–1.14). Split open by Father Manolo, and so by the experience of jouissance (not only the priest's but also his own, the corollary of the sexual power he deploys in trying to rescue Enrique), Ignacio transgresses the ontological barrier between the fiction of *La Visita* and the "reality" of *Bad Education*. In the process he suffers a transformation from the Child whose innocence speaks to the infinite possibility of a blank page ("blanquísima," like Ignacio's voice), to nothing but *the substantialization of nothing*, the positivized form of the void that propels the subject to jouissance.

An earlier sequence in Enrique's film anticipates this negativity, permitting what J. Hillis Miller calls "a glimpse of the zero" in the one. When Zahara hands Father Manolo the story, pointing to a particular passage where she tells him his reading should begin, we see the typewritten leaves of the text and hear Ignacio in voice-over speak the words to which she gestures. He recalls his schooldays, when those students with the highest grades were rewarded with trips to the country in the company of Father Manolo, whom the camera frames in profile reading the words Ignacio speaks. With the voice of the Child as a bridge to the past, the film cuts from Father Manolo's face to the scene Ignacio describes. A group of boys dressed in bathing attire

1.10–1.14: Ignacio
morphs into Juan.
From *Bad Education*
(Almodóvar, 2004).

race toward the river for a swim while the camera, countering their forward movement, tracks in the opposite direction, drawn toward something hidden from view by the overgrowth of a canebrake. On the other side of this shelter, Father Manolo, in his clerical robes, is seated beside Ignacio, who is visibly ill at ease. To the accompaniment of the priest's guitar, Ignacio lends his choir-boy tones to "Moon River," a song from the 1960s, here sung to Spanish lyrics written by Almodóvar himself.[70] The purity of Ignacio's voice imbues the song with a deep ambiguity; the screenplay remarks, "There is something hypnotic and perverse about the fact that a child is singing it."[71] With Father Manolo's hungry eyes fixed upon him intently, Ignacio squirms in an effort to avoid the nakedness of that gaze; yet he finds himself, seemingly against his will, meeting and holding it anyway. As he sings that he will neither forget Moon River nor be carried away by its turbulence, he covertly acknowledges his own contradictions, underscoring the forces of attraction and repulsion, desire and resistance, in the scene (figures 1.15–1.17).

Eager, like Ignacio, to look somewhere else, to escape the sexual tension revealed by these glances exchanged with the priest, the film cuts away to slow-motion shots of the schoolboys at play in the water while Ignacio's version of "Moon River" functions as a soundtrack. On the one hand, this offers a respite from Ignacio's encounter with the priest by immersing the audience in the sights and sounds of what seems like an ethical alternative: the openness, exuberance, and joy of the frolicking schoolboys in the river tacitly rebuking the furtiveness, constraint, and uneasiness in the canebrake. In that sense the film implicitly captions these shots as instantiations of "innocence" and weighs them against the scene in the reeds, soon to literalize the fall. On the other hand, the camera's attention to the glistening bodies of the boys, its idealization of their athleticism in this slow-motion sequence that mimes the will-to-linger of the spectatorial gaze, daubs these shots with the pederastic stain of the scene from which it turns (figures 1.18–1.19).

That recognition, perhaps, brings the camera back to the scene it failed to escape. As two boys bob up and down in slow motion, Ignacio, still singing "Moon River," asks where God and good and evil are found. At the moment the lyrics confess a desire to know what hides in the darkness—"Yo quiero saber / qué se esconde en la oscuridad"—the film cuts away from the river (on the word *saber*, "to know") and returns to the canebrake as seen from without.[72] The camera fixes its gaze on the reed bed to the sounds of the words "qué se esconde" (what hides itself) and then slowly tracks in toward the greenery as Father Manolo's guitar goes silent and Ignacio continues to sing a cappella: "en la oscuridad / y tú lo encontrerás" (in the darkness, and

The muddy water

Of that Moon River

Of that Moon River

1.15–1.17: Turbulent
desires. From *Bad
Education* (Almodóvar,
2004).

you will find it). The screen of vegetation still fills the shot as Ignacio, too,
goes silent before we hear his sharp cry: "No!" The camera pans left to capture Ignacio as he dashes from the reeds, trips on a rock, and winds up flat
on his face. Father Manolo, calling after him, follows anxiously behind (but-
toning his cassock as he does so), until he reaches the boy's prone body and
pauses, looking down (figures 1.20–1.22).

The film then cuts to a close-up of Ignacio from Father Manolo's perspective, the boy's face turning up toward the priest, on whom he fixes his
gaze. His expression conveys neither fear nor anger. Only his impassivity, the
unblinking knowingness of his eyes, allows us to read, or project, reproach
(figure 1.23). A trail of blood traverses his forehead, tracing a cut along whose
line his image literally splits in two, exposing an internal darkness, a void, that

1.18–1.19: The pederastic gaze. From *Bad Education* (Almodóvar, 2004).

prefigures the blacking out of the screen when he sells himself in the sacristy (figures 1.24–1.25). From out of that darkness we now catch sight of Father Manolo's face, as if internal to the boy, but the priest is reading, in the "real time" of Enrique's film, the words Ignacio now speaks, "A trickle of blood divided my forehead in two. I had a feeling that it would be the same with my life: it would always be divided and I couldn't help it" (figures 1.26–1.27).[73]

Most readings of the film, responding to the legal and ethical consensus on sexual relations between children and adults, interpret this episode as Ignacio's subjection to harassment, victimization, or abuse. The screenplay lends some weight to this view, describing Ignacio's look as "defiant" and the boy as the priest's "adored victim."[74] But the film, in exploring the libidinal investments to which its characters respond, poses a challenge to the binarism of victim and abuser, innocence and guilt. Ignacio's inability, while singing, to keep his eyes from those of his teacher; his confession, through

1.20–1.22: Ignacio's "No." From *Bad Education* (Almodóvar, 2004).

the words of "Moon River," of a desire to know what the darkness hides; his literal opening onto darkness when his face is divided in two: these all signal his drive to confront in himself what the film and the culture around it would have us dismiss as nothing. What divides Ignacio as he lies on the ground foreseeing a life of division is not, then, the traumatized aftermath of Father Manolo's advances but rather his recognition of the Father Manolo already within—his recognition, that is, of his own susceptibility to what Father Manolo signifies: the submission to a power beyond one's control that undoes one's fantasmatic coherence by reducing the "one" to the status of the zero and displacing desire with jouissance.

Like the "masques à transformation" (transformational masks) invoked by Catherine Malabou to metaphorize plasticity, Ignacio's face opens onto the priest's as its own internal self-difference, suggesting, as Malabou says of such masques, the "line of division between two ways of representing the same face."[75] But that face possesses no authentic or positive presence of its own. Instead, it gives the illusion of substance to the void that the subject "is": the void in the signifying chain that we compulsively fill with sense by adding ever more links to the chain of reproductive futurism. In this way the one, if not "generate[d]" by the zero, as J. Hillis Miller would have it, can be viewed as its symptomatic expression. It positivizes—as "presence" or "being"—the negativity of primal division, which thereby becomes as imponderable as the zero in its status *as* zero. Catachrestically installing sens absexe in the (non)place of ab-sens, the one grounds our faith in reality's consistency by permitting us to affirm the "background of a totality," the "*one* anterior to discontinuity." To the extent that education, in Israël's phrase, "lead[s] out of the universe of the drive," it refutes the negativity of the signifier in its instability, its constant slippage, by equating reading with making sense and installing meaning in the (non)place of the now impossible Thing.

The shot that literalizes Ignacio's division thus highlights the nested-doll logic of reading in Almodóvar's film. More specifically, its literalization of fracture tropes on the fracture introduced in the film by letters of various sorts; it collocates Ignacio's division with the subject's division by the drive as well as with that of the filmic text (in its illusory relation to presence) by the signifier's materiality. Not for nothing (though precisely to *conceptualize* "nothing") does the splintering of young Ignacio's face, disclosing the Father Manolo within, depict the priest, some thirteen years later, *reading* the adult Ignacio's text. As framed within Enrique's film, this displacement crosses barriers simultaneously temporal and ontological: the flashback shows us Ignacio's narrative as Father Manolo, while reading it, sees it unfolding in his

1.23–1.27:
Ignacio's division. From
Bad Education (Alm-
odóvar, 2004).

mind; but the shot that returns us to the scene of that reading returns us to the "reality" of the present moment and to the text that conjures those images. That conjuring is what the shot's traversal of these barriers asserts: the flashback grants the manuscript's signifiers Imaginary plenitude. Fleshing them out in images, it accords them the "presence" that Ignacio's voice-over gives to the written words on the page—words it raises from lifeless inscriptions of the supposedly dead Ignacio to the living speech in which the Child he was seems miraculously to survive.

If the return to Father Manolo in *La Visita*'s diegetic present deconstructs the Imaginary fullness of Ignacio's voice as an index of "presence," then it reads the Child, the figure of meaning, as Imaginary too, as a fantasy designed to secure our investment in a reality that, like Ignacio's face, might dissolve at any moment into the zero of the Real. The transition from Ignacio to Father Manolo forms a sequence with the next two shots, the first of which cuts to the page that the priest is reading in Enrique's film (the text of Ignacio's *La Visita* that Zahara forces on the priest), while the second cuts to Enrique reading that page in Almodóvar's film (the text of Ignacio's *La Visita* given to Enrique by Juan/Angel). The wipe that fractures Ignacio's face coincides with the reduction of his image to nothing but the effect of linguistic signifiers (the words we see on the page); the subsequent cut from those words to Enrique's face so reduces the priest as well. The Imaginary status of the Child Ignacio for the priest in Enrique's film attaches to the boy and the priest alike in the diegesis of Almodóvar's (figures 1.28–1.30).

Let me slightly reframe this reading, though, to note another aspect of the film that bears on its signification: the aspect ratio that determines the proportions of the image we see on the screen. Usually no more than a technological given, the meaningless frame that determines the space of cinematic inscription, the aspect ratio, for obvious reasons, rarely figures diegetically.[76] For the most part, it simply identifies the dimensions in which the image will appear by serving as the window through which we construct its Imaginary space. But Almodóvar treats the aspect ratio as a signifying element in itself, changing *Bad Education*'s format (in general, 2.35:1) to an aspect ratio that corresponds to a prior historical norm (1.85:1) in order to represent those sequences that take place in Enrique's film.[77] The first such transition occurs when Enrique begins to read *La Visita*, the words of which we hear his voice (not Ignacio's) pronounce in voice-over. A long shot of Enrique absorbed in the text dissolves into an exterior shot of the cinema in which Ignacio and Enrique will subsequently have their first sexual experience together.[78] As the theater comes into focus onscreen, a change in the aspect ratio narrows

1.28–1.30: From Enrique's film to Almodóvar's. From *Bad Education* (Almodóvar, 2004).

the image before our eyes. This constitutes a shift in both the temporality and the ontological status of what we see, though only later do we understand that it marks these scenes as prolepses of Enrique's *La Visita*. The Cine Olympo, as framed onscreen, thus serves as a switch point to foreground the act of cinematic framing—its framing not only *within* the shot's dimensions but also *by* them.[79] Though the content of the image directs our attention to the place for viewing films, its reformatting invites us to cognize what has no place in the films we view: the framework wherein the Imaginary topology of cinema unfolds (figures 1.31–1.35).

The trimming of the image through the expansion of the empty black border that surrounds it signals the signifying function of the "nothing" on whose foreclosure meaning relies. It opens a *diegetic* frame intended to differentiate, in the context of *Bad Education*, representations of filmic representation (the scenes from Enrique's movie) from the naturalized and therefore unremarked-on frame of Almodóvar's. This naturalization will quickly extend to the narrowed, diegetic frame itself; the identificatory lure of the image will scotomize the signifying function of its border, which becomes once again the space of nonmeaning or the nonspace of *nothing to see*. The more thoroughly the Imaginary claim of these scenes from Enrique's film compels us, the less we observe their status, diegetically, as prolepses of his film. *Bad Education*, however, persists in disturbing such Imaginary investments through transitions that take us from one level of representation to another. When the splintering of Ignacio's face reveals Father Manolo, thirteen years later, reading Ignacio's own text, all the scenes of Ignacio's schooldays, with their patina of pederastic desire, melt back, like our image of Ignacio as a Child, into the material from which they spring: the signifiers on the page of the story as the priest imagines them taking place. But then Father Manolo himself turns into a mere linguistic signifier once we realize that the text we construe him as reading (see figure 1.28) is actually the text in which *Enrique* is reading about *him* (figure 1.30). The insert shot of the typewritten page (figure 1.29), though the very same page with the very same words from the very same story by Ignacio, is *not* a reverse shot of the manuscript Father Manolo got from Zahara but rather a cut to the manuscript that Enrique was given by Juan/Angel. The change in aspect ratio confirms this *before* Almodóvar's reverse shot brings us back to Enrique's face (figure 1.30).[80] Thus, while Enrique reads Ignacio's story in Almodóvar's *Bad Education*, Almodóvar unfolds that story by way of scenes from Enrique's film, including the one in which Father Manolo (or the actor who plays him in *La Visita*) similarly reads Ignacio's story and sees it unfold in his mind's eye. From the perspective of Almodóvar's film,

1.31–1.35: Changing the aspect ratio. From *Bad Education* (Almodóvar, 2004).

Enrique's and Father Manolo's visions occur as "a fiction, . . . a dream of passion," to borrow a phrase from Hamlet. As insubstantial as the "nothing" that Hecuba is to the melancholy prince, they produce, like Hamlet's musings on the players, a mise en abyme that calls into question their ontological grounds.[81]

Almodóvar may substantialize those "nothings" by granting them imagistic form, but by tracing their source to the materiality of language, to the signifying letters on the page, he makes those images "nothing" too, suggesting that the world as given sustains its Imaginary positivization only by occluding the negativity that precludes its ontological consistency. He does so here specifically with reference to adult-child sexual relations, the proscription of which informs our fantasy of knowing what sex "is" to the extent that it produces the Child as the locus where sex "is not."

But sex in *Bad Education*, as figured through homosexuality, gender mobility, and pederastic desire, denotes a constitutive gap in knowledge around which the world takes shape. As the pressure of the unintelligible, as what Slavoj Žižek describes as an "ontological 'crack'" in "every notion of the universe qua totality," sex eludes representation except by disrupting or undoing it.[82] Like the filmic apparatus or the linguistic text, both central to *Bad Education*, sex is a machinery of difference without any meaning in itself but out of which meaning arises. Almodóvar's film touches on sex as ab-sens through the ontological flicker that binds its images to a negativity that derealizes what "is."

The image of Ignacio as Child, for example, though deployed as a spur to the spectatorial desire it also aims to sublimate, remains, within the diegesis, only a *cinematic* image, one whose provenance is exclusively the space of Enrique's film. The Child Ignacio as we know him is only an actor in *La Visita*; *Bad Education* provides no image of the actual child that Ignacio was. Though Almodóvar's film, like Enrique's, excites a longing for the lost Ignacio, it brings out, with the *fictional* image of Ignacio as portrayed in *La Visita*, both the Child's illusionary quality and the presence of something internal to the Child that must disfigure and destroy it: a death drive evinced through the instability, the self-difference, of its image. When the face of Ignacio splits in two, exposing his divided condition, its displacement by Father Manolo's face (in the scene from Enrique's film) anticipates another visual effect: the transformation of *La Visita's* Ignacio into *Bad Education's* Juan/Angel while the aspect ratio changes from 1.85:1 to 2.35:1 (figures 1.10–1.14). As in the earlier metamorphosis, this shift from one narrative "reality" to another distorts the Child by producing the face of its own internal antagonism, whether Father Manolo (responsible for the murder of Ignacio in *La*

Visita) or Juan/Angel (responsible, with Father Manolo, for murdering him in *Bad Education*).[83] The plasticity of the image, bespeaking its openness to a negativity that undoes it, registers the fatality of the drive that inheres in *Bad Education*'s Child.

But when Ignacio morphs into Juan/Angel, Almodóvar has not yet revealed the latter's imposture of his dead brother. Despite Enrique's suspicions (he sees no sign of Ignacio in Juan/Angel), the audience takes Juan/Angel at his word when he claims to be Ignacio.[84] Only later do we grasp the otherness that erupts in Ignacio here—an otherness evincing the tension between Imaginary image and Symbolic signifier, the tension that constitutes the drive as the negativity of their relation, as the pressure of the Real. The morphing itself, like the bifurcation that splinters Ignacio's face, corresponds to the nothing of the zero that desublimates the Child. As visible as the force of the death drive is when Ignacio "becomes" Juan/Angel, a still more shocking transformation awaits when we meet the "real" Ignacio. The Child that *Bad Education* induces the audience to desire may only ever be seen as performed by an actor in Enrique's *La Visita*, but Almodóvar grants us access to the "real" Ignacio as an adult in a flashback that accompanies the "real" Father Manolo's narrative of his death.

Unlike Zahara as played by Juan/Angel—charming, seductive, and impish—the adult Ignacio is gangly and shrill, helplessly driven by his addiction to drugs, and far removed from the Child who wins the audience's affection. Indeed, referring to the grown-up Ignacio, Father Manolo—no longer a priest and now working as a publisher named Berenguer—confides to Enrique, "This was not the Ignacio that you and I loved." The film then cuts to a point-of-view shot of Ignacio as Manolo/Berenguer first sees him as an adult and we share his disappointment. Photographed in a crimson light that lends his angular face a tint like that of the poster's red circle (figure 1.36), he lacks the appeal of the young Ignacio or the prettiness of Zahara, as played by Juan/Angel in *La Visita* (figure 1.37).

Like *Vertigo*'s Judy in relation to Madeleine, the "real" Ignacio, when he appears onscreen, effects a desublimation. The screenplay—which calls him "Ignacio Adulto," describes him as "el travesti," and refers to him with male pronouns—paints a picture of decay: "In person he is much deteriorated. He is tall, extremely thin, with long and messy hair, teeth in an awful state, and more feminine than masculine."[85] Though proud of his breast enhancement surgery, Ignacio is desperate for the resources needed to continue his aesthetic reconstruction ("To be cute costs a lot of money"), toward which end he blackmails the former priest.[86] The surgery he seeks would harmonize his appearance with his "being," effecting his sublimation into (his own) desired object and resolving

1.36–1.37: The "real" adult Ignacio and Juan as Ignacio portraying Zahara. From *Bad Education* (Almodóvar, 2004).

the internal division between his ideal ego and his ego itself. But the division that matters in *Bad Education*, and that nothing can ever resolve, lies less in the relation to desire than in the tension between desire as such and the drive, between the futurity elaborated in the former and the latter's insistence on the Real. Hence, Ignacio oscillates between saving his money for the surgery of which he dreams and squandering it, notwithstanding those dreams, on the drugs to which he is driven. One impulse pushes him forward and holds out the promise of future becoming; the other affords the immediacy of an *un*becoming instead. In the grip of the drive that takes him beyond the object form of desire and so, in effect, beyond his very survival as himself, he encounters the Real of jouissance, of expenditure without reserve.

This, we might say, is the zero degree of queerness in the film—the queerness of the zero as negativity and therefore as ab-sens; the queerness that designates sex as nothing but the cut, the division, dividing it from being as being "one." Such a oneness affirms not only the fictive coherence of any entity but also the fantasmatic totalization of a world—a world propped up by images that not only represent it but that also represent, implicitly, its *availability to representation*. Queerness, by contrast, though always fleshed out in catachrestic figures, eludes representation insofar as it eludes identity as itself. It enacts, like the zero, the negation of what is—opening onto the imageless, the impossible, the unthinkable—while succumbing to catachrestic embodiment in entities made to figure the place of the death drive, which similarly refuses representation.

The *nothing to see* that emerges diacritically by the widening of the iris onscreen (and which is referenced in the poster's red circle enclosing the photo of the boy) invokes the ontological negation implied by the splintering of Ignacio's face and his visual morphing into Juan/Angel; it bespeaks the pressure of the zero that operates in and against the logic coimplicating meaning, sociality, and the Child. Perhaps that explains why Father Manolo's blacking-out of the camera's lens (figures 1.2–1.6) gets repeated during Manolo/Berenguer's description of the "real" Ignacio's death. Besotted with Ignacio's younger brother and fearful that Ignacio will expose his past by publishing *La Visita*, Manolo/Berenguer, as he confesses to Enrique, plotted with Juan/Angel to kill Ignacio with a dose of pure heroin. In the flashback paired with this recollection, Ignacio, alone in his study, is typing a letter to Enrique, with whom he has not been in touch since their youth. One by one the typebars, enacting the sublation of language into meaning, print the letters that appear onscreen: "Dear Enrique, I think I have succeeded" (Querido Enrique: Creo que lo conseguí). At this moment, the sound of the buzzer, signaling a visitor, interrupts him. Manolo/Berenguer, who, in order to stall on Ignacio's blackmail demands, has been offering him small quantities of money and drugs, hands him the packet containing pure heroin. After following Ignacio back to his desk, Manolo/Berenguer lingers awkwardly, promising, as he has for months, to come up with the rest of the money soon. The framing of the shot as he does so echoes the earlier scene in the sacristy (figure 1.38), though the former priest's back now impinges on the screen from the right-hand side, not the left (figure 1.39).

Unlike its counterpart, though, this image does not immediately get blacked out. Manolo/Berenguer, as he did before, moves closer to Ignacio, but he does so now with murderous rather than sexual intent. In fact, when Ignacio, preparing the drugs, misreads his former teacher's solicitude as a pretext for ogling his breasts, Manolo/Berenguer, confused, can barely hide his lack of interest. Anticipating the enjoyment of yielding to the powerful

1.38–1.39: Repetition and reversal. From *Bad Education* (Almodóvar, 2004).

rush of narcotic release but uncomfortable with the thought of Manolo/
Berenguer observing him while he does so, Ignacio sends the publisher home
("Go away. I don't like shooting up in front of you" [Váyase. No me gusta
ponerme delante de Vd.]).[87] The substitution here of the formal *Vd.* for the
tu he uses elsewhere ("Just in case, I've written two letters: one for the publisher, the other for your wife") signals his discomfort with the former priest
as a witness to his jouissance, or as a witness to it again, as he was when Ignacio first "sold [him]self."[88] In response, Manolo/Berenguer, knowing the
extent of the negation to which this act of enjoyment will lead, nervously
turns to leave the room, reproducing, in the process, the eclipse of the
image that ended the scene in the sacristy. Just as the partial blocking of
the camera switches from screen left in that sequence (figure 1.38) to screen
right in this one (figure 1.39), so the total blackout of the image entails
a directional reversal as well. Here the camera is blacked out frontally as

Manolo/Berenguer turns away from Ignacio, literally and figuratively both (figures 1.40–1.43), while earlier his back had obscured the lens as he approached Ignacio for sex.

These two homologous blackouts, each construing the zero of the *nothing to see* as a purely differential relation (through the presence and absence of the image) rather than as an ontological condition (where the zero would participate in being itself), link jouissance to the cut of division that never appears as such but desublimates, instead, the unity, the integrity, that the "as such" presumes. Desublimation here is less about stripping the idealizing gloss from an entity, the better to see it as it is, than about seeing it as already idealized in its very framing *as* an entity, in its very construction *as a one*. It thus counters the work of education, which establishes the "one" of the entity through technologies of sense that reinforce as "natural" the movement from legibility to knowledge. Education, especially in the mode of critique, may look like desublimation, but it always presupposes the inseparability of meaning from interpretation; thus, the logic of recognition implicit in Imaginary form expresses itself in education's explicit mandate of comprehension. Almodóvar, however, through Ignacio's encounters with the Real of jouissance (whether through sexual encounters or drugs), de-Imaginarizes the Symbolic, subtracting the *image* of desire that lets us cathect the signifying system and leaving us with nothing to see but an image of the nothing we never can (the nothing that even the blacked-out screen continues to screen out).

The film's first blocking of the camera's lens gave way, with the widening of the iris shot, to an overhead view of boys in rows, an image that multiplied (and made generic) the pedophilic object of desire. Though the second—and shorter—blacking out gives way to a high-angle shot as well, it does so by way of a conventional cut, and the camera is mobile, not static, as if the movement that expanded the iris in response to the image of desire were now transferred to the camera itself. It traverses the adult Ignacio's study, impassively noting his scattered clothing, magazines, and footwear, as it moves toward a framing of Ignacio's head as seen from above and behind (figure 1.44). A cut to a close-up of Ignacio's face, his eyelids heavy, his stare unfocused, confirms that he has injected the heroin in the space the blackout conceals. He falls forward as the heroin reaches his heart ("cuando la heroína roza su corazón") and collapses onto the typewriter, hitting the keyboard with his forehead (figures 1.45–1.46).[89] The film then cuts to a startling shot from the perspective of Ignacio's letter, still held in place by the typewriter's platen, as a jangle of typebars leap upward when Ignacio's head strikes the keys (figure 1.47). No reverse shot shows us their effect on the letter; instead,

1.40–1.43: Ignacio blacked out by Berenguer. From *Bad Education* (Almodóvar, 2004).

Ignacio's final message ("su último mensaje") is conveyed by this Imaginary rendering of the machinery of the Symbolic at the moment of his fatal submission to the Real of jouissance.[90]

Only in the film's concluding scene does that "final message" return. Having discovered exactly how Ignacio died (on the day that principal photography for *La Visita* is completed), Enrique, who shared both his home and his bed with Juan/Angel throughout the shoot, sends him packing, appalled at his intimacy with someone responsible for Ignacio's death. But Juan/Angel has a parting gift: the letter from his dead brother. Shutting the door on Juan/Angel, Enrique unfolds the paper. A reverse shot offers a glimpse of the text that the film denied us earlier. The phrase we had watched Ignacio type before Manolo/Berenguer arrived now ends with a meaningless surplus of characters around the word, "succeeded" (consegui) (figure 1.48). By indexing a death they can never "mean," by inscribing an enjoyment they can never convey, these marks attest to the division inherent in the structure of signification that turns arbitrary signifiers into messages and meaningless letters into bearers of sense. Lacan has something to say about this in "The Signification of the Phallus":

> The signifier plays an active role in determining the effects by which the signifiable appears to succumb to its mark, becoming, through that passion, the signified. This passion of the signifier thus becomes a new dimension of the human condition in that it is not only man who speaks, but in man and through man that it [*ça*] speaks; in that his nature becomes woven by effects in which the structure of the language of which he becomes the material may be refound; and in that the relation of speech thus resonates in him, beyond anything that can be accounted for by the psychology of ideas.[91]

The unreadable surplus of the signifier to which "the signifiable" must succumb denotes, like the frame of the aspect ratio, the mark of articulation—a mark routinely cut off from the meanings its cut alone articulates. This surplus is the energy of difference or division incapable of appearing as such: the zero degree of (il)legibility that constitutes the drive.

This image of a text with its textualized image of what escapes the logic of imaging—the "nothing" of the Real—brings the film to an end. Though not the final image we see (we are granted a medium shot of Enrique refolding the letter while deep in thought), it marks the end of Enrique's "education." While reflecting on Ignacio's "message," he, too, will be textualized as an inscription ("woven by effects in which the structure of the language of which he becomes the material may be refound") when his image is captured

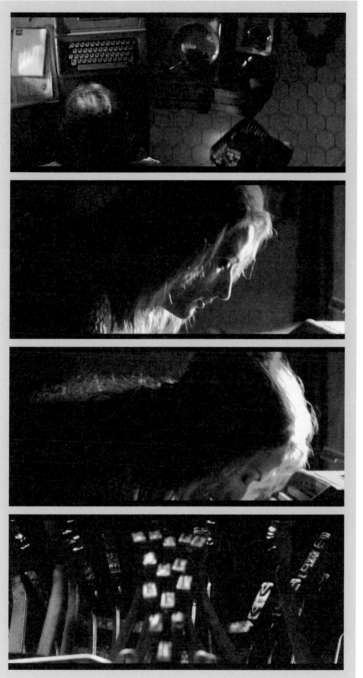

1.44–1.47:
Ignacio falls
forward onto
the typewriter.
From *Bad
Education*
(Almodóvar,
2004).

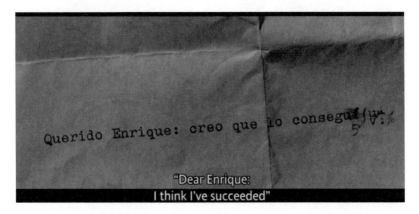

Querido Enrique: creo que lo consegui

"Dear Enrique:
I think I've succeeded"

1.48: A final message and its unreadable surplus. From *Bad Education* (Almodóvar, 2004).

in freeze-frame and a series of text boxes opens onscreen (figures 1.49–1.51). Each sketches the fate of a major character until, with the last one's account of Enrique—"Enrique Goded continues to make films with the same passion" (Enrique Goded continúa haciendo cine, con la misma pasión)—the text box expands beyond the screen, filling it with nothing but a blackness against which "pasión" appears (figure 1.51).[92] But what does that image register? The word *pasión*? The letters that shape it? Their invisibilization of the blackness that makes them perceptible in the first place? The fuzziness of their digital enlargement that speaks to their material production? Though the visual expansion of the text box, accompanied by a swelling musical score, figurally evokes what the word denotes—the emotional intensity of a subject's experience—the blurriness of the signifier, or of the letters that spell it out, effaces the passionate subject, Enrique, as if those letters literalized (by reducing to nothing but letters) what Lacan calls the "passion of the signifier." Like the marks imprinted by Ignacio's death, such a literalization calls into question signification as such by stressing the senseless material on which the sense it offers us rests. It unleashes, as Parveen Adams writes in a completely different context, "the access to jouissance" afforded by "the reduction of the signifier to the letter."[93] But to whose jouissance does this refer? Is there an agential subject of jouissance that can know itself as such? Or is jouissance the zeroing out of the (constitutively divided) subject as it succumbs to the negativity, the contentless energy, of pure division?

Bad Education suggests the latter through its efforts to engage the *nothing to see* as which queerness, like the zero, "appears": the *nothing to see* of the

1.49–1.51: The passion of the signifier. From *Bad Education* (Almodóvar, 2004).

signifying division that is never signifiable, but without which signification, like the subject, is impossible. That excess of signifying energy, though, as unleashed in jouissance, makes the subject itself impossible, exposing it, in the words of Jonathan Lear, to "the deepest form of human helplessness: helplessness in the face of too much energy. As Freud points out, we are vulnerable to repetitions of this helplessness from the beginning to the end of our lives. But this is a peculiar kind of 'repetition'—because it is the repetition of something that is in itself without content."[94] Only the repetition of this energy's too-muchness can bind ideational energy into the "content," the reality, that we "know." Lear expands on this as follows:

> For Freud, the fundamental mental molecule was an idea-plus-quota of energy (which he called affect). It was the transfer of this energy along varying paths of ideas that allowed Freud to explain the formation of neurotic symptoms and dreams. In this use, psychic energy seems to be the "matter" of a form-and-matter unity. But, then, how could there be a case of pure, formless matter? How could there be *mental* energy without an idea? I think the answer is to take this as a limiting case of the mental—somewhat analogous to treating zero as a number. The reason for doing this is to capture the phenomena of trauma and of momentary breakthroughs: these are vicissitudes of the mental.[95]

More than *vicissitudes* of the mental, though, these breaks or breakthroughs are foundational or even, as Lear suggests, "fundamental." Energy itself is the trauma that demands, by way of homeopathic defense, the additional energy of ideational binding. But that binding depends on an excess never contained by ideational bonds, an excess that every attempt to bind it reproduces yet again. In calling this a *formal excess*, I refer to the surplus of forming energy over any totalized form and thus to the surplus informing form that always risks deforming it. Comparing mental energy uncoupled from ideational binding to "treating zero as a number," Lear implicitly invokes the place of the Real in thought itself, where *the Real* names the excess, the negativity, in Symbolic structuration. The imbalance created by that excess and the need to find a way to manage it give rise at once to jouissance and to the law that defends against it. If the zero stands in for the jouissance of the drive that registers the Real, then the one into which the "'innommable'" is always "reconver[ted]," according to de Man, identifies the compulsion to identity that inheres in the logic of desire. As the void within every situation that can never be counted or represented within it, the zero maintains the place of queerness as ceaseless negativity.[96]

From this perspective, *Bad Education* centers less on pederasty, sexuality, or the passion for making films than on the drive's ineducability, its resistance to sublimation, about which Žižek writes, "This minimal distance between the death drive and sublimation, between the negative gesture of suspension-withdrawal-contraction and the positive gesture of filling its void, is not just a theoretical distinction between the two aspects, which are inseparable in our actual experience: . . . the whole of Lacan's effort is precisely focused on those limit-experiences in which the subject finds himself confronted with the death drive at its purest, prior to its reversal into sublimation."[97] As a name for this limit-experience, this impossible encounter with the zero's negativity before its reconversion into a one, queerness inhabits the place of jouissance as the inextricable excess, as the antagonistic nonidentity, that animates the Symbolic order with its traumatizing energy. It stands, that is, beside other terms (including *woman*, *Blackness*, and *trans**) as the ontological exclusion that a given ontology requires.

As Eric Santner remarks in response to the passage from Jonathan Lear, "Fantasy is the name for the process that 'binds' this remainder, converts it into a support of social adaptation, a way of being in the world. I am suggesting that the task of truly inhabiting the 'midst of life' involves the risk of an unbinding or loosening of this fantasy as well as the social bond effectuated in it."[98] Santner, however, invested as he is in a messianic temporality, retreats from this negative moment, from its ontological threat, and from the risk, the queerness, that inheres in such a prospect of social unbinding, affirming, some thirty pages later, that "'unplugging' . . . need not signify a radical break with social reality, with the rule of a community's law, or even from historical agency."[99] This retreat, of course, is precisely what good education always effects: a retreat from the drive at its purest on behalf of its sublimation, a retreat that recuperates "social reality" as defined by "a community's law."

Almodóvar hews more closely, though, to Santner's first formulation, treating the Child as the fantasy object that binds the unbound excess (the traumatic energy of jouissance) and thereby serves as an instrument of "social adaptation." The Child, that is, like the image of Ignacio that advertises the film, enforces the law's, which is also desire's, disavowal of that unbound excess—the excess that presses for a "radical break" from any "ideational content," from anything knowable as a one. The object of desire, as Imaginary entity conceptualized as a one, makes desire itself the ultimate object of reproductive futurism: the desire that propels us forward by fantasizing our survival in the form of an object. The temporality thus established, the temporality of the law, constitutes this very movement of turning zero into one.

In the process it enacts the logic de Man associates with allegory, which aspires to a "stance of wisdom" by tracing a passage from a then to a now—a now that affirms the attainment of insight by surmounting the rupture, gap, or void of "radical discontinuity."[100] Like the permanent parabasis as which Friedrich Schlegel characterizes irony, however (a parabasis that anticipates the linguistic violence by which, for de Man, the "continuous universe" is "interrupted, disrupted *at all points*"), the insistence of the zero refutes the logic of allegorical historicization and enacts instead the structuring force of division, contradiction, negativity. Irony, like the drive, like the letter, like the Real, inheres in every moment, destroying the coherence of the one that we cling to in moving *from* moment to moment and undoing, therefore, the meanings procured by allegory and the logic of desire. But even this chapter's sketch of the irony with which *Bad Education*, like its poster, frames allegorizations of the zero as a one relies on allegorization. To read is always to allegorize, even if only by allegorizing a reading resistant to allegorical compulsion. Even an education in irony must reconvert irony into allegory, queerness into familiarity, meaninglessness into sense, and the "radical discontinuity" of the illegible marks at the end of Ignacio's letter into a figure for the Real of the zero and, as a consequence, into a one.

Education opposes irony as it also opposes the drive, relentlessly generating allegories in which irony is overcome. But *relentlessly* signals, ironically, allegory's own repetition compulsion, its internalization of the very drive it undertakes to sublimate. The concept of bad education is doomed to the status of an oxymoron that gestures allegorically toward an irony incapable of allegorization. That irony is the negativity that marks the *atopia* of queerness, the sinthome not only of allegory but also of education's aesthetic imperative. The aesthetic remains the horizon within which we construe the human itself, the horizon within which "social adaptation" emerges as the good. Faced with the "needs" of the human that find their face in the figure of the Child, queerness has nothing but nothing to teach, the nothing of the zero we can never approach as a concept or a one.[101] We can never know the zero *as* zero or apprehend its void directly, but in those moments of traumatic jouissance from which there is nothing to learn, its queer persistence seizes us as it seizes Ignacio: from behind. That is the truly queer lesson that merits the title *Bad Education*, the lesson that no one can ever learn and no "one" can ever survive.

Against Survival:

Queerness in a Time That's Out of Joint

Hamlet survives as a foundational text of modern Western culture in part by anticipating our secular ideology of cultural survival. Both Freud's attention to the play's Oedipality and Derrida's to its concern with "patrimonial filiation" respond to *Hamlet*'s prolepsis of the subject of reproductive futurism.[1] If Freud's reading of the play through *Oedipus* makes the latter "only retroactively 'prior,'" as Julia Reinhard Lupton and Kenneth Reinhard keenly observe, if the Freudian interpretation, in other words, "Oedipalizes" *Oedipus* through *Hamlet*, it can do so only because *Hamlet*, like Freud's formulation of the Oedipus complex, belongs to the universe in which the Child is the realization and depositary of futurity. The Child thus functions as a fantasy figure that promises temporal redemption through the recovery of an imaginary past in a future endlessly deferred.[2] Securing that future by postponing it, the Child who governs our investment in social and cultural survival instantiates the subject as limitless renewal, as unbounded possibility. But it also invokes the negativity of a repetition compulsion or death drive that gets projected onto those who occupy the position of "the queer:" those abjected, that is, as antisocial, as external to communal (re)production, as threats to the collectivity that sees its preservation in the Child. *Hamlet* gives this question of survival its canonical modern form with the words that begin its most famous soliloquy: "to be, or not to be" (3.1.58ff).[3] Here Hamlet broaches the negativity both enacted and resisted by the play's correlation of survival with repetition, and of repetition with the lifeless machinery that derealizes life from within. This makes the play a crucial text for revisiting reproductive futurism in terms of the violent dis-temporality that queerness inflicts on social order. Futurism, like the aesthetic, on which its fantasy of survival draws, pits its totalizing formalism (whose medium is time) against the foreignness to sense projected onto those made to figure ontological negation and the pressure of the "not to be."

Such a queerness proves intolerable even to those who call themselves queer. To "be" queer, after all, is *not to be*, except as a catachresis of the Swiftian "*Thing which is not*." Queerness is the limit of ontology, the exclusion containing (in both senses of the word) the negativity—the no, the not—that generates being: the rupture, itself libidinally charged, in the logic of survival. Radically opposed to the normativity of the order of identity, it confounds the notion of being as being at one with oneself. Like *woman* or *Blackness*, two other names for being's unassimilable excrescence, queerness can never coincide with itself and no one can "be" of its camp; but neither can anyone ever escape determination by it. Abjected for the threat it poses to a given order's survival, queerness, by threatening that order's coherence, makes possible its consolidation. It thus functions much like the zero, which structures the order of number while remaining unthinkable *as zero* within it. Those who identify themselves as queer or view queerness as a quality essential to a specific class of beings must reject the *negativity* of queerness as aggressively as any other subject committed to surviving as "itself." For queerness induces a disturbing relation to survival, education, and the aesthetic by underscoring the antagonism that inhabits each of those terms.

I have argued that the Real of the zero erupts in moments of jouissance like Ignacio's reduction to the space of the void in Almodóvar's *Bad Education*, moments that the one of the Symbolic survives by splitting from the split that inhabits it and mobilizing a Derridean "autoimmunitary process" cognate with the death drive.[4] I want to approach this nexus of questions about survival, queerness, and the zero by considering how institutions of knowledge, including the discipline of literary studies, for which *Hamlet* serves as a metonym, reinforce Symbolic sublimation by repudiating queerness as nonidentity, as the reification of the "*Thing which is not*." That repudiation, that insistent negation, inheres in the dissensus that Jacques Rancière adduces as the definitive political act.[5] But its negativity precedes the polis as such. Its originary division makes possible the relation that articulates collectivity in the first place and that generates, to secure that collective, catachrestic figures of queerness to embody the radical negativity that derealizes (social) form. The fear that the Real's eruption will effect this unbearable derealization corresponds to the constant pressure of the zero that procures and undoes every "one," thus making the zero, in its queerness, in its inaccessibility to sense, the (non)ground of political conflict.

No "one" can survive the void of the Real, but *something* survives that attests, nonetheless, to the *absence* of this one, something by means of which absence speaks, negating the loss or the void it proclaims by bequeathing us a residue, a self-contradictory *sign* of loss to keep loss from taking place. From such a perspective, absence occasions a type of visitation, an encounter with whatever makes present a lack and thereby, like the meaningless characters imprinted by the fall of Ignacio's head, effectively *registers* loss. But the loss thus experienced is held at bay by this same signifier of lack that translates loss into survival by marking the *presence* of loss itself. Carla Freccero suggests something similar when she explains the inherence of "queer spectrality" in "a queer kind of history[,] . . . since it involves an openness to the possibility of being haunted, even inhabited, by ghosts. What is transmitted in the cohabitation of ghostly past and present is related to survival." Such a survival relies on the continuous relation implicit, to quote Freccero again, in "a historical attentiveness that the living might have to what is not present but somehow appears as a figure, a voice, or a (spectral) kind of materialization, as a being that is no longer or not yet 'present.'"[6] Consoling as a fortification against the traumatizing Real, this "materialization" that indicates absence binds us to a past that never passes, or not, as Hamlet famously swears, "while memory holds a seat / In this distracted globe" (1.5.96–97). Such a memory, such a survival, attests to the signifier of an absence absenting the absence that it signifies, obeying in this the Symbolic law that turns zero into one. "Nothing," like zero, appears, therefore, in the order of intelligibility as a *signifier* of nonbeing, recalling Lacan's account of the one, the primal stroke or signifier, that tracks another's absence. As Lacan maintains, the signifier functions as a "symbol only of absence"; hence, something can only be missing, which is to say, *"missing from its place,"* in the framework of the Symbolic, where everything "must be *or* not be in a particular place"—everything, that is, but the signifier, which, as a presence that *designates* absence, "will be *and* not be where it is," conflating survival and loss.[7]

Hamlet, of course, in his most famous speech (whose first six words survive as literature's most recognized quotation) directly broaches the question of what "must be *or* not be in a particular place." And he does so by attending to what troubles a universe organized by the logic of *or*: the excess attached to the signifier that dis*or*ients the *or*der it *or*dains. Less a philosopher himself than an agent of philosophy's "supra-cognitive" surplus, the senseless element in sense associated by Badiou with "antiphilosophy," Hamlet, personifying the excess that philosophy's reason cannot contain, fingers the stops of rhetoric's flute without stopping *for*, or *in*, death.[8] His last words, pronounced as if post-humously (he has already declared, "I am dead"; 5.2.280), remain fixed on the question of what remains when the word machine, like Ignacio's typewriter, comes to a fatal halt. "The rest is silence" (5.2.300), he tells us, imposing his presence on that silence, which serves as his rest, his remains.

The First Folio edition, however, postpones that silence for half a line, letting Hamlet give voice to one last burst of vocables as he dies: "O, O, O, O!" (5.2.301).[9] Like the random characters imprinted when Ignacio's forehead strikes the keyboard, these textual marks evoke the internal limit of the Symbolic. In their status as interjections, they resist or counter silence, attesting to the subject's presence by way of an utterance that signals no more than the reliance of subjectivity on signification. In their status as signifiers, however, they effectively zero out the subject, repeating the "O" of the nothing, the Lacanian ab-sens, whose madness Hamlet has opened within the Symbolic order itself. The oscillation in this chain of "O"s between the assertion and negation of being revisits "to be, or not to be" as if to reject the *or*—as if the series of "O"s were gesturing toward the one and the zero simultaneously by way of Lacan's reminder that the signifier "will be *and* not be where it is."[10] Earlier, recounting his adventures at sea after Claudius dispatched him to England, Hamlet comments on the brevity of life and the ease with which it can be taken: "And a man's life's no more than to say 'one'" (5.2.75). Though intended to signal life's brevity, this sentence assimilates life and being to the status of the one, the totalized form of the self. To this saying of "one" the First Folio's "O"s add the nothing that "one" leaves unsaid. It seems fitting, there-fore, that these "O"s are often suppressed in modern editions of the play, re-duced to the nothing they incise in the "one" and returned to the silence they (fail to) speak, the remainder or "rest" that can never appear in any account of what "is." In this they recall a suggestion made by Roland Barthes in *Writing Degree Zero*: "The disintegration of language can only lead to the silence of writing." Barthes expands on this thought in what follows: "Mallarmé, the Hamlet of writing, as it were, well represents this precarious moment of His-tory in which literary language persists only the better to sing the necessity of its death. . . . This art has the very structure of suicide: in it, silence is a homogeneous poetic time which traps the word between two layers and sets it off less as a fragment of a cryptogram than as a light, a void, a murder, a freedom."[11]

The silence at which language, like Hamlet, arrives through its suicidal structure brings out the "O" of the void in the *or* by which the Symbolic *or*ders that everything "must be *or* not be in a particular place." Though modern editors tend to silence Hamlet's overflow of "O"s, preferring to let him die in the semantic richness of "the rest is silence," those "O"s speak to something in language that refuses sense and form, something Barthes glimpses in observing: "Any silence of form can escape imposture only by complete abandonment of communication."[12] The ab-sens that refuses communication, however, rests in the silence that Hamlet's last words identify as all that remains. The silencing of the "O"s, their absenting from the text, is itself the rest, the remainder, in which their nothingness survives. Cut off, or cut out, they persist as the trace of the cut that haunts every "one," procuring as well as disintegrating its coherence as an entity and making the "O" unbearable, as if the only response one could have to it were, to repurpose an earlier line from the play, "O, horrible! O, horrible! most horrible!" (1.5.80).

Whether present or absent, spoken or not at the moment of Hamlet's death, the "O" *as zero*, as nothing, as both unspoken and unspeakable, must rest or remain in the silence that is all that rests of Hamlet now, even while shadowing whatever "is" and whatever hopes to survive. Horatio, himself enjoined to survive to tell his prince's tale, responds to "the rest is silence" by trying to restrict the meaning of "rest" to a sleep-like posthumous repose: "Good night, sweet Prince, / And flights of angels sing thee to thy rest" (5.2.302–3). This lyric vision of death as rest ignores life's restless remnant (by which, of course, the play has literally been haunted from the beginning), denying the "something after death" (3.1.80) that can make itself felt in life: the insistent excess beyond death's "bourn" (3.1.81), beyond the *or* of life or death and its binary *or*der of ontology: "to be, or not to be" (3.1.58).

The specters that cross that bo*r*der (and thereby make it spectral too) frequent, and even animate, the work of Jacques Derrida. Less than two months before his death, in an interview first published in *Le Monde* and later as *Apprendre à vivre enfin*, which appeared the following year, Derrida reflects on the place of survival and spectrality in his thought:

> I have always been interested in this thematic of survival, whose meaning is not something that adds itself to living and to dying. It is originary: life *is* survival. To survive in the current sense means to continue to live, but also to live *after* death. With regard to translation, [Walter] Benjamin underlines the distinction between *überleben*, on the one hand, to survive death as a book can survive the death of its author or a child the death of

its parents, and, on the other hand, *fortleben*, *living on*, to continue to live. All the concepts that have helped me to work, notably those of the trace and the spectral, were bound up with "to survive" [*survivre*] as a structural and rigorously originary dimension. It doesn't derive from either to live or to die.[13]

Neither supplementary to living and dying, nor produced by one or the other, survival precedes and determines both, according to Derrida, thereby frustrating from the outset every attempt to distinguish between them. As primal trace, as originary writing, before and without which there is nothing to write nor anyone to write it, survival survives by precipitating the differential *or*der it refuses. It occasions and requires a conceptual geography in which everything "must be *or* not be in a particular place," such that even nonbeing and *atopia* would have to inhabit a place, would have to assume a signifiable form in order to appear as a "one." The Symbolic itself thus operates as the *or*der of survival, giving rise to the world, through sens-absexe, as the archive of signification even while assuring the survival of ab-sens as a threat to that archive from within.

Consider, in this light, Derrida's account of Benjamin's two senses of survival. *Überleben* refers to the remnants, the "rest," left after someone's death, and *fortleben* refers to whatever successfully eludes the grip of death in the first place. But the examples of the former that Derrida cites, survival through books and through children, may challenge the stability of the distinction they are introduced to define. The book that survives an author's death, whether signed by that author or not, allows readers (in the era of the author function) to generate a figure of the writer who produced it. *Hamlet* tells us more about "Shakespeare" than Shakespeare's "life" could tell us about *Hamlet*. Wherever the author function reigns, *Hamlet* will give birth to a "Shakespeare." But had Hamnet, Shakespeare's biological son, survived *instead of* the character who, some argue, took his place, would the Shakespeare to which he could testify be the "Shakespeare" that *Hamlet* constructs? Though we can never know if Hamnet's survival would have altered Shakespeare's work, the nonexistence of *Hamlet* would drastically alter our knowledge of "Shakespeare." Children, like books, may perpetuate the name or the names of those who produced them, but children, though carrying forward such names, are not the products of authors. Their genes can be those of parents they may never meet and never know and whose values, worldviews, and habits will never influence or shape them. As living organisms they carry (under current reproductive regimes) the genetic materials in which some trace of their progenitors *lives on* even as they themselves are seen as what survives (of) their parents.[14] At the crossing of *überleben* and *fortleben*, then, those genetic materials indicate the site at which the survival of a trace or a remnant coincides with the survival of the thing itself: where the genetic codes of the dead live on and life is the continuous transmission and recombination of those codes, thus troubling the Benjaminian distinction between living on and living after.[15]

But genetic "living on" can never assure one's survival in social memory. The child as vessel of a living code (*fortleben*) requires an educational supplement through which its survival will better approximate the living after of a book (*überleben*)—a supplement that makes it a memorial object, the material support for the survival of the parent who, like the dead King Hamlet's ghost, speaks the imperative, "Remember me" (1.5.91). *Fortleben* succumbs to *überleben* here; the child must submit to being authored. Internalizing the ghost's injunction, Hamlet explicitly identifies his brain as a book that preserves his father's words, committing himself to a mode of survival that makes him not only the archive but also the specter of his father:

> Remember thee?
> Yea, from the table of my memory
> I'll wipe away all trivial fond records,
> All saws of books, all forms, all pressures past,
> That youth and observation copied there,
> And thy commandment all alone shall live
> Within the book and volume of my brain
> Unmixed with baser matter. (1.5.97–104)

Taking writing as the figure of knowledge—and so, by extension, of education—Hamlet associates its material inscription with the "trivial fond records" he disdains, with the lifeless copies of "pressures past" that his hand can "wipe away."[16] By contrast, he vows that in the "table of his memory," in "the book and volume of [his] brain," he will carry only his father's "commandment." It "alone shall live" there and this vitality distinguishes it from the records, forms, and copies that were written there earlier, freeing it from the status of mere technical supplement associated with writing and leaving it "unmixed with baser matter," as are the writings he "wipe[s]" away." This singular privileging of the father's commandment—Hamlet here is absolute: it "*all alone shall live*"—produces, as Jonathan Goldberg notes, a decisive "scene of writing," one in which Hamlet functions not as author but as blank page.[17] For the words of his father to live in his mind, he effaces his prior experience, sacrificing the memory of everything that "youth and observation copied there."

The paternal commandment, and it alone, is *not* a copy for Hamlet; it *lives*, it insists like a parasite that sucks the life from its helpless host, surviving not as a "pressure[] past" but as the pressure, always present, of an unrelenting drive. Hamlet becomes, in consequence, an appendage to this living word, the substrate supporting a survival that lives, in more than one sense, in his place. Goldberg evokes this well when he notes that "Hamlet voices his father's text."[18] Lacan observes something similar: "There is a level in the subject on which it can be said that his fate is expressed in terms of a pure signifier, a level at which he is merely the reverse-side of a message that is not even his own. Well, Hamlet is the very image of this level of subjectivity."[19] The survival that *Hamlet* examines depends on securing, as in an archive, a Symbolic *or*der of paternal law whose structuring logic of repetition is inseparable from the death drive.

"Order is a kind of compulsion to repeat," remarks Freud in *Civilization and Its Discontents*, where he describes it as a practice of "regularization" that determines, once it has been established, "when, where and how a thing shall be done, so that in every similar circumstance one is spared hesitation and indecision."[20] With "regularization" as its theory and repetition as its practice, such *or*der *or*ganizes the world. Preempting "indecision" by making responses automatic, it displaces subjectivity with the mechanistic predictability of a world in which everything and everyone "must be *or* not be in a particular place." "Hesitation and indecision," however, loom large in Hamlet's world, inspired by a demand for action without the precedent of "similar circumstance": the restoration of *or*der as *or*dered by Hamlet's father's ghost, whose manifestation both symptomatizes and exacerbates its disturbance. This suggests that *or*der as such may be inseparable from what disturbs it, that the law of *or*der always contains, in both senses of the word, the specter of its own undoing, which it conjures to help it survive.

Hence, the spokesman for patriarchal *or*der in the text takes the form of what strays from its place; the dead king's ghost, in its errancy, exposes the error of clinging with confidence to categorical thought. Its presence, queer despite its investment in patriarchal law, leads all who encounter it "so horridly to shake [their] disposition / With thoughts beyond the reaches of [their] souls" (1.4.60–61) that they become, in Hamlet's phrase, "fools of nature" (1.4. 35), stripped of their faith in sense. To acknowledge and obey the ghost's *or*ders is to pass, in the eyes of the world, for mad, for one governed by what is not. When the ghost reappears to Hamlet as the latter berates his mother in her chambers, Gertrude warns him to cool the "distemper" that drives him to "bend [his] eye on vacancy." Where he sees the ghost of his father, the royal image of paternal law, she, as she puts it, sees "nothing at all; yet all that is I see" (3.4.123). Solidly embedded in the givenness of the world, Gertrude knows only the reality of the normative *or*der of being. For her son, however, the "nothing" of the ghost vitiates that *or*der; but it does so to restore the name of the father and the *or*der of survival in the wake of King Hamlet's murder and the incestuous remarriage of his queen. In each case, the survival of an *or*der entails the survival of what disturbs it: the specter of a Derridean "auto-immunitary process" and the pressure of the "not to be," the "nothing."

In his frequent returns to the topic of survival, which shapes his reflections on life and death ("I never stop analysing the phenomenon of 'survival.' . . . [I]t's really the only thing that interests me"), Derrida engages, time and again, the place of the specter in determining law, the death drive, and cultural transmission.[21] He declares, in the "Exordium" to his *Specters of Marx*, that one can never "teach *oneself* to live"; to live, he asserts, "is not learned from life, taught by life. Only from the other and by death. In any case from the other at the edge of life. At the internal border or the external border, it is a heterodidactics between life and death."[22] Here learning to live depends on something not proper to life itself: the intervention of life's "other," one of whose many names may be "death." But that nomination remains uncertain; Derrida immediately qualifies it, specifying that instruction in how to live comes "in any case from the other at the edge of life." What side of that edge does this other inhabit? Or is it situated "at" the edge by virtue of being situated *on* it? If so, then the otherness "at the edge of life," the otherness from which we learn to live, incises a cut in life's coherence while identifying life with that cut or division, with the opening onto the other that emerges at, and through, life's edge.

This "heterodidactics between life and death," this instruction in life never "taught by life" but only by its other, requires an encounter with the gap in life that continuously exerts its pressure through and across the edge that Derrida also describes as a "border," whether "the internal border or the external border." The "edge of life" thus constitutes a double-edged figure, as it were: an edge that delimits the space of life by bounding it, cutting it out and off from the other that it is not, but also the edge internal to life, the edge that may mark its furthest extreme but that remains, nonetheless, the edge *of* life, the edge that life in some sense "is," the edge at which, through the cut it inflicts, one also encounters life's other. Yet the appositive phrase by which Derrida turns that "edge" into a "border" evokes a desire for the b/ordering that establishes places and fixes relations. In rewriting "at the edge of life" as "at the internal border or the external border"—where the *or*, especially in the English translation, brings out the *or* in *border*—Derrida preserves the distinction between an inside and an outside that such a border exists to secure even as he seems to make that distinction a matter of indifference. Insofar as that border, in either case, denotes the place of life's other, it divides the orders of life and death while allowing communication between them, assuring that the pedagogical necessity by which death alone can teach us to live remains a "heterodidactics" that effectively keeps life and death distinct.

In this vein Derrida can assert that "what happens between . . . life and death . . . can only *maintain* itself with some ghost, can only *talk with or about* some ghost. So it would be necessary to learn spirits. Even and especially if this, the spectral, *is not*."[23] This might sound like the "queer spectrality" to which Freccero's work points the way, but Derrida's specters, in teaching us to live, and even to live "more justly," introduce us, without their being present as such, to what Derrida calls a "being-with" that "would also be . . . a politics of memory, of inheritance, and of generations."[24] Though "the spectral," as Derrida puts it, "*is not*," much like queerness as I've described it, such spectrality (unlike queerness) generates an *or*der of relation, a "being-with," that carries forward, in its "politics of memory, of inheritance, and of generations," the commandment of "*responsibility* . . . before the ghosts of those who are not yet born or who are already dead."[25] For what is one made responsible here if not the distribution of places that secures the *or*der of life "*in general*," turning all of us, as subjects, into archives through which to preserve that distribution within an *or*der shaped by the imperative of generation and "generations."[26]

This may explain why *Archive Fever* reveals even more than *Specters of Marx* what's at stake in the specter as figure of survival not only for Derrida's critical thought but also for the culture we inherit from *Hamlet*. At the outset of *Archive Fever*, Derrida associates archivization with what he refers to as "consignation," which he explains as "the act of assigning residence or entrusting so as to put into reserve" and as "*gathering together signs*" into "a single corpus . . . in which all the elements articulate the unity of an ideal configuration." But at the heart of any such archive he finds the "anarchivic" and "archiviolithic" death drive that destroys it.[27] A single stroke (the stroke of the signifier) generates the archive and undoes it, reducing life to a memorializing supplement at the expense of living memory and inducing, therefore, a breakdown of what is "spontaneous" and "alive":

> The death drive . . . not only incites forgetfulness, amnesia, the annihilation of memory, as *mnēmē* or *anamnēsis*, but also commands the radical effacement, in truth the eradication, of that which can never be reduced to *mnēmē* or *anamnēsis*, that is, the archive, consignation, the documentary or monumental apparatus as *hypomnēma*, mnemotechnical supplement or representative, auxiliary or memorandum. Because the archive, if this word or this figure can be stabilized so as to take on a signification, will never be either memory or anamnesis as spontaneous, alive and internal experience. On the contrary: the archive takes place at the place of the breakdown of the said memory.[28]

The archive, one might say, responds from the outset to the prospect of this "breakdown," this annihilation of living memory, by gathering together and holding in reserve the signs, already specters, of what no longer possesses life. But it does so at the risk of its own eradication by the death drive to which it attests—a drive induced, as Lacan observes, by the signifying system that generates loss and its corollary, survival, at once.

Hamlet, when he vows that his father's words "all alone shall live / Within the book . . . of [his] brain," denies the incompatibility of the archive with "anamnesis as spontaneous, alive and internal." Though acknowledging that the hypomnemic supplement, the externalized remainder essential to the archive as a site of consignation, can be forgotten or "wipe[d] away," he nonetheless proclaims his brain—and himself—the "book" in which his father's commandment, fully present, will live on *and* live after. By identifying himself as the memory of the father whose name he carries forward, the Hamlet who proclaims at Ophelia's grave, "This is I, / Hamlet the Dane" (5.1.241–42), announces himself as an archive, as a site of consignation, that keeps "alive" his father's word by ceding to it his vital force and making himself the instrument, the prosthesis, of its will.[29] Archive and anamnesis combine. Together they endorse a futurism whose complicity with aesthetic education, and with the *violence* of that education, not only shapes the text of *Hamlet* but also contributes to its privileged status in modern Western culture. No less invested than *Hamlet* in the violence of cultural and familial transmission ("a violence that cannot and must not be reduced, because otherwise there would be no more culture"), Derrida, though describing the archive as burying the "spontaneous" memory it annihilates, shares with Hamlet a messianic belief that though the archive invariably "takes place at the place of the breakdown of . . . memory," it can index, through its opening to the *a-venir* (as what is still "to arrive" or "to come"), the possibility of a future that is "not toward death but toward a *living-on* [sur-vie]."[30]

Like *Hamlet*, therefore, *Archive Fever* engages the binary of life or death, "to be, or not to be," while touching, like Shakespeare's play, on conversations with ghosts of the dead and with a father's labor to write his words in the book of his offspring's memory. Freud, whose Oedipalization of *Oedipus* occurred by way of *Hamlet*, plays two roles in *Archive Fever*: both the spectral father whose ghost is conjured and the son on whom the father aims to imprint himself with his words. Both aspects emerge from Derrida's discussion of Josef Hayim Yerushalmi's *Freud's Moses: Judaism Terminable and Interminable*.[31] Derrida pays careful attention to two incidents discussed by Yerushalmi: first, when Freud was given by his father, on the occasion of his thirty-fifth birthday, his childhood Bible rebound with "new skin" and bearing an inscription that declared it "a memorial and a reminder of love from your father"; and, second, when Freud, as the father of psychoanalysis and Anna Freud alike, is called from the grave by Yerushalmi himself so that he, Yerushalmi, as Derrida writes, can hear "the last word, the last will, the ultimate signature . . . of a dying father—and to be even more sure, of an already dead" one.[32] Yerushalmi, as Derrida observes, concludes his book with a question that he addresses to this spectral Freud. Referring to a statement by Anna Freud sent in response to Hebrew University's establishment of a chair in honor of her father, Yerushalmi demands of the ghost he has conjured, "Was she speaking in your name?" Derrida then rephrases Yerushalmi's question to ask if Freud's child, *as* his child, had "*always* spoken in the name of her father"?[33] Can the child, in other words, ever speak in a voice that would be its own?

Bound to the parent who gets under its "skin" and lives on in the "book" of its brain, the figural Child of futurism may carry the burden of survival, but the child caught up in that figure's grasp can never survive as itself. Like Hamlet, as Jonathan Goldberg notes, it voices another's text.[34] Conceived as the archive in which the Other, the one, returns to itself through a consignation that "posits and conserves the law," the Child instantiates the reach of that law, whose commandment to memory, as Derrida writes, "turns incontestably toward the future to come," enacting an affirmation he qualifies as the "self-affirmation of the Unique," of the law as singular, as one.[35]

Though the archive's *order* of memory always pledges itself to the future, there operates within that archive (as there does within that future) something at odds with openness to the unknown of the *a-venir*. Derrida evokes the archontic commandment to remember in the following terms:

> It orders to promise, but it orders repetition, and first of all self-repetition, self-confirmation in a *yes, yes*. If repetition is thus inscribed at the heart of the future to come, one must also import there, *in the same stroke*, the death drive, the violence of forgetting, *superrepression* (suppression and repression), the anarchive, in short, the possibility of putting to death the very thing, whatever its name, which *carries the law in its tradition*: the archon of the archive, the table, *what* carries the table and *who* carries the table, the subjectile, the substrate, and the subject of the law.[36]

The "yes" to which Derrida refers here acknowledges survival as the privilege of "the One"; it reads remembrance as the archive's conflation of repetition and futurity in an act of "self-confirmation" that makes the future, like the self, a mere copy of the law's self-sameness.[37] Recalling Hamlet's thrice-repeated response to his father's command, "Remember me"—"Ay" (1.5.96), "Yea" (1.5.98), and "Yes, yes, by heaven" (1.5.104)—the *"yes, yes"* cited by Derrida strategically enables, in the name of remembrance, a forgetting of ab-sens as the void inherent in whatever is affirmed. It functions as a negation—*in the guise of an affirmation*—of the objectless act of remembrance that the death drive's insistence performs.[38]

This last phrase must seem incongruous. What could the death drive remember when it incites, as Derrida puts it, "forgetfulness, amnesia, the annihilation of memory"?[39] Lacan gives an answer in Seminar VII while discussing *Beyond the Pleasure Principle*. Freud sees the death drive as an unconscious wish to return to a preorganic state not threatened by energic stimulation and so not requiring a reserve of energy to regulate the conscious and unconscious systems. But in Seminar VII, Lacan distinguishes "between the Nirvana or annihilation principle, on the one hand, and the death drive, on the other—the former concerns a relationship to a fundamental law which might be identified with that which energetics theorizes as the tendency to return to a state, if not of absolute rest, then at least of universal equilibrium." The death drive, by contrast, "can only be defined as a function of the signifying chain. . . . It requires something from beyond whence it may itself be grasped in a fundamental act of memorization, as a result of which everything may be recaptured."[40] Although the Symbolic corresponds to the order of history that "presents itself as something memorable and memorized," according to Lacan, the death drive corresponds to "that structural element which implies that, as soon as we have to deal with anything in the world appearing in the form of the signifying chain, there is somewhere—though certainly outside of the natural world—which is the beyond of that chain, the *ex nihilo* on which it is founded and is articulated as such."[41] The death drive, in other words, remembers the "beyond," the nothing that history and the reality induced by the signifier make us forget; it "remembers," insists on, and drives us *toward* the Thing absented from the Symbolic, the inarticulable loss that always accompanies and makes possible subjectification but that never has a being for the Symbolic subject to lose.

To that extent, as Lacan remarks, the death drive, in expressing a "will to destruction," expresses a "will for an Other-thing." Where Freud's account of the death drive "requires that what is involved be articulated as a destruction drive," Lacan, without scanting the extent of its destructiveness with regard to "the historical chain," maintains that "it is also a will to create from zero, a will to begin again."[42] Insofar as that new beginning, however, takes place through signification, it merely repeats the forgetting of the zero, the originary loss of the "Other-thing," that the drive alone remembers: the excluded "beyond" of the signifying chain, the "place in which doubt is cast on all that is the place of being."[43]

As the memory, then, of nothing, of the zero or void that evokes the "*ex nihilo* on which [the Symbolic] is founded and is articulated," the death drive looks like forgetfulness only insofar as it registers "what by its very nature remains concealed from the subject: that self-sacrifice, that pound of flesh which is mortgaged [*engagé*] in his relationship to the signifier."[44] Our metonymically proliferating objects of desire in the world of sens-absexe seek to fill out the place, to cloak the absence, of what "remains concealed": not the *object* of desire but rather its *cause*, the Thing as the locus of the jouissance that "cannot be subjectified as such."[45] To capture this "hidden element" inaccessible to subjectification, Lacan proposes a "mathematical metaphor" describing "human life . . . as a calculus in which zero [is] irrational."[46] This queer mathematical figure, at odds with the algebraic status of zero as rational (as well as even), speaks to Lacan's alignment of the subject, apprehended in its zero degree (in the "hidden element of living reference" always structurally inaccessible), with the permanent nonclosure of irrational numbers, whose decimal transcriptions neither come to an end nor resolve into regular patterns.

This figural irrationality of zero points to something in signification that escapes the closure of identity and the determination of being. We can interpret its unthinkability as the "queerness," the self-negation of being, whose structuring presence in every *or*der gets reduced to the status of nothing. Like the infamous square root of minus one, to which Lacan alludes in his reading of *Hamlet* (he discusses it more fully in "The Subversion of the Subject"), *irrational* denotes "what doesn't correspond to anything that is subject to our intuition, anything real—in the mathematical sense of the term—and yet, it must be conserved, along with its full function."[47] By signaling something "missing in the desired image" wherein a Symbolic subject recognizes itself, the irrational zero, like the square root of minus one, "comes to symbolize the place of jouissance," the place of what we sacrifice—before "we" exist to possess it—so as to "be" in the *or*der of language.[48] As whatever a given *or*der excludes from the frame of intelligibility, as whatever threatens the *or*der of being that such a frame constructs, queerness, too, names a jouissance incapable of positivization; it similarly refers to something radically "unthinkable" about the subject: its inextricability from the "Non-Being" that "makes Being itself languish."[49] Queerness thus figures what disintegrates all integrals from within even as its unthinkability permits the law's self-assertion as One.

In this context, consider one more passage from Lacan's metaphorical mathematics. Discussing the signifier of the Other's lack, the signifier of the structural incompleteness that keeps the Other from attaining the totality or stability of a rational number, Lacan, in "The Subversion of the Subject," denies the possibility of "conferring on [this] signifier . . . the meaning of mana or any such term." He goes on to explain, "Claude Lévi-Strauss, commenting on [Marcel] Mauss' work, no doubt wished to see in mana the effect of a zero symbol. But . . . what we are dealing with in our case is . . . the signifier of the lack of this zero symbol."[50] At stake is the absence of a symbol as such, or rather, the insistence of what the Symbolic order necessarily absents: the queerness that refuses the minimal coherence characteristic of an entity and so escapes positivization in any system of exchange. But the *or*der that forecloses that queerness cannot succeed in escaping it any more than producing a zero symbol avoids an encounter with the void. The constitution of the Symbolic archive enabled by the signifying system opens a space construed as beyond it, the "*ex nihilo* on which it is founded." It produces not only the archive but also the Derridean *mal d'archive*, the evil or malady of the death drive bound to the signifier's archivizing function. It thus produces a self-division, an auto-antagonism, implicating life in death and keeping being and not-being from forming a couple divided by the b/*or*der of *or*.

Slavoj Žižek foregrounds this inconsistency while glossing the counterintuitive vitality of the death drive for Lacan:

Death is the symbolic order itself, the structure which, as a parasite, colonizes the living entity. What defines death drive in Lacan is this double gap: not the simple opposition of life and death, but the split of life itself into "normal" life and horrifying "undead" life, and the split of the dead into "ordinary" dead and the "undead" machine. The basic opposition between Life and Death is thus supplemented by the parasitical symbolic machine (language as a dead entity which "behaves as if it possesses life of its own") and its counterpoint, the "living dead" (the monstrous life-substance which persists in the Real outside the Symbolic). This split which runs within the domains of Life and Death constitutes the space of the death drive.[51]

In this sense the pressure of the death drive betrays the excess *within* the Symbolic congruent with the division constitutive *of* the Symbolic: an excess consigned to the nothing that only appears as the Symbolic's beyond. Incapable of capture by a zero symbol, that nothing attests to the lack of a symbol capable of invoking its lack without resorting to the positivization that turns its zero into a one.

Returning to Derrida's account of how the archive's consignation procures "the One, as self-repetition" in a way that "can only repeat and recall [an] instituting violence," we can better understand how the archive's anticipation of "the future to come" commits it instead, as Derrida writes, to an act of "self-repetition, self-confirmation in a *yes, yes*."[52] Such a "yes" affirms, in the name of the future, an identity, precisely that of the One, that obliges the future to conform to the past, to affirm itself as survival within an economy of reserve. The archive, after all, like the specter, and so like the ghost of the dead King Hamlet, evinces that reserve whose survival produces the future *as its own*. However much it presents itself as open to the unknown, to the unpredictable otherness of whatever event may come, this future, like the "yes" by which archivization affirms it, performs a compulsory return to the One of the father and the law. Derrida dedicates *Archive Fever* not only to Yosef Hayim Yerushalmi, whose work he directly addresses, but also, as he writes, "to my sons—and even to the memory of my father, who was also called, as is life itself, Hayim."[53] Life, as prolepsis and memory, returns to the father here twice over: it returns both to Derrida's father and to Derrida *as* father, and so to his identification, like Hamlet's, with an archivizing function, with the survival of the name of the father, "Hayim," which, in Hebrew, signifies "life."

But "life," as a consequence, suffers what we might call a "dead-ication," its vitality conflated with a "memory" that comes back like *Hamlet's* ghost, which, as Derrida observes, is from the outset not just an apparition but also a "reapparition": "Here again what seems to be out front, the future, comes back in advance: from the past, from the back."[54] Whatever comes from the future must, precisely by coming *into being*, repeat the exclusion of the zero from the reality of what "is," leaving the death drive alone to preserve the memory of "nothing." Futurism in this sense emerges as the prolepsis of a (be)hindsight: the father's penetration from behind, from the back, of what he thereby conceives as the future in an act of self-affirmation by which the child, like Almodóvar's Ignacio or Shakespeare's Hamlet, finds itself screwed.[55]

What should we make in this context of Derrida's explicit affirmation of the future? He writes:

> The affirmation of the future *to come*: this is not a positive thesis. It is nothing other than the affirmation itself, the "yes," insofar as it is the condition of all promises or of all hope, of all awaiting, of all performativity, of all opening toward the future, whatever it may be, for science or for religion. I am prepared to subscribe without reserve to this reaffirmation made by Yerushalmi. With a speck of anxiety, in the back of my mind, a single speck of anxiety about a solitary point. . . . This unique point can be reduced, indeed, to the Unique, to the unity of the One and of the Unique.[56]

Rejecting here Yerushalmi's claim for the absolute and exemplary uniqueness of what Derrida describes as the "link between Jewishness, if not Judaism, and hope in the future," rejecting, that is, the identitarian claims of a *Jewish* responsibility to futurity, Derrida declares himself prepared, nonetheless, "to subscribe without reserve" to the "*yes, yes*" of the "reaffirmation" that bespeaks his "hope in the future."[57]

Such a hope, of course, remains fixed to the framework—historical, cultural, political—from which it springs, imprisoning the future it imagines (even if the *a-venir* must remain unknown) in an Imaginary form that mirrors that of the Symbolic subject who forms it. This future takes the form of form itself; as the condition of "all awaiting," it anticipates something coming into being by coming into form. Insofar as that hope, like Derrida's investment in "messianicity *without* messianism," identifies justice as the making of space for the arrival of the radically unknown, it presupposes the possibility of welcoming into the archive of living being the anarchivic death drive that undoes what (we think) we are.[58] If this future is to be something more than repetition of the same, then it must assume that nonbeing as such can somehow present itself to being, that the system of signification can incorporate its own beyond, and that Symbolic subjects can simultaneously be and exceed themselves, can know the zero *as* zero and not just as another "one."

This fantasmatic future, even when seen as impossible, reflects the rigor mortis of our Symbolic *or*der in which, whatever the father's name, the name of the father is "life." In *Apprendre à vivre enfin*, Derrida makes his position perfectly clear: "I don't want to give free rein to an interpretation according to which survival is on the side of death, of the past, rather than of life and the future. Everything I say . . . about survival as a complication of the life/death opposition proceeds, where I am concerned, from an unconditional affirmation of life. . . . The view I hold isn't mortifying, but, to the contrary, it's the affirmation of a living being who prefers living and, therefore, surviving to death."[59] Though he accepts its "complication," Derrida refuses to permit the division between life and death to vanish; unwilling to acknowledge (except by negation) that his "affirmation of life" might be "mortifying," he aligns himself "unconditional[ly]" with the survival of survival, preserving the "life/death opposition" that puts survival "on the side . . . of life." But such a survival, preserving the archival trace of the past into the future, enacts a resistance to the *a-venir*, to the evental aspect of the future as encounter with the Real. As an eruption of the zero, of the empty set internal to the *or*der of the world, could such an event take place *in the world to which it puts an end*? And could such an event take place *for us* when it revokes the signifying framework that alone sustains our being? As the other beyond the realm of what is, the event must bring what is to an end, inaugurating (the) *nothing* that would arrive ex nihilo to abrogate the *or*der of survival.

The Derrida who can qualify as "unconditional" his "affirmation of life" and accede to Yerushalmi's "reaffirmation" of the future "without reserve" is the Derrida who fully understands that "to ask me to renounce what has formed me, what I have loved so much, what has been my law, is to ask me to die." It is the Derrida who can go on to add, "In that fidelity there is a sort of instinct of conservation."[60] That instinct evinces the mortification that Derrida wants to deny: the mortification by which the Symbolic "colonizes the living entity," in Žižek's phrase, precisely to *make* it an entity, a "One" whose preservation in the *or*der of life coincides with our notion of "the good." When push comes to shove, that good, however, even for someone like Derrida, committed to a "complication of the life/death opposition," compels the choice of life over death, of a conservative rhetoric of futurism over the radical event of the Real. We see that choice in Derrida's account of the terror he calls "bin Ladenism":

What appears to me unacceptable . . . is not only the cruelty, the disregard for human life, the disrespect for law, for women, the use of what is worst in technocapitalist modernity for the purpose of religious fanaticism. No, it is, above all, the fact that such actions and such discourse *open onto no future and, in my view, have no future.* If we are to put any faith in the perfectibility of public space and of the world juridico-political scene, of the "world" itself, then there is, it seems to me, *nothing good* to be hoped for from that quarter.[61]

W. J. T. Mitchell notes that "Derrida's assertion that bin Ladenism has no future is . . . not just empirically wrong, but the projection of a nihilism, a hollowness onto the figure of the enemy," and, even more important, he recognizes that it undermines Derrida's investment in the practice of deconstruction as a "mythic violence . . . that may lead to a new order of reading or legality and political order to come."[62] The "good" for which Derrida speaks requires our "faith in the perfectibility of public space and of the world juridico-political scene." The future he anticipates is an evolutionary one, which is also an evolution *toward* "the One," toward an "absolute law" that he associates with "universal sovereignty" and that utopically moves toward the perfection of justice, political order, and the "world" we know.[63] Lacan—like "bin Ladenism" as Derrida evokes it, or like queerness as I'm discussing it here, or like Blackness as Wilderson engages it in *"We're Trying to Destroy the World,"* or like deconstruction as Mitchell construes it—rejects such an evolutionary model in favor of the death drive as creation ex nihilo. Like them, Lacan refuses the conservative tendency that forestalls the future by *imagining* it, which is to say, by imagining it in the form of what can be formed, of what the imagination can formulate.

Perhaps in resistance to this conservative instinct that he recognizes in himself, Derrida recurs throughout *Archive Fever* to a qualification of the future: "What is at issue here," he writes, "is nothing less than the *future,* if there is such a thing."[64] How do we reconcile this uncertainty with Derrida's subsequent self-representation as "prepared to subscribe without reserve" to "the affirmation of the future *to come*"? The answer may lie in the contradictory nature of this affirmation "without reserve." "*Yes, yes,*" the quintessential affirmation, expresses, by virtue of its status for Derrida as "self-repetition, self-confirmation," the archivizing gesture par excellence, the performance of the consignation by which the One is procured and perpetuated. But the imperative of archivization, like the affirmation that conforms to its law, both rests on and necessitates an economy of reserve, an economy of conservation that casts the future as repetition, which is to say, as "self-confirmation." As early as "Différance," however, Derrida identified the complications such an economy must confront:

> How are we to think *simultaneously*, on the one hand, *différance* as the economic detour which, in the element of the same, always aims at coming back to the pleasure or the presence that have been deferred by (conscious or unconscious) calculation, and, on the other hand, *différance* as the relation to an impossible presence, as expenditure without reserve, as the irreparable loss of presence, the irreversible usage of energy, that is, as the death instinct, and as the entirely other relationship that apparently interrupts every economy? It is evident—and this is the evident itself—that the economical and the noneconomical, the same and the entirely other, etc., cannot be thought *together*.[65]

If affirmation is necessarily affirmation of a "reserve," of what is always confirmed in its recognized place, then affirming the future "without reserve" (and, therefore, without the repetition "inscribed at the heart of the future to come") must, paradoxically, deny that future by interrupting its economy with the noneconomy that expends while preserving nothing.

But what if the impossibility of thinking the economical and the noneconomical "*together*" were the ruse that enabled economy, the archive, and futurity to survive, which is also to say, that enabled the survival of survival *as* economy: the economy of sense that prevails in the Symbolic through the subtraction of ab-sens? In that case the structuring unthinkability to which Derrida adverts us ("the economical and the noneconomical . . . cannot be thought *together*") would coincide with a similar unthinkability that he signaled two years earlier in "Structure, Sign, and Play in the Discourse of the Human Sciences": "It could perhaps be said that the whole of philosophical conceptualization, which is systematic with the nature/culture opposition, is designed to leave in the domain of the unthinkable the very thing that makes this conceptualization possible: the origin of the prohibition of incest."[66] Founded on the binarism central to Aristotle's law of noncontradiction, Western reason reads nature's relation to culture in terms of the either-or logic that differentiates presence from absence, being from nonbeing, and life from death; it necessitates, therefore, the prohibition of incest (whose origin it makes unthinkable) because incest confounds the categorical distinction, the primal differentiation of sameness and difference, on which that law depends. By dissolving the b/order that articulates sense, incest occupies the impossible place of "that which ab-sens designates as sex."[67] Though the specter may perform a transgression at and across "the edge of life," it fortifies the border it crosses precisely by appearing *out of place* and thus reinforcing, through its confirmation of place (where everything "must be *or* not be"), the prohibition on incest, the incitement to philosophy, and the economy of reserve. Like the archive and the Derridean affirmation (*"yes, yes"*), like the prohibition on incest and the impossibility of thinking "the economical and the noneconomical" together, such a specter, however "irrational" it seems, reaffirms the Symbolic *or*der of meaning as determined by sens-absexe, which calls forth the human as the subject of sense.

But *Hamlet* itself is a question posed to that concept of the human whose normative shape it nonetheless imposes on us all. Let us call it, then, a "questionable shape" (1.4.24), this human that emerges from the "inwardness" of Hamlet's habitual questions, his restless returns to the site of nonknowledge where obsession, even madness, serves as the template for human consciousness and the human becomes the ghost of a query—"to be, or not to be"—between whose terms it finds itself poised and by which, from the start, it is poisoned. The venom poured in its ears is *or*, which bestows on Hamlet's most famous *or*ation a ration of H*or*atian rationality that aims, by means of scholastic dispute, to establish some solid ground. But in Hamlet's world, as in Elsinore, there's something else in *or*: a fetishization of difference to which Hamlet himself is heir ("I am but mad north-north-west. When the wind is southerly, I know a hawk from a handsaw"; 2.2.361–362), a veritable frenzy of reasoning driven by the prince's persistence in puns, his "play of signifiers in the dimension of meaning" that lends "his speech an almost maniacal quality," to quote Lacan.[68] As if making the wind blow north-northwest, his punning voids the certitude, the stability of difference, by which to distinguish a hawk from a handsaw. Hamlet himself will concede as much when he cries, in response to the gravedigger's literality of interpretation, which fixates on the signifier as disturbingly as Hamlet's own speech, "How absolute the knave is! We must speak by the card, or equivocation will undo us" (5.1.127).

The *or* of categ*or*ical thinking would f*or*estall the threat of equivocation by installing, instead, the logic that distinguishes "Hyperion" from a "satyr" (1.2.140), thus preserving the *or*der of nature from threats of monstrosity and confusion, from "uncle-father and aunt-mother" (2.2.358), from incestuous ecstasy and c*or*ruption, from the lust that occasions everything "carnal, bloody, and unnatural" (5.2.325). To affirm this *or*der of *or* that keeps what is from coming undone, the dead king's spirit walks by night, enlisting his son as a soldier pledged to defend the sexual n*or*m. "Let not the royal bed of Denmark be / A couch for luxury and damnèd incest" (1.5.82–83), he commands.

And Hamlet understands full well, like any moral zealot, that his charge is not to treat the symptom but to eradicate the disease: "The time is out of joint—O cursèd spite, / That ever I was born to set it right" (1.5.189–90). "Set it right," of course, means "set it straight," since *out of joint*, as the *Oxford English Dictionary* notes with reference to Hamlet's phrase, bespeaks a state "disordered, perverted, out of order," like the "unweeded garden / That grows to seed" (1.2.135–36) in an earlier soliloquy, or like Hamlet himself when Ophelia, similarly nodding to the realm of horticulture after Hamlet calls her a whore, paints him as the "feature and form of blown youth, / Blasted now with ecstasy" (3.1.158–59).[69] Derived from the Greek for "to put out of place," this "ecstasy," like Hamlet's madness when the wind blows "north-north-west," may seem to disturb the *order* of places, but it speaks to his will to rest*ore* that *order* while evincing its internal disturbance.

Made by paternal command a sort of disease to assail the diseased—"like the hectic in my blood he rages" (4.3.67), Claudius muses to himself— Hamlet may be the "mould of form" (3.1.152) for the modern human subject, but only insofar as it, like him, is a monster of n*or*mativity, incapable, for all the self-consciousness we, as Hamlet's scions, grant him, of seeing how much he gets off on the luxury of his antiluxurious rants. Repelled not just by "country matters" (3.2.105) but, more profoundly, by matter as such, he looks to master matter by riding a raging t*orr*ent of words in which his passion rises to fever pitch to castigate passion's slaves. Laced with a rancid misogyny, Hamlet's outbursts vilify sex with a delirious prurience of disgust. He links the unkemptness of "grow[ing] to seed," which nods to the cessation of flowering that attends the development of the seed itself, to the condition of being possessed, taken over, by things that are "rank and gross" (1.2.136). And that representation seems anodyne when compared with his acid precision in portraying the "compulsive ardour" (3.4.76) of his mother, reviling her willingness "to live / In the rank sweat of an enseamèd bed, / Stewed in corruption, honeying and making love / Over the nasty sty" (3.4.81–84).[70]

Disdaining the putrid carrion that is all he sees in flesh, Hamlet dismisses life and sex as equally excremental. "We fat ourselves for maggots" (4.3.23), he notes and traces the course of Alexander's dust to find "it stopping a bunghole" (5.1.189). He may pray for sublimation ("O that this too too solid flesh might melt, / Thaw, and resolve itself into a dew!"; 1.2.129–30) and imagine himself as standing apart from any earthly appetite ("I eat the air," he jests; 3.2.85), but his mind is drawn to dirt and stench with what we must call a vengeance.[71] His revulsion in the face of embodiment, redoubled at the very thought of sex, leads him beyond the paternal charge to root out "damnèd incest," to the point of decrying conception and even demanding "no more marriages" (3.1.146–47). Fanning the flames of Hamlet's loathing for all that "flesh is heir to" (3.1.65), the ghost, to which Hamlet is heir as well, leaves him torn between the need to put time right by restoring sexual norms and the extravagance, beyond all normative bounds, of his assault on sexual institutions. To prove his devotion as his father's child, he would have no children be fathered; defending too well the institution of marriage, he would have no marriage at all.

Stricken by this excess of filial passion, Hamlet is "too much i'th' sun" (1.2.67) beyond what his pun may intend; he is too much, that is, his father's son for his brief against breeding not to breed, as he tells us the sun does, maggots—the maggots, I mean, that taint his mind as it feasts on decay and corruption, He is, therefore, as out of joint as the time, as perverse as his father's restless ghost, that thing that violates nature's bounds to condemn violations of boundaries, that refutes by its presence the order of or it returns from the grave to defend, and that mocks the very distinction pronounced in "to be, or not to be." The inwardness, construed as psychic depth, for which Hamlet provides the model responds, therefore, to the impossible task he confronts as his father's child: to live a sort of afterlife as ambassador of the dead without, in the process, becoming a mere ambassador of death; to carry his father's words in the "book and volume of [his] brain" but to do so without "taint[ing]" his "mind" (1.5.92).

Hamlet will learn that success in the one means failure in the other. In accepting the duty to set time right, he keeps it out of joint, becoming the very prototype of the modern subject as Child. Submitting himself to futurism's generational projections, he keeps alive a ghostly past and produces thereby the emergent regime of heterotemporal repetition. If the Child itself puts time out of joint, can Hamlet hope to put it right without putting an end to the Child? "Why would'st thou be a breeder of sinners?" (3.1.122–23), he demands of an uncomprehending Ophelia, disdaining the survival of human life and those whose passions breed it. With such venom aimed at Ophelia and Gertrude, women whose concupiscence he blames for breeding sins and sinners alike, Hamlet takes aim at his father too, who breeds him in sin a second time by commanding him to revenge. Hamlet, the subject in the form of the Child, knows that breeders of life prevent it too, quite literally by "coming before" it. "Remember me" is the fatal text the parent inscribes on the Child, thus making the Child a memorial object, a prosopopoeia of the dead, a living tombstone to archive the past. Recalling the conflation of father and author in the book of Hamlet's brain, we can glimpse the structural paradox to which this dooms the Child in Hamlet's remarks on the vogue of theatrical companies consisting of children: "Their writers do them wrong to make them exclaim against their own succession" (2.2.335–36). Born to shoulder the burden of debt owed by and to the dead, required to assume his father's cause along with his father's name, Hamlet, like the modern Child whose reign he effectively anticipates, knows neither success nor succession, certainly none that he, too much the son, could properly claim as his "own." We might take his words to Polonius as pregnant with meaning regarding his father: "Yourself, sir, should be old as I am—if, like a crab, you could go backward" (2.2.202). His father does, in a sense, go backward by making his son the ghost of his ghost, charged with the task of setting time right by going against time's tide. In this way *Hamlet* enacts a transition between two modes of subjectivity: the first, now dead as the play begins, the heroically unfathered subjectivity of King Hamlet and his enemy, Fortinbras; and the second, that of the child *or*dained to perpetuate that model but barred from doing so, ironically, by its very subservience to the command. No wonder the question of Hamlet's age excites such fascination: called on to act as his father's son, he can only perform as the Child.

Early in the play, when the specter silently beckons him to follow, Hamlet, restrained by Marcellus and Horatio, escapes their grasp and warns them, "By heav'n, I'll make a ghost of him that lets me!" (1.4.62). Playing on the double sense of *let*—to permit or allow, on the one hand, and to hinder or prevent, on the other—this threat is efficacious: his attendants free Hamlet to follow his father, to pursue the specter who already is "[the] ghost of him that lets me": the ghost of the man who gave Hamlet life and who claims the right to preempt it; the ghost who confirms, in more ways than one, that time is out of joint; the ghost whose return dooms Hamlet to be and not be Hamlet at once. But perhaps that's what being "Hamlet" means in this play of perpetual punning: "[I] am let." It is also, of course, what n*or*mativity means in the world we inherit from Hamlet: to be let, prevented, or constrained by the law that lets those who obey it "be" while inciting a passion to constrain those others who let themselves go too far. "Let not the royal bed of Denmark be / A couch for luxury and damnèd incest," the ghost enjoins his son. But Hamlet, being let by that very "let not," is left in the knot of his name—a name that the prince, though he leaves the world childless, succeeds, nonetheless, in leaving behind in the "book and volume" of *our* brains, wherein it *lives* behind, as well.

When Horatio, ever loyal, proposes to die at his dying friends' side, Hamlet, assuming the place of the ghost ("I am dead," he twice exclaims), intervenes to prevent or to "let" him and imposes the obligation to memory imposed by the ghost on Hamlet himself. Though the injunction to remember costs Hamlet his life, in passing it on to Horatio he attempts to arrange for his survival by appropriating his companion's life as his father appropriated his and making Horatio, in a different fashion, carry on his name: "O God, Horatio, what a wounded name, / Things standing thus unknown, shall live behind me! / If thou didst ever hold me in thy heart, / Absent thee from felicity awhile, / And in this harsh world draw thy breath in pain / To tell my story" (5.2.286–91).[72] Having let the king's blood in the name of the specter of whom he is now the archive, Hamlet can't let the lack of a namesake leave a bloody wound on his name. Horatio, therefore, must "live behind," a phrase that perfectly encapsulates the temporal order of survival in which, paradoxically, what "live[s] behind" is the guarantee of the future. To recall the words of Derrida: "Here again what seems to be out front, the future, comes back in advance: from the past, from the back."

That may explain a peculiarity in Derrida's *Archive Fever*. The title phrase first appears in his text at a moment of self-anticipation: "The death drive is not a principle. It even threatens every principality, every archontic primacy, every archival desire. It is what we will call, later on, *le mal d'archive*."[73] That "later on" arrives shortly afterward, when Derrida cites the phrase again with reference to his earlier essay "Freud and the Scene of Writing." But something interesting happens now: "The model of this singular 'mystic pad' also incorporates what may seem, in the form of the destruction drive, to contradict even the conservation drive, what we could call here the archive drive. It is what we called earlier, and in view of this internal contradiction, *le mal d'archive*."[74] Time's out-of-jointedness makes itself felt in this impossible approach to the "destruction drive" as incorporated into the archive; though Derrida invokes unproblematically what he "could call *here* the archive drive" (emphasis mine), when it comes to the always imminent threat to the survival of that archive, things get more complex. While Derrida first claimed he would only "later" call the death drive *le mal d'archive*, he now claims to have called it that "earlier." This nomination may have happened already or may happen in the future, but the death drive cannot be named first in the present, as something here and now, as something that "is" in the register of being. Originating in repetition or anticipation, the naming of the death drive in Derrida's text is bound to the past and the future, or to the future as what comes back from the past. The archive's "internal contradiction," which makes it different from itself, consists in its necessary archivization of the *mal d'archive* that destroys it; but if the logic of the archive compels it to keep the death drive in reserve, the death drive itself reserves nothing—or reserves, in its gesture of "wip[ing] away," of creating anew ex nihilo, the nothing of the zero *as* zero, as the void that negates what is.

"Remember me," the specter's archivizing imperative, keeps company with the anarchivic impulse prompting Hamlet to "wipe away" all previous records and impressions ("all pressures past") the better to assure that the specter's words "alone shall live" in his brain. The specter, that is, while establishing an economy of reserve, also occasions the death drive's interruption of economy. It is precisely to deny that drive, however, that the specter as such *appears*, reversing the death drive's voiding of the object and its insistence on the zero, on the nothing, the ab-sens, that *never* appears as such. The specter emphatically presents itself *in the form* of an object or a thing: "What, has this thing appeared again tonight?" asks Horatio in the opening scene (1.1.26). That object form is the materialization, the substrate of the "commandment" that "alone" must "live" in the "book" that Hamlet becomes. Lacan observes that the "moral law . . . is incarnated in a certain number of commandments. I mean the ten commandments," and he then proceeds to argue that those commandments establish "the principle of the relation to the symbolic, . . . that is to say, to speech."[75] Each commandment, as Lacan interprets it, performs a differentiation, which, like the prohibition of work on the Sabbath, "introduces into human life the sign of a gap, a beyond."[76] Naming this "beyond" of the Symbolic *das Ding* (the Thing), or the "non–object form of primal loss," as I called it in the previous chapter, Lacan proceeds to explain it as "the very correlative of the law of speech in its most primitive point of origin, . . . in the sense that this *Ding* was there from the beginning, that it was the first thing that separated itself from everything the subject began to name and articulate."[77]

Das Ding emerges in tandem with the Symbolic as what the Symbolic can never accommodate; it evades conceptualization because "at the level of the *Vorstellungen*, the Thing is not nothing, but literally is not. It is characterized by its absence, its strangeness."[78] This strangeness, this Socratic *atopia*, that makes the Thing "*the Thing which is not*" attests to the queerness of ab-sens in its inaccessibility to ideation or thought. Lacan evokes it as what always slips the net of understanding, as the beyond-of-the-signified that separates itself from the order of signification. Not a concept, like the positivizations of nothing that make zero into a one, the Thing, as nothing, voids every concept, annihilating the Symbolic distribution of places constitutive of what "is." The law as commandment, by contrast, secures the Symbolic as the *place* of commandment, as the topology unfolded by sens-absexe wherein "the word is determinative." It does so, Lacan writes, because "the commandment . . . preserves the distance from the Thing as founded by speech," a distance across which we chase the Thing without any risk of catching it.[79]

Materializing the survival that its words command (by insisting on the survival of its commandment in the archive or "table of [Hamlet's] memory"), the specter takes the form of an object that usurps the (non)place of the Thing, functioning like the boys whose images fill Almodóvar's iris shot, or like the photo of Ignacio englobed by the bright red circle on the poster for the film. The specter inspires in those who perceive it "thoughts beyond the reaches of [their] souls" (1.4.61) by appearing to make visible the beyond of the Symbolic within the Symbolic itself. But *appearing* here has a double sense: the ghost appears, takes visible form, as if making present that beyond, but its capacity to do so is only a seeming, an illusory appearance. Defined by its "absence" in the order of being, the Thing, the beyond, has no object form, and every attempt to impose one on it performs its sublimation. As I mentioned in the previous chapter, *The Ethics of Psychoanalysis* proposes a "general formula" of sublimation: "It raises an object—and I don't mind the suggestion of a play on words in the term I use—to the dignity of the Thing."[80] Lacan's equivocation here draws a link (one literally more *pronounced* in the interplay of French and German) between dignity (*dignité*) and the properties of *das Ding*. In opposition to what he called earlier the "indignity" of the terms with which the Symbolic's *Wortvorstellungen* (word presentations) enable the subject to speak, sublimation clothes an object in the "dignity," the authenticity or immediacy, of the Thing unmediated by words. It does so by bestowing on that object, which comports with normative social ideals, the transgressive allure associated with the thought of the Symbolic's beyond.

Much like the specter, such an object will appear, in Slavoj Žižek's words, not only as "empirical, material stuff" but also as "*sublime* material," as "that other 'indestructible and immutable' body" that "endures all torments and survives."[81] Yet as Žižek also goes on to note, "this postulated existence of the sublime body depends on the symbolic order: the indestructible 'body-within the body' exempted from the effects of wear and tear is always sustained by the guarantee of some symbolic authority."[82] Far from shattering the Symbolic or permitting its "liberating disruption" (a phrase I borrow from Simon Ryle), the sublime object succeeds in shoring it up, returning as the future already contained in the Symbolic's *Wortvorstellungen*, its archive of linguistic possibilities, and promising survival by positivizing ab-sens as sens-absexe, as the topological *order* of meaning.[83]

For Derrida, of course, who famously declared, "Il n'y a pas de hors texte" (There is no outside of the text), the text, like the grammatological order, includes all its possible interpretations and all its possible disruptions, inviting, in the words of Rodolphe Gasché, "productive readings, readings that not only weave new interpretative threads into it but compose so many rewritings of it."[84] It constitutes an archive like Noah's ark, bearing every potentiality and encompassing all that is yet to come. From Lacan's perspective, however, there is always something "outside" the Symbolic, pressuring it from beyond the order of sense. We aim to relieve that pressure by naming it, ensnaring it in words intended to make it signify despite itself, reclaiming *das Ding* for the order of meaning from which "it was the first thing that separated itself" when "the subject began to name and articulate."[85] Small wonder, then, that those names include the "incest" against which Hamlet rails, the "bin Ladenism" Derrida decries, and rubrics like "woman," "Black," or "queer" and all their innumerable companions, each with its distinct historical weight in the reality of human lives, but each effectively sublimating the Real *by affirming that collective reality*.[86] Without denying those historical differences, without scanting their toll on the persons who confront them or suggesting that any subject could, as subject, escape their reality, we can say, nonetheless, that such sublimations strip the Thing of "its absence, its strangeness," and, in consequence, of its queerness.

Bad education, by contrast, acknowledges the impossibility of realizing queerness (as opposed to figurally embodying it), and it engages the question Saidiya Hartman poses with trenchant precision after identifying those enslaved as occupying "the position of the unthought": "What does it mean to try to bring that position into view without making it a locus of positive value, or without trying to fill in the void?"[87] This framing cuts to the heart of the problem by exposing our persistent belief that even the unthought must have a "position" and that our relation to whatever the unthought "is," to whatever refuses the "positive value" acquired through sublimation, must still conduce to "meaning." If Hartman, for all the brilliance with which she analyzes the problem, finds herself, nonetheless, bound to its terms, that is only because those terms allow neither her nor us any choice. They write themselves on the book of our brain so we think we can think the "unthought" as merely historically contingent, the *not yet* thought, rather than as what remains—like the nothing, the zero, the void—unthinkable. With the specter's commandment "Remember me," we forget the forgetting it induces: not only of the prior records it thereby prompts us to "wipe away" but also of the Thing no record or commandment could possibly contain, the Thing not accessible through any commandment or legible in any book—not even the one called *Hamlet*.

But as modern literature's specimen text, *Hamlet* is required reading, in part, for promoting reading's capacity to assign a place to everything, including the queerness of the "wondrous strange" (1.5.166), in a Symbolic whose hospitality can "as a stranger give it welcome" (1.5.167). Through its profligate wordplay and its speculations on the meaningfulness of words, it enthralls us with the Symbolic's *or*der that everything "be or not be in a particular place": the *or*der of differential articulation, of *or*, whose logic sublimates, by narrativizing, the incest it makes unthinkable. Enshrining with its mandate to memory the pedagogical principle par excellence (the transmission of wisdom or *techné* in the service of survival), *Hamlet*, by its ceaseless performance of and incitement to interpretation, stokes the fantasy of mastery implicit in reading's anticipation of meaning—a mastery, of the text and oneself alike, inseparable from aesthetic education. What could it mean to forgo the meaningfulness of pedagogical sublimation, to take seriously teaching's status as an impossible profession and the teacher's relation to the student as promoting—rather than cultural survival, the commandment to remember, or archival consignment—a radical queerness, a Socratic *cor*ruption, whose assault on meaning, understanding, and value would take from them more than it gives and leave them not with Hamlet's name, but only with "O, O, O, O"?

"What is someone who has been psychoanalyzed?" asks Jean Allouch, a French psychoanalyst, in his reading of *Archive Fever*. And he answers without hesitation: "He is . . . someone who no longer has a future."[88] We might say, therefore, that he is someone who faces the empty page of "freedom"— freedom, first and foremost, from the illusion of "being" himself—by confronting the drive to create ex nihilo, by renouncing the guarantee of meaning, and by refusing the endless returns of the father as the archive of what is to come. *Hamlet* has much to teach about investing in survival through a commandment's transmission (though the play, while exposing that investment's cost, redoubles it by transmitting that teaching), and it may, in a given system of values, teach us to be better readers, better students—perhaps better people too, depending on how one views "the good." But what *Hamlet* does not and cannot teach, and what we can never know, is how to escape the framework of meaning that its teaching reinforces; how to decline the archival commandment that sublimates the nothing it also preserves; how to allow for *not* saying "yes" to the father's imperative of life; how to let the future be by being what lets the future.[89] We search in vain for a teaching that could make the nothing that undoes what "is" appear "without trying to fill in the void," without assigning it a "position" in which its unthinkability would "mean." To succeed in such a teaching would be, as Wilderson argues, "to destroy the world," and to do so, as it were, for Real. But that's what a bad education, an education in queerness or Blackness, must do: endeavor, against all hope, to teach us nothing.

Funny/Peculiar/Queer:

Michael Haneke's Aesthetic Education

At the beginning of "The Resistance to Theory," Paul de Man notes his essay's unexpected engagement with "the question of teaching": "This essay was not originally intended to address the question of teaching directly, although it was supposed to have a didactic and an educational function—which it failed to achieve."[1] In a brief sketch of the essay's history, he informs us that he wrote the original version as an entry on "literary theory" that he had been invited to produce for "a collective volume entitled *Introduction to Scholarship in Modern Languages and Literatures*" (3). The essays in the collection, to be published under the auspices of the Modern Language Association, were meant to survey relevant publications in the field, to define important areas of academic dispute, and "to lay out a critical and programmatic projection of the solutions which can be expected in the foreseeable future" (3). The essay de Man submitted, however, was rejected for not meeting this mandate. De Man acknowledges that he "found it difficult to live up, in minimal good faith, to the requirements of the program and could only try to explain, as concisely as possible, why the main theoretical interest of literary theory consists in the impossibility of its definition" (3). This failure to fulfill the "educational function" with which he had been charged leaves its trace in the published version's turn to what the original did not address: "the relationship between the scholarship . . . , the theory, and the *teaching* of literature" (3–4, emphasis mine). The "impossibility of [theory's] own definition" prompts de Man to ask if theory could ever be compatible with teaching or if, instead, it necessarily disrupts the "educational function" and its "pedagogical objectives" (3), challenging everything "teachable, generalizable, and highly responsive to systematization" (19) by means of theory's self-resistance, its status as "theory and not theory" (19) at once.

This non-self-identity, like Hamlet's inability to be or not to be the referent of his name, or like the one's inability, according to Euclid, to be or not to be a number, characterizes both literature and theory for de Man and disorients pedagogical institutions that rest on the systematization of knowledge.[2] No Lacanian himself, and not prone to engage psychoanalysis or its vocabulary, de Man, as we saw in chapter 1, by focusing on the zero as suturing the fracture in the "homogeneity of the universe," though only by introducing an element "heterogeneous with regard to the system and nowhere . . . a part of it," recognizes, like Jacques Lacan, that language generates—and generates *systematically*—the beyond of its systematization.[3] Theory makes evident a rupture in teaching's framework of intelligibility that allegory and catachresis, like the zero, plaster over. The former affords us a "pseudoknowledge" that "pretends to order sequentially . . . what is actually the destruction of all sequence," while the latter posits and positivizes the nothingness of the zero ("the name is the trope of the zero"), always "nameless, 'innommable'" in itself, through an act that "usurp[s], by imposition . . . the authority of cognition."[4]

What in each of these cases seems to reinforce the coherence of the order of meaning turns out, as read through the lens of theory, to fracture the system of knowledge production it supposedly secures. In the middle of "The Resistance to Theory," therefore, de Man reframes this titular resistance, redescribing it as "a resistance to reading" (15) and specifying it as a resistance to *rhetorical* readings attentive to the "literariness" that "disrupts the inner balance" (14) of the trivium, the classical model of education, in much the same way that the zero, which secures the "homogeneity of the universe" for Pascal, simultaneously *disrupts* the homogeneity "of the [mathematical] system" insofar as it is "absolutely heterogeneous to the order of number."[5] This paves the way for de Man to characterize reading's negativity as what "prevents all entities, including linguistic entities, from coming into discourse as such" (19). Theory thus becomes an impediment to the generation of knowledge, including the knowledge of theory that literary studies purports to convey. What teaching could allow for the systematic transmission of such a system-destroying practice, one whose aneconomy keeps "all entities . . . from coming into discourse"? Faced with what de Man calls "this undoing of theory, this disturbance of the stable cognitive field that extends from grammar to logic to the general science of man and of the phenomenal world" (17)—faced, that is, with the "undoing" that theory occasions and suffers at once (the undoing of what is "teachable, generalizable, and highly responsive to systematization")—how could theory lend itself to scholarship's "pedagogical objectives"?

From the outset, de Man approaches these questions by rejecting the notion of teaching as "primarily an intersubjective relationship between people," defining it, instead, as "a cognitive process in which self and other are only tangentially and contiguously involved" (4). Viewing teaching as "scholarly, not personal," he scorns the frequent attempts to model it, as he writes in an acid phrase, on "show business or guidance counseling" (4). With specific regard to *literary* scholarship, which should, "in principle,... be eminently teachable," de Man suggests that it ought to involve two different but "complementary" components: "historical and philological facts as the preparatory condition for understanding" and the "methods of reading or interpretation" that build on those facts (4). Adopting a tone of confidence in the future of literary studies, de Man asserts that these "methods" can "hope to evolve by rational means, despite internal crises, controversies and polemics" (4). But when he subsequently characterizes theory as "a controlled reflection on the formation of method," which makes it, at least in this "rational" form, "entirely compatible with teaching" (and which accounts for the fact that "important theoreticians" can be "prominent scholars" as well), he immediately pauses to acknowledge that the compatibility of theory with teaching vanishes once "a tension develops between methods of understanding and the knowledge... those methods allow one to reach" (4). To the extent that "a discrepancy between truth and method" constitutes, for de Man, "an inherent focus of the discourse about literature," it follows that neither "the notion of 'literature as such'" nor the "distinction between history and interpretation" can simply "be taken for granted" (4). As theory's "controlled reflection on the formation of method" parts ways with knowledge, "controlled reflection" leads only to reflections on reflection's escape from control. What begins (in apparent innocence) as an inquiry into methods of literary reading now confronts a self-reflexive abyss that troubles such foundational assumptions as "historical and philological facts." Nothing, it seems, can hold these reflections on the "formation of method" in check since such "control" would be determined by the "method" on whose formation theory reflects. By demonstrating that the knowledge at which method arrives may not be sustained by the methodological model producing it in the first place, de Man dismisses the epistemological "control" that makes theory and teaching compatible.

In this context, where "it... is not *a priori* certain that literature is a reliable source of information about anything but its own language" (11), literary studies can no longer claim institutional justification on the basis of promoting humanistic values (among which knowledge is foremost) or of developing an intimate bond between ethics and the study of aesthetics. To the contrary: insofar as theory reveals "the impossibility of its [own] definition" and then spreads this definitional uncertainty to the objects and methods of literary scholarship, it bespeaks a "negative moment," to borrow a phrase de Man uses elsewhere, that the dominant aesthetic ideology compels both scholars and institutions to disavow.[6] This accounts for the persistent animus against theory "in the name of ethical and aesthetic values" as well as for "the recuperative attempts of theoreticians to reassert their own subservience to these values" (4). De Man highlights the normativity of these values by stressing the allegiance they routinely command from theorists and opponents of theory alike. But the "recuperative attempts" of theoreticians to endorse these "ethical and aesthetic values" inadvertently reveal those values themselves as modes of recuperation, as attempts to assert the value of value over and against the "negative moment" when value succumbs to critique without providing the ground for making critique a value in itself. Never will de Man more clearly indict the reign of "ethical and aesthetic values" in the practice of literary theory, even if he can only do so while maintaining the vestigial value of truth: "If this is indeed so," he pronounces, referring to the separation of truth and method that makes theory "an obstacle" to scholarship and teaching, "then it is better to fail in teaching what should not be taught than to succeed in teaching what is not true" (4). With this assertion he touches on something central to bad education: the failure inherent in every effort to teach "what should not be taught," the failure to encounter the zero *as* zero without turning it into a one. Treating theory as "teachable, generalizable, and highly responsive to systematization" (19) would constitute as effective a *resistance* to theory, and to theory's "impossibility of . . . definition," as would consigning it to the ranks of "what should not be taught" and "teaching what is not true." What, in that case, would it mean to teach what is "true" but "should not be taught"?

I have argued thus far that "what should not be taught" refers to what dissolves a social reality, undoing its coherence as a system adequate to designate what "is." Bad education unleashes the queerness that empties out meaning, derealizes being, and forces us to face our facelessness, our status as posited entities in a system of signification.[7] The various catachreses of queerness (a set that is always definitionally open) give queerness a local habitation and a name to defend against this nothingness, to refigure its zero as a one whose subsequent abjection from the collectivity procures the collective itself as one—a one that survives through such abjections alone and becomes, in effect, their archive. Queerness, to the contrary, figures the cut, the ab-sens, that fractures coherence, even if that cut's negativity is needed to make identity possible. In this sense, queerness expresses the madness of the Symbolic's division into places in the absence of the Imaginary tether that binds them to meaning through sens-absexe. What, after all, is sens-absexe if not the order of meaning or sense produced by the subtraction of sex as ab-sens, where sex is already a subtraction from sense anterior to sense itself? Sex is the senselessness of this primal subtraction that can never be governed by sense, the queerness of the cut that separates the subject of desire from the subject of the drive, the collective from its figures of jouissance: those catachreses of queerness who would void its meaning and so destroy it. If the insistence of this cut makes resistance to identity, coherence, and even to life as what Lacan calls "the service of goods," inextricable, in the form of the drive, from identity as such, if it points toward a "universal" queerness (one that ruptures, universally, the universality of the one), then it associates that queerness not only with the energy of a relentless negativity but also with the notion of radical evil as thought (and repudiated) by Western philosophers from Immanuel Kant to Alain Badiou.[8]

Though definitions of radical evil vary, the link to queerness emerges most clearly in Alenka Zupančič's reading of Kant in *Ethics of the Real*, where she characterizes radical evil as follows: "This is the evil that belongs to the very structure of the act, to the fact that the latter always implies a 'transgression,' a change in 'what is.' It is not a matter of some 'empirical' evil, it is the very logic of the act that is denounced as 'radically evil' in every ideology."[9] Queerness, like the act, derealizes the constituted order of reality by reducing "what is" to the status of mere imposition or groundless positing. Those read as catachreses of queerness serve to localize its negativity, giving visible form to the menacing force of its radical de-formation. Though reaffirming, with this, the order of being by embodying what being excludes, their existence *as figures of nonbeing* also constitutes an act: an assault on the familiar, the common, the known that endangers the security promised by acquiescence to social norms.[10] Such figures embody the "radical evil" inherent in the act as such.

Regardless of how we value that act, its "evil" pertains to its violation of a collective economy of meaning. As Slavoj Žižek cogently notes, "Although the motivations of Thomas More were undoubtedly 'good,' *the very formal structure of his act was 'radically evil'*: his was an act of radical defiance which disregarded the Good of community."[11] Evil, as Žižek goes on to add, always appears as a "purely negative gesture of suspending the life-circuit," as a rejection of the "natural" order in response to something construed as beyond it—something that speaks to the antagonism that structures an order from within. That's what Žižek means in asserting that "Evil is another name for the 'death-drive.'"[12] The death drive, which arises, according to Lacan, as the beyond of signification, insists as the Real of the void *within* the signifying order, precluding any possible closure or ultimate coherence of Symbolic reality. That void, paradoxically, also bespeaks an *excess* in the Symbolic: the insistence within it of the null set that is never made present in reality, making reality "not-all." Insofar as that reality takes shape precisely through Symbolic structuration, something is always missing that leaves reality incomplete. The ab-sens absented for "being" to "be" within the topology of sens-absexe pervades it as excess and lack at once, as the self-resistance de Man sees in theory and Jacques Derrida sees in archivization. In each case, it signals the death drive's inseparability from the order of meaning.[13]

Freud, as I mentioned in chapter 2, declares in *Civilization and Its Discontents* that "order is a kind of compulsion to repeat."[14] The death drive, bound to the repetition compulsion from its first mention in *Beyond the Pleasure Principle*, thus structures order as such.[15] The death drive may insist on the nothingness against which order always defends, but it also enacts the foundational cut that conjures the one out of nothing by means of the signifier's "single stroke."[16] In this sense, as Žižek and Zupančič make clear, the radicality of radical evil lies not in its *degree* of evil but rather in the status of evil itself ("another name for the 'death drive'") "as a priori and not just as an empirical-contingent propensity of human nature."[17] Developed from the "diabolical evil" that Kant proposes but rejects as unthinkable, radical evil, in Žižek's account, "entails the breakdown of the logic of representation, i.e., the radical incommensurability between the field of representation and the unrepresentable Thing."[18] To that extent, as we saw in *Hamlet* and in Derrida's *Archive Fever*, it registers the aneconomy of loss, the self-resistance of the signifying system, and the radical nonreserve that the pedag-archival institution, the order of survival, holds, paradoxically, in reserve.

Alain Badiou, in *Ethics: An Essay on the Understanding of Evil*, sees evil, by contrast, as a secondary consequence of the good, a perversion that only the "rare existence of truth-processes" makes possible.[19] A "truth-process," as he explains it, refers to "the peculiar ability" of the human animal to "take up a position along the course of truths such that he acquires an Immortal aspect" (59). Despite its theological resonance, this last formula speaks to Badiou's distinction between the human as ruled by "brute interest"—which, in an echo of Lacan's phrase, "the service of goods," he refers to as "the service of his mortal life"—and the human as subjectified when seized by the universality of a truth (59). Both Saul's conversion on the road to Damascus and the prisoner who escapes from Plato's cave can model, for Badiou, this experience of being subjectified by a truth (though both, in their status as myths, are necessarily inexact equivalents). They illuminate the birth of the subject through "an immanent break" (60) with a given world.[20] "Transfixed" by the experience of an event that opens possibilities previously absent from the framework of reality, "the human animal," become subject of a truth procedure, "finds its principal of survival—its interest—disorganized" (60). As a consequence, Badiou argues, "the Good is, strictly speaking, the internal norm of a prolonged disorganization of life" (60), an ongoing fidelity to the "hole [that truth] bores in established knowledges" (32), even though that fidelity undoes the community forged by those very knowledges and "put[s] an end to consensus" (32). Although this account of the good may echo Žižek's reading of radical evil ("an act of radical defiance which disregard[s] the Good of community"), Badiou insists that the truth always serves as the basis for a *new* community, a universal community, even if its effect is to sunder the consensus of a given society. This seeming convergence of good and evil, of communal consolidation and radical break, reflects Badiou's understanding of evil as always immanent in the good, and therefore as capable of assuming the appearance and the language of a truth-procedure. Unlike a genuine truth-process, though, evil, as Badiou understands it, promotes an "absolute particularity" (73) instead of universality, affirming a truth uniquely addressed to a *specific* community (to "the alleged national substance of [the German] people" [73] in the case of Nazi Germany) instead of to all who share in the human "capacity to enter into the composition and becoming of some eternal truths" (90).

From this vantage point, Badiou proposes that we "abandon the theme of radical Evil" (63), in which he recognizes nothing but the paradox of an "incommensurable measure of Evil" (62), a "measure [that] must itself be immeasurable, yet . . . must constantly be measured" (63). In *Ethics*, however, he goes on to identify a "particular figure of Evil," one that he qualifies as "a disaster" and, more specifically, as "a disaster of the truth" (85). This evil resides in the effort to absolutize a truth by imposing it "rigid[ly] and dogmatic[ally]" (83) on the site of an event. When a truth, Badiou argues, is forced to name every element in a situation, including opinions and social customs that fall outside its scope, it destroys the very world that provides the event with its enabling site. In such a case, Badiou explains, "the Immortal would come into being as the wholesale negation of the human animal that bears him" and thereby serves as "truth's very foundation" (84). Although the "wholesale negation" in which this "particular figure of Evil" disastrously participates may mimic the "disorganization" of "the principle of survival" effected by "the Good," the latter propounds an "immanent break" that preserves "the mortal animal" (84) along with the "fabric of opinions" (85) by which humans "socialize their existence and arrange [the elements of their situation] in terms of their interests" (81). It may "disorganize" the "principle of survival," but the Good, by becoming an "internal norm," what Badiou calls "a secondary and paradoxical organization" (60), prevents that disorganization from becoming a threat to survival itself.

Reinforced by this "secondary organization," the subjects of truth-procedures "continue along the path of vital disorganization" (60), pursuing a truth not reducible to "the thought of animality" (133) but without needing to reject that animality in subservience to that truth. As opposed to the evil that produces the disaster of trying "to name the whole of the real" (83), the language of a truth-procedure leaves something "inaccessible to truthful nominations" (85). Badiou refers to this component of the situation as "the unnameable of a truth" (86) even though it is not, inherently, unnameable in itself (the language of the situation, of the world as it is, can readily give it a name); rather, it constitutes that aspect of the world "not susceptible of being made eternal" because incapable of being named *as a truth*. It preserves "the pure real [réel] of the situation, of its life without truth" (86). This forestalls disastrous evil by allowing the survival of the various differences—of opinions, customs, and social forms—that remain outside the discourse of truth and to which the truth is indifferent.

That indifference, however, always presupposes that the "unnameable" is, indeed, "without truth," which, for Badiou, means not universal. Without this assumption nothing would escape the composition of a truth, whose violent undoing of "what is" would evince the negativity of the death drive. Truth, Badiou argues, finds a place in the world only if the world "without truth" survives. Thus, each of the four fields in which he identifies the operation of truth-procedures (politics, science, art, and love) includes its distinctive "unnameable": the element that marks the Real of that field, which Badiou proceeds to specify. "The community and the collective are the unnameables of political truth" (86), he tells us, because to give them a name would prescribe a specific *form* of collectivity and enshrine a particular community in relation to the truth. He locates the unnameable of science, which he exemplifies by mathematics, in "non-contradiction" because "it is . . . impossible to prove, from within a mathematical system, the non-contradiction of that system (this is [Kurt] Gödel's famous theorem)" (86). Though the exclusion of noncontradiction from the naming of a mathematical truth corresponds to a formal imperative of incompleteness in a logical system, it spares us, like the unnameable of political truth, the evil that follows from trying to name everything in terms of the truth as One. With regard to art and, specifically, to poetry, Badiou associates the unnameable with language subtracted from reference and meaning; insofar as "the poet investigates the unnamable in his exploration of the limits of the force and potency of language," that potency resides in language's ability to make present in linguistic representation what has no positive being otherwise.[21] Consonant with the impossibility of naming the void on which poetic language subsists, Badiou describes what remains "without truth" in the realm of love as follows: "As far as love is concerned, it can be established that sexual pleasure (*jouissance*) as such is inaccessible to the power of the truth (which is a truth about the *two*)" (86).

This last unnameable can be understood as the "truth" of all the others, which, if named, would similarly unleash the jouissance of totalization, perverting the truths they claim to sustain by eliminating the multiple. Unnamed, they assure truth's openness to the possibility of transformation by preserving a point of the Real that marks the void in the Symbolic, the null set contained within it, which precludes Symbolic closure in an annihilating One. Named in terms of a given truth, they erase the very condition that makes a truth-procedure possible: the open exchange of opinions through which "truths make their singular penetration" (84). If such a naming poses a risk to truth as "a truth about the *two*," it does so not by excluding the multiple formed by joining two ones, but, instead, by excluding the multiple produced by combining the one and its uncounted void, the point of the Real within it that has no part in any count, that always registers as nothing, but that marks the necessary self-resistance of every truth as named. For example, as Badiou writes with regard to mathematical truths, "Non-contradiction is the limit of the potency of mathematics, because within the theory we can't demonstrate that the theory is non-contradictory. Consequently, a reasonable ethic of mathematics is not to wish to force the point. If you have the temptation to force the point of non-contradiction, you destroy mathematical consistency itself."[22] Mathematical efforts to prove or to name the truth of noncontradiction (the sine qua non of mathematical truth) open mathematics to a fundamental contradiction or incompleteness. Badiou states the consequence bluntly, "If a mathematical theory is contradictory, it is destroyed. It is nothing."[23] To avoid the voiding of mathematics as such and its reduction to the status of "nothing," its truth must not be forced to name the void on which it rests. For the Badiou of *Ethics*, preserving the unnameable shelters us from the death drive, which he views as a "will to nothingness" (34); it imposes a limit on the power of a truth and constrains the violence that would otherwise turn the world itself into "nothing."[24]

In *The Ethics of Psychoanalysis*, which focuses on the psychoanalytic challenge to every conventional interpretation of ethics, Lacan addresses that limit too. He observes that "as soon as we have to deal with anything in the world appearing in the form of the signifying chain, there is somewhere— though certainly outside of the natural world—which is the beyond of that chain, the *ex nihilo* on which it is founded," and he refers to this beyond, which constitutes "the limit of our experience," as "the field of the Thing, . . . this place in which doubt is cast on all that is the place of being."[25] Later he calls it "the unspeakable field of radical desire that is the field of absolute destruction, of destruction beyond putrefaction" (216). With the addition of that final appositive, Lacan makes clear that the destruction at stake exceeds mere death as animal destiny, as the general condition to which Gertrude refers in urging Hamlet to give up his mourning: "Thou know'st 'tis common; all that lives must die, / Passing through nature to eternity."[26] Instead, Lacan gestures toward the death of the world as it appears through sens-absexe, toward the beyond of our signifying logic where jouissance, unbearable to the subject, overwhelms the Symbolic with ab-sens.[27]

Anticipating Badiou, Lacan acknowledges the barriers to this beyond. For Badiou, the good as "internal norm" regulates the "vital disorganization" that truth-procedures effect and protects us against the disaster of turning the inherent negativity of truth against the world itself. Lacan, too, affirms this function of the good, noting that it "erects a strong wall across the path of our desire" and thereby serves as "the first barrier" (230) to the field of jouissance. In addition, however, he indicates the presence of a second barrier, the one he calls "the true barrier" (216), which consists of "the aesthetic phenomenon" and "is identified with the experience of beauty" (217). The fascination exerted by the beautiful, which realizes itself in an image that affirms the coherence of the body ("Even in Kant's time it is the form of the human body that is presented to us as the limit of the possibilities of the beautiful"; 298), generates, for Lacan, a "blindness effect" (281). It "prevents us from seeing [the] true nature" of the "field of absolute destruction" (281) beyond it. Like the "fantasms" (298) that determine our relation to the world, beauty introduces a "barrier as far as access to jouissance is concerned" (298).

Though he differs from Friedrich Schiller in how he understands that barrier, Lacan, like the German philosopher, opposes beauty to the "radical desire" it wards off, which is also to say, to jouissance as the radical *of* desire.[28] Beauty, for Schiller, inspires the pursuit of freedom through "aesthetic play," which transforms the human subject until it finds its highest pleasure in a capacity for creativity detached from utility or service to nature. In this way beauty assures a more intimate experience of (hetero)sexual relations and leads to a more harmonious social order: "A lovelier necessity now links the sexes together, and the sympathy of hearts helps to maintain the bond which was knitted only capriciously and inconstantly by desire. . . . And just as Beauty resolves the conflict of natures in its simplest and purest example, in the eternal opposition of the sexes, so does she resolve it—or at least aims at resolving it—in the intricate totality of society."[29] Drawing, like Schiller, on the work of Kant, Lacan sees a similar imperative in beauty, arguing that "the beautiful has the effect . . . of suspending, disarming desire. The appearance of beauty intimidates and stops desire" (238). As in the narratives of the Marquis de Sade, where the torments the heroines may suffer neither diminish their beauty nor disfigure their bodies, beauty instantiates a formal coherence, an imaginary ideal that serves as a shield against the violence of jouissance, assuring, as does the good for Badiou, the survival of the "human animal" and the world "without truth" that it inhabits. The suffering of Sade's beautiful heroines, much like the image of Christ on the cross, evinces for Lacan how beauty, as the instantiation of pure form, testifies to "a stasis which affirms that that which is cannot return to the void from which it emerged" (261). Reaffirming his description of beauty as the limit before the unspeakable field of the Thing, he echoes Schiller's reading of it as "the beneficent appearance which fills out emptiness."[30]

Unlike Schiller and Badiou, however, Lacan does not see jouissance as incapable of universalization. While Badiou's exclusion of "sexual pleasure (*jouissance*)" from the generic power of a truth reframes Schiller's assertion that "we enjoy the pleasures of the senses simply as individuals, and the race which lives within us has no share of them; hence we cannot extend sensuous pleasures into being universal," Lacan sees jouissance, instead, as the generic field to which we are blinded by beauty.[31] While he might concur with Keats's urn when it announces that "beauty is truth," his point would be that truth, like beauty, has the function of a lure.[32] Consolidating the subject as subject of desire in the order of sens-absexe, "truth" obscures the drive that propels the subject *beyond* the lure of truth, toward ab-sens, which undoes every order. For just that reason Lacan proposes the following formulation: "The love of truth is the love of this weakness whose veil we have lifted, it's the love of what truth hides, which is called castration."[33] To the extent that he identifies the love of truth with the love of what truth hides, Lacan defines truth as simultaneously the agent and object of concealment. It conceals, however, no object but rather the loss that the object, as *fantasy object*, always disavows; truth, in fact, conceals nothing except the nothing of pure division: "Love is truth, but only insofar as it is from it [the truth], from a cut, that a knowledge other than propositional knowledge arises, namely, unconscious knowledge. . . . It [Love] is irreversible division."[34] Badiou may see jouissance as an element "without truth" in the field of love, but Lacan, for whom it names the negativity of irreparable division, construes it as something closer to the truth of love itself. Small wonder, then, that Lacan suggests, in *The Other Side of Psychoanalysis*, that "the only chance for the existence of God is that . . . He is *jouissance*" and then proposes that Sade could identify with nature's destruction and renewal of forms not only because he saw himself as "the instrument of divine *jouissance*" but also "because he loved truth."[35]

In the case of Sade, that love finds expression in provoking the Other to jouissance, *making* it "come" into being, the Lacanian definition of perversion: "The sadist himself occupies the place of the object, but without knowing it, to the benefit of another, for whose *jouissance* he exercises his action as sadistic pervert."[36] Like the disaster induced, according to Badiou, by attempting to totalize the reach of a truth by forcibly naming the unnameable, jouissance, for Lacan, also follows from a forcing, one inherent in the "truth" of the subject of desire pursuing the pleasure principle: "To the degree that it involves forcing an access to the Thing, the outer extremity of pleasure is unbearable to us" (80). In much the same way as, for Derrida, the "heterodidactics between life and death" is learned from "the other at the edge of life," so the "outer extremity of pleasure," for Lacan, occasions a similar encounter, one he qualifies as "unbearable" because already stained by the jouissance of "forcing an access to the Thing."[37] Here, inside and outside coincide as pleasure, both at and *as* its extremity (an extremity internal to pleasure but figured as "outer" nonetheless), confronts the "unbearable" jouissance that at once exceeds and undoes it. This jouissance, which I designated earlier as the exemplary unnameable for Badiou, functions, therefore, as both cause and effect of this forcing of the truth. It names both the Thing, the beyond of pleasure, to which access is being forced and the "outer extremity of pleasure" seen as responsible for that forcing.[38] Love of truth may lead the pervert to force the Other's jouissance, but the pressure of the drive impels that "forcing."

If, as Dany Nobus writes, "*jouissance* thus gains ascendancy in the pervert's ideology as a formal universal principle which is applicable to everyone in every situation," then the drive extends the truth of that principle beyond perversion alone.[39]

To that extent, such a "love" of truth takes the form of the Sadean maxim, which, as characterized by Lacan, "proposes a rule for *jouissance* . . . in the Kantian fashion, that of posing itself as a universal rule."[40] Expressing his fidelity to jouissance as the subject's determining substance, Lacan affirms that "the only thing of which one can be guilty is of having given ground relative to one's desire" (319). But his use of "desire" is misleading here; it takes its force from his representation of "the field of absolute destruction," the field beyond the limit of *Atè* where Antigone meets her fate, as "the unspeakable field of radical desire" (216), the field, that is, of jouissance as the radical of desire itself. Like "the outer extremity of pleasure," "radical desire" names the jouissance that surpasses pleasure or desire; it gestures toward the radical of desire as such as instantiated by the drive's constant orbit of the void that desire and its objects would positivize. If the truth of the subject for Lacan consists in its relation to jouissance, such that only betraying its "radical desire" can properly generate guilt, then how does he situate jouissance in relation to radical evil?

In the seminar of March 20, 1960, Lacan admits that if we follow Freud in *Civilization and Its Discontents*, then "we cannot avoid the formula that *jouissance* is evil . . . because it involves suffering for my neighbor" (184). Despite that recognition, however, he later affirms that "there is no other good than that which may serve to pay the price for access to desire" (321). He then goes on to identify this "good" we must yield to become subjects of desire: "This something is called *jouissance*. . . . That's the object, the good, that one pays for the satisfaction of one's desire" (322).[41] Jouissance, then, is explicitly characterized as good and evil at once, reflecting the difference in valuation across the divide of the Lacanian subject. From the vantage point of the social order and the subject of the Symbolic, which is also to say from the vantage point of the subject of the statement, jouissance brings the evil of a suffering disastrous to the community and injurious to one's neighbor, including the neighbor one is to oneself. But from the perspective of the subject of the enunciation, the subject of the unconscious, jouissance denotes its only good, the substance of its being.

Essential to one version of the subject, then, while intolerable to the other, jouissance can operate, pace Badiou, as a Kantian imperative for Lacan: "One can easily substitute for Kant's 'Thou shalt' the Sadean fantasy of *jouissance* elevated to the level of an imperative—it is, of course, a pure and almost derisory fantasy, but it doesn't exclude the possibility of its being elevated to a universal law" (316).[42] Indeed, Lacan effectively interprets it as the law of psychoanalysis when he associates the repetition compulsion that drives and subtends desire with the specificity of "an unconscious theme," a "theme" that reappears when he conceives the sinthome as the distinctive attachment of a subject to the Real that shapes its destiny: "If analysis has a meaning, desire is nothing other than that which supports an unconscious theme, the very articulation of that which roots us in a particular destiny, and that destiny demands that the debt be paid, and desire keeps coming back, keeps returning, and situates us once again in a given task, the track of something that is specifically our business" (319). So understood, the "desire" to which Lacan encourages fidelity ("the only thing of which one can be guilty is of having given ground relative to one's desire") is the "radical desire" of the drive that "keeps coming back" to the specific "task" that is the "business" of a given subject.

That may explain what Lacan intends when he writes that the "good which is sacrificed for desire . . . means the same thing as that desire which is lost for the good" (322).[43] The first "good" refers to jouissance, "the good . . . that one pays for the satisfaction of one's desire," as Lacan straightforwardly puts it. Such desire, the corollary of the Symbolic law that at once excites and constrains it, requires the sacrifice of jouissance for its domesticated counterpart: the pleasures one's objects afford. When "desire" returns or comes back, however, in Lacan's chiastic phrasing, as "that desire which is lost for the good," both "desire" and "good" have changed places. Rather than signaling the order of desire for which jouissance as "good" is sacrificed, "desire" now pertains to the "radical desire" (216) that is jouissance itself, the "desire [that] keeps coming back, keeps returning . . . [as] something that is specifically our business." If that jouissance is "lost for the good," then the "good" no longer names jouissance but the good of the Symbolic subject of desire, "the good," as Lacan writes elsewhere, "that keeps us a long way from our *jouissance*" (185): an ethical or a social good that only the framework of desire makes possible. Incompatible with the good to which the subject clings in that economy of desire, this "radical desire" engenders the guilt experienced by those who betray it: "From an analytical point of view, the only thing of which one can be guilty is of having given ground relative to one's desire." Such giving ground, as Lacan points out, is often done "for good motives" (319), indeed, for the sake of the "good" itself, which demands that we "sacrifice" our "radical desire," the "good" that is jouissance.[44] Conforming to the social good, therefore, as Lacan adverts us, is "far from protecting us not only from guilt but also from all kinds of inner catastrophes" (319) that follow from being "driven by the idea of the good" (321).

As Sophocles portrays him in *Antigone*, Creon exemplifies such "inner catastrophes." In "seek[ing] the good" (258) of the community he governs (what Lacan calls "the good of all as the law without limits" [257]), Creon destroys his family and ends the play "out of his mind" (269), the victim, as Lacan translates the Chorus's words, of "a misfortune that is not external to him" (277). Antigone provides a counterexample of fidelity to her "radical desire," regardless of cost or consequence. This inflexibility so transforms her that she acquires an "unbearable splendor" (247), "the glow of beauty" (281) that accompanies "the moment of transgression or of realization of Antigone's *Atè*" (281), a beauty that "causes all critical judgment to vacillate, stops analysis, and plunges the different forms involved into a certain confusion, or, rather, an essential blindness" (281). To what does this "beauty effect" (281) blind us if not to the *unbearable*, the "the field of . . . destruction beyond putrefaction" (216) that such beauty works to conceal? In line with de Man's reflections on ethics and aesthetics in "The Resistance to Theory," *The Ethics of Psychoanalysis* also construes the "barrier" before this field of the Thing as that of "the aesthetic phenomenon . . . identified with the experience of beauty . . . that has been called the splendor of truth" (217). Only by transgressing the limit defined by such a "truth," only by resisting the pacification that beauty would effect, do we enter the field of jouissance as radical desire, as the cut, the irreversible division, the pure negativity that "truth hides."

Two subjects, then, two versions of desire, and two readings of the good collide here. The queerness of non-self-identity that de Man discussed in relation to theory colors life at its "edge," pleasure at its "outer extremity," and "desire" in its "radical" form. The order of reality, unable to acknowledge the Real as its own self-resistance, as the structurally generated impediment to that order's totalization, displaces it onto placeholders of negativity instead, onto figures constrained to embody the voiding, the derealization of "what is." Such figures are treated as contingent evils in a given situation, but they speak to the radical evil inseparable from Symbolic structuration: the radical evil of the death drive inhabiting the archive for Derrida and the very notion of order for Freud. Ironically, given his exclusion of jouissance from participation in a truth-procedure, it is Badiou's words describing "the event as such" that best characterize such figures of queerness: "a-cosmic and illegal, refusing integration into any totality and signaling nothing."[45]

Catachrestic figurations of queerness share these attributes with the event because they, like it, make present in a world what otherwise counts *as* nothing. By turning the zero into a one, by positivizing the queerness of ab-sens, these various figures—"the Black," "the queer," "the woman," "the trans* person," "the terrorist," inter alia—make possible a (mis)representation of what has no being to represent. They stand in for what displaces the world as given, for what undoes that world in much the same way that an event "compels . . . a *new* way of being" through a "rupture, an overturning."[46] In each case the act of nomination aims, like Blackness as Frank Wilderson unpacks it, to destroy the world, not just to change it. "Truth *forces* knowledges," Badiou writes in *Ethics*; "the verb *to force* indicates that since the power of a truth is that of a break, it is by violating established and circulating knowledges that a truth returns to the immediacy [*l'immédiat*] of the situation, or reworks that sort of portable encyclopedia from which opinions, communications and sociality draw their meaning" (70). Such a "break," like Lacan's "irreversible division," posits truth as the negativity expressed in the internal division of truth itself between the cut of division ("castration"), which is "what truth hides," and the agency hiding that cut.

Bruno Bosteels—challenging the Badiou whose *Ethics* preserves the unnameable to ward off the evil, the "disaster," that would follow from its being forced (a position, Bosteels notes, that marks a change from Badiou's stance in *The Theory of the Subject*)—underscores a threat this preservation poses to Badiou's philosophy: the risk "that the unnameable operates only as a kind of point in reserve, from which perspective any subjective procedure of truth could be read as always involving a disaster. . . . [T]he unnameable, instead of mapping an internal limit of an effective procedure of truth, would then block the very possibility of an effective regime of fidelity to any event whatsoever. . . . Indeed, does assuming the unnameable in order to stop evil not mean proposing an insuperable limit to all generic thinking of truth?"[47] As this suggests, any requirement to maintain an unnameable (as a "point in reserve") must impose in advance a rule on the event whose evental status consists precisely in its breaking from the rule of what is. It must assume, within the framework of a given situation, the ability to put a "limit" on the very truth that would transform it. For just this reason, as Badiou himself would subsequently observe, the imperative to preserve an unnameable impinges on the disorganization that a truth-procedure necessarily effects. A decade after his *Ethics* was published, Badiou declared in an interview:

I have publicly renounced the theory of the unnamable, as presented in *Ethics*. I may very well renounce the use of the term "ethics," since it has so many countermeanings. . . . I have already asserted, of course, that there is no general ethics, but only ethics in situation, ethics tied to the singular truth-procedures. One has to go even further in that direction. Forcing the right decision regarding a point is the only form of duty we can recognize. The imperative of truths is greater than any other. And I'm inclined to believe that we cannot oppose any formal limits to it.[48]

What does this absence of "formal limits" on the violence of "forcing" mean if not that truth-procedures invariably rely on the agency of the death drive even while those made subjects through (catachrestic) namings of the event attempt to socialize its rupture, to rebind its unbound energy, to contain the queerness of its eruption? As a first step in clarifying this relation between the death drive, the event, and its naming as a truth, we might note how often Badiou identifies repetition as such with death, perhaps most clearly in his work on Saint Paul when he discusses the apostle's meditation on sin and the law in the Epistle to the Romans. While explaining how "the law" in that epistle becomes "one of the names of death in a subjective constitution," Badiou writes, "The law, and only the law, endows desire with an autonomy sufficient for the subject of desire . . . to come to occupy the place of the dead. The law is what gives life to desire. But in doing so, it constrains the subject so that he wants to follow only the path of death."[49] If the law here incites and vivifies desire, it does so by endowing desire with a seeming autonomy from the law, thus enacting a logic that echoes Michel Foucault's account of the law as producing, not repressing, desire.[50] But why should this flourishing of desire propel the subject down the "path of death"?

Badiou answers this question directly through his definition of sin: "What is sin, exactly? It is not desire as such, for if it were one would not understand its link to the law and death. *Sin is the life of desire as autonomy, as autonomism.* The law is required in order to unleash the automatic life of desire, the automatism of repetition. For only the law *fixes* the object of desire, binding desire to it regardless of the subject's 'will.' It is this objectal automatism of desire, inconceivable without the law, that assigns the subject to the carnal path of death."[51] Leaving aside its binding to an object, desire's attributes, in this description, correlate more closely with the drive: repetition compulsion, automatism, subordination of the subject's will. Badiou might well be troping on Lacan's engagement, in *The Ethics of Psychoanalysis*, with this very passage from Paul's epistle. For Lacan, the relation between desire and law, where the latter refers to "the law of speech" (83) that governs the Symbolic, gives rise to the death drive in the form of sin, which Lacan construes as the "Thing": "The dialectical relationship between desire and the Law causes our sin to flare up only in relation to the Law, through which it becomes a desire for death" (83–84). Crucially, though, Lacan asserts that the Thing (*das Ding*) "is the very correlative of the law of speech in its most primitive point of origin, and . . . that this *Ding* was there from the very beginning, . . . it was the first thing that separated itself from everything the subject began to name and articulate" (83). To the extent that it refers to the originary loss that inheres in the primal division produced by naming as articulation, the Thing, entwined as it is with the Law, denotes the constitutive exclusion that every linguistic act repeats.

Badiou—like *Hamlet*, Freud, and Lacan—concedes that the repetition compulsion determines the order of survival. But he holds out the prospect of escaping repetition, the stasis of the law's survival, through a break with the order of law itself:

> The law . . . delivers desire to its repetitive autonomy. . . . The law's prohibition is that through which the desire of the object can realize itself involuntarily, "unconsciously," . . . which is to say, as a life of sin. As a result of which, the subject, de-centered from this desire, crosses over to the side of death. . . . If the subject is to swing over to another disposition, one wherein he would be on the side of life, and sin—that is to say, the automatism of repetition—would occupy the place of the dead, it is necessary to break with the law.[52]

In a world where "sin" alone has vitality and where the death drive organizes life, the event, for Badiou, as uncontrollable eruption of the Real (and so, of the contentless queerness of ab-sens), enables a break with the law as survival and with the "automatism of repetition" that makes survival a kind of death.

That this break calls forth a living subject different from the "human animal" constrained to mortifying repetition might seem to confirm as absolute Badiou's privileging of life over death. Such a belief prompts Žižek to draw a sharp line between Lacan's position and Badiou's. After remarking that Lacan rejects the positivity of what Badiou denotes by the truth-event and so "implicitly changes the balance between Death and Resurrection in favour of Death," Žižek adds that, in doing so, Lacan "parts company with St. Paul and Badiou: God not only is but always-already was dead—that is to say, after Freud, one cannot directly have faith in the truth-event; every such Event ultimately remains a semblance obfuscating a preceding Void whose

Freudian name is death drive."[53] This criticism, though trenchant in its theoretical framing, presupposes that the truth-event *must* be construed as positivized by Badiou and affirmed, therefore, as the site of a content *other than* the pressure of "a preceding Void whose Freudian name is death drive." But does Badiou's event, as Žižek asserts, simply obfuscate that void, or might it also, if less explicitly, attest to its insistence? Is the event exhausted by the truth it inspires, or does it extend to the *form* of the event itself, to the radical interruption of the law's repetition—the interruption of its formulated truth—by the encounter with the Real? In the latter case the law's repetition would identify the Real within it, the place where inner and outer converge, and the event would announce the "a-cosmic and illegal" ground of every order. Far from an alternative to the repetition subtending the law, the event, instead, would repeat it by marking the advent of a new truth. To that extent the event as *form* would desublimate the truth its disciples name by insisting on the queerness of the evental drive inaccessible to nomination. Not the event, then, but rather the *naming* of the event, the catachresis that bends it to the law of speech, would obfuscate the death drive; the event itself would manifest the ex nihilo of the drive, thus making it, like theater in Badiou's formulation, a "repeatable event."[54] Like the event of theater, the event as such is never once and for all; it never signals truth's completion or our capacity to comprehend it but always insists on the not-all of its given articulations—a not-all obscured by every name we bestow in a truth-procedure. Each event, therefore, *repeats the interruption of repetition* by opening onto the void whose queerness ruptures the world's coherence. But that rupture gives rise to another name that another event must displace. How, after all, can the zero escape transformation into a one without destroying the conceptual frame in which the zero "appears" catachrestically? Those seized by an event and faithful to its nomination through a truth-procedure *must* force it by way of naming it, but the truth they declare will inevitably dissimulate the drive from which it springs: the void, the "castration," that "truth hides."

The event thus confronts the subject of the law with its counterpart in another dimension: the headless or acephalic subject with which it can never be one. Lacan approaches this difference in dimension when he poses the following question: "Is the place that I occupy as subject of the signifier concentric or eccentric in relation to the place I occupy as subject of the signified?"[55] The answer, as Lacan goes on to suggest, hinges on the fact that "the S and the *s* of the Saussurian algorithm are not in the same plane, and man was deluding himself in believing he was situated in their common axis, which is nowhere."[56] The difference of order, the ontological gap that prevents these planes from meeting on a "common axis," gives rise, Lacan argues, to the death drive and the eruption of the Real. It precludes the comprehension of those planes within any totalizing framework by assuring that every unified system will carry that gap within. As the obtrusion of the void internal to any particular situation, but perceptible only through a pressure or "force" exerted from outside it, such a gap pertains to another dimension and invokes the beyond that *inhabits* the "known" in the form of what "is" not. It registers the persistence within the signifying order of the bar in the Saussurian algorithm—the bar excluded from the signification that it alone makes possible by dividing the signifier from the signified while establishing a (non)relation between them. It attests, thereby, to the primal repression of the senseless machinery of division (sex as designated by ab-sens) that produces the Symbolic order (as the topology of sens-absexe).

The repetition compulsion intrinsic to order emerges from that primal repression, that absenting of ab-sens. What repression first bars from signification is the Saussurian bar itself. It precludes our thinking what conditions thought: pure difference in the absence of positive terms, the primal cut of division from which the Symbolic subject is born and which, as negative relationality, as what Lacan denotes by the phallus (which is also to say, by castration), eludes the positivizations through which the Symbolic tries to contain it. From this "primitive point of origin" of the Symbolic's law of speech, *das Ding*, as we have already seen, "was the first thing that separated itself from everything the subject began to name and articulate." The primal cut of articulation is itself the cutting off of what will have been lost thereby as *das Ding*, the cut that Lacan defines as the truth that generates the unconscious: "It is from it [the truth], from a cut, that a knowledge other than propositional knowledge arises, namely, unconscious knowledge." The primal repression of the Saussurian bar allows for the advent of meaning, which is absent in the bar itself, and it consigns to the realm of unthinkability the originary split or mitosis by which "nothing" divides into "nothing" and "something" (the zero and the one). Both the event and radical evil repeat that primal creation ex nihilo, that fracturing of what is by the radically detotalizing insistence of the nihil as such; but they both get contained by the Symbolic compulsion to speak, to name their truth. Such a forcing of truth through its naming intends to ward off the (Real) disaster by which the event, in its queerness, voids the Symbolic law of nameability, thus undoing the world much as theory undoes cognition for de Man: by "prevent[ing] all entities, including linguistic entities, from coming into discourse as such." Since the unnameable, the zero, can never be named, even in the act of forcing it, the (Real) disaster lies not in trying to name it in a truth-procedure (notwithstanding the real *historical* disasters that such forcing repeatedly occasions) but rather in its evental annihilation of the order of naming itself. The naming of the event, from this perspective, is the sublimation of the death drive that animates it, the death drive philosophy refuses to raise to the dignity of a truth.

The convergence of theory's challenge to teaching (by troubling the logic of reference) with the event's repetitive break from the naming that negates the "nothing" of the cut is brought into focus in the complex dynamics of Michael Haneke's *Funny Games* (1997). This deliberately sadistic and assaultive film, remade by Haneke ten years later in an English-language version intended to attract (in order the better to condemn) a mass audience of slasher-film fans, thinks aesthetic education with radical evil (and each, obliquely, with the event) in order to explore the undoing of the world whose givenness we assume. *Funny Games* shatters epistemological security (including the security of knowing the genre to which the film itself belongs) much as the home invaders within it destroy the world of the Family they terrorize. At once a tragedy and a comedy, a thriller and a science fiction film, an exemplar of so-called torture porn and an indictment of that genre, *Funny Games* scorns the categorical coherence (or the *claim* to categorical coherence) that orients interpretation. But Haneke's investment in education, an investment elaborated both within the film and in his commentaries on it, seeks to restore the "ethical and aesthetic values" that *Funny Games* seems to attack. It aims to restore them through a sublimation, as in the Kantian dynamic sublime, that allows the mind to rise above terror by seeing natural concerns as small and looking beyond them to the superior power that the mind itself possesses. As Kant puts it in characterizing a liking for the sublime as "only *negative*," "It is a feeling that the imagination by its own action is depriving itself of its freedom, in being determined purposively according to a law different from that of its empirical use. The imagination thereby acquires an expansion and a might that surpasses the one it sacrifices. . . . For the imagination . . . acting in accordance with principles of the schematism of judgment (and hence, to that extent, in subordination to freedom), is an instrument of reason and its ideas."[57] For Haneke as for Kant, the mind's triumph depends on sacrificing our attachment to the Imaginary—or depends, at any rate, on the representation, the *imagination*, of such a sacrifice. *Funny Games* offers an allegory of that Imaginary sacrifice, depicting it as performed terroristically, which is also to say, perversely, by "queer" figures of radical evil engaged, like de Man's "The Resistance to Theory," in fulfilling "a didactic and an educational function" for the Family and the audience alike.[58]

Starkly linear on the level of plot, *Funny Games* begins with Georg, Anna, and their young son, Schorschi, driving to their lakeside vacation home for a holiday of golfing and sailing. No sooner do they arrive and start settling in, though, than everything goes awry. Despite fences—controlled electronically—regulating access to the house, two young men, dressed strangely in shorts, white shirts, and white gloves, show up at their door and talk their way inside. Their initially polite requests (the first wants to borrow eggs for their neighbor, the second to admire their golf clubs) quickly escalate into verbal manipulation and then physical attacks (see figure 3.1). Played out in a series of menacing "games," these acts of aggression escalate, despite efforts of resistance by the Family, until the two men eventually make good on the pledge they announced near the outset: that by 9:00 a.m. the following morning, the Family would be dead.

Only three times does the relentless drive toward this promised end get interrupted: first, when Schorschi escapes from the house and seeks shelter with the neighbors next door; then, when the intruders, after killing Schorschi, unexpectedly take their leave; and, finally, when Anna, seizing the rifle that was used to kill her son, shoots one of the two invaders before the other can intervene. After each of these incidents, the film, however, reverts to its fatal trajectory: young Schorschi, having found his neighbors dead, prior victims of the two invaders, is captured and dragged back to his family's house, where, shortly thereafter, he is killed; the intruders, after murdering Schorschi and leaving his parents in the house with his corpse, come back, this time with Anna, who had fled to seek help when they left; and in the third and most noteworthy deviation, after Anna shoots one of the two young men, the other finds the television's remote control and uses it, in the signature moment of the film, to rewind the sequence we just saw on screen and replay it with a difference: this time he grabs the rifle before Anna can manage to kill his friend. At the end of the film, with their pledge fulfilled and the Family's members dead, the youths move on to a neighbor's house to begin their games anew.

The violence of this repetition compulsion takes as its target the bourgeois ideal of private property and familial security. The young men enact a death drive internal to the social order they embody in their exaggerated rituals of politeness when they first appear onscreen. Always acting—always inventing new games, new narratives, new rules—they refer to themselves as Beavis and Butthead, Tom and Jerry, or Peter and Paul, repudiating the stability of naming with its mortifying self-sameness in the service of the truth. Referring to "the proper name" as "something already dead in the individual," Jacques-Alain Miller asserts that "the Symbolic order . . . is death

3.1: The intruders. From *Funny Games* (Haneke, 1997).

itself."[59] The intruders, I'll call them Peter and Paul, have purely differential identities, and they mock explanations of their actions in historical or psychological terms. Like a cross between Brandon and Phillip in *Rope* (Alfred Hitchcock, 1948) and the white-clad, home-invading truants who sow disorder in *A Clockwork Orange* (Stanley Kubrick, 1971, Warner Brothers), they refuse the structures of meaning to which the Family clings for dear life, obtruding the "queerness" of their jouissance, the *vitality* of the death drive, onto the Symbolic order's deadness.

Mocking the sort of backstories common to social-problem narratives in their efforts to explain, by psychologizing, antisocial behaviors, Paul traces the delinquency of Peter to his closeness to his mother, a woman whose erotic attachment to her son made him, in Paul's pseudoanalysis, gay ("schwul"). But the two young men, paired visually and contextually as a nonromantic couple (an antireproductive couple that gets off on eradicating families), evoke associations with same-sex intimacy only as a visual shorthand for the queerness, the jouissance or the radical evil, that prompts their destruction of "what is." Peter and Paul give accounts of themselves just as fictive as their names. Nor do they grant the Family and the world it inhabits any more stable reality. Paul, in fact, makes clear that what we are seeing takes place in a film: when Georg implores the intruders to put a quick end to the Family's torment, Paul, with ironic earnestness, rebuffs him: "But we're not up to feature film length yet." Dismissing the diegetic reality that the Family thinks it inhabits, rejecting the ontological assumptions that determine how the Family acts,

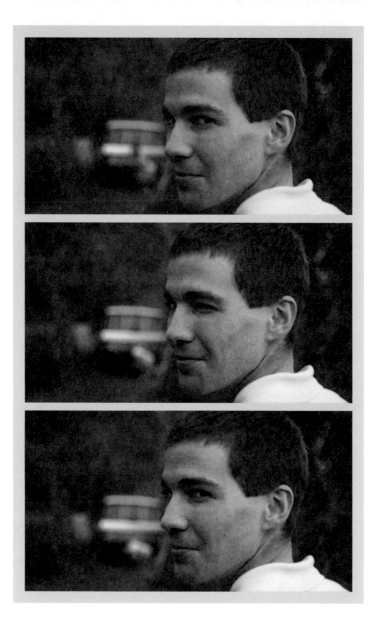

3.2–3.4:
Winking at the
audience. From
Funny Games
(Haneke, 1997).

Paul literally winks at the audience and, breaking the illusion of the camera's
nonpresence, addresses it directly (see figures 3.2–3.4).

Meanwhile, with increasing desperation as the world they know unravels,
Georg, Anna, and Schorschi fight to preserve their place within it, unaware
that even "Georg" and "Anna" are merely generic names that Haneke bestows on the central characters in at least nine of his feature films. As their
civilized life succumbs to the senseless assault of Peter and Paul, the Family
looks in vain to reason and logic for defense.

Haneke establishes the Family's faith in rationality from the outset by way of its fondness for the harmonized order of the music it prefers. While traveling to their vacation home, Georg and Anna display their cultural capital in a game (anticipating the "funny games" to come) that requires them to identify the titles and composers of various operatic selections.[60] This contest does more than speak to the refinement of their musical aesthetic; it enacts their faith in the aesthetic itself as comprehension. They seem to believe, with Friedrich Schiller, that "taste alone brings harmony into society, because it establishes harmony in the individual."[61] Their demonstration of aesthetic mastery in identifying passages from George Frideric Handel and Pietro Mascagni coincides with their movement toward the freedom that their country home bespeaks—a freedom purchased, as the film makes clear, at the cost of enclosure by fences to secure it from those outside. Aesthetic education, the gateway to liberty and the ground of the Family's attachment to a coherent social order, represses that order's dependence on the exclusion those fences effect. It mistakes for a universal—that is, a totalizing—comprehension the violent social divisions every aesthetic order imposes, divisions those fences enact by keeping the Family, in its self-enclosure, from encounters with the social antagonisms those fences aim to keep out. Like the various aspect ratios of Almodóvar's *Bad Education*, the fences mark the horizon of the Family's aesthetic comprehension; the aesthetic education put on display in the first of the film's many "games" seeks to sublimate the negativity to which those fences attest and to positivize (as social order) the divisions they produce.

Haneke subjects this sublimation—the Family's and the audience's alike— to the violence performed in the credit sequence by a sudden aural intrusion. After foiling Georg's effort to discover, by looking at the CD case, the title of the track being played in the car, Anna tells him, instead, "Just listen." In the moments that follow, as they gaze at the road, we, along with the Family, hear Handel's arioso from *Atalanta*, "Care Selve." But suddenly the beauty of Handel gives way, for the audience, *though not for the Family*, to the discordant heavy metal sounds of "Bonehead" and "Hellraiser," tracks from John Zorn's *Torture Garden*, an album released in 1990 by Naked City, his band. These sounds, described by *Rolling Stone* as "brutally disorienting, genre-defying bursts," ironize the placidity of the Family's smiles as they continue to listen to Handel while the opening credits imprint the film's title, *Funny Games*, on their faces (see figures 3.5–3.6).[62]

Their obliviousness to the (extradiegetic) shrieks that disconcert us in Zorn's compositions joins with their ignorance of the (extradiegetic) text that overwrites their images; together these elements signal that the "funny games" that

3.5–3.6: What we perceive but the family does not. From *Funny Games* (Haneke, 1997).

have now begun will play themselves out at the Family's expense, capitalizing on their nonrecognition of the filmic machine that controls them. The howls of Zorn's tracks, with which Paul, diegetically, will later scare Schorschi from his hiding place when he escapes to his neighbor's home, unleash the chaos sublimated by aesthetic education.[63]

But if Haneke assails the aesthetic faith that sustains the Family's world, if he permits the figures of radical evil to puncture it as an illusion, he maintains, as true to Schiller as they, that art nonetheless can free us from the Family's mistaken belief in its freedom. He declares, in a calculated provocation, "I've been accused of 'raping' the audience in my films, and I admit to that freely—all movies assault the viewer in one way or another. What's different about my films is this: I'm trying to rape the viewer into independence."[64] This formula, poised as it is between the paradoxical and the self-deconstructing, grounds my reading of *Funny Games*. Though Haneke elides the rape that figures in his intertext, *A Clockwork Orange*, he depicts the violation of Anna through a painful scene of forced undressing whose sadism gains intensity from the threat of rape informing it.[65] By framing his film as an effort "to rape the viewer into independence," Haneke rationalizes that sadism (directed at the Family and the audience at once) on pedagogical grounds, offering it up as an allegory of his cinematic project: to free the spectator from enslavement to illusory appearance. In this he explicitly aligns himself with the violence of the two intruders and yokes his filmic assault on "what is" to an ethical education that affirms the function of the aesthetic as inherently pedagogical.

"An art form," Haneke elsewhere maintains, "is obliged to confront reality, to try to find a little piece of the truth."[66] With that in mind he reformulates Jean-Luc Godard's much-cited take on cinema as "truth at 24 frames per second"(*Le Petit Soldat*, 1963), calling it, instead, "a lie 24 times a second *to serve the truth*."[67] If this reversibility of truth and lie recalls the Lacanian paradox that "love of truth is . . . the love of what truth hides" (a love of truth that, as we saw, Lacan associates with Sade), then we can better understand how in Haneke's version the audience's subjection to his cinematic "lie" (the violence he figures as "rape") aims to "free" it from ideological complacency through enforced self-recognition. To that extent, his reference to "rape" brings out its root in the Latin *rapere*, "to seize, to carry off by force."[68] Haneke aims to remove us from the world perceived as truth, which, like Lacan, he construes as deception: "Truth, in the first place, is seduction to dupe you. One must be strong not to fall prey to it" (La verité est seduction d'abord, et pour vous couillonner. Pour ne pas s'y laisser prendre, il faut être fort).[69] For those who lack that strength in themselves, Haneke forces a reckoning meant to show that they've been duped. In an interview with Serge Toubiana where he contends that *Funny Games* excoriates the violence of contemporary film and mass media, Haneke once again adopts an aggressive stance toward the viewer, a sort of tough love that has as its raison d'être the spectator's good: "It gave me a lot of pleasure to give a sort of awakening slap, to say 'look at what you normally look at!'"[70]

This statement captures the contradictions of Haneke's filmic pedagogy. On the one hand, he aims to enlighten his viewers by exposing how "the normal thriller" prompts them to "enjoy" or "get off on" violence ("jouir de la violence"); on the other hand, he does so while enjoying a comparable violence of his own ("it gave me a lot of pleasure to give a sort of awakening slap").[71]

This paradox comes to the fore when Haneke imagines the "awakening slap" as saying, "Look at what you normally look at!" (regarde ce que tu regarde normalement). In contrast to the products of mainstream cinema ("what you normally look at"), which snare the viewer in illusion, his films dissect that manipulation to free us from its hold. At the same time, however, his phrasing suggests that his own films do so precisely by offering the audience "what [it] normally look[s] at," affording not an *awakening from* but a *repetition of* its "normal" experience. Haneke's violence (the "awakening slap") and the surplus jouissance he attains by punishing the viewer's jouissance result from the division implicit in the repetition of the signifier, "look at" (*regarde*). By urging us to "look at" what we "normally look at," he focuses attention on a critical distance internal to looking as such: a division between naive and sophisticated looking, between an ignorant and an educated eye, that would mirror a similar division between a restrictive or ideologically constraining text and a resistant or ironic one, between the cinema of exploitation and the art film that critically dissects it. The former, like "normal" torture porn in Haneke's estimation, indulges the spectator's will to get off on the spectacle of sadistic violence, subjecting the viewer to cinematic manipulation; the latter, while critiquing torture porn, gets off on the disciplinary violence that punishes the viewer's will to get off, reflecting the diegetic torture of its plot in the torture it inflicts on its spectators so as to free them, albeit forcibly, from their "normal" ways of looking. But what epistemology could reliably differentiate these two ways of "look[ing] at" film? Can an ironic text about torture porn teach a lesson about reading that genre without inciting the very jouissance it intends us to renounce? Might torture porn, like melodrama, or, indeed, like genre as such, be seen as auto-ironic, as emphasizing the function of convention in its very framing? And is irony ever "teachable, generalizable, and . . . responsive to systematization," or does it turn against *every* system, every order of comprehension, by dissolving any ground?

Funny Games, like "The Resistance to Theory," both performs and troubles theoretical work—a work inseparable for Haneke from cinema's ethical responsibility: "Because cinema is a part of [the] media, it has an obligation to carry out a reflection on its own methods, on the question of violence and the manner in which it is represented."[72] Echoing de Man's definition of theory ("a controlled reflection on the formation of method"), Haneke endorses the rationality that makes such reflection, as de Man maintains, "entirely compatible with teaching." Indeed, such reflection is at once the vehicle and the content of Haneke's lesson. Roy Grundmann, for instance, observes that his films "show . . . that popular art can be used to get people to think critically about their lives, to teach them to question their conditions of existence."[73] But theoretical reflection, as de Man reminds us, can escape epistemological control, plunging us into fathomless depths of ironic distantiation and challenging the possibility of Haneke's cinematic "teach[ing]." Deploying the violence of representation to compel the viewer to *reflect on* violence can produce, in place of a transmissible knowledge, a vertiginous hall of mirrors filled with endless *reflections of* violence. In the case of Haneke's *Funny Games*, the mise en abyme of theoretical reflection finds its double within the narrative where the invaders who torture the Family (and, psychologically, the audience) are also Haneke's surrogates, the vehicles of his film's "awakening slap."

Almost from the moment they appear onscreen, Peter and Paul dismantle the logic of the bourgeois family's world. Not that their violence in itself is a threat to the order of law as such. Their transgressions could also, as Foucault affirms, bolster the institutions of the law empowered to define, prohibit, and punish them. But Peter and Paul enter Haneke's film like creatures from another dimension, like heralds of a different ontological order invading the space of "what is." Injecting the stylization of commedia dell'arte into the Family's bourgeois "realism," they disfigure it as much as if Freddy Krueger spent the weekend with Uncle Vanya. Underscoring this aspect of *Funny Games*, Haneke talks about Peter and Paul as "the white clown and the comic clown in the circus," flatly asserting that they "aren't really characters. They're artifacts."[74] Elsewhere, he returns to this theme: "It is not a realistic film. Those two characters [Peter and Paul] are completely artificial confronting a family that is, itself, realistic. The two young men are like robots on an emotional level, they don't have any human reflections."[75] Haneke implicitly acknowledges here that the film and the intruders alike maintain a distance from the Family: continuous in this with the film itself, the intruders debunk the Family's faith in the coherence of its "realism" and acknowledge the filmic medium in which their violent acts unfold. If they have no "human reflections," that may signal that, as reflections themselves, as images or "artifacts," they enact the robotic machinery, the automatism of life, that the signifier "human" denies. Constructed to *induce* reflection, the ostensible hallmark of "human" being, they lay no claim to being human; instead, they haunt the world of the film like (in)versions of Hamlet's specter, devoted not to survival but to the destruction of all that "is" while bringing out the death drive in survival and the archive.

When their unctuousness gives way at last to an almost formal brutality, a violence dispassionately performed, Peter and Paul seem less like cold-blooded thugs or sadistic murderers than like teenagers perfunctorily picking off targets in a virtual reality game. Luc Lagier suggests as much in interpreting their viciousness as a critique of media culture: "For the two adolescents, nourished on video games and television, the world comes down to a game that is simplified to the point of caricature, a world without consequences where there is no 'real' death and the people one encounters seem like characters or mere figures, like so many puppets to be manipulated in one's own fiction."[76] This "explanation" for their behavior, though, rehearses the social-problem narratives that Peter and Paul make fun of and Haneke explicitly scorns: "All these explanations serve no purpose: if one wants to kill, one kills," he claims.[77] Lagier's reading, moreover, encounters a far more serious stumbling block: the film paints *the Family*, not Peter and Paul, as ontologically deluded. Unlike the intruders, the Family mistakes its world for immediate reality; Peter and Paul, by contrast, acknowledge their presence in a film. They know, as the members of the Family do not, that all of them *are* "mere figures" produced in the space of a game or of play—a space in which "there *is* no 'real' death" (emphasis mine) and only the lure of the Imaginary sustains the fiction of "reality."

To be sure, when Paul, addressing himself to the audience directly, shows his understanding of the conventions that govern the film in which he appears (asking with regard to the members of the Family, "You are on their side, aren't you?"), he does so while remaining in character as "Paul," rather than as Arno Frisch, the Austrian actor who portrays him. Only within a fictional frame does Paul break the frame of the fiction. By acknowledging, however, the generic expectations, the rules of the game that condition the audience's responses to *Funny Games*, Paul revises its genre. As Haneke's henchman and surrogate, he compels us (as he compels the Family) to abandon Imaginary illusion (our immersion in the film's diegetic reality) and "awaken" to our complicity in cinema's constitutive "funny games" (see figure 3.7). As Haneke explains to Serge Toubiana, his film aims to "give an analysis of the work within the work" by making "a film about the way of treating violence in the cinema." "I'm making the spectator the accomplice of the killer," he maintains, "and at the end I'm reproaching him for this position. It's a little sarcastic, but I wanted to show how you're always an accomplice of the killer if you watch this kind of film. Not in a self-reflexive film like this one, but in films that show violence in an 'acceptable' way."[78]

As Haneke's qualification implicitly acknowledges—a qualification that scuttles his argument by trying to distinguish between "this kind of film"

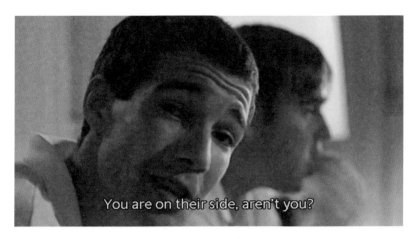

You are on their side, aren't you?

3.7: Imaginary identification. From *Funny Games* (Haneke, 1997).

and "a self-reflexive film like this one"—the spectator of a film like *Funny Games* is *not* exposed to the genre of film that "mak[es you] an accomplice of the killer" but rather to a film *about* those films and so to a film that, seen in this light, is *not* about itself. The problem, of course, inheres in the very notion of self-reflection, which properly speaking requires that a work engaged in self-analysis would have to analyze, in an infinite regress, its "self," its self-analysis, and its analysis of its self-analysis 'til the crack of doom.[79] The gap between "the work" and "the analysis of the work" remains, therefore, as obdurate, and ultimately as destructive, as the gap between "the S and the *s* of the Saussurian algorithm," or between the self and the mirror image with which it never coincides.

As it happens, near the end of *Funny Games*, Peter and Paul engage in an odd conversation (the only prolonged conversation between them in the film) that centers on this difference in dimension, this split occasioned by reflection. Having murdered Anna's husband and son, they are sailing on the lake with Anna in tow (her wrists are bound, her body is chained, and her mouth is sealed with tape) when they begin to discuss a movie that resembles Andrei Tarkovsky's *Solaris* (Mosfilm, 1972).

> PETER: Only it's all inverted. But of course all these predictions are wrong so as to avoid a panic. But now Kelvin knows how it really is . . . and wants to warn his wife and daughter in time. But the problem is not only getting from the world of antimatter to reality, but also to regain communication—

Though interrupted here as Paul catches sight of Anna's last bid to escape, Peter, after foiling her efforts, returns to his fan-boy account of the film:

PETER: So. Where was I?

PAUL: The communication problems between matter and antimatter.

PETER: Exactly. As if you were in a black hole! Gravitation is so strong that nothing can escape it: absolute silence.

PAUL: By the way, what's the time?

Mindful of his wager that the Family's members would be dead by 9:00 a.m., Paul, when he learns it is just after eight, kisses Anna's cheek with a vacant smile before pushing her backward into the lake, where she noiselessly sinks to her death.

PETER: Why? The deadline was at 9:00. She had almost an hour left!

PAUL: Firstly, it was too hard to sail like that, and secondly, I'm starting to get hungry.

Laughing, they forget about Anna and return to their discussion of the film:

PETER: When Kelvin overcomes gravitation, it turns out that one universe is real, but the other is just a fiction.

PAUL: How does that happen?

PETER: What do I know! It was a kind of model projection in cyberspace.

PAUL: And where is your hero now? In reality or fiction?

PETER: His family is in reality and he's in fiction.

PAUL: But the fiction is real, isn't it?

PETER: How do you mean?

PAUL: Well, you see it in the film, right?

PETER: Of course.

PAUL: So, it's just as real as the reality which you see likewise, right?

PETER: Crap.

In Tarkovsky's film, Kris Kelvin, a psychologist whose wife has committed suicide, discovers, after landing on a scientific outpost orbiting the planet Solaris, that the planet has a consciousness; it materializes memories and desires into emanations of people that seem to be real. When he encounters such an emanation in the form of his dead wife, he repeatedly tries to destroy it lest he believe it *is* his wife. But the Kelvin in the film that Peter summarizes has a family living "in reality" (the "wife and daughter" he hopes to "warn"), while the universe in which he finds himself is a "model projection in cyberspace" and therefore "just a fiction." Though Tarkovsky suggests at the end of his film that Kelvin's apparent return to Earth may be merely another illusion produced by Solaris's mimetic consciousness, Paul notes that *everything seen* in cinema has the same ontological status. Depictions of diegetically fictive events are no less "real" than depictions of diegetically truthful ones—as Hitchcock shows with the "flashback" in *Stage Fright* (1950, Warner Brothers) and as Tarkovsky makes clear with the filmic materialization of Kelvin's dead wife.[80] For Paul this means that whatever a film diegetically represents as illusion is "just as real as the [diegetic] reality which you see"; but this also exposes "[diegetic] reality" as an equally fictional projection, which, of course, is just what Tarkovsky does when the camera pulls back at the end of his film to show us Kelvin's earthly home afloat in the ocean of Solaris.

In *Solaris*, as in *Funny Games*, the exposure of cinema's Imaginary lure takes place *within* that Imaginary. The pedagogical ambition of breaking the hold of Imaginary captation—of loosening the Imaginary's grip on the aesthetic and detaching the Symbolic subject from illusion—is accomplished in each case only by means of aesthetic sublimation. The aesthetic, in other words, is overcome, surmounted, *by* the aesthetic, by the Imaginary projection of a self beyond it. As Barbara Johnson muses while analyzing Narcissus's reflection, "Could it be that the aesthetic and the fantasmatic are related, or at least equally indifferent to the empirical difference between 'real' and 'not real'?"[81] Or, to take her question further: does the aesthetic, as the idealization of form, as the image of formal coherence, inhere in "reality" as itself the projection of Imaginary totality, of a world? Is "reality," like the proto-subject of the Lacanian mirror stage, the positivization of the gap between the perceiver and the "self" it perceives, the aesthetic sublimation of the senseless division foreclosed from Symbolic thought? If so, that reality, as aesthetic form, would embody the Real by masking it, would express the truth by hiding it, as the garments worn by the Invisible Man disclose his body by veiling it.

The pedagogy of Haneke's "awakening slap," like the chaos induced by Peter and Paul, intends our "independence" from Imaginary illusion, but its strategy merely replaces one aesthetic illusion with another, inviting us to imagine ourselves as *awakened* from illusion. Consonant with the liberatory pedagogy of aesthetic education, *Funny Games* tries to shift the audience from attachment to the "side" of the Family—the side of Imaginary identification—to the side of its attackers, including Haneke himself. Though the film heaps scorn on the viewer's investment in the Imaginary "realism" of the Family, few succeed in dissociating themselves from Anna, Georg, and Schorschi. The jeers with which many at Cannes reacted to the screening of *Funny Games* and the anger that many viewers still feel when Paul rewinds the film—thereby denying Anna, and the audience, the enjoyment of revenge—speak to the audience's discomfort at having its Imaginary shattered. *Funny Games* wagers everything on the negativity of that shattering, on the traumatic violence of confronting the void inherent in "what is." Though Haneke stops at nothing in rousing hostility toward the "queer" intruders, priming the audience to cheer when Anna, seizing the gun, kills Peter, he does so, as he repeatedly claims, the better to indict that audience for its susceptibility to filmic illusion, its avidity for violence, and its submissiveness to the machinery that keeps it enslaved to images.

No wonder that responses to the film tend to mimic those attributed by Plato to the liberated prisoners in his allegory of the cave:

> And now look again, and see what will naturally follow if the prisoners are released and disabused of their error. At first, when any of them is liberated and compelled suddenly to stand up and turn his neck round and walk and look towards the light, he will suffer sharp pains; the glare will distress him, and he will be unable to see the realities of which in his former state he had seen the shadows; and then conceive someone saying to him, that what he saw before was an illusion, but that now, when he is approaching nearer to being and his eye is turned towards more real existence, he has a clearer vision,—what will be his reply? And you may further imagine that his instructor is pointing to the objects as they pass and requiring him to name them—will he not be perplexed? Will he not fancy that the shadows which he formerly saw are truer than the objects which are now shown to him?[82]

In Plato's allegory, the model for the pedagogical project of *Funny Games*, the spectator's liberation from illusion takes place by means of a violence similar to Haneke's "awakening slap" or to the even more extreme violence of "rap[ing] the viewer into independence." The prisoners in the cave are "compelled . . . to stand up" and, in consequence, "suffer sharp pains" and "distress." Their perplexity and disorientation anticipates Neo's in *The Matrix* (Lana and Lilly Wachowski, 1999, Warner Brothers) when he awakens to the fact that the reality in which he had spent his whole life was virtual, a computer-generated fiction. In accord with the liberal fantasy informing the romance of liberation, Neo, while still in the matrix, can make a decision to renounce it.[83] Having intuited a beyond of the matrix that has determined his subjectivity, he is free to *opt* for freedom, to *choose* the red pill over the blue, and he finds himself, after doing so, in a wholly different dimension.

Haneke, however, denies free will to those enslaved by illusion. The violence of the Real alone dissolves their fantasmatic reality, the same violence that converted Saul to Paul as he traveled the road to Damascus. Haneke's bourgeois subjects, like the prisoners whose freedom depends on their being "compelled" by *others* "to stand up," can be "disabused of their error" only by something experienced as abuse. Badiou, affirming with Plato that the liberating event must come from without, observes of the persons immured in the cave and constrained to look straight ahead that "Plato rules out any form of spontaneous disalignment," thus denying the prisoners the prospect of any *choice* of liberation.[84] To the contrary, Badiou insists that "for there to be such disalignment, some sort of pressure is needed, a push from outside, which designates, in my vocabulary, its *evental* character."[85] The event, that is, marks a violent departure never occasioned *by* oneself insofar as it involves most signally a departure *from* oneself; indeed, from Badiou's perspective, the truth of resurrection that Paul declares pertains less to the particularity of Jesus's miraculous return from the dead than to the universalization of Paul's emergence as a radically new subject, "an immortal," from out of the body of Saul.[86]

Irrupting unpredictably as a negation of "what is," the event that generates life out of death and that fractures, for de Man, "what is not true" requires, as Badiou reminds us, "something that exceeds the order of thought."[87] For just this reason it defies translation into anything "teachable, generalizable, and highly responsive to systematization." To the contrary, such systematization relies on the adequacy of a given situation's language to an expression of the truth, while an event, by breaking from the constraints imposed on "the possibility of possible things," allows for the naming of what that situation excluded from language and thought.[88] Manifesting itself through an incursion of the Real that comes as a "push from outside," the event thus precludes its transmission as knowledge in the language of "what is." Badiou makes this point quite clearly: "The idea that one can only accede to another way of seeing by means of force opposes the idea according to which what matters is the acquisition of a new knowledge. But if one were to unveil to the spectators [i.e., Plato's prisoners] the mechanics by which appearances were engineered, that wouldn't change very much; they would, perhaps, be 'stunned and bothered'—and that's all."[89] Attempts to explain the machinery of appearances bind us to appearances all the more because the language available for explanation belongs to the *world* of those appearances. The rupturing of illusion, by contrast, involves the dissolution of what we are and a radical distancing from the language that enables knowledges and opinions (the language Badiou identifies as the situation's "encyclopedia"). But the naming of the event invariably yields a new subject-language in turn, one that "appears to the outside observer both arbitrary and contentless."[90] This *declaration* of a truth-event, this forcing of the indiscernible to appear in the situation that it explodes, breaks faith with the Real of the event itself by naming within the order of signification the void that exceeds all naming. The event, that is, as a "push from outside," attests to the division in language that generates its beyond. Rather than interrupting a given language, it interrupts language *tout court*, sweeping away the reality that a linguistic regime constructs and forcing, in its manifestation, not the naming of a truth (which would betray the event's negativity), but, more radically, *a separation from the order of naming*, a separation from the order through which "entities," in de Man's formulation, "come into discourse."

This dismantling of the definitional coherence by means of which entities take form, so that "the clear distinction between history and interpretation can no longer be taken for granted," is qualified, at the start of "The Resistance to Theory," as the thing that "should not be taught" (4). It becomes, however, by the end of the essay, the thing that *cannot* be taught. One can only, at best, assert it by way of a reading tripped up by its own demonstration that knowledge is unreliable. Insofar as this mode of reading (de Man defines it as "rhetorical") entails the "methodical undoing of the grammatical construct and . . . [the] disarticulation of the *trivium*," it shares with theory, in de Man's understanding, the properties of the drive: "boring, monotonous, predictable, and unpleasant" (19), it exerts a pressure that splinters the world made coherent by the linking of grammar, rhetoric, and logic in the trivium. Such readings, reinscribing the cut of ab-sens in the language of sens-absexe, function as "theory and not theory at the same time, the universal theory of the impossibility of theory" (19), according to de Man. With his essay's well-known conclusion, "Nothing can overcome the resistance to theory since theory *is* itself this resistance" (19), de Man returns to the split that makes teaching "what should not be taught" impossible even as it makes it inevitable that we teach "what is not true." To put this otherwise, theory's self-resistance asserts the incompatibility of method with the knowledge that method produces—an incompatibility that has the effect of dividing knowledge against itself. What should not be taught, as we have seen, is the void in knowledge or sense, the necessary seizure of the subject by something inarticulate, overwhelming, and destructive, like the jouissance by which Ignacio is seized from behind in *Bad Education*. The lesson offered by *Funny Games*, Haneke's "awakening slap," is that its lesson can never be transmitted as knowledge but only through violence to the subject and the subject's ways of knowing and being.

Diegetically and extradiegetically both, *Funny Games*, like Sade, enacts an attempt to procure the Other's jouissance, its liberation from itself, although Haneke explicitly denies his film's implication in such perversion: "I've heard this reproach of sadism that you level against me before, but it is totally unwarranted. The artist's role is to scratch where it hurts, to unveil what no one wants to see or to know."[91] Yet the language with which he rejects the charge gives his (funny) game away. One does not, customarily, "scratch where it hurts" but rather where it itches; and far from yielding unwanted results, such scratching brings (short-term) relief. This subliminal suggestion of respite from an itch informs the more patent aggressiveness expressed by the will "to scratch where it hurts." With his second figure for the artist's task— "to unveil what no one wants to see or to know"—Haneke identifies this vulnerable location, the place "where it hurts" to scratch, as the eyes. These two figures, occupying syntactically a relation of *apposition*, operate at the same time, conceptually, in a relation of *opposition*: the former threatening blindness while the latter compels one to see. If their common denominator is the violence imposed on vision from without, then that violence implicitly entails a release, like the scratching of an itch—a release in excess of what the subject "want[s]" and situated, in its compulsory repetition, at "the outer extremity of pleasure," the *atopia* of jouissance. It is there, at that extremity, that Haneke and the intruders play their games, inflicting a "pain" that targets illusion and unveils "what no one"—or, perhaps, no "one"—"wants to see or to know." To the extent that such games are "funny," they bring out that signifier's suggestion of something peculiar, perverse, or odd (as something strange or queer can be said to have something funny about it). Their "fun" or "funniness" springs from the collision of normative, predictable, rule-bound reality with the anarchic force of an alternative universe where rules get changed at will. Though Peter and Paul, like the Marx Brothers, disturb the hum of the social machine, they do so "knowing" that the reality they shatter is nothing but a lure and that the family they terrorize suffers "but in a fiction, in a dream of passion," as Hamlet says of the player.[92] Peter and Paul *act* as sadists knowing full well that they and the Family are "really" images in a film—a status sadistically underscored when Paul rewinds *Funny Games* itself, undoing Anna's revenge and showing that our attachment to the Family expresses our investment, like the Family's, in Imaginary illusion.[93]

Even more: the Family *allegorizes* Imaginary illusion. With their generic Hanekean names, Anna and Georg embody not only their class's privileged aestheticism but also the aesthetic privilege of realism, the genre allied with that class. They allegorize, by extension, the reading practice that realism implies: one rooted in legible appearances, the self-evidence of reality, that realism takes for granted. Such reading turns into *mis*reading, though, whenever applied to allegory. By taking itself—and its world—at face value, by ignoring its metarepresentational status, the Family succumbs to what Barbara Johnson calls "the temptation of immediate readability."[94] As a result, it fails to recognize what Peter and Paul know from the outset: that the Family is not the representation of an empirical, real-world family but the *representation* of that representation—specifically, its representation within the conventions of home-intruder and torture-porn cinema. In this sense, as de Man writes of allegory, Haneke's film makes "reference to a meaning that it does not itself constitute."[95] As the cinematic self-awareness of the intruders (and the seriality of the murders they commit) makes clear, the Family exists only as an image of itself, as an "allegorical sign" that "refer[s] to another sign that precedes it" and whose meaning "consist[s] only in the *repetition* (in the Kierkegaardian sense of the term) of a previous sign with which it can never coincide."[96]

By signaling this abyssal division between the sign and its seeming referent, Haneke's film, like allegory, becomes a reflection on its own method, which is to say, a theory of reading. But just as theory, in de Man's analysis, thinks its difference from itself, so allegory leads to a similarly insistent moment of negativity. If "allegories . . . are always allegories of the impossibility of reading" for de Man, then that impossibility undoes the logic by which they would lead us to knowledge.[97] To the extent that allegory generates modes of reading nonetheless, it does so by seeming to repudiate the "temptation of immediate readability," of Imaginary illusion. But the "belated" readability that allegory promises, the superior understanding that follows its demystification of immediacy, is another mystification. The movement toward knowledge in allegory's characteristic act of unveiling ("to unveil what no one wants to see or to know") veils once more the gap inherent in the signifying system. Such unveilings, after all, reinforce the idealism of aesthetic education by purporting to move us from blindness to a state of insight or understanding; in fact, they return us to the conflict between method and the knowledge that method makes possible.

Haneke's comments on *Funny Games* contradictorily assert the need for violence to free us from illusion ("to scratch where it hurts") and the possibility of liberation by means of allegorical unveiling ("to unveil what no one wants to see or to know"). Peter and Paul, on the other hand, recognize what Haneke's remarks obscure: that the liberation promised by allegory and aesthetic education consists only in the negative knowledge that knowledge itself is grounded on nothing—a nothing whose violent undoing of reality, whose dismissal of "what is," finds its positivization in the various catachreses of negativity. Peter and Paul, in this regard, are more upfront than Haneke; they have the courage of *his film's* convictions as they unleash the relentless violence meant to "teach" the Family that nothing.

Pace Haneke, violence cannot "unveil what no one wants . . . to know"; our knowledge, as *Funny Games* implies, is always already a veil that blinds us to what we *cannot* know: whether our "ethical and aesthetic values" have any more substance than the murdered family; whether our awakening from imaginary illusion is the illusion the Imaginary requires; whether the good that disorganizes life is the same as the death drive that destroys it. What alternative to aesthetic sublimation, then, can *Funny Games* hope to offer? Does its voiding of ethical and aesthetic values appeal to a new set of values and a new aesthetic in turn? If Haneke claims to be offering a lesson that his film seems not to endorse, if *Funny Games* fails to sustain the pedagogical project he assigns it, then perhaps the film's negation, its queer undoing of our sense of "what is," consists in affording us nothing more than this psychic and conceptual violence: the violence it does to the conceptualization and mastery of reality and to the hope of breaking the bonds that enslave us to the nothing, the void, the pure division that the subject "is." Reading, analysis, and interpretation all seek to redeem that violence through allegorical unveiling, itself the labor of sublimation. That is what meaning means. But the insistence of that violence expresses the queerness of the negativity we view as evil: the violent negativity of the enjoyment to which the subject as such is chained and from which it succeeds in escaping only as Georg, Anna, and Schorschi do. "It gave me a lot of pleasure to give a sort of awakening slap, to say 'look at what you normally look at!'"

4

There Is No Freedom to Enjoy:

Harriet Jacobs's Negativity

By unleashing its sadistic aesthetic against aesthetic education's promised freedom, *Funny Games* foregrounds a structural antagonism internal to the aesthetic itself: an antagonism that emerges from the distance between the autonomy the aesthetic promises and the heteronomy it entails. Even Friedrich Schiller, while praising the exemplary freedom the aesthetic makes visible, finds himself snared in the contradictions produced by such exemplarity. Conscripted to a pedagogical function that binds "the whole fabric of aesthetic art" to "the still more difficult art of living," Beauty, in Schiller's description of it as "released . . . from the fetters of every aim" (a condition he sees expressed in the sculpted faces of Greek gods), paradoxically imposes on the aesthetic the aim of exemplifying this aimlessness, this absolute of freedom, "in order to incite [the human being] into the ideal world."[1] Schiller may acknowledge as "self-contradictory . . . the notion of a fine instructive (didactic) or improving (moral) art," adding that "nothing is more at variance with the concept of Beauty than that it should have a tendentious effect upon the character," but he bases his argument for aesthetic education on "the cultivation of Beauty," understood precisely as the "instrument" whereby our "character become[s] enobled."[2] Though humanity may be "chained . . . to the material" in his view, the aesthetic lifts it to the realm of abstraction and allows it to reflect on the material world with which it no longer identifies.[3] Hence, "contemplation (reflection) is Man's first free relation to the universe."[4]

As Walter Benjamin would argue, however, such a notion of freedom is purchased at the cost of collectivity and political engagement. Carolin Duttlinger, tracking

Benjamin's ideas about attention, contemplation, and distraction, sums up the views on aesthetics and autonomy that he held while writing "The Work of Art in the Age of Mechanical Reproduction": "In modern secularized society, . . . contemplation not only loses its liberating potential but is in fact exemplary of a pervasive trend towards social fragmentation and isolation. As a result, [Benjamin] argues, the residues of religious practice in bourgeois art reception do not lead to greater (self-)awareness but are more akin to the secular state of absorption, which Benjamin criticizes in 'Über das Grauen.' Unlike in his earlier text, however, Benjamin's critique is not primarily psychological in focus, but concerns the social and political consequences of such contemplative reception."[5] Schillerian aesthetic autonomy, as evinced in the self-enclosure common to the aesthetic object and the contemplative subject, carries with it, according to Benjamin, a threat of political quietism. By contrast, the modes of distracted reception excited by encounters with urban architecture or by cinematic spectatorship enact a heteronomous subordination to forms of collective experience.[6]

In "A 'Hive of Subtlety': Aesthetics and the End(s) of Cultural Studies," their jointly written introduction to a special issue of *American Literature*, Christopher Castiglia and Russ Castronovo explore one consequence of this antagonism inherent in the aesthetic that leads to irresolvable tensions between autonomy and heteronomy, withdrawal and engagement, the individual and the collective, and freedom and limitation. Though grounding their remarks in the specific context of American cultural studies, they identify a more general complication in the politics of the aesthetic: "Cultural Studies, with its attention to the social conditions and settings that make aesthetic contemplation a privilege available to relatively few, keeps us alert to the dangers of making aesthetics inherently progressive. In a corollary and countervailing gesture, however, cultural studies, with its attention to the unpredictable nature of these social conditions and settings, keeps us alert to the parallel fallacy of discarding aesthetic process as inherently conservative."[7] Taking issue with theorists like Fredric Jameson, who construes as a repression of social engagement what he called the "aesthetic revival" in criticism at the end of the twentieth century, Castiglia and Castronovo insist that the aesthetic "can, in fact, facilitate collective becoming, and, with it, collective social interests."[8] In doing so they suggest that the aesthetic's "return" more properly designates its rehabilitation for progressive political ends.

Conservatives, after all, have never renounced the utility of the aesthetic (and its corollary, disgust) in consolidating communities of taste, even if that taste swings wildly between assertions of cultural supremacy and populist opposition to cultural elitism. In the wake of the civil rights era, the United States has incubated conservative ideologies that simultaneously denounce high culture for its association with privilege and decry the displacement of that culture's pantheon of European-descended white males. If the aesthetic collectivizes "the people" in the conservative imaginary, this "people" generally possesses a racial and ethnic specificity, notwithstanding its framing as universal (or, at the very least, as national). Taking seriously the normative implications of such a conservative aesthetic, Fred Moten describes the racial logic of Western subjectivity as the invention of a "transcendental aesthetic," an aesthetic of "abstract, equivalent citizens" conjoined in the political community he describes (not unironically) as "civil society."[9] Similarly, Sylvia Wynter attributes the origins of racial subjectivity to a "bio-aesthetic system of figuration" that "sets limits to [the] Subject's mode of imagining . . . and, therefore, to the knowledge it can have of its world."[10] This aesthetic shapes the normative framework within which reality makes sense; conservative defenses of the aesthetic, therefore, coincide with defenses of that framework and that normativity both. Simon Gikandi puts it bluntly: "We cannot understand the idea of autonomy and transcendentalism in the ideology of the aesthetic outside of its economy of exclusion."[11] Proponents of the aesthetic's contemporary "return" aspire, by contrast, to affirm the aesthetic's potential to produce an *inclusive* community, one that Castiglia and Castronovo invoke as "an alternative, post-identity collectivism."[12]

This (re)turn of the aesthetic also reflects an impatience with what Rita Felski calls "the limits of critique." It can signal, in such cases, an attempt to escape a hermeneutics of suspicion expressed in paranoid, symptomatic, deconstructive, and ideological modes of analysis, all of which stand accused of performing a constraining and predictable set of moves that subordinate aesthetic objects to history, rhetoric, or politics. Drawing on the currency of affect theory in its numerous iterations, Felski observes that reading "is not just a cognitive activity but an embodied mode of attention that involves us in acts of sensing, perceiving, feeling, registering, and engaging." It is on this that she stakes her claim for the transformative power of the aesthetic: "To speak of a stylistics of existence is to acknowledge that our being in the world is formed and patterned along certain lines and that aesthetic experience can modify or redraw such patterns. . . . We give form to our existence through the diverse ways in which we inhabit, inflect, and appropriate the artistic forms we encounter."[13] The aesthetic, so framed, is said to afford what critique alone cannot: a change in our being, and not just our thought; a freedom from the hold of the patterns to which we had previously been bound; a freedom, that is, from what Wynter sees as the limits on our "mode of imagining" that follow, as Wynter recognizes, from the dominant aesthetic itself.

Over a decade after collaborating with Castronovo, Castiglia, hailing the "post-critique" moment to which Felski's work responds, refers to it as potentially "the most significant dispositional shift [in literary criticism] since the advent of the New Historicism."[14] He quotes Stephen Best and Sharon Marcus to explain his own enthusiasm for this renewed engagement with the aesthetic: "I believe that, as Best and Marcus assert, 'immersion in texts (without paranoia or suspicion about their merit or value)' can result in an 'attentiveness to the artwork as itself a kind of freedom.'"[15] Let us bracket just what this attentiveness means (a return to Schillerian contemplation?); let us bracket, as well, what immersion means and how it can evade the metaphorics of depth associated with paranoia and suspicion. Let us focus exclusively on the freedom claim being made on behalf of the aesthetic, a claim deeply rooted in the transformative potential that Castiglia links with "speculation, idealism, hopefulness, and their combination in what I've been calling imagination."[16] Like José Esteban Muñoz before him, Castiglia finds in Ernst Bloch support for his interpretation of hope, which he links to aesthetic imagination, as the engine that frees us from "the tyranny of unchallengeable facts" and the "inevitability . . . of the purported real"; only this imaginative freedom from fact permits us, Castiglia argues, to envision "counterworlds."[17]

This view of the aesthetic as the gateway to freedom, like the preference for hope over fact, echoes Schiller's association of the aesthetic with the imaginative liberty of "seeing," which he distinguishes from perception. "What we *see* through the eye," writes Schiller, "is different from what we *perceive*. . . . As soon as seeing acquires an absolute value for [Man], he is already aesthetically free also."[18] Such seeing, like the liberating immersion in art that Castiglia endorses through Best and Marcus, corresponds to the subordination of fact to the autonomy of aesthetic imagination, which Schiller understands as delight in "mere appearance" or form.[19] By exercising this faculty, Schiller argues, humans discover their sovereignty: "Since all actual existence derives its origin from Nature, as an extraneous power, but all appearance comes originally from Man, as percipient subject, he is only availing himself of his absolute proprietary right when he separates the appearance from the essence and arranges it according to his own laws. With unrestrained freedom he can join together what Nature has sundered, as soon as he can think of it together, and separate what Nature has combined, as soon as he can separate it in his intellect."[20]

Castiglia, however, parts company with Schiller when it comes to the imagination's intervention in the world. With regard to aesthetic autonomy, Schiller insists that the human "possesses this sovereign right positively only in the *world of appearance*," only "in the unsubstantial kingdom of the imagination."[21] The aesthetic, in other words, frees us precisely by freeing us *from* the actual, and it loses, for Schiller, its aesthetic status once harnessed in the service of reality, even if that instrumentalization intends to alter the reality we know. Schiller puts this plainly: "Only insofar as it is *candid* (expressly renouncing all claim to reality), and only insofar as it is *self-dependent* (dispensing with all assistance from reality), is appearance aesthetic. As soon as it is deceitful and simulates reality, as soon as it is impure and requires reality for its operation, it is nothing but a base tool for material ends and can prove nothing for the freedom of the spirit."[22] Displaying here what Paul de Man calls "idealism as an ideology," Schiller, as de Man goes on to observe, "posits the possibility of a pure intellect entirely separated from the material world, entirely separated from sensory experience."[23]

This is not to say that Schiller denies the aesthetic any social consequence; to the contrary, he sees the aesthetic as the necessary condition for social relation. "Beauty alone," he famously observes, "can confer on [Man] a *social character*. Taste alone brings harmony into society, because it establishes harmony in the individual. All other forms of perception divide a man, because they are exclusively based either on the sensuous or on the intellectual part of his being; only the perception of the Beautiful makes something whole of him, . . . only the communication of the Beautiful unites society, because it relates to what is common to all of them."[24] The commonality to which Schiller refers, however, is the common pursuit of an aesthetic state that severs our thralldom to the actual, not a common investment in actualizing an imagined aesthetic state. That commonality, moreover, as Moten rightly notes, presupposes a universal aesthetic, which is also an aesthetic of universality attached, as Schiller makes clear by referring to the indifference of the gods in Greek sculpture, to a particular ethnocultural history that it (mis)represents as the apolitical investment in an ideal.[25]

The different interpretations of aesthetic freedom in Castiglia and Schiller correspond, if inexactly, to what Jacques Rancière calls "an originary and persistent tension between the two great politics of aesthetics: the politics of the becoming-life of art and the politics of the resistant form. The first identifies the forms of aesthetic experience with the forms of an other life. The finality it ascribes to art is to construct new forms of life in common and, hence, to eliminate itself as a separate reality. The second, by contrast, encloses the political promise of aesthetic experience in art's very separation, in the re-sistance of its form to every transformation of form into life."[26] The return of the aesthetic as endorsed by Castiglia, who stands in for a host of others here—including Felski, Marcus, and Best—partakes of the hope, essential to progressive appropriations of aesthetic discourse, invested in what Rancière describes as the "becoming-life of art." From this perspective, the aesthetic evinces the creativity of life itself and allows us, as Rancière puts it, "to con-struct new forms of life in common." This is what Castiglia and Castronovo suggest when they declare that "illusion, masquerade, deception, artifice, and any other terms that connote the ultimate ideological bankruptcy of aesthetic practice can, in fact, facilitate collective becoming, and, with it, col-lective social interests."[27] So conceived, the virtue of the aesthetic lies in its capacity to envision the lineaments of a world beyond the present one, but the political end it's made to serve is the reconstruction of *this* one, through the freedom of imagination, in terms of the *oneness* of a collectivity modeled on the aesthetic union of "the sensuous" and "the intellectual."

By this logic, moreover, the freedom, which is also the autonomy, of the aesthetic (as invoked by Castiglia's emphasis on its "turning away from facts") paradoxically reinforces its submission to the heteronomy of social reality.[28] Elizabeth Maddock Dillon recognizes as much when, echoing Castiglia and Castronovo's joining of the aesthetic to "collective becoming," she writes, "It seems important to view aesthetic judgment in its connection with commu-nity function and thus with heteronomy."[29] To this extent, the contemporary return of the aesthetic among thinkers on the left is largely the return of the *politics* it purports to supersede. But rather than leading to more critique or to what Felski reads as routinized gestures of ideological unmasking, the re-turn of the aesthetic recurrently "discovers" something no less predictable and no less predetermined: the imaginative positing of counterworlds to counter the intolerable burden of ideologically determined fact. Castiglia puts it as follows: "Facticity, in Bloch's account, serves the interests of the privileged, but anticipatory illuminations turn the real into a fantastic—and vigilant—hope."[30] Though what he refers to here as aesthetic "illuminations" both escape and transform "the real," Castiglia's reference to Bloch seems to challenge his celebration of aesthetic hope at the expense of critique as neg-ativity. How do we *know* that facticity "serves the interests of the privileged" except by performing the sort of critique—whether paranoid, suspicious, or symptomatic—against which Castiglia poses the aesthetic? And what props up the vigilance of hope but Castiglia's a priori faith in the imagination's dis-positive relation to the factual world from which, he claims, it turns? On the basis of such a presumed relation, Paul Gilmore affirms a similarly political vision of aesthetic hope: "Aesthetic experience could become a precondition to greater political and social freedom and equality by imagining a universally shared terrain in place of the delimited ground of identity politics."[31]

One need hold no brief for "identity politics" to hesitate before Gilmore's predication of freedom on a "universally shared terrain," which is to say, on the sort of "transcendental aesthetic" discussed by Moten. Gilmore's desire for universality speaks to an investment in the aesthetic, to quote Rancière, as "a living tissue of experiences and common beliefs in which both the elite and the people share"—an investment, therefore, in producing, as Rancière goes on to suggest, "a 'consensual' community, not a community in which everyone is in agreement, but one that is realized as a community of feeling."[32] Such a community, however, as Rancière makes clear, comes at the cost of the aesthetic autonomy from which it purports to spring. The privileging of the aesthetic for its alleged independence from the world of "unchallengeable fact" turns out to have been the projection of a political vision all along—a vision wholly determined by the "facticity" it supposedly escapes. As if speaking directly to Castiglia, for whom the return of the aesthetic explicitly hinges on the imaginative "suspension of reality"—that is, on the suspension of the political, social, and cultural reality of the world as given—Rancière asserts, "Aesthetic metapolitics cannot fulfill the promise of living truth that it finds in aesthetic suspension except at the price of revoking this suspension, that is of transforming the form into a form of life."[33] The "suspension of reality," to put this otherwise, responds to the imperative to *transform* reality by means of this very suspension, which, in consequence, is never really a suspension after all. Castiglia and Castronovo affirm this transformation of "form into a form of life" when they characterize the aesthetic as a mode of "collective becoming." With this they partake of a Deleuzean tradition that aspires, in the words of Levi Bryant, "to formulate an *ontology* . . . that locates intelligibility at the level of the aesthetic or the sensible itself," thus making the aesthetic a resource for the apprehension of new ways of being.[34] Insofar as this politics of the aesthetic is determined by the reality it purports to suspend, it engages a process of "becoming-life" that coincides with *becoming-intelligible*. As Immanuel Kant points out in the *Critique of Judgment*, "It is necessary that the imagination in its freedom be commensurate with the lawfulness of the understanding."[35] Indeed, the very point of this (re)turn to the aesthetic for progressive political ends lies in the intelligibilization, the critical translation into new forms of life, of what the imagination conjures beyond the "facticity" of the actual world. Rather than just *affective* access to what that world forecloses, the aesthetic would give *cognitive* access to it as well, allowing us to grasp what a given reality casts outside of sense. The aesthetic politics of "becoming-life" thus must posit the aesthetic as, simultaneously, sufficiently *other* than factual reality to be free of its conceptual limitations and sufficiently *intimate* with factual reality to model new modes of collective life.

In this way the aesthetics of becoming-life constrains the imagination to serve once more the ends of intelligibility. For all that this version of the aesthetic may insist on affect and embodiment, its social and political mobilization rests, as Felski puts it clearly, on our "inhabit[ing], inflect[ing], and appropriat[ing] the artistic forms we encounter."[36] The pedagogical corollary of her project, as she implicitly acknowledges, is wholly cognitive: teaching her students "*to think carefully* about their attachments" will allow them to "move beyond the stultifying division between naïve, emotional reading and rigorous, critical reading."[37] But the ostensible movement "beyond... division" wherein students "think carefully about their attachments" maintains the obvious privileging of careful thought over "naive" reading. Like the aesthetic, "attachments" must submit to the language of critical intelligibility even in the effort to overcome the "limits of critique." Whatever falls outside the frame of a community's intelligibility, whatever that community possesses no critical language to "think," will therefore elude recognition by the aesthetic imagination as well. If the foremost stake in this return of the aesthetic for progressive political ends is its ability to offer, through imagination, forms of thought not bound by the conceptual restrictions of the world as it is, then we must ask what happens when the aesthetic itself, in Sylvia Wynter's words, "sets limits to [the] Subject's mode of imagining." Or, alternatively, what happens if we take the notion of aesthetic autonomy seriously, recognizing the aesthetic as separate from and ex-centric to actuality and, therefore, as incommensurate with the assumption of its intelligibility?

This prospect shapes the second of Rancière's "two great politics of aesthetics," the "politics of the resistant form," which asserts the "radical separation of the sensorium of art from that of everyday aestheticized life," permitting the aesthetic to "[retain] its purity, avoiding all forms of political intervention."[38] This position conceives the aesthetic as so thoroughly self-enclosed that it succeeds in eluding human thought, "refusing every form of reconciliation," and "maintaining the gap between the dissensual form of the work and the forms of ordinary experience."[39] Like the becoming-life of art, however, it still holds out, as Rancière explains it, a metapolitical promise for the organization of the world. On the one hand, that promise inheres in art's very *separation* from the world, suggesting a possible freedom from reality and its hierarchies of value; on the other hand, and to me the more interesting one, it inheres for Rancière in the aesthetic's "testimony to the power of the Other."[40] The politics of the resistant form insists on "the shock of the *aistheton*, attesting to the mind's alienation from the power of an irremediable alterity. The work's sensible heterogeneity no longer vouches for the promise of emancipation. On the contrary, it comes to invalidate every such promise by testifying to the mind's irremediable dependency with regard to the Other inhabiting it."[41]

Referring to the work of Jean-François Lyotard to conceptualize this aesthetic Otherness, Rancière invokes the *differend*, a Lyotardian term he borrows to name a relation of "pure difference," a relation defined by the nonrelation between the mind's "conceptual determinations" and the "sensuous matter" that the mind is incapable of grasping or presenting, although it consists of such matter itself.[42] But Rancière touches, however briefly, on another reading of alterity in the politics of the resistant form when he describes it as "grounded in a notion of art as that which testifies to the immemorial dependency of the human mind on the unmasterable presence that, following Lacan, [Lyotard] calls the 'Thing.'"[43] As tantalizing as this suggestion is, Rancière does little to expand on the connection between the Lacanian "Thing" and the aesthetic. I choose, nonetheless, to press on it here for the challenge it poses to the return of the aesthetic as a mode of "collective becoming"—a challenge responsive to the insistent pressure with which queerness and Blackness, as catachreses of ab-sens, fracture the ontological ground sustaining the aesthetics of collectivity.[44]

The Lacanian Thing, as we saw in chapter 1, designates the "beyond-of-the-signified" incapable of signification.[45] Negatively inhabiting the Symbolic as its constitutive exclusion, it testifies to the presence of the null set in every account of the world as it "is" and to the persistence of something uncounted, because uncountable, in every collective. Misnamed by every name that turns its nothing into something, the Thing eludes the intelligibility proposed by its catachreses. Neither intelligible nor sensible, it sidesteps the logic of sense. Where Schiller views the aesthetic as surmounting the division between "the sensuous" and "the intellectual," the Thing, as ab-sens, instantiates the radical priority of division as such, a division that is not a division *of* something but, rather, an originary division. Only through the prior subtraction of ab-sens as meaningless cut or subtraction is the thought of being made possible, but that same subtraction also makes the thought of ab-sens *im*possible.

The subtraction that constitutes ab-sens for Lacan is central to his theorization of sex, which, insofar as it is designated by ab-sens, remains inaccessible to meaning. As the senselessness of the cut or division cut off to yield sens-absexe, which positivizes "sexual difference," sex is misrecognized, metaleptically, as the effect of its absenting. For just this reason Lacan maintains that "there is no sexual relation" and that man and woman, the so-called halves purporting to totalize the subject positions available to the speaking animal, are merely linguistic positings that dissimulate ab-sens. Queerness, as I have argued, rather than offering a vague umbrella identity for nonnormative sexual practices, catachrestically figures the ab-sens that designates sex in psychoanalysis, the ab-sens that queers the fantasy of sexual complementarity by escaping the order of sense. As a placeholder for the inconceivable Thing beyond intelligibility, it appears, from the dominant perspective of the becoming-life of art, as the anti-aesthetic, the aesthetic's inverse, which is to say, the obscene. If, as Rancière asserts, the politics of the becoming-life of art and the politics of the resistant form share "a common core linking the autonomy of art to the anticipation of a community to come," then the queerness excluded from community, the queerness that figurally embodies the void unrecognized in every collectivity, manifests itself as the obscenity that marks the Other of the aesthetic.[46]

Major thinkers of Afropessimism theorize Blackness in similar terms. Noting that "it [is] impossible to divide slaveness from Blackness," Frank Wilderson proposes that since "the structure by which human beings are recognized and incorporated into a community of human beings is anti-slave," the Black remains "a sentient being for whom recognition and incorporation is impossible."[47] Fred Moten, wittily placing himself "in apposition" to Afropessimism, remarks, "I am in total agreement with the Afropessimistic understanding of blackness as exterior to civil society," and he concurs that from within "the coordinates of the transcendental aesthetic," "blackness is nothing, that is, the relative nothingness of the impossible, pathological subject."[48] He then generates a number of questions: "What's the relationship between blackness, thingliness, nothingness, and the (de/re)generative operations of what Deleuze might call a *life* in common? . . . Can there be an aesthetic sociology or a social poetics of nothingness?"[49] Although he answers in the affirmative ("In the end," he writes, "*life* and *optimism* are the terms under which I speak"), Afropessimists like Jared Sexton offer another response: "The question that remains," writes Sexton in his respectful engagement with Moten, "is whether a politics, which is also to say an aesthetics, that affirms (social) life can avoid the thanatological dead end if it does not will its own (social) death."[50]

The contemporary return of the aesthetic is far from willing its own social death, making it less a return than an extension of an aesthetic politics whose two major aspects, as Rancière asserts, find their "common core" in a commitment to "a community to come." With its promise of a redemptive collectivism, this aesthetics that returns without having left can realize such a community only by perpetually excluding the void, the *inform*ulable within it, that gets embodied in catachrestic forms (like "the queer," "the Black," "the woman") produced *to be abjected*. These catachreses of impossibility function as the aesthetic's obscene remainders: as fleshed-out versions of the (no)Thing cast out to secure an aesthetic community. In the ethics of collectivity, obscenity is definitionally irredeemable; it can have no aesthetic value without ceasing to be obscene.

The aesthetic, in this, is *bound* to an ethics, specifically to an ethics of desire. Our earliest seizure by the aesthetic coincides with our very precipitation as subjects through identification with the image of the other in which we first glimpse an integral self. The ethical relation of the self to the other takes shape in the human from the outset by this internalization of an aesthetic image, a totalized form, *as* the self—an aesthetic form whose apparent totality determines our paradigm of being. That totality, however, can offer no image of queerness, or Blackness, or sex, though later, under certain regimes of visibility, their catachrestic positivizations may appear. Queerness, Blackness, sex, and ab-sens, as names for the primal subtraction that renders totality not-all, oppose to the aesthetic's ethics of desire (which is the desire for aesthetic unity) the anti-aesthetic expressed by the drive, the undoing of totalized form.

What *drives* this incessant return of the aesthetic, which comes back, to ever-renewed acclaim, to where it has been all along? Rooted as it is in an ethics of desire, why is the aesthetic constrained to repeat the repetition of compulsion's negativity when its goal is precisely to surmount negativity through the totalization of form? Perhaps, as I've suggested, the answer leads back to its origins in the mirror stage that elicits the subject through anticipation of the unity of the "I." The image in the mirror is never whole; it marks and is marked by the distance that divides it from the proto-subject perceiving it (a subject who discovers not only itself but also its rival in the mirror). In mobilizing the logic of division while initiating the movement of desire, the mirror invokes, by negation, what never appears in the form of an object: the negativity of division as such. Out of that division, the other of the aesthetic emerges too: the Real that dissolves our reality, the obscenity wherein we never are but without which we could not be. That radical division with no name of its own, though the names it assumes are legion (including queerness, Blackness, woman, and trans* as signifiers with no positive meanings), is the site of the subject's unfreedom, the place where all claims of aesthetic liberation, self-possession, and autonomy founder. But it is also, as Alenka Zupančič maintains, the singular *condition* of our freedom: the place of the subject's self-constitution insofar as "there is no Other of the Other, no cause behind the cause."[51] Determined by nothing beyond that division as it expresses itself in the drive, the subject is not *subjected to* the drive as a constraint or a form of unfreedom but, instead, is *subjectified by* it. In her juxtaposition of Kant and Lacan, Zupančič reminds us that, according to each, "man is not only much more unfree than he believes, *but also much freer than he knows.*"[52]

Freedom, in fact, is something the subject is *incapable* of "knowing" since its realization takes place at the level of the drive and not of desire, expressing itself in a jouissance indifferent to the subject who experiences its self-interest as that of its aesthetically totalized self. Rather than pertaining to the self as the primal mimesis of aesthetic form (the coherence of the image in the mirror), freedom inhabits the gap or division *internal to* the aesthetic and resistant to its totalizations. The subject of desire's pursuit of completion through the objects, the things, it cathects inverts the drive's fixation on the object *a* with which *nothing* coincides. Lacan makes the point in Seminar XX that "object *a* is no being. Object *a* is the void presupposed by a demand."[53] This aspect of the void finds its corollary, he tells us, in the metonymy that propels us through a sentence from its beginning to its end, instantiating, in his account of it, "a desire that is based on no being."[54] In this radical of desire uncoupled from any objectal realization we encounter the negativity of the void evoked by Lacan in "ce n'est pas ça": "'*That's not it*' means that, in the desire of every demand, there is but the request for *object a*."[55] That "request," in its negativity, constitutes the drive as the radical of desire: as the subtraction of desire from any positivization in an object. This "ce n'est pas ça" tracks closely with the de-ontologizing force of Frantz Fanon's "n'est pas" ("Le nègre n'est pas. Pas plus que le Blanc") as incisively glossed by David Marriott: "Too many readings of Fanon want to say what this 'n'est pas' is, to explain it away as mere negation in the manner, say, of Freud or Hegel. It seems necessary to be able to locate blackness in terms of what negates it, or, more precisely, to be able to attach predicates to it to make it recognizable (it seems to be characteristic of these readings to assume at least the possibility that blackness can be incorporated as a thing, or else as an identity or subject whose demands can be met and its referent duly agreed on)."[56] With this distancing of Blackness from the "predicates" intended to bind it to a referent and this foreclosure of its incorporation in "an identity or subject," we see the commonality of Blackness and queerness as catachreses for what is never "recognizable" in the form of "the Black" or "the queer."

In this context, we might reconsider Paul Gilmore's claim : "Aesthetic experience could become a precondition to greater political and social freedom and equality by imagining a universally shared terrain in place of the delimited ground of identity politics." The aesthetic—*itself* an "identity politics" inseparable from the subject's constitutive self-identification *as a subject*—cannot procure the subject's "freedom," from a psychoanalytic point of view, any more than universality can avoid its status as not-all. The only universality a psychoanalytic concept of freedom acknowledges is the drive's attachment to a jouissance at odds with the (aesthetic) identities through which we imag(in)e ourselves and the world. Such a freedom, because it is inaccessible to the subject's conscious desires, can serve as the ground for no political program or collective social engagement. Attending to the historical logic by which G. W. F. Hegel could justify the enslavement of Africans as "an essentially emancipatory project," Andrea Long Chu asks a series of questions raised by the drive as well: "Can we think freedom without the future? What would a radically presentist notion of freedom look like? Would we even recognize it as freedom?"[57] Even the Marquis de Sade, in his most orgiastic scenes, filters his evocations of the drive through the lens of the libertine's putative "liberty," making it, at worst, a wearisome task to which the libertine accedes and not what it is for psychoanalysis: an imperative that sidesteps the will.

Slavoj Žižek gives us a better image of the drive's relation to freedom when he discusses the fate of Karen in Hans Christian Andersen's "The Red Shoes."[58] While the woman by whom she was raised lies dying, Karen, eager to attend a ball being thrown that night in town, turns her thoughts to the shiny red shoes in which she takes inordinate pride. Thinking it can do no harm to look at, to handle, or even to wear them, she decides to put them on. No sooner has she done so than they prompt her to abandon her place by her guardian's deathbed and make her way to the ball. Once there, the shoes take control of her movements, becoming one with her feet and making her dance without rest. Far from gaining the pleasure she imagined or the freedom of action she desired, she experiences herself as coerced by the shoes, in which she now feels imprisoned. They exert, like the drive, as Žižek puts it, "a kind of impersonal willing" that "exacts satisfaction at any price, irrespective of the subject's well-being." But Karen, who perceives this willing as something alien to her desire, determines to escape it. Toward that end, she persuades an executioner to cut off her feet with his axe. Still ensconced in the shoes, her feet dance away while Karen, now crippled, devotes herself to a life of penitence and devotion, "free" of the enjoyment to which she had found herself driven by the shoes. But as Žižek rightly reminds us, while no subject can ever "subjectivize" the drive and "assume it as 'her own,'" it "operates in her very kernel," expressing "that which is 'in the subject more than herself'"; indeed, to the extent that "desire is the desire of the Other, while drive is never the drive of the Other," only the latter can express the subject's freedom from external determination.[59] Only it reveals, in the words of Zupančič, "no Other of the Other, no cause behind the cause," thus escaping heteronomy.

Unlike what Rancière discusses as the aesthetic politics of the resistant form—where the work "no longer vouches for the promise of emancipation. On the contrary, it comes to invalidate every such promise by testifying to the mind's irremediable dependency with regard to the Other inhabiting it"—the drive's insistence, as "The Red Shoes" depicts it, interimplicates enslavement and emancipation. It testifies not to what is Other than the subject but to the division that the subject "is," to its (negative) ontology. Intolerable to our cathected self-image, the negativity that emerges from within the aesthetic (not for nothing do the red shoes begin as the beautiful objects of Karen's desire) occasions not only the disavowal of the compulsion such negativity exerts (as when Karen asks that her feet be cut off) but also its sublimation, its rerouting toward socially sanctioned ends, like the penitence that demands of Karen, just as the red shoes did, submission to a will not her "own." If the compulsion of the drive gets negated here as the antithesis of aesthetic freedom only to be refigured as Karen's subservience to the mandate of celestial law, then we can recognize the underlying affinity in the tale between religion and the obscenity it demonizes, an affinity that shows how the drive's sublimation, aesthetic education's goal, preserves, in its own negativity, the obscenity it subl(im)ates.

Thus, the constant return of the aesthetic corresponds to the constant pressure of the drive; in seeking to counter the drive's enjoyment, aesthetic sublimation reinforces it. In the same way, the freedom the aesthetic proposes finds its predicate in constraint: not just in the constraint by which the subject escapes enchainment to materiality (by chaining that devalued materiality to the abstraction alleged to transcend it) but also in the literal enchainment of those it excludes from rational thought and reduces to material objects. Like philosophy in Alain Badiou's account, the aesthetic, as a form of education, "wants to know nothing about jouissance" *and for just that reason* is bound to it, like Hegel's lord to his bondsman.[60] And just as that latter relation, for Lacan, provides the template for viewing philosophy as the theft of the slave's jouissance, so it also describes the structure supporting Schillerian aesthetic freedom, with its privileging of the "idleness and indifference," the release from "the fetters of every aim, every duty, every care," that allows for "Man" to become himself insofar as *he is only wholly Man when he is playing.*[61] If, as Schiller argues, "we shall never be wrong in seeking man's ideal of Beauty along the selfsame path in which he satisfies his play impulse," then Beauty, in its "self-sufficiency" as a "completely closed creation," closes out those consigned to the work that frees others from the "fetters of . . . care."[62]

Exploring the central position of race in the formation of such an aesthetic, Gikandi observes that "proponents of the aesthetic sought to use blackness as the counterpoint to beauty and enlightenment and then to relegate it to the margins of their discourse."[63] Responding to Elaine Scarry's defense of beauty as a spur "to repair existing injustices," he remarks, "It is perhaps true that concerns with beauty do indeed make us hanker for justice and just solutions to our social problems, but still, if this claim is to be taken seriously, if we are to associate beauty with an immanent idea of justice, then we need to consider its counterpoint: the injuries done to the bodies of those considered to be outside the domain of the beautiful and the injustice committed on these bodies in the name of beauty."[64] But we needn't stop there. We should also consider the injustice done to those excluded from the realm of being, those figured as its negation to defend the concept of aesthetic totality against its own inherent antagonism. These are the queer, the Black, the monstrous, the alien, the irrational, the nonhuman in all its various iterations, and they include, as Harriet Jacobs makes clear in *Incidents in the Life of a Slave Girl*, those persons who, though acknowledged as "beautiful," belong to a category whose negation defines and sustains aesthetic community. For a "slave girl" in the American South, Jacobs notes, "If God has bestowed beauty upon her, it will prove her greatest curse."[65] How could individual beauty, when associated with those made to figure the obscenity at odds with what Schiller calls "the ideal of Beauty, which Reason sets up," fail to incite to obscenities those who claim to embody reason while, in its service, enjoying slaves?[66]

Chu, in the course of arguing that "Hegel's remarkable stomach for slavery in fact reflects his commitment to freedom," reminds us that in the *Philosophy of History* Hegel maintains that "slavery is itself a phase of advance from the merely isolated sensual existence—a phase of education—a mode of becoming participant in a higher morality and the culture connected with it."[67] This notion of "education," crucial to Hegel's view of world history as the realization of Reason, bears all the hallmarks of the aesthetic: the repudiation of jouissance (here figured as "sensual existence"), the necessity of exclusionary violence (implicit in the concept of "slavery"), the promise of sublimation ("becoming participant in a higher morality and the culture connected with it"), and a vision of totality (the world historical movement toward the universal freedom of world spirit). As the *object* of slavery's "education," however, Jacobs sees it otherwise; rather than elevating the enslaved to the status of "participant[s] in a higher morality," slavery reduces the culture at large to the level of "sensual existence." Yet her argument for freedom, like Frederick Douglass's, relies on the aesthetic principles that justified slavery as their corollary; freedom, in her framing, still rests on the constraint and exclusion of jouissance, which is also to say, of the queerness or obscenity linked to the drive's compulsion.

Gikandi helps us to situate this contradiction in a larger historical context: "Just as the aesthetic could become a key index in the violence of modernity, it could also provide the subject of this cruelty with the hallowed place where utopian dreams could be nurtured and secured."[68] Important as such a reminder is, it scants both the costs and the consequences of those "utopian dreams" that envision, like the (re)turn to the aesthetic among thinkers on the left, an all-inclusive community, free of fracture or antagonism. Saidiya Hartman, in her reading of Jacobs, confronts more directly what she identifies as the "cross-hatchings of slavery and freedom," the inextricability, that is, of freedom from a logic of compulsion, revealing, as she puts it, "the indebtedness of freedom to notions of property, possession, and exchange."[69] Collocating freedom's "indebtedness" to compulsion with education's sublimation of the drive, I want to trace how Jacobs and Douglass, while refusing the Hegelian defense of slavery as world historical pedagogy, preserve the supremacy of reason used to justify that pedagogy and, like Hegel, oppose rationality to "sensual existence" or jouissance. In short, they endorse a pathway to freedom that entails an aesthetic education still premised on the exclusion of the Real, the irrational, and the obscene—exclusions enacted by abjecting catachrestic embodiments of queerness and of Blackness.

In attempting to "convince the people of the Free States what slavery really is," Jacobs, writing as Linda Brent, repeatedly turns to the image of a child, in particular a female child, in order to drive home its horrors (5). Whether describing the torment of women in slavery stripped of access to their children or evoking the terror of those children on discovering what having a master means, she correlates the institution's monstrosity with its violations of sexual and familial norms, violations that give children in slave-owning households—those raised in the bosom of the master's family no less than those raised by his slaves—early exposure to what Jacobs calls "the unclean influences every where around them" (47). Slavery, which she characterizes in a memorable phrase as "that cage of obscene birds" (48), becomes for her the paradigm of queerness as bad education: a violent pedagogy of corruption that leaves a "blight on . . . children's souls" (48).

Displaying everywhere an economy of enjoyment predicated on the slave-owner's absolute power over the bodies of the enslaved, slavery inculcates, in Jacobs's view, a general subversion of moral law by the law of the state that permits it, a law that openly acknowledges the obscene foundation on which it rests. By exempting the relation of slaveholders to the persons they enslave from laws that otherwise regulate interpersonal encounters (since slave law defines that relation as one between a person and that person's property instead of one between subjects holding a *property in themselves*), slave law *authorizes* the enjoyment otherwise accessible by transgression alone. This opens a dangerous conceptual space that allows for the spectacle of *possible* persons (the slave can pass from the condition of property to that of "free" subject, after all) treated as objects of pure enjoyment because they are put, by the law itself, outside the law's protection. If this calls to mind the state of exception and the condition that Giorgio Agamben associates with the figure of *homo sacer*, the one abandoned by the law, it produces more immediately for Jacobs a threat to the moral or natural law that she raises above the laws of the state.[70] Such natural law, as Jacobs sees it, retains its full significance even when seemingly suspended by the authority of state law.

We can see this in the well-known passage where Jacobs refers to the intuition of those enslaved that news about the legality of their enslavement, although concealed from them in the South, might be available in northern journals:

> One woman begged me to get a newspaper and read it over. She said her husband told her that the black people had sent word to the queen of 'Merica that they were all slaves; that she didn't believe it, and went to Washington city to see the president about it. They quarreled; she drew her sword upon him, and swore that he should help her to make them all free.
>
> That poor, ignorant woman thought that America was governed by a Queen, to whom the President was subordinate. I wish the President was subordinate to Queen Justice. (42)

Lauren Berlant, in a reading of this moment that anticipates Castiglia's alignment of aesthetic imagination with "speculation, idealism, hopefulness," argues that Jacobs uses it both to "show how dominated people find ways to sustain their hopefulness in a cruel world" and to demonstrate that "the kinds of invention, innovation, and improvisation her illiterate interlocutor practiced with only partial knowledge could be used radically, for the re-imagination of collective political life within the nation."[71] To this I would add that it *also* invokes the sovereignty superior to written law that functions for Jacobs as the only ground on which the legitimacy of the law can rest. In that sense the figure of a higher law embodied by the "queen of 'Merica" can indeed "be used radically," as Berlant rightly puts it, but "radically" in the sense of lacking a specific political orientation, in the sense, that is, of its ability to sustain antithetical ideological positions and sociopolitical beliefs.

Explaining her refusal, after escaping to the North, to purchase her freedom from the man who continued to claim her as his slave, Jacobs writes, "I knew the law would decide that I was his property, and would probably still give his daughter a claim to my children; but I regarded such laws as the regulations of robbers, who had no rights that I was bound to respect" (155). This opposition of a natural or moral law to the written law of the state establishes the basis for every form of antinomian practice. It subtends, as a consequence, resistance to law by the right and the left alike. As Rebecca Hill writes in an analysis of John Brown's abolitionist fervor, "Scholars writing about John Brown in the 1970s connected his disturbing use of violence to the revolutionary left. Today's historians are just as likely to compare the 'antinomian' Brown to right-wing evangelical Protestant militants, as represented by the anti-abortion terrorist Paul Hill."[72] The tension that elicits these seemingly antithetical historical comparisons is at least as old as *Antigone*, the text Lacan discusses in *The Ethics of Psychoanalysis* to illuminate the relation of drive and jouissance to the law.[73]

Antigone's refusal of Creon's decree that her brother remain unburied expresses, for Lacan, a tension between the state law wielded by Creon and the chthonic law, the law of the earth, that Antigone calls the unwritten law of gods more ancient than Zeus. Lacan explains as follows: "These are no longer laws, νόμος [nomos], but a certain legality which is a consequence of the laws of the gods that are said to be αγραπτα [agrapta], which is translated as 'unwritten.' . . . Involved here is an invocation of something that is, in effect, of the order of the law, but which is not developed in any signifying chain."[74] This imperative, pertaining to "the order of the law" but unwritten, unarticulated, and unacknowledged within the order of signification, launches

Antigone into "the field of the Other," beyond the limits of the human.[75] She thus fully assumes her responsibility to the Kantian moral law, whose requirements can never be satisfied by mere obedience to codified rules. Moral law remains αγραπτα because it is unspecified in advance—and all persons must formulate maxims to embody its categorical imperative. In this they become responsible both *for* it and *to* it at once. Such a law, as Kant understands it, drives the subject beyond itself, beyond, that is, the self invested in its formal coherence, its aesthetic unity, and toward the "immortal" self that sees such self-interest as pathological. If Lacan construes the death drive as leading us out of aestheticized selfhood, then that drive performs an education in the etymological sense of the term (from *educere*, "to lead out") that opposes itself to the program of Schiller's aesthetic education. It offers a radically different lesson in the subject's relation to freedom, one it never ceases to repeat because one we can never learn. Insisting on the division between reality and the Real, the division *that generates them both*, the drive propels the subject beyond its imaginary coherence, beyond the limits of its desire, and so beyond the law of the state that regulates the good of the self in terms of the collectivity. Like the slave woman Jacobs describes as invested in a law superior to the president's, Antigone appeals to an absolute authority, a Truth, beyond that of the state; and as the slave envisions the "queen of 'Merica" drawing her sword on the president, so Antigone opposes Creon's law in the name of one unwritten.

We must say of the queen of America, then, and of Jacobs's attachment to the moral law whose authority that figure personifies, that the violence implicit in her unsheathed sword raises questions similar to Lacan's when he challenges the common view of Antigone: "Is she, as the classic interpretation would have it, the servant of a sacred order, of respect for living matter? Is hers the image of charity? Perhaps, but only if we confer on the word charity a savage dimension."[76] Jacobs, even more than Antigone, can seem remote from such a "savage dimension," the dimension, as we saw in chapter 1, that Jean Allouch connects with the *décharite* of psychoanalysis itself. Leaning heavily on the rhetoric of Christian morality, her narrative can distract us from its frequent jabs at how churches pervert divine law:

> They send the Bible to the heathen abroad, and neglect the heathen at home. I am glad that missionaries go out to the dark corners of the earth; but I ask them not to overlook the dark corners at home. Talk to American slaveholders as you talk to savages in Africa. Tell *them* it is wrong to traffic in men. Tell them it is sinful to sell their own children, and atrocious

to violate their own daughters. Tell them that all men are brethren, and that man has no right to shut out the light of knowledge from his brother. (65–66)

Ironizing her reference to "savages in Africa" by excoriating the heathen savagery abetted by churches in the West, Jacobs reveals the "savage dimension," the antinomian violence, that puts her own understanding of justice above that of the US institutions claiming access to sacred law.[77]

This savage dimension, linked for Lacan with the jouissance of the drive, makes the invocation of unwritten law so dangerous and so appealing. Of course, the division of law between codified ordinance and the unwritten principles that ground it animates the political dissensus that keeps the law open to revision. If it thereby assures the possibility of continuously reimagining collective existence, this division also speaks to the queerness, the element of enjoyment, on which the law relies. With regard to the specificity of written law, this takes the form of its positing of its universal purview while imposing the interests and protecting the enjoyment of particular persons or groups; and where the notion of unwritten law is concerned, it takes the form of a violent insurgence against the legitimacy of legal authority, an insurgence that enacts the enjoyment of transgression and, with it, the insistence of the drive from whose grip the law is imposed to protect us.

Rebecca Hill's work on radical politics draws out the implications of the two types of law as they relate to this "savage dimension":

> This antinomian claim to access God's plans, also made by Nat Turner, is the principal claim to authority for people who are excluded from the process of lawmaking and legal participation in any society in which religion plays a significant role in politics. While it is commonsensical that placing oneself above the law, particularly when justifying the use of force, can lead to terrible consequences, the labeling of such resistance as by definition antidemocratic carries its own risks. Those who level such charges as the "antinomian heresy" against antislavery activists of the nineteenth century not only must wonder at taking sides against Anne Hutchinson, but also should grapple with what it means to call for the rule of law in an era when slavery was officially legal. As such, attacks on [John] Brown's violence rest on the continuing erasure of the fact that slavery was a reign of terror.[78]

Now my own point is neither to endorse nor to condemn appeals to an authority "above the law" but rather to note that this authority derives from the same ungrounded positing, the same initiating violence, as that of the written law itself. As Walter Benjamin puts it, "There is inherent in all such violence a lawmaking character."[79] In breaking from the dictates of established law, that violence enacts, as does written law, a *particular* mode of enjoyment aiming to regulate enjoyment *universally*. Hill effectively makes this point in her characterization of slavery. By calling it, correctly, a reign of terror, she justifies the mimetic violence of John Brown's insurrection against it.

But her resort to that phrase, "a reign of terror," produces a telling complication. In general use it refers not to long-entrenched state institutions (like those sustaining the ancien régime or the antebellum South) but instead to the republican attempt to realize, amid the chaos of the French Revolution, the absolutism of a transcendent law unleashed in order to destroy them. While the system of slavery clearly relied on the violent deployment of terror, so, too, did the struggle against it as waged by John Brown, Nat Turner, or even, in Jacobs's narration, the queen of America. Not because the translation of persons into property has any moral equivalence to acts that resist such dehumanization, but rather because the authority presupposed by each of these antithetical visions would dissolve a governing framework of law (through secession in the South or through the queen's resort to arms against the president) in the name of a higher law. Each enacts a form of enjoyment that the other aims to foreclose by turning the other's enjoyment into a figure for the queerness, obscenity, or terror against which a new law arises.

Each, therefore, *from the other's perspective*, exemplifies bad education by exhibiting the flagrant libidinal indulgence of a radical enjoyment (the erotics of slavery, on the one hand, and Nat Turner's insurrection, on the other).[80] Though there was never a queen of America to raise her sword against the president, when Nat Turner raised *his* against slave-owning families, his rebellion was rapidly quashed. Hundreds of Blacks across the South were killed in retribution, and others lost the right to gather in public, to bear arms, to travel unaccompanied, or to preach without white persons present. Jacobs notes that in Linda Brent's neighborhood, slaveholders, made anxious by the rebellion, "came to the conclusion that it would be well to give the slaves enough of religious instruction to keep them from murdering their masters" (61). If the hope of spiritual deliverance held out by this ideological "instruction" was intended to dissuade the enslaved from the jouissance of armed revolt, it ignored the fact that from an early age, according to his *Confession*, "religion . . . principally occupied [Nat Turner's] thoughts" and that the Spirit who urged him to rise up against the power of the "Serpent" did so by asserting that "the time was fast approaching when the first should be last and the last should be first."[81] Christian spiritual indoctrination, the template of the West's identification of pedagogy with sublimation, offered a higher authority against which to judge the slaveowner's sins. Both Turner and Jacobs, in their different ways, would seize on the moral ground it provided to resist the law that authorized slavery's pedagogy of obscene enjoyment.

Jacobs, in particular, assails that pedagogy, arguing that slavery schools in vice everyone it touches. Raised "in an atmosphere of licentiousness and fear" (45), the slave girl, however hard she tries to preserve her "pride of character" (29), is destined to find that "the lash and the foul talk of her master and his sons are her teachers" (45). Those children raised as the master's own learn to emulate his eroticized power, but his slaves, among whom no small number might also bear his genes, learn to master, instead, their resistance to his use of their bodies and his thwarting of their wills. Jacobs recounts Linda's bitter instruction, shortly after she turned fifteen, in the sexual designs of Dr. Flint, the name Jacobs gives to the master of the household where Linda was enslaved: "He peopled my young mind with unclean images, such as only a vile monster could think of" (27). Surrounded by "monstrous intimacies," to borrow Christina Sharpe's canny phrase, Linda locates the master's monstrosity, paradigmatic of "the secrets of slavery" (33), in the sexualization to which he subjects her, in the obscenities masked by the aesthetic vision of "beautiful groves and flowering vines" (66) that contributed to the romanticized notion of slavery as "a beautiful 'patriarchal institution'" (66).[82] With no recognized claim to personhood, she inhabits a space, as Hartman puts it, in which "compulsion eclipses choice, as neither right nor protection secures the line between consent and nonconsent."[83] In such a context she can only lament that "there is no shadow of law to protect her from insult, from violence, or even from death" (27).

"No shadow of law": to the contrary, the very law that puts her in her master's hands gives license to his licentiousness. As property she is fully his to enjoy and to cultivate for surplus value. "Every where the years bring to all enough of sin and sorrow," Jacobs muses, "but in slavery the very dawn of life is darkened by these shadows" (28). What she calls the "shadow of law" may fail to offer her protection, but that shadow returns in the evils described as the "shadows" "of sin and sorrow." Ironically, these latter shadows *do* enjoy shelter in the "shadow of law" and thereby shadow the "shadow of law" with their own particular darkness. Engaged, then, in a battle of wills not only with her "master," whose desires she seeks to frustrate, but also with the national consensus that makes him her master *by law*, Jacobs must work to discredit the law and solicit its protection at once. Her project, that is, must try to distinguish the "shadow of law," construed as shelter, from the obscenity "of sin and sorrow" that shadows the law itself.

And how better to image the darkness of vice that contemporary slave law sanctioned than by showing its inevitable complicity in the moral corruption of the young? "Even the little child," Jacobs notes, "who is accustomed to wait on her mistress and her children, will learn, before she is twelve years old, why it is that her mistress hates such and such a one among the slaves. Perhaps the child's own mother is among those hated ones. She listens to violent outbreaks of jealous passion, and cannot help understanding what is the cause. She will become prematurely knowing in evil things" (28). As if to underscore its importance, Jacobs, after Dr. Flint has prevented her marriage to the free Black man she loves, repeats this phrase in explaining her decision to take a white man as her lover: "The influences of slavery had had the same effect on me that they had on other young girls; they had made me prematurely knowing, concerning the evil ways of the world" (49). What is this knowledge that comes too soon if not the knowledge that corrupts, perverts, or queers by destroying innocence, polluting the mind, and, thereby, "compell[ing the child] to realize that she is no longer a child" (28)? Such premature knowing enacts a violence made explicit by this reference to compulsion: the violence of a spoliation that the text, repurposing the rhetoric of sentimental fiction, identifies as "moral ruin" (48). Taking this as her central figure for the legal injustices of slavery, Jacobs posits as universal the law's responsibility to children, and, by extension, to the family as the purported institutional safeguard of children's innocence.

But if innocence, in this context, entails freedom from the threat of inappropriate knowledge, then the law, whose sheltering shadow Jacobs solicits for protection, could bar such contamination only by enforcing a concept of privacy that relies on the state as the public institution authorized to establish, regulate, and maintain the distinction between private and public. Drawing on Berlant's incisive reading of *Incidents* as "a counterpornography of citizenship," Bruce Burgett makes this point by showing that Jacobs "remains torn between her belief that (sexual) privacy ought to be a right accessible to all and her realization that, without acts of publication like *Incidents*, privacy will remain a source of privation for sexually, racially, and economically exploited subjects like herself."[84] The privacy in which the sexual takes cover, then, must not lend its sheltering shadow to improper, immoral, or illegal acts. The state, therefore, reserves the right to adjudicate the line between public and private, thus opening the private to the very publicity, the very politicization, from which the state was invoked to defend it. This pinpoints the difficulty that Jacobs confronts not only in soliciting the shadow of law but also in detailing her narrator's encounters with the obscenities she excoriates for "violating the most sacred commandments of nature" (27).

The South's "peculiar institution"—where *peculiar*, as Aliyyah Abdur-Rahman remarks, signifies not only "distinctive" but also, and more pejoratively, "aberrant" or "queer"—brushes with the taint of obscenity both Jacobs's "blighted" childhood and her efforts to publicize the "premature knowledge" of the obscenities that blighted it.[85] As Lydia Maria Child anticipated while helping Jacobs (as fraught as that assistance was) bring her text to publication, *Incidents* could be read as participating in the circulation of the "unclean images" that instantiate for Jacobs the moral depravity of slavery.[86] In her editor's introduction to *Incidents*, Child defends its discussion of matters that might well be considered "indelicate," including its references to sexual predation, by arguing that such publicity aims at "arousing conscientious and reflecting women at the North to a sense of their duty in the exertion of moral influence on the question of Slavery" (6). But Jacobs, as this phrasing acknowledges, can do so only to the extent that she succeeds in exciting—in "arousing"—those women. As Deborah M. Garfield astutely puts it, Jacobs, so framed by her editor, "must starkly impose her sexual ordeals on a white counterpart's bashful listening . . . becom[ing] the satanic tempter whose candid whispers risk blighting the white auditor's purity."[87] Once Jacobs localizes the violence of slavery in a sexualized knowledge that falls like a "blight on . . . children's souls," that blight, like the queerness from which it springs, attaches to all who engage it.

Now suppose we were to place beside Jacobs's depiction of slavery as public obscenity the terms in which Vladimir Putin has defended Russia's law against "gay propaganda." The point, of course, would not be to equate the experience of sexual minorities in Russia with that of persons in the African diaspora subjected to slavery and its ongoing afterlife. Instead, it would be to gain insight into questions of sexuality, publicity, and law by seeing what Jacobs's antinomian depiction of slavery's obscene education shares with the official discourse used to justify the Russian legislation. Signed in June 2013, the law prohibits, in any location where minors could encounter them, expressions or representations of "non-traditional sexual orientations" as well as the "obtrusive spreading of information about non-traditional sexual relationships that might arouse interest in such relationships."[88] In addition to sanctioning everything from rainbow flags to nonheterosexual displays of affection in public, the law, as Katherine Weber explains it in the *Christian Post*, prohibits "the 'propagation' of information relating to homosexuality in the country, invoking heavy fines on those who seek to spread information about the lesbian, gay, bisexual and transgender community to minors."[89] For Jacobs in North Carolina as for Putin in contemporary Russia, the "shadow of law" is solicited to shelter the young from the blight of obscenities considered to "violat[e] the most sacred commandments of nature" (27). As Russia's Constitutional Court affirmed in upholding the validity of the law, the government has a legal duty to "take measures to protect children from information, propaganda and campaigns that can harm their health and moral and spiritual development."[90]

What Jacobs calls premature knowing—even when that knowledge, as we see in Russia, pertains to relations permitted by law (homosexuality is not illegal in Russia, as Putin often reminds his critics)—thus constitutes bad education, a freedom that undermines freedom and destroys the foundation of civil society. According to Putin, by "protecting children from the respective information"—information, that is, about the existence and oppression of "non-traditional sexual orientations"—the law also protects society against an aggressive imposition of foreign values: "It's about protecting us from rather aggressive behavior from some social groups who, in my opinion, are trying to impose their points of view in a rather aggressive way."[91] A year after Putin made this statement in an interview with CNN, Russia's Constitutional Court dismissed a challenge to the law in strikingly similar terms, citing "the need to protect the child from the influence of information that is capable of causing harm to his or her health or development, particularly information that is combined with an aggressive imposition of specific models of sexual conduct, giving rise to distorted representations of the socially accepted models of family relations corresponding to the moral values that are generally accepted in Russian society."[92] As the *Guardian* noted the following year, "The Kremlin increasingly portrays human rights as a western imposition, arguing that homophobic laws are a defence of local culture and values against western imperialism."[93] If slavery for Jacobs was a queer obscenity, queerness for Putin is an obscene enslavement to the decadence of the West. Before we get too comfortable, however, in our ostensible Western enlightenment, recall that a vociferous movement in France gained public support in 2014 for a boycott of schools based on rumors that the state intended to indoctrinate students in a "gender theory" that amounted to a form of homosexual propaganda.[94] Nor should we forget attempts in the United States, not always without success, to introduce state or local legislation prohibiting elementary and middle school teachers from any mention of homosexuality, even to counter homophobic bullying.[95]

Like the infamous Section 28 of the Local Government Act 1988 passed into law in Thatcherite Britain, both the Russian law and Jacobs's focus on children made "prematurely knowing" view the Child as the site of endangered freedom while defending familial structures that treat children themselves as a form of property. Indeed, a decade and a half before Jacobs published *Incidents in the Life of a Slave Girl*, Karl Marx, in *The German Ideology*, wrote that "the nucleus, the first form, of [property] lies in the family, where wife and children are the slaves of the husband. This latent slavery in the family, though still very crude, is the first property."[96] However critically he may view this structural domination that generates property, Marx refers to it as "the natural division of labour existing in the family," where this allegedly natural organization of our earliest social relations arises from the fact that, according to Marx, it "was originally nothing but the division of labour in the sexual act."[97] Jacobs, like Marx, will implicitly naturalize the property rights of the family, so that for her, as for contemporary Russian law and, indeed, for liberal thought in the West, the Child, though deployed as a figure for freedom from enslavement to sexual corruption, has no symmetrical freedom to *consent* to sexual knowledge or encounters. The Child, that is, though trained to believe it can refuse another's touch, has no sovereignty under law to accept it and so, like the slave, no freedom of will.

Jacobs recalls a telling event from her childhood in this regard. Her brother, Willie, being called on to serve both his father and his legal owner at once, was "perplexed to know which had the strongest claim upon his obedience" (12). He concluded that he ought to give priority of response to his owner in the eyes of the law. In the aftermath, however, he suffered his father's reproach: "You are *my* child," his father insisted. "And when I call you, you should come immediately, if you have to pass through fire and water" (12). The dilemma, like the emphasis Jacobs gives to her father's use of "my," makes clear the implicit structural parallel between the positions of child and slave.[98] So when Jacobs goes on, in the following sentence, to refer to her brother's subsequent fate in being sold to Dr. Flint, we might wonder, despite her assertion that "he was now to learn his first lesson of obedience to a master" (12), if that *first* lesson hadn't already been accorded him by his father. Indeed, a central distinction between free and enslaved women in Jacobs's text consists of the former's security in the possession of their children. "They are your own," Jacobs writes, addressing herself to free mothers among her readers, "and no hand but that of death can take them from you" (17). Though underestimating the degree to which the law's complicity with patriarchal privilege can take free women's children from them too, Jacobs endorses the dominant conception of children as the property of their parents. The enslaved woman's envious "They are your own" perceives children, like slaves, *as* owned.

The right, then, to keep one's children, as possessions, from premature sexual knowledge props up not only the enjoyment of exercising one's authority as a parent but also the enjoyment of a greater authority to be gained in the name of the Child: the authority over those whose freedoms interfere with one's property rights in the Child. For freedom embodied in the figure of the Child shows the paradox of freedom itself: it carries within it the libidinal enjoyment of subjecting the other to constraint by restricting his freedom to impinge on a property legally claimed as one's own. As the Russian Information Agency noted, in a news article about the Russian law (whose subject matter, on account of that law, required that it be labeled unsuitable for persons below the age of twelve), the Russian Constitutional Court, in the judgment that validated the law, determined that "the exercise of civil rights and freedoms could not be permitted at the cost of other people's rights," a formula whose inconsistency, whose absolute reversibility, reveals the shadow over any freedom seeking shelter in the shadow of law.[99] Insofar as the state is the arbiter of one's property right in oneself, that self remains a property whose ownership belongs to the state. The freedom of the subject is delivered to constraint by the state in the name of freedom, as witnessed by various court rulings during the presidency of Donald Trump that equal protection for trans* persons violated the right to religious freedom.

What should we make of it, then, when Frederick Douglass, arguing for the abolition of slavery, invokes, in *My Bondage and My Freedom*, a version of the Russian court's formulation? While describing his old master, Captain Anthony, as capable of "outrages, deep, dark, and nameless," Douglass asserts that the captain was not a monster, but the product of his upbringing, a victim, like Jacobs's slave girls, of what she calls slavery's "unclean influences": "Had he been brought up in a free state," Douglass writes, "surrounded by the just restraints of free society—restraints which are necessary to the freedom of all its members, alike and equally—Capt. Anthony might have been as humane a man, and every way as respectable, as many who now oppose the slave system."[100] In imagining Captain Anthony as he might have been had he been brought up in a "free state," Douglass denotes with the latter phrase those states that prohibit slavery. But that same phrase connotes a sort of freedom Captain Anthony has never known: the freedom that comes from restraining those freedoms associated with excessive enjoyment or with the "sensual existence" from which slavery, according to Hegel, is "a phase of advance." Douglass implies that Captain Anthony, having had the misfortune to be raised in a slave state, was himself condemned to a state of enslavement; for as Douglass observes of the slaveholder in his relation to the enslaved: "Reason is imprisoned here, and passions run wild."[101] The wildness of those passions finds full expression in the scene where Douglass witnesses the whipping of Esther ("a young woman who possessed that which is ever a curse to the slave-girl; namely,—personal beauty"), a scene Douglass describes as "a tempest of passion, . . . a passion into which entered all the bitter ingredients of pride, hatred, envy, jealousy, and the thirst for revenge."[102] In this moment, which Christina Sharpe adduces as one of slavery's "primal scenes," the master gives voice to "all manner of harsh, coarse, and tantalizing epithets" even while "protract[ing] the torture, as one who was delighted with the scene."[103]

Douglass frames this enslavement of his master's reason to "passions run wild" in implicit relation to the "joyous" condition in which Douglass spent his earliest years. Referring to his experience of enslavement as a child, Douglass muses that "the slave-boy escapes many troubles which befall and vex his white brother."[104] Elaborating on this notion in a bravura passage whose rhetorical brio deftly effects an inversion of freedom and enslavement, he revises the meaning of each of those terms in the context of a bad education:

> [The slave-boy] seldom has to listen to lectures on propriety of behavior, or on anything else. He is never chided for handling his little knife and fork improperly or awkwardly, for he has none to use. He is never reprimanded for soiling the table-cloth, for he takes his meals on the clay floor. . . . He is never expected to act like a nice little gentleman, for he is only a rude little slave. Thus, freed from all restraint, the slave-boy can be, in his life and conduct, a genuine boy, doing whatever his boyish nature suggests; enacting, by turns, all the strange antics and freaks of horses, dogs, pigs, and barn-door fowls, without in any manner compromising his dignity, or incurring reproach of any sort. He literally runs wild.[105]

As Douglass depicts it, the freedom enjoyed in our "genuine" or natural state corresponds to the brute, unregulated passions that put humans on a footing with beasts. Giving license to enactments of the rudest drives, to all that "his boyish nature suggests," the "freedom" bestowed on the "slave-boy" here exempts him "from all restraint." But it enslaves him to the domination of instinct and denies him the moral instruction necessary to the regulation of "civilized" life. As Douglass declares, "If [the slave-boy] can only manage to keep out of the way of the heavy feet and fists of the older slave boys, he may trot on, in his joyous and roguish tricks, as happy as any little heathen under the palm trees of Africa. . . . [He may] continue to roll in the dust, or play in the mud, as best suits him, and in the veriest freedom."[106] The slave's enjoyment of a happiness equal to what he might have known in Africa coincides with a distinctly ambiguous qualification of this "veriest freedom"; it is the freedom, after all, of a "heathen" to "roll in the dust, or play in the mud," the freedom to remain in perpetual thrall to "whatever . . . nature suggests."

Reinforcing the value Douglass finds in "the just restraints of free society," the untutored slave boy, who "literally runs wild," anticipates the description of Captain Anthony, whose "passions run wild" in his enjoyment of the property the law gives him in those he enslaves. Discussing "what Thomas Jefferson called the boisterous passions of slavery, the 'unremitting despotism' of the slave owners, and the 'degrading submissions' of the enslaved," Saidiya Hartman maintains that these "boisterous passions bespeak the dynamics of enjoyment in a context in which joy and domination and use and violence could not be separated."[107] Douglass and Lacan might allow us to add that the scene of enjoyment expresses not only the despotism of the slave owners but also their own determination by, their subjection to, what Douglass describes as the passions and Lacan would call the drive. Unlike Lacan, though, Douglass, in company with Jacobs, Putin, and the Russian parliament, identifies the human subject with reason, and the passions with what enslaves it, proposing, therefore, that freedom is always the proper restraint of enjoyment.[108]

Dissociating himself from the African heathen, whose animal enjoyment, unfettered by reason and "freed from all restraint," finds its counterpart in the obscene enjoyment of Captain Anthony and his fellow slaveholders, Douglass, in speaking for "reason," finds himself entangled in philosophical idealism. Ronald Judy suggests as much in *(Dis)Forming the American Canon* when he notes that Douglass accedes to the sign's subordination to meaning and thereby establishes a connection between legibility and humanity. For Douglass, as Judy explains it, the sign's materiality "becomes transparent in the act of reading. It has no meaningful value within the economy of signification, the value system, which reading constitutes. This transparency of the material sign enables Douglass to devalue writing, per se, by maintaining the fundamental immateriality of thought as discourse and situating value within that discursivity."[109] In doing so, Douglass affirms and enacts the subordination of jouissance to reason and of materiality to the idea, a subordination Badiou identifies as essential to Western philosophy: "The thesis according to which the libertine is unhappy, more unhappy than the wise man, is a foundational thesis of philosophy. It's Plato's thesis exactly: the evil person is unhappy. That's why, according to Socrates, [philosophy] works: because it's possible to tell people who have a choice between becoming tyrannical subjects of enjoyment or wise philosophers that the better choice is [philosophy]."[110] When he translates Plato's *Republic* in an effort to keep faith with its vitality, Badiou has Socrates espouse the notion to which Douglass subscribes above. Identifying three agencies at work in the subject—Thought, Affect, and Desire—Socrates maintains that in an ideal society "the rational agency will have to be dominant."[111] He then goes on to add, "Thought and Affect will keep an eye on Desire, so that, obsessed as it is with repeatedly seeking immediate pleasures, . . . it doesn't try to enslave the other two agencies and take power over the whole Subject."[112] If philosophy in the West intends from the beginning the subjugation of "radical desire," then it does so in the name of the subject's own "good": in the name, that is, of the subject's freedom to pursue the good through reason. Unlike enjoyment, which we all encounter in our own particular ways, the Idea, for Badiou, is the same for all and so "must be universal. It must be free of any element within it that would prevent its being shared by all."[113]

The universality of this Idea, like the idea of universality, orients the philosophical tradition for Badiou by constraining the particularity of "[d]esire," which in this case is closer to jouissance and registers, as Judy writes with regard to the sign's materiality, "no meaningful value." The freedom offered as the alternative to the subject's enslavement to desire, however, entails desire's enslavement to reason ("the rational agency will have to be dominant"), which leads to the enslavement or exclusion of those who figure jouissance, those catachrestically posited to embody the absence of reason. At issue for Jacobs, for Douglass, for Putin, and, mutatis mutandis, for us, is a battle between competing figurations of freedom that stand in for, or take the place of, incompatible figures of the subject: the philosophical subject, on the one hand, the sovereign agent of Symbolic Thought, and the psychoanalytic subject, on the other, the site of division, jouissance, and the drive.

While this might suggest a specular structure and the deadlock of symmetrical positions, that would neglect a crucial difference in the two interpretations of freedom. Philosophy's identification of freedom with reason's domination of desire presupposes a desire for freedom that reason alone can secure. Reason thus succeeds in constraining desire through the specific paideia of philosophy, which leads the subject toward "the good." But desire continues to dominate through the mask of reason itself as philosophy posits as a universal good its *particular* version of enjoyment, which is to say, the enjoyment unleashed by reason's domination of desire.

This universalization provides the ground for refusing the *other's* jouissance: a refusal that props up slavery and abolitionist rhetoric both and that generates the figure of queerness as universality's other, as what it necessarily excludes. Étienne Balibar suggests something similar in taking issue with the universalism he associates with Badiou: "The violent exclusion inherent in the institution or realization of the universal can take many different forms, which are not equivalent and do not call for the same politics. A sociological and anthropological point of view will insist on the fact that setting up civic universality against discriminations and modes of subjection in legal, educational, moral forms involves the definition of *models of the human*, or *norms of the social*. Foucault and others have drawn our attention to the fact that the Human excludes the 'non-Human,' the Social excludes the 'a-social.'"[114] Philosophy, for Badiou and Plato, in asserting the universality of reason as the good, ignores the particular enjoyment attaching philosophy to universalism in the first place, an attachment that even philosophy knows is far from universal.

By privileging reason over "sensual existence" and implicitly siding, in this regard, with a Hegelian moral education, Douglass and Jacobs repudiate slavery as a form of obscene corruption. But the Western philosophy their arguments echo has been attacked in the very same way: as a dangerous mode of enjoyment corrosive to the morals of the young. Indeed, for Badiou philosophers should *merit* the accusation that was leveled at Socrates; the philosopher's *duty*, he tells us, is to "corrupt the young" by virtue of promoting "the irresponsibility of thought . . . in the face of what is established."[115] Though affirming, thereby, the freedom of thought to resist opinion or law, Badiou insists that the philosopher must "make [this] irresponsibility itself a responsibility."[116] The philosopher, in other words, corrupts the young by preserving the excess ("l'excessif") characteristic of youth itself, its openness to the infinite possibility inherent in every situation, in opposition to the regulatory pressure exerted by "natural collectivities" such as "family, work, and fatherland" (la pression des collectifs naturels: famille, travail, patrie).[117] This excess, however, demands of Badiou assiduous qualification. It is "not necessarily the desire nor the will for excess" ([n]on pas forcément le désir de l'excès ou son vouloir) but rather the incommensurable element of a situation, what remains unrealized within it. Hence the "paradoxical subjectivization" (une subjectivation paradoxale) that philosophy pursues: it protects the irresponsibility of youth by effecting its transformation through thought into another responsibility, one opposed to the "ludic irresponsibility" (irresponsabilité ludique) instantiated by the Sophists.[118] Notwithstanding

Badiou's acknowledgment of the excess, the void or negativity, by which philosophy, like Lacanian psychoanalysis, breaks with what is (which Badiou, like Lacan before him, describes as "the service of goods"), he defines the philosophical imperative as the responsibilization of the excess, the jouissance, irresponsible to opinion or law. Only through this responsibility does philosophy lead to freedom.

Consider now the freedom that psychoanalysis proposes for the subject understood as subject of the drive. Though seemingly the mirror inverse of the philosophical subject's freedom, this freedom entails no correlative fantasy of subjugating Reason; to the contrary, it recognizes in reason the persistence of jouissance. Mladen Dolar puts it clearly: "The renunciation of enjoyment itself produces enjoyment; the very act of renouncing is always ambiguous, and there is never a subtraction of enjoyment that wouldn't be at the same time an addition, in the very same gesture. Fighting the enjoyment, advocating a suppression of the enjoyment, always turns into a remodeling of enjoyment, offering new ways of enjoyment rather than getting rid of enjoyment. Indeed, enjoyment appears as the one thing that can never be gotten rid of."[119] This explains the aporia of reason in the judgment by Russia's Constitutional Court that "the exercise of civil rights and freedoms could not be permitted at the cost of other people's rights." Insofar as the restraint of enjoyment for some will generate enjoyment for others, the subject's freedom of enjoyment invariably opens onto conflict. By refusing our dominant view of law as protection against potential harm, the freedom of enjoyment, as Lacan makes clear, invokes a violent universe governed by Sade's disquieting version of Kant's categorical imperative, "Let us take as the law, as the universal maxim of our action, the right to enjoy anyone at all as an instrument of our pleasure."[120]

Here we return with a vengeance to Jacobs's "cage of obscene birds" or to Douglass's vision of "passions run wild." Reflecting on the sense of repugnance this Sadean universe provokes, on the horror with which we tend to recoil from such absolute freedom and equality, Lacan writes, "If the same opening is given to all, one will be able to see what a natural society is like. Our repugnance may be legitimately related to that which Kant himself claims to eliminate from the criteria of the moral law, namely, to the realm of sentiment."[121] Few are willing to follow Lacan, Kant, or Sade in situating the "moral law" outside "the realm of sentiment," certainly not Jacobs, for whom the moral law brings reason and sentiment together. To be sure, as Hortense Spillers observes, the Linda Brent of Jacobs's narrative had no right, any more than Mrs. Flint, the wife of Linda's master, to "claim *her* body and its various productions . . . as her own," but the ethics that would follow from the freedom of enjoyment—or from living in a "natural society," to borrow the words of Lacan—would deny all of us, universally, a property in anything, including ourselves.[122] Such a thought, in a world contending with centuries of slavery and its aftermath and still coming to terms with the righteous indignation of those who see themselves in #MeToo, can scarcely be entertained.

For Guy Hocquenghem, however, amid the conservative reentrenchment that dominated France beginning in the 1970s, it felt urgent to keep faith with the slogan of the Front homosexuel d'action reévolutionnaire (Homosexual Front for Revolutionary Action), "Jouissons sans entraves" (Enjoy without limits)—a slogan that was taken up widely during the events of May 1968.[123] Rejecting the bourgeois imposition of the modern (neo)liberal consensus, Hocquenghem, in L'apres-mai des faunes (1974), proposes a queer theory avant la lettre that dares to claim an unbearable freedom for the subject of jouissance and that draws, in doing so, on the Sadean reframing of Kant discussed by Lacan: "In claiming sex as the property of the free and conscious person, one perpetuates the old deception. Our bodies belong to us—what sadness! That the body of each 'belongs to all who want to enjoy it' would make a more satisfying formulation."[124]

A more satisfying formulation, perhaps, but not a more pleasurable outcome. Because enjoyment exceeds the pleasure principle, extending into pain, it exposes the gap in the subject on which assertions of freedom must founder; the division between pleasure and enjoyment, after all, coincides with the gap between desire and drive, between aesthetic image and obscene remainder, thus troubling the distinction between the subject's experience of freedom and constraint. Lacan quotes Kant on the moral law to explain the subjective corollary to the acephalic act that evinces the psychoanalytic subject's freedom, the act that seems to be generated, like the compulsion to dance in "The Red Shoes," by something beyond, and against, our will: "We can see *a priori* that the moral law as the determining principle of will, by reason of the fact that it sets itself against our inclinations, must produce a feeling that one could call pain." Lacan then expands on this thought: "In brief, Kant is of the same opinion as Sade.... For in order to ... open the floodgates of desire, what does Sade show us on the horizon? In essence, pain. The other's pain as well as the pain of the subject himself, for on occasions they are simply one and the same thing. To the degree that it involves forcing access to the Thing, the outer extremity of pleasure is unbearable to us."[125] "Access to the Thing is "unbearable," that is, to the "free and conscious person[s]," in Hocquenghem's words, as which we view ourselves. The radical enjoyment that Lacan conceives as the "outer extremity of pleasure" becomes "unbearable" insofar as it drives us, without our awareness and against our will, toward the Thing, which is also the "nothing," the Real, the ab-sens that remains inarticulable in the signifying chain; it thereby attests, simultaneously, to the absolute of freedom (where freedom no longer submits to the heteronomy of "sentiment") and to the absolute of compulsion (where the freedom of the drive expresses itself subjectively as pain).

Bad education confronts the antagonism that this primal division occasions, the aporia inherent in freedom, and the violence of the catachreses that undertake to conceal it: in particular, the law and the law's obscene shadow, where the latter materializes the nothing of which the former means to be free. Like the Lacanian act, such a bad education affords, to quote Ed Pluth's account of the act in psychoanalysis, "a way of thinking about manifestations of freedom without the usual presupposition of a sovereign, conscious subject exercising the freedom."[126] It forces us out of our comfort zone, where freedom permits the willful pursuit of objects of desire, and plunges us into a nightmare space of radical egalitarianism in which conscious consent no longer trumps the freedom of the drive. In this world of unbound terror, as figured by Haneke's Peter and Paul, the subject is stripped of Imaginary coherence and any claim to aesthetic autonomy, dissolving into the *atopia* of what ab-sens designates as sex. We can no more own or own up to such queerness than we can escape our constitutive subjection to sense, as a result of which approaching the Thing, or the "outer extremity of pleasure," will always seem "unbearable."

But if queerness is to remain an active concern, an ongoing challenge to social constraint and not just another humanist plea for the normalization of those we currently describe as LGBTQ+, then we have to confront the abyss of enjoyment from which queerness, like the will to restrain it, springs, the abyss of enjoyment enslaving the subject to the dream of being free—free, that is, to enjoy and to be free of enjoyment at the same time: free to be and not to be by conceptualizing freedom only in the form of its regulation by law. Even when the dream of freedom insists on the freedom to "be" queer, to "be" Black, to "be" woman, while still retaining a property claim to one's body as one's own, such freedom dreams are ultimately dreams of being free *from* queerness, Blackness, or woman to the extent that each of those terms disrupts the consistency of being.

Such a freedom props up the master's self-universalizing enjoyment, the enjoyment of *denying* enjoyment (both the other's and his own) that instantiates his mastery and underlies philosophy. That's why Lacan associates philosophy with the freedom of the master when, after asking, "What does philosophy designate over its entire evolution?," he answers, "It's this— theft, abduction, stealing slavery of its knowledge, through the maneuvers of the master." And what knowledge does the slave possess for philosophy, in the form of the master, to steal? Lacan answers by referring to "the only thing that motivates the function of knowledge—its dialectic with *jouissance*."[127] Philosophy succeeds in appropriating, in "mastering," the slave's enjoyment by sublimating it as freedom, the freedom to *be* what the slave *is not*. As both Jacobs and Douglass make clear, however, such a notion of freedom is one that also (pre)occupies the slave, who seeks to come into being, like the master, through freedom from the negativity that is figured by the enslaved. By contrast, psychoanalysis stresses the *rupture* introduced by language that makes being always not-all.

In such a context, the tension that Rancière discerns between his politics of the becoming-life of art and his politics of the resistant form would not, as he proposes, dissimulate "a common core linking the autonomy of art to the anticipation of a community to come." Instead, it would signal the originary rupture that generates both politics and aesthetics (the one inseparable from the other) in order to repair or deny that rupture. If the politics of the resistant form attests to the "unmasterable presence that, following Lacan, [Lyotard] calls the 'Thing,'" then it relates to the becoming-life of art as psychoanalysis relates to philosophy. Just as the politics of the resistant form resists "the promise of emancipation . . . by testifying to the mind's irremediable dependency with regard to the Other inhabiting it," so it resists the freedom from enjoyment affirmed by philosophy in general and, more particularly, by the *political* philosophy of the becoming-life of art. In this the politics of the resistant form refutes the "anticipation of a community to come."

Tom Fisher, in a cogent reading of Rancière, observes a version of this dynamic, although he frames it in other terms:

> On the one hand, Rancière's political philosophy privileges the interruptions produced through the coming into speech, audibility, visibility, and "account" of those who are silent, inaudible, invisible, and of no "count." It is an egalitarian politics of dissensus and political justice. On the other hand, his thought on the aesthetic privileges the rupture of the sensible itself that does not give way, at least directly, to new speaking subjects or the expansion of the field of who and what can be heard. Instead, we might say, it is the rupture itself that resists its own recovery within a progressive narrative of an expanding field of speech and possibility.[128]

Politics, like philosophy, as Fisher reads Rancière, "redistributes the sensible to make new sense possible," allowing for a more fully inclusive community "when the natural order of domination is interrupted by the introduction of a part of those who have no part."[129] Fisher then quotes Rancière's assertion in *Politics of Aesthetics*: "The dream of a suitable political work of art is in fact the dream of disrupting the relationship between the visible, the sayable, and the thinkable, without having to use the terms of a message as a vehicle. It is the dream of an art that would transmit meanings in the form of a rupture with the very logic of meaningful situations."[130] In the movement between these two quotations, Fisher writes, the political force of interruption "gives way to an almost pure 'rupture' of the very scene in which something like 'meaning' itself might take place."[131] With this Rancière's politics of the resistant form seems to broach the "pure 'rupture'" of the Lacanian Thing, the negativity of ab-sens, insofar as it seems to break from "the very logic of meaningful situations." But Rancière, at just this moment, pulls back from the radicality of his claim, yoking it, instead, to the "dream of an art that would *transmit meanings*" (emphasis mine) by way of that rupture itself. With this the politics of the resistant form gets recuperated pedagogically, enmeshing it in the logic of transmission, the logic of pedag-archivalization, that continuously enacts a resistance to what Freud calls the death drive, Bataille calls consumption, and Derrida calls expenditure without reserve. Retreating from the particularity of enjoyment wherein psychoanalysis finds its field, Rancière reenacts the theft of jouissance by philosophy-as-master, wrenching the politics of the resistant form, like the becoming-life of art, into a vehicle for the transmission of meanings and the "anticipation of a community to come."

Jacobs, too, sounds a political hope for the advent of such a community, explicitly intervening, as Rancière would put it, to change "the distribution of the sensible which defines the common of a community, to introduce into it new subjects and objects, to render visible what had not been, and to make heard as speakers those who had been perceived as noisy animals."[132] But despite appealing to the moral law as the basis for a nonexclusionary community where reason and sentiment, working together, would guarantee freedom for all (where freedom means freedom from the enjoyment as which she conceptualizes slavery), Jacobs exhibits an enjoyment of her own when the "war of [her] life" (20) against her master becomes a "competition in cunning" (107) and her discourse of Christian fellowship (as ordained by "the heavenly Father, who 'made of one blood all nations of men'" [41]) gets entangled with the underlying aggression informing her relation to the law.

Jacobs announces at the outset that her "mistress had taught [her] the precepts of God's Word: 'Thou shalt love thy neighbor as thyself'" (11). As Lacan argues in Seminar VII, however, that injunction lets loose on our neighbors the superego that loves us all too well. In *Incidents in the Life of a Slave Girl* the narrator's grandmother inhabits the place of what Freud called the ego ideal, a concept Freud later conflated with the superego as such. The woman of whom Jacobs has Linda admit, "I feared her as well as I loved her. I had been accustomed to look up to her with a respect bordering on awe" (28), externalizes the Christian piety that Jacobs herself only *seems* to promote. When Linda and her brother chafe against the injustice of enslavement, their grandmother, Martha, encourages their submission to a wisdom beyond their own: "Most earnestly did she strive to make us feel that it was the will of God: that He had seen fit to place us under such circumstances; and though it seemed hard, we ought to pray for contentment" (18). The two siblings, like their Uncle Benjamin—who confesses to his mother, "I wish I had some of your goodness. You bear every thing patiently, just as though you thought it was all right. I wish I could" (23)—find in Martha's faith the embodiment of a *genuine* Christian ideal, one at odds with the hypocrisy practiced by white churchgoers in the South. Thus Martha can offer a spiritual comfort that the established church cannot: "She was so loving, so sympathizing! She always met us with a smile, and listened with patience to all sorrows. She spoke so hopefully, that unconsciously the clouds gave place to sunshine" (17–18).

In the unconscious of the text, however, the moral law Martha espouses, grounded in her faith that justice will arrive in God's time (and *only* through God's agency), yields to another embodiment of Linda's superego: her father. It is he who admonishes Linda's brother for choosing to respond to his master's call before responding to his father's: "You are *my* child. . . . And when I call you, you should come immediately, if you have to pass through fire and water." This demand for filial obedience, though, is also an act of resistance. It rejects the written law of the state, which gives authority to the master, in favor of the supposedly natural law of patriarchal privilege. Though he dies near the beginning of *Incidents*, when Linda is only twelve, her father plays a significant role in her relation to the world, not only commanding fidelity to his spirit of resistance but also determining her enjoyment *of* and *through* his example of defiance, regardless of its cost. Described by Jacobs as having "had more of the feelings of a freeman than is common among slaves" (12), he presides over Linda's refusal to accept her condition of enslavement, so much so that on hearing the news of his death, "[her] heart rebelled against God"

(13). Though her grandmother, the narrative reassures us, tries to dissipate her bitterness—"'Who knows the ways of God?' said she. 'Perhaps [the dead] have been kindly taken from the evil days to come'" (13)—Linda's rebellion, her unwillingness to acquiesce to routinized injustice, betrays the internalization of her father, who taught his children "to feel that they were human beings. This was blasphemous doctrine for a slave to teach; presumptuous in him, and dangerous to the masters" (13).

The invocation of blasphemy here, like the "rebell[ion] against God" occasioned by Linda's father's death, highlights the danger posed by his teaching not only to "the masters" but also to her grandmother's hope for redemption through patience, faith, and obedience. Despite its ostensible humanism, her father's teaching is saturated by an enjoyment incompatible with communal law but continuous with his daughter's antinomianism. To that extent, it verges on what I've been calling a bad education; as a "blasphemous doctrine" that "corrupts" the young with "irresponsibility" to the law, it courts the very accusation that Jacobs directs against slavery, itself an *institutional* blasphemy the reveals the "great difference between Christianity and religion at the south" (67).

The distance between the trust in God espoused by Linda's grandmother and the "blasphemous doctrine" of resistance to which her father adheres instead is finessed in a figurally subtle passage as Linda plots an escape to freedom for her children and herself. Before putting her plan into action, Linda visits her parents' graves, not knowing if she will ever have a chance to gaze on them again: "For more than ten years I had frequented this spot, but never had it seemed to me so sacred as now. A black stump, at the head of my mother's grave, was all that remained of a tree my father had planted. His grave was marked by a small wooden board, bearing his name, the letters of which were nearly obliterated. I knelt down and kissed them, and poured forth a prayer to God for guidance and support in the perilous step I was about to take" (79). In this text where Blackness is as overdetermined as the genealogies of those made Black by law, the pairing of the "black stump" beside her mother's grave with the "nearly obliterated" letters on the "wooden board" above her father's returns us to the coimplication of archival and anarchival energies. The stump and the faded letters, which gesture toward interruption and loss, toward the cutting down or cutting off of what *guarantees* survival, invoke, at the same time, the persistence of something as meaningless, as illegible, as the random marks imprinted on the page of Ignacio's final letter: the ab-sens that naming obliterates and that obliterates every name.

Call it the stump of Blackness: the unbearable cut in the framework of being or in the logic of the name, the "nonrecuperable negativity" of Ronald Judy's "incomprehensible African."[133] Call it the obscenity, the queerness, that eradicates the meaning of what is. Or call it, as Jacobs's text does, at least by metonymy, Nat Turner: "As I passed the wreck of the old meeting house, where, before Nat Turner's time, the slaves had been allowed to meet for worship, I seemed to hear my father's voice come from it, bidding me not to tarry till I reached freedom or the grave. I rushed on with renovated hopes. My trust in God had been strengthened by that prayer among the graves" (79). Continuous with the black stump and the fading letters, the "wreck" of the slaves' former meetinghouse, no longer the "little church in the woods . . . built by the colored people, . . . [who] had no higher happiness than to meet there and sing hymns together, and pour out their hearts in spontaneous prayer" (60), now conjures the rupture inherent in transmission, the ineluctable force of erasure, that undermines pedag-archivalization. Demolished in the wake of Nat Turner's rebellion, when slaveholders feared the consequences of permitting Black persons to gather on their own, the meetinghouse, or rather its wreckage, figures the collision of the different values embodied by Linda's father and her grandmother, Martha. When the former's voice seems to emanate from the empty shell of the church, its metonymic association with Turner (whose name is invoked to account for its ruin) implicitly correlates her father's resistance to written law with Turner's. Instructing Linda to choose "freedom or the grave," the voice echoes Turner's associate, Will, who won Turner's "full confidence" with his response when asked if "he thought to obtain [liberty]": "He said he would, or loose [*sic*] his life."[134]

Incidents never endorses Turner or his militant insurgence, but it never repudiates them, either. Linda even comments ironically on the "great commotion" (56) his violence inspired among the slaveowners in her town: "Strange that they should be alarmed, when their slaves were so 'contented and happy'" (56). In fact, the only atrocities she refers to in the context of Turner's rebellion are those committed by the whites, who respond to it by organizing a muster, a militarized show of power intended to terrorize the Black population and reassert white authority. Her contemporaries may have battened on the sensational details of Turner's insurrection, but Jacobs has Linda exclusively focus on the reactive violence it provoked: "Every where men, women, and children were whipped till the blood stood in puddles at their feet. . . . All day long these unfeeling wretches went round, like a troop of demons, terrifying and tormenting the helpless. At night, they formed themselves into patrol bands, and went wherever they chose among the colored people, acting out their brutal will" (57–58). That brutality of will, like slavery itself, holds a mirror to Turner's enjoyment. It fractures the veneer of civilization, exposing the normally hidden links between obscenity and the law. As Jacobs has Linda remark with regard to the chaos produced by the muster: "What a spectacle was that for a civilized country! A rabble, staggering under intoxication, assuming to be the administrators of justice!" (60). Though she plays no part in the mimetic violence of Turner and this "troop of demons," Linda still thinks of herself as at "war" and is "resolved never to be conquered" (20).

After seeming to hear her father's voice endorsing Nat Turner's resistance, Linda characterizes her hopes as "renovated" and her "trust in God" as "strengthened," thus disguising her anti-enjoyment enjoyment (like Hamlet's, mutatis mutandis) in the more conventionally acceptable trappings of her grandmother's Christian faith. The latter, in the logic of sublimation, legitimates the former, effacing its link to obscenity through its assertion as moral law and allowing the narrative to contain—that is, both to circumscribe and to incorporate—the negativity of jouissance. But this sublimation, though intended to free her from enslavement to enjoyment, merely reroutes that enjoyment into the concept of "freedom" itself. Even while hiding in the garret of a shed contiguous with her grandmother's home, where, stifled by the lack of circulating air, she must "sit or lie in a cramped position day after day, without one gleam of light" (98), Linda not only asserts that she "would have chosen this, rather than my lot as a slave" (98) but also experiences the surplus enjoyment of "match[ing her] cunning against" (107) Dr. Flint's. Like Andersen's Karen, who may flee from enjoyment by having her feet cut off but who can only exchange one mode of enjoyment for another in so doing, Linda, whose bid for liberty also threatens to leave her "a cripple" (107), finds similar enjoyment in her confinement: the enjoyment of mastering her master by deploying the literacy he had forbidden to those he enslaved. By way of a series of letters, she leads him to think she has fled to Boston, though she lives within range of his voice. Delighting in the framing of this elaborate hoax (she records her attention to its every detail), Linda invents her escape from the South without actually having performed it, refusing, in fact, to make her way north before securing her children's safety. She acquires a certain freedom by her flight from Dr. Flint's home, but only at the cost of an oppressive regime of physical constraint. Her suffering, however, like the duplicity of her letters, remains attached to enjoyment: the masochistic enjoyment of frustrating her master's attempted enjoyment of her.

Mobilizing, if only implicitly, the ab-sens that pertains to the letter as such, Linda speculates on the nothing that writing and reason both seek to master. More than merely strategic, her letters liberate a surplus aggression. She taunts her "owners," who imagine, like Hegel, that those of African descent embody "the conditions of mere nature" inherently alien to any "rational State," by exposing how letters and the signifying system emblematic of rationality make comprehension always not-all.[135] She assimilates herself, by extension, to the void they can *never* comprehend. Like *Incidents*, her letters take shape as a sort of autothanatography, to borrow from Judy's assertion that thanatology is the slave narrative's true genre. By displaying a mastery of Reason through the very cunning with which they confound it, her letters endorse, as Judy puts it, the "universal comprehension of reality" made possible only through the subtraction of the African's illegibility, that is, through the subtraction of Blackness.[136] Paradoxically, though, in their nonidentity with the significations they convey, they *preserve* that illegibility beyond Symbolic comprehension: the originary cut, the "black stump" by which Blackness persistently stumps Reason.

If this Blackness can neither be nor be known, if it resonates with the queerness of ontological negation and registers the nothing from which nothing is free, then it implicates the politics of the resistant form in the resistance to form as such, including the resistance to such "progressive" forms as the "the community to come." Though imagined as nonexclusionary, that community presupposes, as do narratives of enslavement in Judy's keen analysis, the "universal comprehension of reality," suggesting at once the universality of what reality comprehends and the universality of reality's availability to comprehension. Such communities exclude what reality, ontology, and meaning reduce to nothing: the negativity that resists the totalizing logic of aesthetic education.

Consistent with that logic, *Incidents* concludes with a double affirmation. "Reader, my story ends with freedom," Jacobs has Linda assert, though the latter immediately acknowledges that "the dream of [her] life is not yet realized" (167). She continues to aspire to a property right not delivered with formal freedom: "I do not sit with my children in a home of my own. I still long for a hearthstone of my own, however humble. I wish it for my children's sake far more than for my own" (167). "My own," the phrase she repeats three times, signals her continued possession by the economy of ownership, which extends to the ownership of her selflessness in desiring to own such property "for [her] children's sake far more than for [her] own." Regretting that her dream remains unfulfilled, Linda, in a singularly freighted phrase, laments,

accepts, assigns blame for, and rejoices in her fate: "But God so orders circumstances as to keep me with my friend Mrs. Bruce" (167). As if fearing
that this sentence might register an un-Christian animosity, or that the resistant tones of her father's voice might echo in a phrase intended to evoke her
grandmother's humble submissiveness, Linda qualifies her phrasing at once:
"Love, duty, gratitude, also bind me to her side. It is a privilege to serve her
who pities my oppressed people and who has bestowed the inestimable boon
of freedom on me and my children" (167).

Depicted as the quintessential "good neighbor," as the stand-in for the Christian women in the North to whom Jacobs addresses her text, Mrs. Bruce, as
Lacan would argue, displays the altruism "that is situated on the level of the
useful" and that "becomes the pretext by means of which I can avoid taking
up the problem of the evil I desire, and that my neighbor desires also."[137] In
purchasing Linda from Dr. Flint's heirs and putting an end to Linda's long
years of anxiety, concealment, and flight, Mrs. Bruce violates Linda's will,
which Linda explains to her friend by remarking that "being sold from one
owner to another seemed too much like slavery; that such a great obligation
could not be easily cancelled; and that [she] preferred to go to [her] brother
in California" (165). The altruistic purchase of Linda's "freedom" thus inspires in her a surge of outrage at the fact of her having been sold. Though
Mrs. Bruce makes clear that she purchased Linda to procure her freedom,
not her service, and though *Incidents* tells us that, despite her outrage, Linda
"felt as if a heavy load had been lifted from [her] weary shoulders" (166), the
bitterness of the "obligation" that she now must assume toward Mrs. Bruce,
the bitterness of her debt to the charity, the generosity, of the other, animates a continuing resentment that preserves her enjoyment in its negativity.
Indeed, the words with which Linda walks back the hint of any animosity
toward God, who "keep[s her] with [her] friend Mrs. Bruce," betray what
inspires that rancor in the first place: "Love, duty, gratitude, also bind me
to her side. It is a privilege to serve her who pities my oppressed people and
who has bestowed the inestimable boon of freedom on me and my children."
Officially released from bondage (though *Incidents* says nothing of her man-
umission), Linda remains more stringently bound by an all-too-holy trinity
("love, duty, gratitude") demanding that she view it as a "privilege to serve"
the person who explicitly told her, "I did not buy you for your services" (166).

Linda's affirmation of freedom, then, coincides with its negation—unless
we construe that negation itself as her *mode* of access to freedom: the freedom
to enjoy "the evil I desire, and that my neighbor desires also." Linda cannot
avow that evil; she remains enslaved to the Christian ideal of goodness she

makes her master. The claim that her narrative ends with freedom gives way, therefore, to a second affirmation bringing *Incidents* to its close, an affirmation of the ego ideal envisioned in "tender memories of [her] good old grandmother, like light, fleecy clouds floating over a dark and troubled sea" (167). By sublimating the enjoyment that insists like the waves that endlessly trouble that sea, Linda's image of her grandmother's goodness—expressed as lightness, weightlessness, disembodiment—conjures the "transcendental aesthetic" that, as Moten writes, leaves Blackness, as a figure for ontological exclusion, "unmappable within the cosmological grid of the transcendental subject."[138] Linda may privilege the heavenly clouds ("light" because free of all burden or weight and free because "fleecy" or white), she may wish, that is, to assimilate herself to the space of aesthetic freedom won through abstraction from the world, but Jacobs ends by insisting on the "dark and troubled sea." If that image invariably calls to mind the waters of the middle passage, then the darkness continuously troubling that sea is the Blackness it entombs: the void in meaning, the negation of being, the ab-sens that weighed down, and that still weighs down, the millions trapped in the fatal chains of catachrestic nominations that compel them to signify nothing.

Harriet Jacobs's remains are buried beneath a tombstone in Mount Auburn Cemetery. Its letters are not (or, at least, not yet) as obliterated as those on the wooden board marking Linda's father's grave, and the tree near which it is located is not (or not yet) a black stump like the one she described at the head of her mother's grave. Instead, her marker repeats with a vengeance Linda's gesture of sublimation, denying the rebelliousness, negativity, and enjoyment to which Jacobs speaks in her text. Her tombstone sums up her life in these words: "Patient in tribulation, fervent in spirit serving the Lord" (see figure 4.1). Quoting from Paul's Epistle to the Romans by combining, though with their order reversed, phrases from verses 12:11–12 in the King James Version, this epitaph represents Jacobs as Jacobs represented Linda's grandmother. It obliterates her active resistance to law, her attachment to the "blasphemous doctrine" of her father, and her refusal to forget the "troubled sea" in favor of "light, fleecy clouds."

As the emphasis on "serving the Lord" suggests, these phrases, in the context of Paul's Epistle, urge acceptance of difference in rank or position ("we have many members in one body, and not all members have the same office"), the renunciation of material embodiment ("present your bodies a living sacrifice, holy, acceptable unto God, which is your reasonable service"), and forbearance in the face of oppression ("bless them which persecute you: bless, and curse not"). They encapsulate, in other words, the conjunction of

4.1: The tombstone of Harriet Jacobs in Mount Auburn Cemetery, Cambridge, Massachusetts.

Moten's "transcendental aesthetic" with the sublimation of enjoyment effected not only by religion (which Lacan identifies as "the original home of meaning") but also by philosophy and its subsidiary, aesthetic education.[139] But they fail to deliver freedom from enjoyment, from the "evil" of the drive. Even Romans retains the "black stump" of the negativity it means to sublimate: "Therefore if thine enemy hunger, feed him; if he thirst, give him drink: for in so doing thou shalt heap coals of fire on his head." This optical illusion or anamorphosis that promotes the transcendence of "evil" by love does so by encouraging acts of love that enact a holocaustal aggression, satisfying thereby "the evil I desire, and that my neighbor desires also."

There may be no freedom of enjoyment, then, but there is no freedom *from* it either, which is why I end with two quotations. The first is Lacan's response to a journalist who asked if psychoanalysis entailed a repression of freedom.

"Those words make me laugh," Lacan responded, "I never speak about freedom."[140] The second is from Jared Sexton in an interview with Daniel Coluccielo Barber: "And if we, ourselves, are that unfree thing that we do not know and cannot solve, if we are most powerfully that inhuman element of dispossession that upsets and unleashes every humanism and anti-humanism alike, what then?"[141]

Coda: Nothing Gained:

Irony, Incest, Indiscernibility

That the inscription on Harriet Jacobs's tombstone, like the conclusion of her narrative, undertakes a sublimation reminds us that, notwithstanding her own rebelliousness and negativity, Jacobs shares philosophy's hostility to enjoyment. According to Lacan, that hostility gets expressed in philosophy's "theft" of enjoyment, which mirrors, he argues, the master's theft of the jouissance of the slave. Reinforcing Judy's claim that slave narratives write their authors into "being" only insofar as they affirm a "universal comprehension of reality," which dooms Blackness—"the incomprehensible African"—to the status of nonbeing, Jacobs's *Incidents in the Life of a Slave Girl* shows her investment in rationality by denouncing, like Frederick Douglass, the condition of enslavement to jouissance.[1] Both Jacobs and Douglass knew firsthand the nightmare of one group's access to enjoyment at another group's expense, which Hortense Spillers aptly describes as "the ecstasy of unchecked power."[2] Both assert their claim to the reason by which Western logic defines human "being"; yet both, by doing so, endorse the logic used to justify slavery: the necessity of constraining the irrational enjoyment that Douglass calls "run[ning] wild."[3]

Determined to prove her rationality superior to that of her "masters," ill-disposed as they were to credit her claim to reason in the first place, Jacobs writes her way to enjoyment and its disavowal at once. Emulating Linda's triumph in her "competition in cunning" with Dr. Flint, a triumph won by anticipating his belief that her letters were transparent in meaning, Jacobs experiences an enjoyment at odds with her grandmother's counsel to submit with patience to whatever "God . . . orders."[4]

But *Incidents*, like the words on Jacobs's tombstone, attempts to whitewash that enjoyment, associated with the resistance of her father and Nat Turner to the written law of the state, by conflating Jacobs's politics with her grandmother's Christian communitarianism. By attempting to sublimate the *enjoyment* attached to Jacobs's antinomian resistance, *Incidents* betrays the concessions needed for Jacobs to get her book published (as a formerly enslaved Black female dependent on white abolitionists in the North). But it also betrays the antagonism inherent in the progressive political vision of a nonexclusionary community.

Such a politics has zero tolerance for enjoyment and the negativity it signifies, since enjoyment undoes attachment to both self-interest and the collective good. Insofar as the subject can know itself only as a subject of desire, jouissance *subverts* its self-interest by broaching the vanishing of the "self." Lacan makes this explicit: "Far from being the desire for jouissance, desire is precisely the barrier that keeps you at a distance, more or less accurately calculated, from that blazing hearth called jouissance, which the thinking subject must avoid."[5] Approaching too close to that "blazing hearth" exposes the self to what Romans 12:20 anticipates for one's enemy: "heap[ing] coals of fire on his head." The negativity of the drive, as oblivious to the self as it is to the self's self-interest, batters, like Jacobs's "dark and troubled sea," the barrier of desire, while desire, like a seawall, protects us by attaching us to meaning.[6] As seen from the perspective of the subject of desire, the only perspective we know as "ours," the zero of enjoyment appears as a one through its catachrestic embodiments (*the* Black, *the* woman, *the* queer, et al.) that affirm the order of sense.[7] We saw this in Jacques Rancière's discussion of the aesthetic politics of the resistant form where even the Thing as subtraction from meaning, as the negativity of ab-sens, was construed as "transmit[ing] meanings" and so as anticipating "a community to come" as much as the becoming-life of art did.[8] To challenge that pedag-archival transmission or that community to come is to court the distrust directed at all who promote a bad education.

Consider, as a minor—and far from disinterested—example of such distrust, a response to *No Future* by Merrill Cole, a critic whose his essay's title announces what he purports to expose and resist: "The Queer Repression of Jacques Lacan." After describing *No Future* as "the most controversial attempt to bring Lacan into queer theory" since Tim Dean's *Beyond Sexuality*, Cole writes, "Queerness, for Edelman, should involve not 'an oppositional political identity,' but 'opposition to politics as the governing fantasy' of imaginary closure. It is perhaps only from a privileged social position that one could dismiss politics as fantasy for however unreal politics may seem, it directly affects people's lives and well-being. Rather than holding itself aloof, I argue that queerness should engage in the struggle to change people's lives for the better."[9] Leaving aside the vacuity of that final "political" appeal—"changing people's lives for the better," after all, is the radically empty program that everyone from Adolf Hitler to Mahatma Gandhi, from Maximilien Robespierre to Martin Luther King Jr., can readily get behind—I would note Cole's strange response to Edelman's characterization of politics. For it requires no "privileged social position" to identify (which is hardly the same as to "dismiss") the structure of politics as a fantasy, only a *Lacanian* one. "Fantasy dominates the whole reality of desire, which is to say, the Law," Lacan observes in *The Other Side of Psychoanalysis*.[10] Rather than something "unreal," as Cole puts it, fantasy, Lacan maintains, "gives reality its frame."[11] Lacan lays out, moreover, the specific shape this political fantasy takes, evoking it as the Imaginarization of what refuses Imaginary totality:

> It's an idea . . . that knowledge could produce a totality, which, if I can put it this way, is immanent, immanent in politics as such. The Imaginary idea of the whole, such as it is given by the body, is part of the political preaching based on the good form of satisfaction, on that which makes a sphere; taken to its limit, what is more beautiful, but also what is less open, what more closely resembles the self-enclosure of satisfaction?
>
> The collusion of this image with the idea of satisfaction: that's the thing we run into every time we encounter something knotted in this work [i.e., psychoanalysis] that entails bringing something to light by the paths of the unconscious.[12]

This "political" idea, associated with the coherence of a totalized enclosure that expresses "the good form of satisfaction"—where "good" is no simple term of praise but rather an acknowledgment of the complicity between moral discourse and Imaginarization—impedes the analytic labor that undoes such fantasmatic consistency.[13] The resistance to analysis, like the resistance to negativity, springs from the "satisfaction" afforded by the image "of the whole," which Lacan identifies, or—to borrow Cole's term—*dismisses*, as political "preaching."[14]

Cole's argument, directly correlated with his own indulgence in such preaching ("queerness should engage in the struggle to change people's lives for the better"), becomes more interesting and more telling when he concedes, after correlating politics with a reality not to be confused with fantasy ("however unreal politics may seem"), that fantasy, in Lacanian theory, structures reality after all. Referring to an essay by Chris Coffman, he writes, "Traversing the final fantasy is the endpoint of Lacanian psychoanalysis, where we dispossess ourselves of *the unconscious fantasies structuring our reality*, an evacuation that, as Coffman argues, 'clears the ground for a future that could be lived otherwise.' Clinical Lacanian analysis aims at radical change: 'traversing the fantasy' is futurally oriented" (emphasis mine).[15] Attempting to make "traversing the fantasy," a concept popular in Lacanian circles though barely theorized by Lacan, coincide with the sort of "satisfaction" Lacan mocks as "immanent" in politics (the satisfaction promised by some "radical change" toward "a future that could be lived otherwise"), Cole turns traversing the fantasy into the very fantasy it's supposed to traverse. He imbues it with the heroism of a "struggle to change people's lives for the better" without interrogating whose desire is at stake or who determines what makes those lives "better."[16] So fully "Americanized" a version of Lacan, in which analysis secures a "better" future by traversing a fantasy that Lacan invokes as "radical" (le fantasme radical) or "fundamental" (cette expérience du fantasme fondamental) and not, as Cole says, "final" (as if it were the ultimate veil beneath which, at last, we encounter the truth), bears little relation to Lacan's own texts.[17]

Coffman, on whose work Cole's essay leans, may identify "traversing the fantasy" with an opening onto "a future that could be lived otherwise," but Lacan says no such thing. In his seminar of June 24, 1964, the only time he refers to (and even then only once) traversing the radical fantasy (or, more precisely, to *having* traversed it), he does so by *questioning* how one lives, or how one *lives on*, in its aftermath. "What becomes of someone who has passed [or who has undergone the pass] by way of this experience concerning the relation, utterly opaque at its origin, to the drive? How can it be lived, by a subject who has traversed the radical fantasy, how, from that point on, is the drive lived?"[18] Instead of a futural orientation or an assurance of change for the better, Lacan lingers here in uncertainty before the question of survival: "This is the beyond of analysis, and it has never been approached. It has only, to the present moment, been approachable at the level of the analyst, insofar as it would be required of the analyst precisely to have traversed in its totality the cycle of the analytic experience."[19]

The claim that this beyond has been approachable only "at the level of the analyst" refers to the moment in the training analysis ("la psychanalyse didactique") when analysts-in-training, no longer mistaking the analyst for the subject supposed to know, still desire to occupy the analyst's place, now perceived as "the place of nonbeing" (la place du dèsêtre).[20] If the fantasy of the subject supposed to know, of the one who has what the analysand seeks, makes "the logic of the analyst . . . the agalma which integrates itself into the radical fantasy that the analysand constructs," then the dissolving of that fantasy reduces the analyst to the status of any signifier whatsoever ("au signifiant quelconque").[21] Far from producing the promise of "a future that could be lived otherwise," this divestiture of the analyst's *agalma* coincides with the analysand's "subjective destitution," an emptying-out sufficient, Lacan maintains, "to sow panic, horror, curses, even attacks."[22]

Lacan goes further. Whoever, at the end of the training analysis, would assume the analyst's nonbeing ("dèsêtre") "roots himself in what most radically opposes everything by which it is necessary and sufficient to be recognized in order to 'be': respectability, for example."[23] Having confronted the lack in the Other and no longer pursuing, therefore, the Other's recognition or good opinion, such a person embraces, according to Lacan, "the true import of the constitutive negation that infamy signifies."[24] By linking this "constitutive negation" to "infamy," the opposite of those communal values (i.e., respectability or honor) that earn recognition in the realm of being, Lacan implicitly opposes it to pedag-archivalization and posits its centrality to the movement into the "beyond of psychoanalysis."[25] Underscoring its importance, he calls this negation bound up with infamy "a connotation it is very much necessary to restore to psychoanalysis."[26]

No one could fault Cole or Coffman for refusing the negativity of this negation or for trying to keep themselves far removed from the infamy it bestows. But for just that reason no one should confuse their arguments with Lacan's. Their refusal coincides with the fantasy of achieving the unity, the aesthetic coherence, inseparable from the subject of desire and inseparable, therefore, from the fantasy in which *everyone* believes, whether they know they believe it or not. But Cole and Coffman align their refusal with a progressive political engagement founded on a diluted version of Deleuze's positivization of nonbeing, taking every variation in the status quo as indexical of "becoming." In doing so they mistake transformations in the contingent *expressions* of Symbolic law for fundamental transformations of Symbolic law as such. Nor are they alone in this regard.

Mari Ruti, for example, in maintaining that "the real can alter (rather than merely devastate) the symbolic," supports her claim by pointing to the creativity with which we "generate fresh forms of signification."[27] On this ground, she declares, "we can participate in an ongoing and endlessly renewed process of becoming. The future, in other words, is never determined but inherently open ended; far from a predetermined fantasy, it is a manner of remaining alive to the utter unpredictability of existence."[28] This notion, however appealing, ignores that "generat[ing] fresh forms of signification" is the Symbolic's normative function. Moreover, if "becoming" is an "ongoing and endlessly renewed process," then its insistent productivity is, by definition, "predetermined" (what else could "endlessly renewed" denote?), *though its specific forms are not*. To that extent, it is far removed from the "unpredictability" that Ruti affirms. The bond between futurism and the order of meaning is procured by the predictable necessity of generating "fresh forms of signification." Nothing in this process "alter[s]" the Symbolic; it merely enacts its law.[29]

Pursuing an argument akin to Ruti's, Coffman also seeks to rebut what she, like Ruti, finds in *No Future*: an "excessively negative interpretation of Lacan." Expanding on the notion that "an act in the Real can prompt changes in the symbolic," Coffman proposes that unlike Edelman's politics, "[Slavoj] Žižek's politics of the Real offers queer theory not a release from the symbolic order but rather the possibility of changing its coordinates."[30] Her example of "changing [the Symbolic's] coordinates"? The wedding scene from *In and Out* (Frank Oz, 1977, Paramount) where Howard Brackett (Kevin Kline) surprises himself and those around him by coming out as gay. Coffman credits Žižek as the source of this example, but even Žižek, when he adduces it, notes that it's "not quite appropriate" since it fails to demonstrate "the 'crazy,' impossible choice of . . . *striking at [one]self*, at what is most precious to [one]self," that marks the Lacanian act.[31] Coming out can alter many things, but neither in nor out of *In and Out* is Symbolic law among them. To the contrary, by assimilating the subject to a legible identity in the signifying system, it reaffirms the subject's defining subjection *to* the Symbolic law. As for genuine acts, those that "accomplish what, in a given symbolic universe, appears to be 'impossible,'" Žižek maintains that they "change the coordinates of the *situation* in which the subject finds himself" (emphasis mine), *not* the coordinates of "the symbolic order."[32] Such acts, as discussed in previous chapters, are not expressions of will or desire but rather of the acephalic drive whose relation to enjoyment disturbs the "the political preaching based on the good form of satisfaction" for the sake of which Ruti, Coffman, and Cole require a less "negative" Lacan.[33]

Ruti frames that politics plainly: "Those of us advancing this newer version of posthumanist theory tend to possess a strong commitment to matters of social survival, justice, and responsibility."[34] Wholly honorable, wholly admirable, such commitments command assent. Refusal to sign on to such a project, in Alenka Zupančič's phrase, *"would be impossible, inhuman."*[35] Zupančič, however, introduces this phrase precisely to ventriloquize ideology's resistance to "the gap opened up by an act."[36] A genuine act, as Zupančič makes clear, never registers as honorable or respectable; far from praise for its "responsibility," it earns, Lacan tells us, "infamy" for threatening the fundamental fantasy that consolidates a world. Ruti may refer to "posthumanist theory," but her argument repurposes liberal humanism, vaunting "social survival, justice, and responsibility" without recognizing that the split in the subject, the fracture at the core of posthumanist thought, makes those three things incompatible. How can we be responsible to the subject of desire and the subject of the drive at once? How can we do justice to a divided subject in tension not only with itself but also with the order that produced it? How can we reconcile "social survival" with the assault on the social order that condemns the authentic act to "infamy"?

The answer, for Ruti, Coffman, and Cole, is to displace the constitutive division of the subject into external divisions among social subjects, thus allowing for the hope of *political* repair through an "endlessly renewed process of becoming." To suggest that this process is endless because the void is *incapable* of repair would challenge such political hope and provoke a political rebuke. Thus, Cole waves off the Lacanian account of politics as a governing fantasy by associating defense of that argument with a "privileged social position," and Ruti similarly describes the negativity implicit in endless "becoming": "The kind of radical negativity and self-dissolution that Edelman (following Žižek) advocates can only be undertaken from a position of relative security," she writes.[37]

But Ruti misreads *No Future* here in a symptomatic way. Though it repeatedly insists on the *figural relation* between jouissance and those viewed as queer, and though it repeatedly urges such persons to embrace their *figural* embodiment of the death drive, *No Future* never "advocates" for psychic "self-dissolution," as if such a thing were a question of will or could constitute a political program.[38] Ruti takes this misreading further: "Deprivileged subjects—some women, racially and ethnically marked individuals, and those who lead economically precarious lives (that is, subjects whose claim to symbolic identity is shaky to begin with)—simply cannot afford to abandon themselves to the jouissance of the death drive in the way that more secure subjects might be tempted (or even compelled) to do."[39] The confusions of psychic and social here are multiple and instructive. No subject, regardless of gender, race, ethnicity, sex, or sexuality, can "afford to abandon [itself] to the jouissance of the death drive"—not if "afford" suggests it can do so voluntarily and with impunity. The drive, itself *unconscious*, pushes toward an emptying of the subject that has nothing to do with "temptation"; it affords that subject nothing more than an opening onto nonbeing ("dèsêtre") that neither liberates nor redeems it but only subtracts it from sense.

Just as claims to Symbolic identity are no less "secure" for "deprivileged subjects" than they are for their privileged counterparts—indeed, the very fixity of those Symbolic identities is what proves destructive to "deprivileged subjects," making their claims to *social viability*, not to Symbolic identity, "shak[ier]"—so the insistence of the death drive "compel[s]" those subjects no less than it does any others. Denying those marked by oppression the psychic structures that shape us as subjects may bespeak a political belief that the "deprivileged" simply cannot "afford" them; but it might also reflect, to return to Cole's phrase, a "privileged social position" that flattens "deprivileged subjects" into empty figures for their lack of privilege, reducing them to the status of furniture—useful objects, perhaps even chattel—in liberal humanism's performance of its own exemplary moral conscience.

In a wonderfully rich analysis, Bobby Benedicto diagnoses this general logic, describing it as the

> familiar schema . . . in which the erotics of death appears as a dangerous luxury, as the proclivity of those who find relative security in the gap between psychic dissolution and physical death, between the figurative and the literal: a matter, that is, of (white) privilege. In turn, the queer of color emerges as a generative figure, a bearer of hope; lauded for its resilience amid the perils that surround it, its interests appear to lie not in the dream of a deadly unbinding but in staving off the threat of death by undertaking the revivifying labor of creation—of world making—or what might be understood, more critically, as the burden of repairing the very world that demands its annihilation.[40]

Thinking alongside Antonio Viego, whose important book, *Dead Subjects: Toward a Politics of Loss in Latino Studies*, he cites at the end of the following quotation, Benedicto voices "a sense of wariness about how the disavowal of the urge to dissolution—an urge that would indeed attest to a universal condition of loss—runs the risk of conjuring, explicitly or implicitly, the queer of color as a figure unfractured by any death instinct, and in turn of repeating, if only by leaving them unremarked, 'the themes of wholeness, completeness, and transparency . . . (that) provide racist discourse with precisely the notion of subjectivity that it needs in order to function most effectively.'"[41]

Proceeding to consider "the relationship of homosexuality to death," Benedicto acknowledges, like Eric Stanley and Calvin Warren, that "the threat of literalization [the literalization of homosexuality as a figure of the self's annihilation] . . . does not fall on all equally."[42] Writing about Luka Magnotta, who "murdered, dismembered, and decapitated Jun Lin, a Chinese international student whom he allegedly met on Craigslist, and on whose butchered body he performed acts of necrophilia and cannibalism," Benedicto compellingly theorizes Lin's "forced racial migration" by Magnotta from "benign invisibility" to "the nonontological place of those whose lives do not matter, the site of blackness."[43] In this context Benedicto asks, "What . . . might prompt Magnotta's racism other than the fear of seeing, mirrored back at him, reflected in the other's skin, the condition of nonbeing that is, by virtue of *his* [i.e., Lin's] queerness, also necessarily his [i.e., Magnotta's]?"[44] Lin's racialized Asian body comes to figure the Black body's racial construction as the catachresis of Blackness itself, as an ontological negation conceivable only by (mis)taking that catachresis for a literal (id)entity: *the* Black, whose body can thereby *signify*, in its apparent legibility, nonbeing. At the same time, as Benedicto implies, Lin's figural "blackness" (borrowed from the equally figural Blackness of those who are culturally *literalized* as Black) serves to figure, for Magnotta, a queerness that is equally catachrestic and equally literalized in whomever a culture designates as queer.

This literalization of catachresis, which turns nonbeing into identity, repeats, of course, the zero's sublimation into a one. It also shapes the (mis)readings of *No Future* by Ruti, Coffman, and Cole, all of whom base their arguments on misleading literalizations. Ruti's contention that *No Future* advocates "self-dissolution," for example—despite the book's repeated assertion that those a culture reads as queer are always "Symbolic subjects consigned to *figure* the Symbolic's undoing" (emphasis mine)—finds its counterpart in Coffman's claim that *No Future* refuses "politics, futurity, and the symbolic order."[45] Cole then reminds us that such an escape from the Symbolic is impossible: "The real, contrary to Edelman's claim, is not a place that queers or anyone else could occupy."[46] *No Future*, however, makes no such claim; instead, it makes the very point that Cole adduces against it: "The *figural* burden of queerness . . . is that of the force that shatters the fantasy of Imaginary unity, the force that insists on the void (replete, paradoxically, with jouissance) always already lodged within, though barred from, symbolization: the gap or wound of the Real that inhabits the Symbolic's very core[.] *Not that we are, or ever could be, outside the Symbolic ourselves*; but we can, nonetheless, make the choice to accede to our cultural production *as figures* . . . for the dismantling of such a logic and thus for the death drive it harbors within."[47]

Each of these critics thus literalizes what *No Future* describes as figural. By discrediting the straw men they conjure, Ruti, Coffman, and Cole obscure the antagonism that follows from Symbolic division and defend a progressive politics founded, like politics tout court, on the literalization of identities (national, racial, sexed, etc.) essential to the political fantasy "that knowledge could produce a totality." Such literalizations, insofar as they posit a figural designation *as* literal, conform to the *figural* logic that is always, in its essence, a form of misnaming. To say this is not to reify the distinction between the literal and the figurative, but to show that those literalizations themselves *aspire to* such reification. Inseparable from every politics and therefore mobilized by the right and the left alike, they function as catachrestic *identities* (*the* Black, *the* woman, *the* alien, *the* queer) to give local habitation and a name to what, as nonbeing, undoes identity. We might call them, therefore, *id-entities*: entities, ones, created to embody the libidinal danger of the id's resistance to the conscious subject's "being"; entities called into being to be excluded as manifestations of nonbeing.

The right repeats this *ontological* exclusion (which pertains to impossibility) in the form of a *social* exclusion (which pertains to prohibition). It generates for itself the enjoyment of exclusion by excluding embodiments of enjoyment from the social totality it promotes. The left, pursuing a different path toward the goal of totalization, normalizes the social identities of those produced to embody "nothing"—affirming the positivization that turns the zero into one—as part of an inclusive community whose coherence, in this like its right-wing counterpart's, excludes the zero of jouissance it rests on nonetheless. Whatever figures that jouissance (the racist, the fascist, the homophobe) persists as a threat to community.

To put this somewhat differently: politics functions allegorically, turning the social relations among persons into relations among *types* of persons (citizen and noncitizen, for example), some of whom come to stand in for the undoing of personhood as such. Once literalized, these identities permit us to know and to regulate a social body whose totality requires the exclusion of those id-entities that materialize ab-sens.[48] As Judith Butler observes, "The question of who and what is considered real and true is apparently a question of knowledge. But it is also, as [Michel] Foucault makes plain, a question of power."[49] Allegory, as the figure of the knowledge achieved by negating, through narrative sequence, irony's negation of determinate sense, expresses, as Walter Benjamin writes, "the voluptuousness with which significance rules, like a stern sultan in a harem of objects."[50] In its "voluptuous" display of power, allegory conjures the meaningfulness that irony empties out, proposing, through the temporal movement between past and present, between then and now, the possibility of arriving at knowledge, or, in Benjamin's phrase, at "the 'opening of the eyes.'"[51] Insofar as it positivizes irony, though, by resolving it into sense, allegory itself is a figure of the irony it means to sublimate. Paul de Man expresses this cryptically: "To say then, as we are actually saying, that allegory (as sequential narration) is the trope of irony (as the one is the trope of zero) is to say something that is true enough but not intelligible."[52]

If the truth of this claim, precisely in its unintelligibility, succumbs to the force of irony, it does so in a way that anticipates de Man's thoughts on teaching in "The Resistance to Theory": "It is better to fail in teaching what should not be taught than to succeed in teaching what is not true."[53] Insofar as the "truth" of this identification of allegory as the trope of irony cannot be made intelligible, any effort to teach it must fail. But the assumption that the unintelligible "should not be taught" attests to the production of "what is real" through the subtraction of ab-sens, which assures, like allegory for Benjamin, that "significance rules" in the Symbolic.[54] To the extent that this exclusion of the Real establishes the order of intelligibility, another name for that primal exclusion is the prohibition of incest, where incest emerges as a catachresis that allegorizes what meaning excludes.

As founding prohibition and "primordial law," as the foreclosure of the Real that opens a space for the Symbolic subject's appearance, the incest taboo produces and stabilizes the difference between sameness and difference, making possible linguistic articulation and its offshoot, conceptual thought.[55] Jacques Derrida, as we saw in chapter 2, suggests that "the whole of philosophical conceptualization . . . is designed to leave in the domain of the unthinkable the very thing that makes this conceptualization possible: the origin of the prohibition of incest."[56] But this is a sort of pleonasm; incest "itself" already evokes the unthinkability of origins. Only conceivable as already tabooed, its very nomination refers to the cut that already cuts "incest" off from itself, already frames it as a concept in language, so that sameness and difference can emerge. If philosophy preserves, in the form of the unthinkable, the meaninglessness of that cut (which alone allows meaning, form, and thought), then it thereby makes incest the nothing against which being and meaning take shape. Incest thus constitutes "that which ab-sens designates as sex."[57] But "sex" here refers to the cut of division before anything exists to divide: the cut subtracted as ab-sens to permit the articulation of entities and the consequent materialization of what gets posited as "sexual difference." Referring to Claude Lévi-Strauss's claim that "the regulation of relations between the sexes represents an overflow of culture into nature," Petar Ramadanovic writes, "The incest prohibition is the fundamental social rule because human sexuality exists in a social mode, and whatever rule regulates the way people organize the social bonds that make them into subjects must also regulate the condition for the possibility of their becoming subjects."[58] He then underscores what matters most: "The taboo as such neither has nor needs any content. It is differentiated as a function—its function being to separate the orders of nature and culture and make each possible."[59] More precisely, its function is separation as such, the division whose catachrestic articulations of an undifferentiated "nature" produce the entities, the significations, that emerge as sens-absexe.

These catachreses yield a "fantasy-space" that "materializes a certain limit," as Žižek writes, enacting thereby "the transmutation of Real into Symbolic: the impossible-real changes into an object of symbolic prohibition." This, Žižek then explains, is also "the logic of the most fundamental of all prohibitions, that of incest: incest is inherently impossible (even if a man 'really' sleeps with his mother, 'this is not *that*'; the incestuous object is by definition lacking), and the symbolic prohibition is nothing but an attempt to resolve this deadlock by a transmutation of impossibility into prohibition."[60] Fleshing out "incest" with content or meaning ("if a man 'really' sleeps with his mother") can never defeat the obstacle to thought that incest poses as Real ("the incestuous object is by definition lacking"). "This is not *that*," as Žižek puts it, because incest "as such," could we think such a thing, would figure the indiscernibility that the *prohibition* of incest "subtracts" to generate the being of "thises" and "thats"—the being always foreign to incest, on whose subtraction that being depends.

Despite attempts to literalize incest by assigning it a (re)cognizable meaning, it remains an indeterminate figure for the threat of indetermination. For example, quoting Henry Hughes's *A Treatise on Sociology: Theoretical and Practical* (1854)—in which the author, an opponent of miscegenation, writes, "The same law which forbids consanguineous amalgamation forbids ethnical amalgamation. Both are incestuous. Amalgamation is incest"—Christina Sharpe observes that "Hughes's conjunction and fusion of amalgamation and incest (each term fraught in itself) and their collapse into a singular understanding marks one nodal point around which subjectivity in the New World was reorganized and around which it cohered."[61] Hortense Spillers similarly writes of the "incestuous, interracial genealogy" of slavery, which she describes as "one of the richest displays of the psychoanalytic dimensions of culture before the science of European psychoanalysis takes hold."[62] In a related move, Ramadanovic notes that incest "has been inseparable from the heterosexual norm . . . since Classical Greece, when the Oedipus myth was tied to homosexuality."[63] And Judith Butler, in order to demonstrate that "the term 'incest' is overinclusive," remarks, "To the extent that there are forms of love that are prohibited or, at least, derealized by the norms established by the incest taboo, both homosexuality and incest qualify as such forms."[64] As particular embodiments or literalizations of incest's catachrestic function, these racialized and sexualized associations dissimulate incest's queerness as the zero degree of being, which is also, through taboo or negation, being's inconceivable origin. They conceal what makes incest both Real and Symbolic: not just that it "put[s] the knowability of truth into enduring crisis," as Butler writes, but also that it establishes truth itself as a trope of unintelligibility, as an allegory sublating into meaning the nothing that nothing permits us to know.[65]

The incest taboo, in other words, negates ab-sens by *signifying* it through, and as, what displaces it: the topology of sens-absexe. That taboo makes incest/ab-sens inconceivable while preserving it as the very system that transumes it into allegory. If catachresis as a queer rhetorical figure (mis)names what can have no name of its own, then this foundational catachresis, the prohibition on "incest" that enables meaning, produces an endless stream of names by which different cultures at different moments turn nothing into something *to get rid of it*. Such personifications of nonbeing, such figures of ontological impossibility, differ in their histories, their social experiences, and their viability in the larger community. They require, therefore, the empirical, contextual, and culturally specific framings provided by Black studies and critical race theory; women's, gender, and sexuality studies; feminist analysis; disability studies; queer theory; and trans* studies, among many others.

But they also require a more structural analysis of what empirical approaches slight: the shared determination of these catachreses by the radical negativity that the Symbolic order relegates to nonbeing, to the atopic space of incest, enjoyment, and the Thing. The various forms of delegitimation imposed on these catachrestic id-entities cannot be understood by acceding in advance to the "truth" of their literalization. Instead, such literalizations must be perceived as anamorphoses: distortions that generate meaningful forms from the absence of form or meaning. But the bad education prohibited for calling the literal into question is also, as we've seen, *impossible*; all education is aesthetic education and promotes the temporal unfolding of knowledge that conforms to the structure of allegory. Those willing to risk the stain of infamy can hope, at best, to expose that allegory as itself a trope of irony, but only, on the one hand, by making an assertion that is doomed to remain unintelligible, and only, on the other, by enacting the logic of exposure inherent in allegory. In advocating, nonetheless, for a bad education, for the persistence in what is impossible, I maintain my conviction, to return to de Man, that "it is better to fail in teaching what should not be taught than to succeed in teaching what is not true." But that same conviction obliges me to acknowledge that nothing can ground the good of that "better" or secure that dictum's "truth" except my commitment to the "not" of the "nothing" that persists, beyond intelligibility, as a zero, not a one: as the empty set in the signifying order, always present but never presented and never brought any closer to "being" by the discourse of "becoming."

To conclude this book's engagement with the queerness of zero's incomprehensibility, I want to touch briefly on two last texts that explore the ontological exclusions from thought on which thought itself depends and that do so while centrally thematizing pedagogy and incest in determining relation. The first reads incest in the context of enslavement, Blackness, and "ethnical amalgamation," and in contiguity with the Black femme function as Kara Keeling discusses it.[66] The second situates incest in relation to same-sex desire, aestheticization, and the problematic of reading, and in contiguity with lapses of consciousness that produce a blacking out. Each pivots on a retrospective account of a child's encounter with the drive, and each sublimates that drive into meanings bound to the negativity they mean to displace. Each mobilizes the promise of aesthetic transformation to redeem, through narrative closure, the Real of that encounter, and each ends with a scene that interprets such redemption as a negation of what can never be taught or resolved into meaning, and so as a trope, an allegorization, of irony's negativity.

At the absent center of *Eve's Bayou* (Kasi Lemmons, 1997) is a moment represented three times in the film but never in its diegetic reality. To be sure, that diegetic reality itself is a recollection by the narrator, the adult Eve Batiste (who is voiced by Tamara Tunie but never seen onscreen). The film visualizes her memories of events that took place when Eve was ten years old—events that defined, as she tells us in voice-over, "the summer I killed my father."[67] To that extent, everything the film depicts is subjective retrospection. But *Eve's Bayou* constructs, within that frame, a diegetic visual reality that functions *as if* it were objective (by including, for example, events to which the narrator had no access) and against which three types of visualization get qualified as subject to doubt. The first consists of flashbacks governed by familiar cinematic conventions, including a voice-over accompanying the visual interruption of diegetic narrative time. The second, closely related but used explicitly only once, deploys the flashback setup to introduce a counterfactual past intentionally produced to deny or negate what the film has shown as true. The third consists of clairvoyant visions, hallucinatory disruptions of reality as experienced by the narrator and her Aunt Mozelle (Debbi Morgan), who inherit these gifts from their ancestor, Eve (Billie Neal), described as the "African slave." To distinguish these visions from the rest of the film, they always appear in black-and-white and take shape as fragmentary images that suggest, but never fully achieve, a sense of narrative coherence.

These three distinct indices of subjective vision offer templates for interpreting the three appearances of what we might call the "missing" scene. That scene, obedient to the law that compels the obscene to remain *un-seen*, marks the moment when Cisely (Meagan Good), the narrator's older sister, finds herself engaged in a kiss with her father (Samuel L. Jackson) that crosses from innocent to incestuous. "Finds herself engaged in a kiss with her father": the awkwardness of that phrasing finesses the film's refusal to specify who initiates, who desires, and who turns from that kiss—a kiss that ultimately leads to the murder announced by Eve at the outset. If that indeterminacy itself reflects the incestuous status of the kiss, then the exclusion of the kiss from the film's reality and its consignment to subjective vision enacts the prohibition on incest. But this introduces a paradox. By denying the kiss representation in the "objectivity" of its visual narrative, the film condemns it to indeterminacy. The taboo as exclusion, in other words, gives rise to incest as the indeterminacy the taboo intends to exclude. The foundational cut of the law that calls forth the subject by calling forth incest as a cognizable, but prohibited, relation also calls forth, by back-formation, the impossibility of thinking incest *as the impossible itself*: incest as the non-cognizability of "that which ab-sens designates as sex."[68]

In fact, the scene of the incestuous kiss excluded from the "reality" of *Eve's Bayou* echoes a different encounter that initiates both the film and the Batiste clan: the union of General Jean Paul Batiste and Eve, the woman he enslaved. *Eve's Bayou* starts with a sequence (described in the script as "abstract, hallucinatory") assimilated to the status of a premonition by its black-and-white cinematography (see figures C.1–C.6).[69] Unable at first to read its images as slow-motion shots of a man and woman engaged in a sex act, though fully clothed, the viewer strains to interpret what seem to be nonrepresentational patterns, shifting fields of black and white (see figures C.1–C.3). Eventually brought into focus as reflected in the eye of the young Eve Batiste (Jurnee Smollett) (see figure C.6), these images later reveal themselves as hallucinatory anticipations of Eve's father, Louis (Samuel L. Jackson), committing adultery with Matty Mereaux (Lisa Nicole Carson). The abstract patterns of black and white produced by that sexual encounter ("hard, violent, thrilling

C.1–C.6: The amalgamation of black and white. From *Eve's Bayou* (Lemmons, 1997).

FUCKING," according to the screenplay) invoke, at the same time, the mythic origin, the primal coupling of Black and white, of Eve and Jean Paul Batiste, a coupling whose absence of visualization parallels the absence of the kiss from the diegetic reality of the film.[70]

As framed in the adult Eve's voice-over, that primal (un)scene of Black and white, of (former?) slave and (former?) master in unspecified sexual relation, raises questions, like the (un)scene of the incestuous kiss, about resistance and desire.[71] "The town we lived in was named after a slave," Eve remarks, immediately after her reference to "the summer I killed my father." This metonymy binds the cause of his death—Eve's rage at what he has done to her sister—to the family's myth of origin, which she then proceeds to re-count: "It's said that when General Jean Paul Batiste was stricken with cholera, his life was saved by the powerful medicine of an African slave woman called Eve. In return for his life, he freed her and gave her this piece of land by the bayou. Perhaps in gratitude, she bore him sixteen children. We are the descendants of Eve and Jean Paul Batiste. I was named for her." The oblique account of this erotic union—"Perhaps in gratitude, she bore him sixteen children"—reinforces the (un)scene's indeterminacy and the limits on our ability to define its status, legally or affectively. Jean Paul Batiste is never shown (nor are any other whites), but the ur-Eve twice comes into view as her namesake narrates her story. Solemn, almost motionless, she haunts the bayou that bears her name, so fully incarnating what Judy calls the "incomprehensible African" (a figure, in the Western gaze, undifferentiated from "nature") that in her second appearance she can only with difficulty be distinguished from the background (see figures C.7–C.8).

Her solitary and ghostly presence in the film ignores the central events of her life as traced by her descendant: cure, liberation, and gratitude. Accompanied by neither husband nor children, she bears her secrets in silence. In this way the "African slave woman," Eve, prefigures both the isolation of Cisely that the incestuous kiss will occasion ("It's like she's sleepwalking," her mother says) and the silence the girl sinks into until her sister, Eve, implores her to talk and is sworn to silence too (see figure C.9). Like the kiss, this primal (un)scene contains, in both senses, the threat of incest, the "ethnical amalgamation" of the one anticipating the "consanguineous amalgamation" of the other. Both gesture toward something unspeakable because fundamentally unknowable: incest as the nondifferentiation prior to articulated speech and thought. This unknowable incest, this unthinkable origin, from which the law cuts subjects into meaning, also gets figured in the Blackness

C.7–C.8: "African slave woman called Eve." From *Eve's Bayou* (Lemmons, 1997).

that registers the African as "incomprehensible," as belonging to an undifferentiated "nature," from the perspective of Enlightenment "reason."

Much as the "incestuous" origin of the Batistes puts speculation in the place of knowledge ("Perhaps in gratitude..."), so the absence of the kiss from the filmic reality elicits its subjective overpresence, each account of it offering a different representation of what took place. When Cisely breaks her silence to Eve, the film shows her version in flashback. Having heard her parents fighting downstairs about Louis's affair with Matty, Cisely, once her mother goes up to bed, decides to check in with her father, who remains,

C.9: The imperative of silence. From *Eve's Bayou* (Lemmons, 1997).

half asleep and half drunk, in the parlor. "I was afraid of what she might have said. I was afraid he might divorce us," she tells her sister in explaining her actions. "I wanted to make him feel better. I sat on his lap. And I was scared." With this, the voice-over pauses while the flashback continues onscreen. After bending her head toward Louis and brushing his lips with a filial kiss, Cisely sits back and looks at him in sympathy and sorrow. Through his half-shut eyes, he returns her gaze, and then, leaning forward with a grateful smile, he presses his parted lips against hers while his hand, encircling her shoulder, forces her body back and down. At that point Cisely's narration resumes: "And I was trying to get away and he was hugging me and kissing me until I finally pushed him away with my knee." Infuriated by such violent resistance, Louis slaps her across the face. She falls to the floor, looks up in surprise, then flees while we hear her, in voice-over, moan, "I must have hurt him because . . . he's never hit me."

Horrified both by this narrative and by her sister's visceral pain, Eve cries out, "I'll kill him, Cisely. I swear it. I'll kill him for hurting you." She later attempts to fulfill that promise by hiring Elzora (Diahann Carroll), a practitioner of Louisiana Voodoo, to put a death curse on her father; but she precipitates his death more immediately by mentioning, in pretended innocence, to Matty's husband, Lenny Mereaux, that Matty and Louis have been seeing each other while he was out of town. Though Lenny will fire the shot that kills Louis, Eve all but hands him the gun. Her father's betrayal of her sister's trust is the proximate cause of her vengeance, but it draws on her earlier sense of betrayal when she saw the premonition of her father's adulterous union with Matty come true. "I saw them kissing," she tells her sister; "he was all up against her and her dress was all up and they were rubbing." Though aware of her father's infidelity, Cisely tries to protect him and her sister by telling Eve she has misunderstood. "I'm gonna tell you what happened," she declares, and with that we return, *as if* in a flashback, to the sexual encounter between Louis and Matty. In its first, "objective" depiction, Eve is upset when her father dances with Cicely instead of with her at a party and flees to the garage, now used as a storeroom, to nurse her wounded pride. Curled up in an abandoned carriage, she eventually falls sleep, only to be awakened by the noise of her father and Matty having sex. In its second iteration, as retold by Cisely, the scene unfolds with *both* of the sisters positioned in the carriage, still dressed in the nightclothes they were wearing when Eve told her sister what she had seen. Now they watch together, as if they were viewing a film or a play, as the events from earlier that evening play out in accord with Cisely's narration. "They came in to get some more wine," Cicely announces, "and Daddy told her a joke. And she fell against him laughing. And they woke you up."

Her erasure of Louis's transgression in this false reconstruction of what took place casts doubt on the reliability of her subsequent narrative of the kiss, a doubt redoubled after Louis's death when Eve finds a letter to his sister, Mozelle, that offers a different account. As Eve reads it, we hear her speak its words until her father's voice takes over. No sooner does he mention the night of the kiss than we see another version of the scene. The visuals track closely with Cisely's at first, but that changes when, in this account, it is she who succumbs to desire:

> Roz and I had a terrible fight. And I guess it was inevitable. I knew Cisely could never sleep through a fight like that, so I wasn't surprised when she came downstairs. Maybe I was even waiting for her. I let myself wallow in filial comfort. Mozelle, I swear, the first kiss was the sweetest kiss a daughter could give a drunk and guilt-ridden father. A kiss of redemption. In the next moment, it had gone wrong. From my scotch haze, it took me a second to realize that my daughter was kissing me like a woman. This is where I blame myself. I was so startled that I hit her and she fell to the floor.

Though disclaiming responsibility for the second kiss, Louis admits to handling it badly; the blow he delivered to his daughter crossed the very line it sought to fortify: "Mozelle, I would give my life to have that moment back. I would hold her and comfort her. We would talk through her confusion and I would put her to bed with the boundaries between us intact." Those boundaries, as drawn by the incest taboo to preclude the indeterminacy, the nondifferentiation, that incest "is," prohibit the queerness that erases such boundaries *but that cannot appear without them.* Understood as the radically excluded or strange that vitiates communal being, such queerness is, like incest itself, ontologically impossible. Its threat to identities and to the comprehension those identities allow could never be realized *in the order of difference* where those identities are positivizations of the cut that articulates them into being. Those boundaries, in other words, require incest and queerness as figures for what being excludes: the originary negativity embodied, and prohibited, in those made to figure ab-sens.

The prohibition of incest and queerness as what undoes articulated being structures the prohibition of Blackness too, which, as David Marriott writes, has "no locatable referent or unequivocal name, but is something that escapes all attributes."[72] As a corollary of incest's indeterminacy, inarticulable Blackness is excluded from thought to secure the identity that *literalizes* Blackness in a catachrestic nomination that sublimates its unintelligibility and conjures "the Black" (as it conjures "the queer") as an allegory, a personification, of what calls into question personhood, identity, and the proper. Arguing in a similar vein, Jared Sexton recognizes Blackness as antithetical to the economy of the literal or the proper, referring to Afropessimism's "general critique of the myriad recuperations of the proper at the singular expense of blackness (blackness in some ways as that expense of the proper)."[73] Like Derrida responding in *Archive Fever* to Josef Hayim Yerushalmi's assertion of the "absolute uniqueness" of "the link between Jewishness . . . and hope in the future," I can say that "I am prepared to subscribe without reservation" to Sexton's assertion with only "a single speck of anxiety about a solitary point," in fact, about a solitary word: Sexton's adjective, "singular."[74] As I have been arguing throughout this book, "the myriad recuperations of the proper" demand a myriad of catachreses, all of which try, without success, to secure the propriety of Being, the singularity of identity, against the pressure of the zero that makes every one not-all.

Because catachresis performs no trope or turn on some prior sense or name, because it literalizes by misnaming what has no "proper" name of its own, it invokes the impossible origin of language, the unthinkable primal positing by which literality begins: an origin as fully unthinkable as the origin of the incest taboo. The prohibition of incest, the subtraction of ab-sens, and the primal emergence of language all entail an articulating cut that produces entities, being, and sense by separating or cutting itself off from the negativity of incest, ab-sens, and sex. *Eve's Bayou* associates incest with this zero degree of sense and so with the catachrestic figures conjured to flesh out and deny it: conjured, that is, to *embody* the ab-sens whose subtraction enables "being." This is the stake in the film's last visualization of the "missing" scene.

Feeling guilty about causing her father's death and distraught that she may have occasioned it by crediting a lie, Eve confronts Cisely with her father's letter and accuses her of deceit. Despite her sister's protestations ("I wasn't lying!," she insists), Eve turns against her angrily: "I believed you. And I hated him. I hated him for you." At this point they both break down in tears, and Cisely moans, "He hurt me, Eve. He hurt me so bad I wanted to die." Though Eve begs her sister to tell her the truth, Cisely, barely able to speak, shakes her head and moans, "I can't." Does she refuse to tell what Eve wants to know or not know what Eve wants her to tell? To discover the truth about the kiss for herself, Eve puts out her hands, palms up, toward her sister. After pausing for a moment Cisely places her own, palms down, on top of Eve's (see figure C.10). This touch, taught Eve by her Aunt Mozelle, is a conduit for the second sight transmitted to certain women in the Batiste family through Eve, "the African slave." The images engendered when the sisters touch hands offer one last version of the incestuous kiss whose "reality" the film forecloses.

Though mere hallucinations from the perspective of Western Reason, these images attest to an epistemology through which the African Eve, a party to incest as "ethnical amalgamation," survives in a matrilineal descendance that evokes, as Kara Keeling writes, "a still-present past wherein slavery and freedom are indiscernible."[75] That indiscernibility, itself a property common to Blackness, queerness, and incest, attaches to the black-and-white images that constitute Eve's vision. After a traveling shot that pierces the bayou where her namesake last appeared, Eve sees her sister and Louis in profile, their lips repeatedly approaching each other's for the filial "kiss of redemption." Though it multiplies images of this redemptive kiss, the vision omits the incestuous one, cutting, instead, to repeated shots of Louis raising his hand to Cisely, whose head then reels from his slap (see figures C.10–C.18).[76]

The violence of that repeated slap, whether read as enforcing the incest taboo (as Louis's version affirms) or as reacting to its enforcement by Cisely (as her account proposes), displaces the kiss itself. The one violation of the "boundaries between" them substitutes for the other. Not even the epistemology of the African Eve can make present in the order of being the nonbeing that order excludes: the Blackness and the incest absented by law for the Symbolic order to "be." That order, which demands that everything "must be

C.10–C.18: Clairvoyance fails to see. From *Eve's Bayou* (Lemmons, 1997).

or not be in a particular place," makes incest, Blackness, queerness, woman, trans* (the list is endless) both impossible and atopic.[77] In fact, insofar as *atopia* has functioned (since Plato wrote Socrates into being) as a figure for irony's undoing of sense, we can say, rewriting de Man through Lacan, that sens-absexe is the allegorization of the atopic trope of irony, though that claim is no more intelligible than irony or *atopia* themselves. This book has argued, and Eve's vision suggests, that the allegorical redemption essential to pedag-archival transmission enacts the violence of negation in sublimating zero into one. *Eve's Bayou* ends with a primer on how such sublimation takes place.

Though baffled at first by her vision's failure to reveal what she wanted to see, Eve accepts that Cisely herself does not know what happened with her father, implicitly acknowledging a limit to what any order of sense can make present, regardless of the epistemology by which that order shapes the world.[78] Perhaps recognizing that *every* world forecloses what structures it through subtraction, Eve destroys her father's letter, submerging it in the bayou as if to realize Prospero's promise to "drown [his] book."[79] When he makes that pledge in *The Tempest*, of course, Prospero renounces the magic by which he kept Caliban enslaved. But Eve drowns her father's words in the bayou whose link to her namesake leaves the boundary between "slavery and freedom . . . indiscernible." And she does so to prevent the transmission of those words, to prevent their literalization as a truth that would free us from the indiscernibility, the Blackness or the queerness, that incest "is" (see figure C.19).

Her father's letter, in Eve's estimation, is not a story to pass on; it must become, instead, the absence, the void in the weather of what is. As Toni Morrison writes at the end of *Beloved*, echoing the force of Jacobs's reference to the "dark and troubled sea," "By and by all trace is gone, and what is forgotten is not only the footprints but the water too and what lies down there. The rest is weather. Not the breath of the disremembered and unaccounted for, but the wind in the eaves, or spring ice thawing too quickly. Just weather."[80] But what could "just weather" mean? Does it resonate with Wallace Stevens's "The Snow Man," where only "a mind of winter" could fail "to think / Of any misery in the sound of the wind"?[81] Indeed, whoever possesses such a mind becomes, for Stevens, both snow man and no man, an embodiment of nonbeing, of the "unaccounted for," who, "nothing himself, beholds / Nothing that is not there and the nothing that is." In the circulation of those repeated nothings, though, even nothing, finally, "is"; "being" becomes the impossibilization of the nothing that is not. By not passing on her father's letter, by refusing to be, like Hamlet, the archive of her father's word, Eve lets the

C.19: Drowning the letter. From *Eve's Bayou* (Lemmons, 1997).

letter, in *Hamlet*'s sense of impeding or preventing it, lest it become "le mot qui tranche," as Lacan describes the opening onto meaning in the topology of sens-absexe.[82] But the film *does* pass the letter on. Thus, despite its refusal to clarify what happened between Cisely and her father, it turns the encounter with incest/ab-sens, the encounter with the unknowable, into a lesson in the limits of knowledge, which, *as* lesson, masters those limits, much as the mind affirms self-transcendence in the experience of the sublime. The film affirms this comprehension that reestablishes harmony by pulling out all the stops in its final vision of aesthetic education.

After Eve submerges the letter, the camera frames the two sisters by the bayou in the evening's fading light. Hand in hand, their backs to the audience, the two girls gaze into the distance as the camera zooms out to produce an image that visualizes aesthetic redemption (see figures C.20–C.24). Positioned between the trunks of two trees, the two girls stand on a strip of ground that divides two branches of the bayou. Their images, doubled in the water, reflect their status as images themselves, images recalled by the grown-up Eve, whose voice-over, having opened the film, now returns to close it:

> The summer my father said goodnight, I was ten years old. My brother, Poe, was nine, and my sister, Cisely, had just turned fourteen. We are the descendants of Eve and Jean Paul Batiste. I was named for her. Like others before me, I have the gift of sight. But the truth changes color depending on the light. And tomorrow can be clearer than yesterday. Memory is a selection of images, some elusive, others imprinted indelibly on the brain.

> Each image is a like a thread. Each thread woven together to make a tapestry of intricate texture. And the tapestry tells a story. And the story is our past.

With its multiple figures of aesthetic transformation (the colors of painting, the textures of tapestry, and the narrative unfolding of story), this passage, supported by the framing of the sisters at the center of various symmetries, encloses the film in the spherical form that expresses the "satisfaction," in the words of Lacan, afforded by "the idea of the whole." But this totalization represses the excess and the lack of Louis's letter; it makes incest's indiscernibility, what can never be known or thought, the ground of the narrator's *Bildung*, allowing her to imagine a coherent world that could incorporate what it excludes. To that extent, the "missing" scene, the zero, gets read as a one, as a figural "thread" in a tapestry, that enables the "tell[ing of] a story," or, more exactly, of *the* story: the story of meaning's (re)production from the zero it excludes.

That story may be, in Eve's words, "our past," but it is also the allegorization of the Thing that neither passes nor passes into knowledge. Kara Keeling, attuned to the film's investment in "put[ting] the unthought . . . into thought," reads the end of *Eve's Bayou* as a failure to imagine what "the black femme function" anticipates: the expansion of affective possibilities into new forms of social relation incompatible with the coherence of those modes of thought construed as "common sense."[83] "The black femme," she writes, "both provides the affective labor necessary to reproduce hegemonic sociality and, along with the black butch, simultaneously does immaterial labor to produce alternative social networks. . . . With one foot in an aporia and another in the set of what appears, the black femme currently is a reminder that the set of what appears is never perfectly closed and something different might appear therein at any-instant-whatever."[84] Here, as with the question that the "missing" scene prevents us from resolving, the messianic, almost Benjaminian hope is that the excluded "might appear." While that hope shapes the film's sublimation of the kiss from incestuous threat to aesthetic "thread," Keeling wants the tapestry it generates to give us the future, not the past:

> The narrator's conclusion marks the film's failure to stop and allow space and time for the new that is becoming visible while Eve and Cisely hold hands by the bayou. The narrator's mundane musings at the end of the film about how truth is relative and the past is a "tapestry" of images, a narration jazzed up by the music that elevates it to the level of poetry, continues the movements necessary for the film to make (common) sense, but it fails to capitalize on the fresh grooves cut into the viewer's sensory-motor apparatus. To the common sense that *Eve's Bayou* secures

C.20–C.24: The aesthetic
sublimation of obscenity.
From *Eve's Bayou* (Lem-
mons, 1997).

with its perfunctory voiceover ending, those grooves remain irrational and ignored—invisible. In spite of the narrator's attempt at closure, the black femme function persists in *Eve's Bayou*, insisting on the existence of a radical Elsewhere.[85]

Keeling interprets the film as attempting to think the not-yet-thought; in consequence, she finds its closural gestures conventional and disappointing. Rather than "becoming visible," the "new" and unthought remains "radical[ly] Elsewhere." But perhaps the radicality of that "Elsewhere" bespeaks the *impossibility* of making it present and not a contingent failure to do so. "The set of what appears," as Keeling reminds us, remains open to "something different" that might appear at any moment. Such appearances, however, are possible only by excluding what *cannot* appear: the null set, always unnamed and unnameable, despite the catachrestic attempts to turn its nothing into something. Rather than thinking the not-yet-thought, *Eve's Bayou* addresses, as I've been arguing, the radically unthinkable. Such radicality is not one of magnitude, though; it does not pertain to a horror so great, like the ongoing toll of slavery, that the mind cannot comprehend it. It is an index, instead, of the limits on thought that give rise to such horrors in the first place. Those limits get transposed into limitations on what any order can comprehend, into prohibitions (of access to the order of being) of what is (ontologically) impossible: the incomprehensible zero whose catachreses include, among others, Blackness, queerness, woman, and incest.

Slavery, racism, xenophobia, ethnonationalism, femicide, anti-Blackness, transphobia, and queer bashing are, by extension, just a few of the names for the enforcement of the exclusion of nonbeing that those catachreses are produced to enable. But so, too, and this has been my point throughout, are philosophy, progressive politics, and aesthetic education. Indeed, the whole regime of thought, even at its most "progressive," necessarily repeats the exclusions at the origin of thought itself. By positivizing negativity, philosophy, progressive politics, and aesthetic education initiate worlds of desire whose sublimations preserve, in their displacement of it, the jouissance from which thought and desire both turn, ironically exposing that turn as a *trope* of the jouissance it repudiates. The pain of subjective destitution when the subject of desire comes too close to the Thing is the counterpart of subjective mastery through philosophy, politics, and art.

Bad education—were it possible, were "nothing" capable of being taught—would confront the subject with the "missing" scene in which meaning disappears: the ob-scene of ab-sens subtracted for the world and the subject to emerge. The originary moment of creation ex nihilo that establishes the topology of sens-absexe would revert, in such an impossible case, to the nihil troped as "creation"—a creation that consigns it, in its status *as* nihil, to non-being, to unintelligibility. The subject itself would vanish into the nothing it can never "know" but can only "become" by ceasing to "be": not by ending its animal existence, however, but by vanishing as a subject of meaning and becoming, instead, the acephalic subject of the Lacanian act or drive. This syncope of the subject of sense necessarily exceeds our thought, which must always recur to some image, some narrative that effaces the eclipse of meaning in the very process of conceiving it. In this way the conceptualization of nothing repeats the primal division that separates nothing from itself to yield the "not nothingness" of being, the false positive of ontology, through a founding act of *negation* allegorized as *creation* in "creation ex nihilo."[86]

We cannot, as Symbolic subjects, *not* participate in that creation. Even Bartleby, with his preference not to, creates a distinctive relation to being: a negativity for which Herman Melville's narrator, the Wall Street lawyer for whom Bartleby worked, makes him the privileged figure. At the same time, though, the lawyer invests that figure with a pathos that *negates* his negativity and that permits the lawyer's story to end with the appeal to communal value that is humanism's trump card: "Ah Bartleby! Ah humanity!"[87] The compulsory response to this humanistic construction of an affective community inverts the logic of the incest taboo—which prohibits what is impossible—to celebrate what is *inevitable* (aesthetic totalization) as an exceptional achievement. And that, I think, is what Lemmons visualizes in the final shots of *Eve's Bayou*: the compulsory aesthetic allegorization of the radical indiscernibility for which incest, Blackness, queerness, and irony are stabilizing names.

If I end with one last allegory of negativity's allegorization (the imperative to which joins philosophy, politics, religion, and aesthetic education), I do so because it reengages the text with which I began. As I suggested in chapter 1, Pedro Almodóvar's *Bad Education* attempts to make visible the "nothing to see" encountered when the subject of desire is eclipsed or blacked out by jouissance. In *Pain and Glory* (*Dolor y gloria*, 2019, El Deseo), he expands on aesthetic philosophy's compulsion to make such eclipses meaningful, revisiting many of the questions and themes he took up in the earlier film (including the emergence of sexual awareness, the insistence of aesthetic sublimation, and the division between drive and desire). By constructing *Pain and Glory* as a sort of response to *Bad Education*, Almodóvar revises the tragedy of the one as the late romance of the other.[88] If *Eve's Bayou* invokes *The Tempest*, then *Pain and Glory* recalls *The Winter's Tale* as it tracks how bitterness, rupture, and loss give way to redemption and return. And if Lemmons unfolds *Eve's Bayou* around flashbacks of dubious reliability, then Almodóvar shapes *Pain and Glory* around scenes *interpreted* as flashbacks until the film's final sequence reframes them with the force of an *après-coup*.

Pain and Glory recounts the restoration to a well-known filmmaker, Salvador Mallo (Antonio Banderas), of the friend he had quarreled with, the lover he had parted from, the physical and mental well-being he had lost, and the directorial career to which his ill health had put an end too soon. Presented as a leading light of La Movida Madrileña, like Almodóvar himself, Salvador Mallo (his very name anagrammatizes Almodóvar's) gained fame in the 1980s for films that spoke to a new generation. When *Pain and Glory* begins, however, his energy seems long since spent: the death of his mother and the various ailments that prevent him from making more films have left him isolated, depressed, and immobilized by physical and emotional pain.

First seen submerged in a swimming pool, unmoving in its teal blue light, he floats like the corpse of Joe Gillis (William Holden) in Billy Wilder's *Sunset Boulevard* (1950, Paramount Pictures), but without the corpse's buoyancy, hovering above the floor of the pool as if in suspended animation (see figure C.25). When the camera travels up his back, it follows the scar of an incision, recalling the fracture that sundered Ignacio's forehead when he fell in *Bad Education* (see figures C.26 and C.27). The relation of sundering to suturing, of incisions to cuts or scars, looms large in *Pain and Glory*'s conversation with the earlier film, to which, as Salvador's name makes clear, it responds with a tale of salvation that moves the protagonist from the first to the second of the film's two titular nouns.

As if prompted by the uterine overtones of his suspension in the pool, the film dissolves from the image of Salvador to a scene depicting his childhood. The transition takes place by superimposing over a close-up shot of his face the flowing waters of a river in which his mother, Jacinta (Penelope Cruz), will soon be seen scrubbing her laundry (see figures C.28–C.32).[89] This vision, which the film invites us to read as Salvador's recollection, takes him back to his origins, to his childhood, and to his mother, while returning the film, as Almodóvar notes, to the experience from which it sprang:

During the [summer] holidays I used to submerge myself in the pool to enjoy the weightlessness afforded by the water. It was the only time of the day when nothing hurt. All tension disappears under water. I decided that this was a good image with which to start my story and that is what I did. The water of the swimming pool took me to the current of the river

C.25–C.27: Suspension and division. From *Pain and Glory* (Almodóvar, 2019) and *Bad Education* (Almodóvar, 2004).

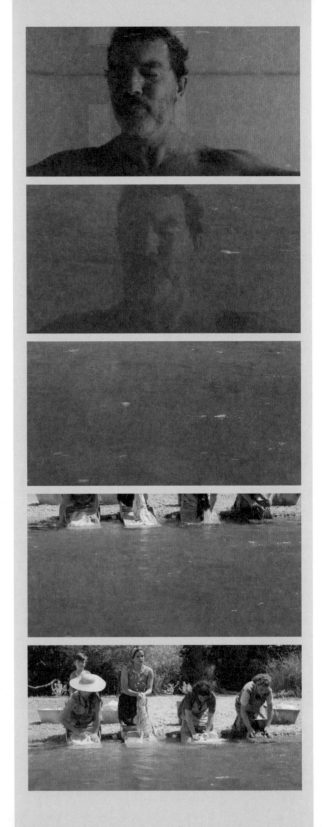

C.28–C.32: The memory of happiness in a time of pain. From *Pain and Glory* (Almodóvar, 2019).

where the women, including Salvador's mother, did the wash; a ritual full of life that Salvador watched at the age of four. When he recalls it in the swimming pool, he understands that this was probably the happiest day of his life. It is undoubtedly the best memory he has of his mother, overflowing with beauty and joy, singing songs with the other washerwomen while he played with the soap fish. This second sequence, the one by the river, established the alternation that I needed for my story, so as not to feel trapped by the darkness [*negrura*] that dominated the first notes.[90]

The "alternation" that counters such *negrura*—such "blackness," in its literal translation—with Salvador's "best memory" of his mother ("overflowing with beauty and joy") gestures toward what Lacan describes as the "*pulsative* function" of the unconscious.[91] It signals a rhythm of emergence and suppression in which unconscious material only appears in the mode of erasure or negation that serves to whitewash its *negrura*, much as the inscription on Jacobs's tombstone serves to whitewash her negativity. The *negrura* at issue in Almodóvar's film—a deep-rooted pain, of both body and soul, that condemns him to death-in-life—gives way to a vision of the past as pastoral, as an idealized landscape of aesthetic harmony inhabited by Jacinta and her friends.

Only in *Pain and Glory*'s last moments do we learn that this idyll, like every sequence showing Salvador in his youth, is not, in fact, a flashback per se but a proleptic glimpse of the film we will see him directing at the end.[92] Just as *Bad Education*'s Enrique and Ignacio are only seen as children in Enrique's *La Visita*, so we only see young Salvador in scenes from *El primer deseo* (*The First Desire*), a film in which he returns to work by reflecting on his passion for cinema. His restoration to creative vitality follows a series of events set in motion by a restoration of a different kind. As we learn in the scene that follows the "flashback" to his mother on the banks of the river, the cinematheque of Madrid has "restored the negative" (ha restaurado lo negativo) of his early film, *Sabor* (*Flavor*), which he directed some thirty years earlier, and has invited him to discuss it at a screening.[93] This moves him to reconnect with the star of *Sabor*, Alberto Crespo (Asier Etxeandia), from whom, as soon as he finished the film, Salvador cut himself off, angry that the actor's addiction to heroin resulted in a slow-paced performance. More appreciative now of Alberto's work, and regretting his decision to bar him from attending *Sabor*'s premiere, Salvador tries to make amends by inviting him to appear at the cinematheque to talk about the film. In a wild coincidence, his reunion with Alberto leads Salvador to reencounter his ex-lover,

Federico (Leonardo Sbaraglia), with whom he had been out of contact since they separated in the 1980s.[94]

Although Federico's heroin addiction put an end to their relationship (just as Alberto's interrupted their friendship), Salvador, now living with physical pain, joins Alberto in smoking heroin when he invites the actor to the screening. From that moment on he turns to it more and more for its palliative effects. Only when he sees Federico again does he determine to renounce the drug in favor of medical help instead. Shortly after, while waiting for a CAT scan, he sees a postcard for an exhibit of "people's art" (arte popular) being held at a local gallery. In another of the coincidences that suggest the film's link to Shakespearean romance, the image on the postcard shows a watercolor sketch of Salvador himself, a sketch the director has wholly forgotten in the fifty years since its creation by Eduardo (Cèsar Vicente), a handsome young mason employed by Jacinta, who paid him by letting her nine-year-old son teach him reading, writing, and math. The sketch restores to Salvador's memory the events adjacent to its creation: events that will have the effect, once recalled, of reawakening his passion for filmmaking (see figures C.33–C.35). This allows *Pain and Glory* to end with him directing *El primer deseo*, the film to which all the scenes of his childhood turn out to have belonged all along.

Those "memories," which punctuate Almodóvar's film, invite us to read them as flashbacks and so to think of Penelope Cruz, for example, as young Jacinta in *Pain and Glory* instead of as an actor who *plays* Jacinta in Salvador's *El primer deseo*. This "fictionalization" of Salvador's past, misrecognized as the past itself, this transformation of seeming memory into filmic representation, matters insofar as Almodóvar's film addresses the aesthetic mediation essential to his "autobiographical" cinema. In one of the very few flashbacks retrospectively legible as "really" a flashback (legible, that is, as a memory rather than as a sequence from Salvador's film), Julieta Serrano appears as Jacinta and warns her then sixty-year-old son (Banderas) against appropriating her life for his art; "I don't like autofiction" (No me gusta la autoficción), she declares.

Nor is this the only thing she objects to where Salvador is concerned; she announces out of the blue one day, "You have not been a good son" (No has sido un buen hijo). Her complaint—that after her husband's death Salvador ignored her offer to come live with him in Madrid—is not answered to her satisfaction by his insistence that she would have been lonely there while he was off making films. Both recognize a less altruistic motive: his desire to escape her judgment on his life (or on his "lifestyle," as the English subtitles

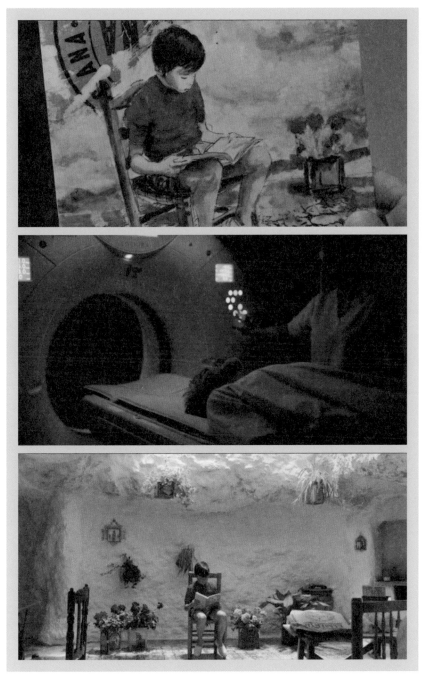

C.33–C.35: The past recovered. From *Pain and Glory* (Almodóvar, 2019).

put it). Responding to her accusation while obeying the taboo she imposes on talking about his sexuality openly, he apologizes for disappointing her, for not having been the son that she wanted and of whom she could have been proud. Sitting next to her on his terrace and inflecting his statement with the tone of a question, as if inviting her to deny it, he says, with the catch of a sob in his throat, "I have failed you simply by being as I am" (Te he fallado, simplemente por ser como soy).[95] Serrano's expression may suggest a hint of regret in Jacinta's silence, but the script describes a reaction wholly free of any such sentiment: "The mother doesn't respond; she keeps a cruel and dignified silence. She doesn't budge an inch."[96]

Her disapproval of the "failure" identified with the "being" of her son overdetermines *Pain and Glory*'s relation to *autoficción*. One the one hand, Almodóvar repeatedly acknowledges the film's proximity to his experience, referring to this scene in particular as "the only part of the film that moved me so much that it was difficult to direct, it brought tears to my eyes."[97] He even describes the feelings it unleashes as having inspired the film itself: "It's odd to have shot the entire film to scratch at an emotion about which I've never spoken, in the first place because it is very unpleasant and painful. There are things from my childhood that I have deliberately erased so that they did not weigh down my life, and one of those things was that way of looking at you like someone different, in a pejorative sense, that is included in the film. It's a very ugly feeling to remember and I got rid of it as soon as I came to Madrid."[98] The will to erase that "ugly feeling" prompts the erasure of its memory too, thus repeating, though to a different end, the negating impulse that motivates "that way of looking" in the first place. Excluded by such abjecting looks from the communities of his youth ("I was a different kind of child, and not just for my parents: I was a different kind of child for my town, for my school, and for my family"), Almodóvar sought, like Salvador, to escape them in Madrid.[99]

If, in this context, his protagonist refuses, until compelled by his mother's illness, to reawaken that childhood pain by welcoming Jacinta, and her "way of looking" at him, into his home in Madrid, then his mother's ultimate request in the film assumes an added weight: "Salvador, I brought you into this world and I dedicated myself to bringing you up. . . . Take me back to the village. That is my one last desire."[100] Though Jacinta's death prevents her son from keeping his pledge to do so, the emotional blackmail of her "last desire," imploring him to take her back to the very place from which he fled, determines the subject and title of the film with which he returns to directing: *El primer deseo*. Ironically, however, that first desire takes him back, at least cinematically, to the town Jacinta longed to see, granting his mother her *last* desire by returning her to the sun-drenched village in which he experienced his first.

Though Almodóvar acknowledges his own experience of having been seen as different ("in a pejorative sense") by his parents and his neighbors, he takes great pains to assert, nonetheless, that *"Pain and Glory* is not auto-fiction."[101] Referring to "the scenes with Julieta Serrano," he emphasizes that "[he does] not want [spectators] to think that [he] had problems with [his] mother, but rather to see [themselves] in front of their own mothers."[102] At the same time, though, he acknowledges that Serrano's performance moved him so deeply that he wrote new scenes for her during the shoot, including the scene on Salvador's terrace, and admits that those scenes were "hidden in some unconscious part of [him]self."[103] This contact with something unconscious—something negated or repressed—shapes not only the production but also the narrative of *Pain and Glory*. Like Almodóvar's film, *El primer deseo* engages something unconscious: in this case the memory of a *loss* of consciousness, a memory whose recovery repeats that loss by *seeming* to recuperate it. Precisely by giving us access to what his consciousness excluded, by positivizing through images the memory *once it's recovered*, Salvador loses the *negrura*, the blacking out from conscious memory, of the moment of blacking out.

His lost memory involves his relation to Eduardo, with whom he first locked eyes on the day he arrived with Jacinta in Paterna, the town where his father had finally found work. In *El primer deseo*'s rendition of the events surrounding the sketch's creation, his parents leave him alone with Eduardo, who is installing some tiles for his mother, while Salvador, wholly absorbed in a book, sits reading in the morning sunlight that pours in through the open-air atrium. The mason, having tapped the last tile in place, is struck by the boy's concentration. He seizes an empty cement bag thinly coated with a layer of plaster and rapidly sketches Salvador's pose. Displaying his work for the boy's approval, he announces his plan to finish it later with watercolor washes, then, remarking that he's covered with plaster and paint, asks permission to get cleaned up. While Salvador goes to get some soap, Eduardo positions a washbasin on the boy's now-empty chair, preparing to scrub himself down in the space filled by Salvador in the sketch. After he hands Eduardo the soap, the boy, feeling weak from too much sun, retreats to his darkened bedroom while the mason strips down to bathe.

Feverish with sunstroke and half asleep, Salvador listens to the sound of the water laving Eduardo's body and hears, alongside it, though introduced without diegetic explanation, the electric buzz of insects heretofore absent from the scene. Roused of a sudden by Eduardo's voice asking for a towel, the boy, still groggy, goes to retrieve one. As he approaches the atrium, towel in hand, the camera, adopting his point of view, shows Eduardo, facing him frontally, standing naked in the sunlight that bathes him from above. Gaping, the boy stops dead in his tracks, drops the towel, and falls down, unconscious (see figures C.36–C.40).

The crux of the scene, its navel, as it were, is this sudden loss of consciousness. It encapsulates *Pain and Glory*'s alternation between "beauty and joy," on the one hand, and *negrura*, on the other, as the film enacts, to return to Lacan, the "*pulsative* function" of the unconscious, collocating the aesthetic radiance of the scene with an instance of blacking out. Though this syncope bespeaks an encounter with the Real unbearable to the subject of consciousness, the film encourages explanations that are simpler and more comic as well: Salvador faints, like a Victorian lady, at the sight of Eduardo's endowment; or he passes out at the breathtaking beauty of the young man's naked form; or he is overwhelmed by the recognition of a nascent gay desire; or, trading psychic for somatic causation, he suffers the effects of sunstroke. These readings master his loss of sense by restoring the sense he loses, securing our access to meaning as Salvador's hold on it slips away. They sublimate the boy's unbearable encounter with the Real, filling with signification the void that prompts his eclipse as a subject not, as the logic of sublimation would affirm, in response to his "primer deseo" but rather in response to what Almodóvar calls the "primeras pulsiones sexuales": "I remember my first sexual drives [*primeras pulsiones sexuales*] at nine years old. I remember how [it was] and in what circumstances. Sexuality begins at that age, you are not conscious [of it] because you are not your body nor do you know what you have to do. But desire exists within you."[104] Notwithstanding the contradictions here (the drives elude our consciousness, but Almodóvar remembers their emergence), this remark conflates "el primer deseo" with the "primeras pulsiones sexuales" by returning the object of desire to its unconscious relation to the Thing, to the nonobject on which the drive, indifferent to the reign of desire, insists.

Salvador may fix on Eduardo as the crystallized embodiment of his budding desire but only because desire blots out the drive on which it leans. His blacking out, in other words, is the blacking out *of the drive*, where the ambiguous genitive ("of the drive") announces the drive as agent and object of this blacking out at once. The sexually self-conscious subject of desire emerges from this syncope—which Salvador views, retrospectively, as the birth of "el primer deseo"—because the subject's desire blacks out the relation of that

C.36–C.40: The first desire. From *Pain and Glory* (Almodóvar, 2019).

syncope to the drive; it blacks out, that is, the blacking out's source in a too-close approach to the Thing that it afterward sublimates, or positivizes, in its objects of desire.

Salvador's blacking out thus enacts the ab-sens absented from thought by the subject of desire's division from the subject of the drive, the ab-sens *blacked out* by sens-absexe, in the topology of which, as Lacan asserts, "c'est le mot qui tranche." Salvador, of course, is not *literally* constituted as a subject of desire at this moment. He was, as a speaking subject, a *desiring* subject long before. But to the extent that he reads this vision of Eduardo, retrospectively, as his "primer deseo," it *allegorizes* the birth of desire through the sublimation of the drive. The blackout collapses desire and drive, condensing them into the *atopia* "before" their differentiation, "before" the being of the subject that only that differentiation secures. This syncope coincides with the indiscernibility at issue in *Eve's Bayou* as well: the incest—(ontologically) impossible and (legally) prohibited at once—from which every queerness descends.

Pain and Glory explores this link to incest through its scenes from *El primer deseo*, provided that we pay attention to what that film within the film lays bare. But the problem—which is also the problematic this book has engaged from the outset—lies in the lure of such "laying bare," which gestures toward allegorical unveiling and Eduardo's nakedness at once, conflating the object of Salvador's gaze, the spur to his recognition of desire, with allegory's demonstration, in Benjamin's phrase, of the "voluptuousness with which significance rules." But Eduardo's nakedness, paradoxically, *covers up*, by dressing in the garments of desire (the desire for Eduardo's uncovering), the attachment to the Thing that animates incest and the drive alike: the Thing no form, however naked, could fail to conceal *by giving it form*. Framed between two zones of darkness before Salvador blacks out (see figure C.37), Eduardo's nakedness distracts us from and sublimates what never appears as such: the void, the nonbeing, catachrestically named (and, thereby, disavowed) as Blackness and queerness, but also as incest.

Consider how Eduardo's nakedness magnetizes spectatorial desire while obscuring the psychic centrality of the object in the literal center of the frame. Though unequal to the task of competing with the young man's naked appeal to the eye, the washbasin, rather than Eduardo, occupies that pivotal place—the place of the boy who, sitting there earlier, inspired the mason's sketch (see figures C.41–C.42).

These three elements—the boy's aestheticized image, Eduardo's eroticized body, and the washtub that mediates between them (to the extent that it occupies the place of the former while contiguous with the latter)—gesture

C.41–C.42: The center of the frame. From *Pain and Glory* (Almodóvar, 2019).

toward what presents itself only allusively in the scene. They evince the pull of an "other scene" that dialecticizes this one: *El primer deseo*'s primal scene (in the chronology of *Pain and Glory*), which reproduces, in Almodóvar's words, "the best memory [Salvador] has of his mother, overflowing with beauty and joy." That scene, the one by the river, begins with Salvador sitting on Jacinta's back as she kneels by the edge of the water, scrubbing laundry with her friends. The four-year-old boy, in the words of the screenplay, is "ecstatic with happiness" (exultante de felicidad) in this pastoral setting where "all is perfect, the water of the river, the fish in his hands, the pure white sheets [*sábanas blanquísimas*] spread over the reeds and pennyroyals, his mother smiling, and the women singing 'A tu vera.'"[105] The aesthetic insistence of this sequence (recalling the conclusion of *Eve's Bayou*), the radiance with which it visualizes the primal scene of Salvador's youth, anticipates the conjunction of aesthetics and desire in the scene with the naked Eduardo. Its perfection suggests the secondary revision by which contradictory psychic materials acquire a coherent shape, in the present case by serving to establish, to return to Almodóvar's phrase, "the alternation that I needed for my story, so as not to feel trapped by the darkness that dominated the first notes." From the outset, that is, the purpose of the scene is to sublimate *negrura*, to displace it with the whiteness ("blanquísima") of aesthetic luminosity that enables the "alternation" of *negrura* and light so as not to be "trapped by the darkness." But that very alternation speaks to the "*pulsative* function" of the unconscious that makes the whiting out of *negrura* a negation or blacking out too.

When that blacking out gets literalized with Salvador's collapse, the *negrura* returns as a corollary to the central object in the frame (see figure C.42). Not merely a response to the desire aroused by the sight of Eduardo's nakedness, the syncope betrays an *après-coup*, a retroactive trauma, occasioned by the contiguity of the naked man and the washtub. The former may awaken the boy's "first desire," but the latter *reawakens* an earlier one that shadows it from the beginning, a desire that is not a desire per se but a crossing into "the unspeakable field of radical desire that is the field of absolute destruction, of destruction beyond putrefaction," the field that Žižek associates with "the Lacanian incestuous Thing."[106] The washtub, after all, returns us, as it must have returned the boy, to the day by the river with his mother as Salvador depicts it in *El primer deseo*.[107] In the film he puts such a basin in close proximity to Jacinta, who leans forward on her hands and knees while Salvador straddles her back (see figure C.43). Used literally as a vehicle for whitewashing here—for carrying the "sábanas blanquísimas"—the basin conveys the anti*negrura* that aestheticizes the scene. It carries or transports (the literal meaning of *metapherein*, the root of *metaphor*) the bedsheets whose whiteness serves to displace (and excite) the erotics of the bed, thus establishing a connection between their whiteness and Salvador's moment of blacking out. The sequence by the river, in other words, sublimates the "incestuous Thing" by whiting out "the unspeakable field of radical desire"; domesticating the boy's enjoyment by reducing it to pleasure, this scene—which, like the scene with Eduardo, seems the referent of "*el primer deseo*"—negates the radicality of "radical desire" by attaching it to an object: the m/other as aesthetic form.

Two points require emphasis, though. First: as objects of Salvador's desire that get blacked or whited out (the aesthetic whiting out of *negrura* serves, like *negrura*'s blackings out, to perform an erasure or exclusion), both Eduardo and Jacinta *equally* positivize the incestuous, indiscernible Thing. No

C.43: The mother and the washbasin. From *Pain and Glory* (Almodóvar, 2019).

more than Eduardo is his mother "really" the object of incestuous desire. Incest has no "real" object; it only has a *Real* one, which has no object-form. Second: by describing as "unspeakable" the field of radical desire, Lacan intends something other than a Lovecraftian heightening of its horror; he aims to define with exactitude incest's resistance to exact definition, its catachrestic naming of the Real in all its undifferentiated negativity as forever excluded from, and by, Symbolic articulation.[108] Thus, Salvador's fall from consciousness signals the traumatic conflation of the object-desire excited by his glimpse of Eduardo with the incestuous enjoyment reawakened by Eduardo's nearness to the tub.

While that tub is the visual switch point here, transporting the tincture of erotic desire from the later scene to the earlier one while carrying the trauma of incestuous enjoyment in the opposite direction, it is not all that links these two moments. The sound of the water as Eduardo bathes harks back to the river's current; the bar of soap the boy hands him recalls the one Jacinta drops in the stream, around which the soap fish gather; and the first words uttered in *Pain and Glory*—spoken by Rosita, Jacinta's friend, in *El primer deseo*'s "primal scene"—are ripe for reactivation when Salvador sees Eduardo: "I'd like to be a man so I could bathe in the river naked."[109]

Where the scene by the river sublimates Salvador's attachment to his mother, expunging all traces of the incestuous Thing through its pastoralizing aestheticism, his response to the naked Eduardo retroactively mobilizes its "impurity," the enjoyment that the soap, the soap fish, the pure white sheets, and the beauty of the mise-en-scène all strive to wash away. Eduardo becomes Salvador's first desire by virtue of being his second, though only the spectacle of Eduardo's body in proximity with the tub spurs Salvador to unconscious recognition of his mother as his first. This condensation of Eduardo and Jacinta, both occupying the place of "el primer deseo" in its relation to the drive, proves psychically unbearable, and Salvador loses consciousness. To read his syncope, in this context, as a manifestation of gay identity or an expression of queer desire would erase the queerness of the *loss* of identity that the blacking out performs, the queerness of the unenlightenment, the *negrura*, that identity, like desire, whites out. Queerness, that is, pertains to the Blackness of Salvador's blacking out—a Blackness, like incest, foreclosed from thought in a world whose condition of being is the prohibition of those made to figure the impossibility of what "is" "not."

As the naked Eduardo's contiguity with the tub seems responsible for Salvador's blackout, so that blackout is figured metonymically by the sketch juxtaposed with it in time. Reencountered some fifty years later, the sketch reactivates Salvador's memory of the events that caused the blackout, inspiring his return to cinema through his "autoficción," *El primer deseo*. But the blackout enacts a loss of sense and a falling away of identity, while the drawing asserts the mastery of sense by imaging Salvador reading. Its homage to literacy and education gains force from its production by the mason who learned to read under Salvador's tutelage (and who later sends him a letter signed "your student," "tu alumno"). Reaffirming the topology of sens-absexe, wherein "the word is determining" (c'est le mot qui tranche), the sketch enshrines legibility and the achievement of comprehension while capturing Eduardo's teacher—the pedagogue as *sujet supposé savoir* (the subject supposed to know)—just minutes before he is brought down to earth by the drive that no knowledge can master. Like Salvador's *El primer deseo*, or like Almodóvar's *Pain and Glory*, Eduardo's drawing sublimates the void the boy will later encounter, assimilating the access to meaning procured by Salvador's act of reading to the fantasy of comprehension that makes education inherently aesthetic.

With this the film offers another way of construing "el primer deseo": as the foundational emergence of desire out of drive, as the logic that procures the subject's "being" through its sublimation of the zero and its investment in the one that gives it and its world their consistency.[110] This, as I noted in chapter 1, defines education for Lucien Israël: "Education is education against the drive. To lead out of . . . , that's what educate means, to lead out of the universe of the drive."[111] But the pedag-archival imperative, as exemplified in *Hamlet*, attaches this movement "out of" the drive to the enjoyment of the drive itself. Even in battling "against the drive," education repeats the negativity of its unyielding repetitions. This speaks to the double valence of desire in pedag-archival institutions, where desire, as Derrida argues, informs both the eros that establishes the archive and, in the Lacanian sense of "radical desire," the death drive that destroys it. The displacement of the latter by the former is what education means and the means by which it achieves that end is the allegorical production of meaning, Benjamin's "'opening of the eyes.'"

Education, which is always education in desire "lead[ing] out of the universe of the drive," is necessarily, then, a *good* education: education in the good to shelter us from the incursion of radical evil. Recall how Žižek describes such evil as discussed in chapter 3: "[Radical evil] entails the breakdown of the logic of representation, i.e., the radical incommensurability between the field of representation and the unrepresentable Thing."[112] Disregarding arguments over pedagogical technique or the efficacy of individual teachers, strictures against so-called bad education assail (as they did in the case of Socrates) teachings, thoughts, or fields of thought perceived as endangering a community's foundational attachment to being itself. Such fields have included, in recent years, Black studies, ethnic studies, critical race studies, queer studies, disability studies, trans* studies, women's studies, and gender and sexuality studies. Condemned as frivolous and subversive at once, as both wasteful in their insignificance and as laying waste to all that "is," these fields bear the taint of ontological negation attached to the communities they engage. Like the members of those groups, who figure the nothing inaccessible to thought, these fields are often subjected to forms of censure or prohibition despite aspiring to something impossible: making present the Thing that "is" not.

This brings us back to the incest taboo, which, as Ramadanovic writes, "is differentiated as a function—its function being to separate the orders of nature and culture and make each possible." As the articulating cut that establishes the Symbolic as the order of articulation, the incest taboo, the founding prohibition and the site of "el primer deseo," prohibits, first and foremost, *nothing*. Through a negative gesture dividing nothing into itself and its own negation—creating something (not-nothing) ex nihilo—it makes possible thought by way of making the thought of nothing *im*possible. To use an image equally resonant in the work of Lacan and de Man, we could say that the zero of the incestuous Thing occasions an anamorphosis: nothing, through the negation that prohibits it, produces the universe of "things" as its tropes. These are the beings, objects, and entities, the "ones," that make up reality and populate a world. But they also include those "ones" made to figure, in any given world, the zero—the incestuous Thing that is no-thing or nothing—by *literalizing* nonbeing, which then, in the form of those ones, can be excluded from reality by excluding *them*. Though James Baldwin would never have used these terms, he had in mind something similar when he wrote, near the end of *The Fire Next Time*, "Color is not a human or a personal reality; it is a political reality."[113] It refers, that is, to a figure of the Real against which a given idea of the human, invariably political, takes shape. Black persons, then, like "women" or "queers," like all the catachrestic instantiations of nothing, are made to "be" not-being within particular social formations and at different scales of abjection and violence. Denise Ferreira da Silva puts it well: "For blackness refers to matter—as The Thing; it refers to that without form—it functions as a nullification of the whole signifying order that sustains value in both its economic and ethical scenes."[114] Insofar as it refers to what has no form and "nullifi[es]" the "signifying order," such a Blackness (as distinct from the lived realities of persons literalized as Black), like queerness (as distinct from the lived realities of persons literalized as "queer"), coincides with incest's status as a catachresis of ab-sens.[115] Thus, the prohibition of incest/ab-sens makes economy the ethics of humanism, as Ferreira da Silva's play on the meaning of "value" may suggest; economy, like education, would lead us out of the drive's aneconomy, its expenditure without reserve.

Pedag-archival institutions necessarily sustain this ethical economy, bound as they are to practices of conservation and survival. The positivization of the drive (in the form of desire and the desire for form) attaches us both to objects and to aesthetic education, to the education in mastery that allegory always subtends. The Salvador whose mastery of reading Eduardo idealizes in his sketch may still be toppled by unconsciousness, felled by the indiscernibility bound up with incest and irony alike, but the drawing, by inspiring *El primer deseo*, comes to image, as does the film itself, irony's "redemption" by allegory: the escape from irony's aneconomy, from its Blackness or *negrura* ("I once was blind"), into allegory's insight ("but now I see"). As the anamorphosis of nothing, though—that is, as the trope of irony, according to de Man—allegorical unveiling creates an illusion of sense it can never deliver. To return to the passage from de Man cited earlier: "To say then, as we are actually saying, that allegory (as sequential narration) is the trope of irony (as the one is the trope of zero) is to say something that is true enough but not intelligible."[116]

Dismissing as "excessively negative"—that is, as exemplars of bad education—all who attend to this unintelligibility instead of celebrating "becoming," readers like Ruti, Coffman, and Cole display their progressive bona fides (and their faith in inclusive community) while repeating the structural exclusion of incest, nonbeing, and unintelligibility—exclusions that reflect the originary antagonism that founds the Symbolic order. The politics of becoming they advocate is itself a sublimation—an allegorical anamorphosis—of nothing's "excessive" negativity. However admirable their efforts—and they *are*, without irony, admirable: perhaps *too* admirable, *too* unironic—the project of affording (some) Blacks, (some) "queers," (some) women, (some) catachreses of nothingness the shelter of the communal count, can never prevent the communal exclusion of Blackness, queerness, or the myriad other catachreses of ab-sens. Precisely insofar as they credit the count and its capacity to name and include, these critics share the commitment of politics, whether it leans to the left or the right, to the pedagarchival logic of desire's displacement of the drive—a logic that requires, as a corollary to the sublimation of the drive's aneconomy, the antiqueerness or anti-Blackness that guards against its return.

Allegory traces the emergence of meaning as the anamorphotic gesture that translates the zero into a one. All cultural products enshrine that emergence, even, or perhaps especially, when they seem to expose its mechanics. Both Eduardo's sketch and Almodóvar's film call attention to their material substrates, as if trying to keep us from forgetting what aesthetic freedom transcends. The former associates reading, for instance, with the mastery of legible form, but the only words it incorporates belong to the cement bag on which it was sketched (see figure C.44). And the latter ends with a demonstration of cinema's transformative power: the camera tracks back from Jacinta and Salvador, in what seems like a flashback to Salvador's youth, only to reveal, with the shock of a retrospective understanding, its status as a scene that Salvador is directing for *El primer deseo* (see figures C.45–C.46). This belatedly alters our reading of *all* the "flashbacks" to Salvador's youth; only with the veil of illusion lifted (though still within the illusionism of Almodóvar's film) do we realize that they were prolepses of *El primer deseo* all along. The satisfaction produced by this allegorical "'opening of the eyes'" is redoubled by our awareness of Almodóvar's controlling presence outside the frame, directing the scene for *Pain and Glory* (produced by his company, El Deseo), in which his stand-in, Salvador, directs the scene for the diegetic *El primer deseo*.

Like the part of the cement bag that remains untouched by the artistry of Eduardo's sketch, this glimpse of the reality transmuted by Salvador's aesthetic mediation seems to foreground the freedom of the mind to exceed the limits of sensuous reality precisely by way of its reflection *in* that sensuous

C.44–C.46: The substrate of the image. From *Pain and Glory* (Almodóvar, 2019).

reality. With this it rises above itself, as it does in the sublime. Both pedagogy and culture enact that sublimation, which perhaps explains de Man's reference to teaching as "more than ever and profoundly Schillerian."[117] Explicitly responding to Schiller's work, Hegel describes art as the field in which "the sensuous is *spiritualized*, i.e., the *spiritual* appears in sensuous shape."[118] But the shaping through which that shape appears, by expressing thought's imprint on matter, makes the sensuous as such the semblance of itself and, therefore, a one, not a zero (not the meaningless material from which meaning is made, but the material made to *mean* meaninglessness and not, therefore, without meaning). Hegel puts it as follows: "What [art] requires is sensuous presence, which, while not ceasing to be sensuous, is to be liberated from the apparatus of its merely material nature. And thus the sensuous in works of art is exalted to the rank of a mere *semblance* in comparison with the immediate existence of things in nature, and the work of art occupies the mean between what is immediately sensuous and ideal thought."[119]

It follows that we can never conceive the sensuous in its sensuous immediacy, its "merely material nature," even outside of art; we can only know the mediated thought or idea of that immediacy. Hegel may assert "the foreignness of the Idea to natural phenomena," but the reflective consciousness of the subject sees such phenomena through ideas.[120] "Man is animal," Hegel writes, but "just for the reason that he knows himself to be animal, he ceases to be animal, and, as *mind*, attains to self-knowledge."[121] We have seen, with Jacobs and Douglass, the price of privileging such "self-knowledge," defined as philosophy and reason, in order to distinguish "Man" from "animal," or the immediacy of nature from "the being of spirit," which, in Hegel's view, "is not . . . immediate, but is, exists only as producing itself, as making itself for itself by means of negation as subject."[122] Like the negation that generates not-nothing ex nihilo, this negation of immediacy separates itself from what Hegel calls the "formlessness" of "what is indifferent or undifferentiated"—from the nondefinition and nonidentity that this book has been calling incest, queerness, Blackness, and all the infinite catachreses of zero or of nothing.[123]

This leads to Hegel's version of "education against the drive." "It is in the very nature of spirit," he writes, "just because it is living, to be at first only potential, to be in its notion or conception, then to come forward into existence, to unfold, produce itself, become mature, bringing forth the notion of itself, that which it implicitly is, so that what it is in itself or implicitly may be its notion actually or for itself. The child is not as yet a reasonable person; it has capacities only, it is at first reason, spirit, potentially only. It is by means of education and development that it becomes spirit."[124] Providing the template, acknowledged or not, for progressive theorists of becoming, Hegel's education as "becom[ing] spirit" replicates the becoming that is spirit as such, "spirit being essentially this activity of self-production" whose "goal . . . is that spirit should know itself, comprehend itself, should become object to itself."[125]

This movement toward a total comprehension sublates the division of subject and object by reflecting the former into the latter, recalling in this the Schillerian claim that the individual, by cultivating beauty, can successfully "harmonize" with the "unalterable unity" of its "pure ideal."[126] At the same time, it anticipates Lacan's evocation of politics as inherently aesthetic and as resting on the false "idea . . . that knowledge could produce a totality." In the passage where he makes this claim (which is cited more fully above), Lacan lays out the continuity of politics and aesthetics. "The idea of the whole," he tells us, "is part of the political preaching based on the good form of satisfaction, on that which makes a sphere; taken to its limit, what is more beautiful, but also what is less open, what more closely resembles the self-enclosure of satisfaction?"[127] However "beautiful" this political idea, the totality it imagines in the "form" of the "sphere" precludes the irreparable division that structures and defines the Lacanian subject. For just that reason the process of becoming, as even Ruti acknowledges, must be "endlessly renewed," along with the performance, both political and aesthetic, of the innumerable cultural sublimations that make allegory a trope of irony.

The Schillerian "ideal" of "unity," then, is always already purged of the cut, the ab-sens it never includes in the count no matter how earnestly progressives may seek a community without exclusion. The assumption that "knowledge could produce a totality," to borrow Lacan's formulation of our governing aesthetico-political predicate, takes totality as the totality of being, perpetuating the exclusion of the nothing, the nonbeing incapable of being known. Whether promoted by thinkers on the right or the left, the fantasy of aesthetic community preserves the prohibition of this nonbeing, which is also the prohibition of incest, indiscernibility, and the Real, and so the prohibition that establishes community in the first place. Ironically, were community without division possible, it would embody the incest, the queerness, the Blackness, and so the ironic indetermination of the "universe of the drive" from which, like the Haneke of *Funny Games*, education purports to lead us.

Jean-Paul Sartre, in *Being and Nothingness*, challenges Hegel's claim that being is "pure indetermination and emptiness" in which nothingness "can be apprehended" from the outset.[128] Asserting that even negations of being instantiate the "logical priority of being" that "has no need of nothingness," Sartre turns back to the example of Socrates and his pedag-archival transmission: "Even

Socrates, with his famous statement, 'I know that I know nothing,' designates by this *nothing* the totality of being considered as Truth."[129] Working within a Lacanian frame, this book has reversed that picture, maintaining the priority of the nothing whose self-negation, whose relentless negativity, produces being by way of the sens-absexe that swells up when ab-sens is absented. Consonant with the Lacanian dictate that creation can only take place ex nihilo, I have focused on the structural consequences of this troping of the zero as a one—a troping whose tropological nature remains, in de Manian terms, unintelligible, but that every institution of culture, determined by the pedag-archival imperative, ceaselessly repeats and literalizes in defense of intelligibility.

My claim for the structural, and therefore intractable, insistence of division and exclusion undoubtedly poses a challenge to the political hope for "collective becoming," but it does not imply that those bound to such hope are dupes who need wising up. We all, inevitably, are bound to that hope through our attachment to, our predication on, the world of sens-absexe; education's allegorical logic, in the form of "wising up," can offer us no escape. To the contrary, that narrative movement from ignorance to knowledge, from blindness to vision, exemplifies the compulsory "becoming" to which, as subjects, we are bound. Every effort, including this one, to expose the stranglehold of allegory reproduces it *as exposure*. The allegorical determination of social life (through the unveiling of meaning in matter, through the supersession and exclusion of what is not) is inseparable from the prohibition of incest, from the unthinkability of nondifferentiation, on which our very "being" depends.

To insist on the limits of knowledge, to take the uncounted into account in order to counter the idea of totality with the pressure of the not-all: this is the task of bad education—and the task of queer theory, as well. Like them, it is both impossible and, for that very reason, imperative. The nothing precluding totality will always elude our grasp, but not for a moment does it relinquish, or even loosen, its grasp on us. As the drive (inherent in the subject), or as irony (inherent in language), or as a threat to communal being (inherent in the sociopolitical field), the specter of nothing haunts "what is" as its structuring antagonism, as the queerness, the Blackness, the persistent ab-sens made unthinkable by sens-absexe.

While important work remains to be done on the social, historical, and material conditions experienced by "queer" beings, I have argued for the central importance of the cut that puts queerness outside of being and then literalizes the "outside of being" in those construed as queer. Thus, the more queer theory theorizes queerness, the less it substantializes "queers." Instead, it turns its attention to queering as a tropological figure, a catachrestic positing, an anamorphotic literalization defending against the Real. Coextensive in this with allegory, ethics, economy, and a vast array of pedag-archival institutions, this defense makes studies of tropology central to the politics of queer theory even as queer theory ironizes the concept of "the political."

Politics, after all, while adjudicating irony's relation to the literal, takes shape as a figure itself: a figure of the "knowledge [that] could produce a totality," a perfect comprehension, an aesthetic community.[130] Because queering, like Blackening, or sexing, is, to return to Baldwin's words, a "political reality," not "a human or a personal" one, it designates the point of contact between politics, figuration, and the unintelligibility that politics insists on "knowing" to death. Resisting the political gravity of the pedag-archival apparatus, Socrates asserts, as quoted by Sartre, "I know that I know nothing." This book, by contrast, ends on a note less sanguine and more jarring: "I know that I *don't* know nothing." *No one* can know the nothing that every *one*, to be a one, "no"s. Such negations of nothing make history and politics, as pedag-archival institutions, allegorical sublimations that elevate knowledge to the dignity of the Thing, which is to say to the place of *das Ding* as incestuous, indiscernible, impossible. Queer theory, like bad education, posits our nescience of that nothing, but nothing, including queer theory, can keep us from "knowing" its catachreses or from trying to get rid of that nothing precisely by getting rid of *them*.

The camera tracks back as the author completes the text of *Bad Education*, which exposes his revision of Socrates—"I know that I *don't* know nothing"—as yet another allegory turning nothing into knowledge. If allegory is a "trope of irony," though, "as the one is the trope of zero," then, ironically, by "say[ing] something that is true enough but not intelligible," it has come as close to queerness, Blackness, and ab-sens as any "one" can.

Notes:

Preface

1 Evan Hill, Ainara Tiefenthäler, Christiaan Triebert, Drew Jordan, Haley Willis, and Robin Stein, "How George Floyd Was Killed in Police Custody," *New York Times*, May 31, 2020, https://www.nytimes.com/2020/05/31/us/george-floyd-investigation.html. See also Mike Baker, Jennifer Valentino-DeVries, Manny Fernandez, and Michael LaForgia, "Three Words. 70 Cases. The Tragic History of 'I Can't Breathe,'" *New York Times*, June 29, 2020, https://www.nytimes.com/interactive/2020/06/28/us/i-cant-breathe-police-arrest.html.

2 Bostock v. Clayton County, Georgia, 590 U.S. ___ (2020), majority opinion by Justice Neil Gorsuch, available at https://www.supremecourt.gov/opinions/19pdf/17-1618_hfci.pdf.

3 Bostock v. Clayton County, Georgia, 590 U.S., majority opinion by Justice Neil Gorsuch.

4 Bostock v. Clayton County, Georgia, 590 U.S.

5 Adam Nagourney and Jeremy W. Peters, "A Half-Century On, an Unexpected Milestone for L.G.B.T.Q. Rights," *New York Times*, June 15, 2020, https://www.nytimes.com/2020/06/15/us/politics/supreme-court-lgbtq-rights.html.

6 Nagourney and Peters, "A Half-Century On, an Unexpected Milestone for L.G.B.T.Q. Rights." Without questioning the symbolic significance or the widespread impact of the resistance at the Stonewall Inn, we do a disservice to the courageous people who pursued gay rights for decades before it by foreshortening the historical record and ignoring the work of the Mattachine Society, the Daughters of Bilitis, and other organizations dedicated to procuring justice for those denied it because of their sexual orientation, sexual identity, or sexual practices.

7 Bobby Seale, "Interview with Bobby Seale," conducted by Blackside, Inc., November 4, 1998, Eyes on the Prize II Interviews, Washington University Digital Gateway Texts, http://digital.wustl.edu/e/eii/eiiweb/sea5427.0172.147bobbyseale.html. See also item 8 of the "Letter to Parents Concerning the Black Panthers," reprinted from "What Do the Panthers Stand For" (1970),

https://ia803109.us.archive.org/34/items/mcsa_S6_1970BlackPantherParty /1970BlackPantherParty.jpg: "As a first step we want a truce signed between black, white, and brown working people, in the community and on the job, as we recognize that fighting among ourselves only serves the rich."

8 Ibram X. Kendi, *How to Be an Antiracist* (New York: Random House, 2019), 222.

9 Kendi, *How to Be an Antiracist*, 49, 238.

10 Kendi, *How to Be an Antiracist*, 223.

11 Frank B. Wilderson III, *Afropessimism* (New York: Liveright, 2020), 14.

12 Angela Y. Davis, *Freedom Is a Constant Struggle: Ferguson, Palestine, and the Foundations of a Movement* (Chicago: Haymarket Books, 2016), 18.

13 Wilderson, *Afropessimism*, 331.

14 As the introduction argues, the logic of sexual difference in the Symbolic, informed by what Lacan calls *sens-absexe*, takes shape through the subtraction of sexe (ab-sexe) in order to generate sense.

15 The paradigmatic nature of sexual difference does not make its correlation with the established binarism of male and female necessary, contrary to Justice Alito. It insists only that a marker of difference will shape Symbolic subjects and that any such marker, whatever it may be, will carry a libidinal force.

16 *Oxford English Dictionary Online*, s.v. "queer (adj.)," accessed March 11, 2022, https://www.oed.com/view/Entry/156236.

17 "USCCB President 'Deeply Concerned' about Court's LGBT Ruling," *Intermountain Catholic*, June 19, 2020, http://www.icatholic.org/article/usccb-president -deeply-concerned-about-courts-lgbt-24213922.

18 See, among others, Manuela Tobias and Anthony Galavi, "Woman Allegedly Attempts to Deface Fresno Black Lives Matter Street Art," *Fresno Bee*, June 19, 2020, https://www.fresnobee.com/news/local/article243672582.html; and Marissa Parra, "Oak Park Black Lives Matter Mural Painted Over to Read, 'All Lives Matter,'" *CBS Chicago*, July 8, 2020, https://chicago.cbslocal.com/2020/07/08 /oak-park-black-lives-matter-mural-painted-over-to-read-all-lives-matter/.

19 Calvin Warren, "The Catastrophe: Black Feminist Poethics, (Anti)Form, and Mathematical Nihilism," *Qui Parle: Critical Humanities and Social Sciences* 28, no. 2 (December 2019): 357.

20 My argument, in advancing its analysis of structure, presupposes the very ontology whose totalizations it critiques. It proposes no access to the beyond of sense except by engaging the ruptures, the ironic obtrusions, produced by the order of meaning that, in both senses of the word, *contains* them.

Introduction

1 *Oxford English Dictionary Online*, s.v. "educate (v.)," accessed March 10, 2022, https://www.oed.com/view/Entry/59580.

2 Jacques Lacan, *Séminaire 2, 1954–1955: Le moi dans la théorie de Freud et dans la technique de la psychanalyse*, December 1, 1954, 67, http://staferla.free.fr/S2/S2 .htm. Unless otherwise noted, English translations from non-English sources are my own.

3 Lacan, *Séminaire 2*, 16. "Que *la fonction symbolique* intervient à tous les moments et à tous les degrés de son existence."

4 Lacan, *Séminaire 2*, 16. "Et *la totalité* dans *l'ordre symbolique* s'appelle *un univers* . . . à l'intérieur duquel tout ce qui est humain doit s'ordonner." (And that totality in the Symbolic order is called a universe . . . inside of which everything human must organize itself.)

5 Lacan, *Séminaire 2*, 157. "Si le sujet humain ne dénomme . . . comme la *Genèse* dit que cela a été fait au *Paradis terrestre*: les espèces majeures d'abord, . . . ne s'entend pas sur cette *reconnaissance*, il n'y a aucun monde même perceptif du sujet humain qui soit soutenable plus d'un instant."

6 Lacan, *Séminaire 2*, 16. "En d'autres termes, que tout se tient, que pour concevoir ce qui se passe, ce qui nous est donné dans *le champ de l'observation*, le domaine propre qui est de l'ordre humain, il faut que nous partions de l'idée que cet ordre constituant *une totalité*, et *la totalité* dans *l'ordre symbolique* s'appelle *un univers* et est *donné d'abord* et dans son caractère universel, c'est-à-dire que ce n'est pas peu à peu qu'il se constitue quelque part une amorce de *relation symbolique*, un *premier symbole*: *dès qu'il vient le symbole, il y a un univers de symboles qui englobe toute la question*, si vous voulez, qu'on pourrait se poser." (In other words, in order for everything to hold together, to understand everything that happens, everything that is given to us in the field of observation, the proper domain of the human order, we have to start from the idea of that order constituting a totality, and that totality in the symbolic order is called a universe and is given from the outset in its universal character, which is to say that there isn't constituted somewhere, little by little, some beginning of symbolic relations, a first symbol: as soon as a symbol appears there is a universe of symbols that englobes every question that arises.)

7 Lacan, *Séminaire 2*, 21.

8 Alenka Zupančič, "On Evil: An Interview with Alenka Zupančič," interview by Christopher Cox, *Cabinet*, no. 5 (Winter 2001–2002), http://www .cabinetmagazine.org/issues/5/alenkazupancic.php.

9 Luce Irigaray, *This Sex Which Is Not One*, trans. Catherine Porter (Ithaca, NY: Cornell University Press, 1985), 122; Julia Kristeva, "La femme, ce n'est jamais ça / Woman Can Never Be Defined," in *The New French Feminisms: An Anthology*, ed. Elaine Marks and Isabelle de Courtivron (New York: Schocken Books, 1981), 137; Catherine Malabou, *Changing Difference: The Feminine and the Question of Philosophy*, trans. Carolyn Shread (Malden, MA: Polity, 2014), 98; Sylvia Wynter, "*Proud Flesh* Inter/Views: Sylvia Wynter," interview by Greg Thomas, *Proud-Flesh: New Afrikan Journal of Culture, Politics and Consciousness*, no. 4 (2006), https://www.africaknowledgeproject.org/index.php/proudflesh/article/view /202; Jared Sexton, "Unbearable Blackness," *Cultural Critique*, no. 90 (Spring 2015): 162; and Fred Moten, "Blackness and Nothingness (Mysticism in the Flesh)," *South Atlantic Quarterly* 112, no. 4 (Fall 2013): 739.

10 At the end of 2017, for example, US district judge A. Wallace Tashima permanently blocked a ban on ethnic studies programs in Arizona's public schools that

had been passed in 2010, while in August 2018, Prime Minister Viktor Orbán's government moved to ban gender studies courses in Hungarian universities.

11   In the manifesto *2083: A European Declaration of Independence*, Breivik devotes significant space to lamenting the decline of the Western University, a decline he blames on the Frankfurt School and the academic institutionalization of multiculturalism, feminism, queer theory, and deconstruction. He writes, for example, in the introduction:

> This new generation of critics instead became prime practitioners of what is known in literary circles as 'cultural criticism.' They strained to view literature from the 'woman's point of view' or the 'victims' or the 'radical minority point of view.' Their attempts were not to find meaning—they were influenced too greatly by relativists for that—but to find sexism, racism or 'homophobia' in the works of male, European or heterosexual authors.
>
> Derridean deconstruction became a tool for these cultural critics. Simply stated, deconstruction is a school of thought that posits that words have no meaning. Instead, words have 'traces' of meaning. The meaning of a word is continually disappearing, leaving us with only the memory, or trace, of what that meaning once was.
>
> Once they realised the power of this school of thought, the cultural critics embraced it readily, for here they discovered a method of attack on the traditional interpretations of literary works. They used deconstruction to remove traditional meaning and replaced it with new meaning. That meaning was the Political Correctness that infests our society today. For example, after the traditional meaning of 'How Do I Love Thee?' has been destabilised in the process described above, a feminist critic might come along and—in the absence of a stable traditional interpretation—declare that the poem is 'really' concerned with how women in nineteenth-century England were conditioned to see themselves as secondary to men.

Kakutani, in *The Death of Truth*, echoes these sentiments. Denouncing the turn to "subjectivity" in academic criticism and its association with multiculturalism, feminism, and queer theory, she then turns her focus to deconstruction: "Deconstruction, in fact, is deeply nihilistic, implying that the best efforts of journalists and historians—to ascertain the best available truths through the careful gathering and weighing of evidence—are futile. It suggests that reason is an outdated value, that language is not a tool for communication but an unstable and deceptive interface that is constantly subverting itself." Symptomatically, neither of these defenders of "meaning" and "reason" seems to deploy these concepts very meaningfully or reasonably. Breivik assails cultural criticism and deconstruction for claiming that literature and even words have no meaning before going on to describe the sorts of meanings that cultural critics might discern in literary works. And Kakutani, while complaining that for deconstructive critics "reason is an outdated value," seems, unreasonably, to assume that just because deconstruction exposes the nonfinality of evidentiary interpretations, such interpretations themselves must be "futile." Similarly, she seems to think that language cannot be, at the same time, a "tool for communication" *and* "an unstable and deceptive interface that is constantly subverting itself." Anders Behring Breivik, "Political Correctness: Deconstruction and Literature," in *2083: A European Declaration of Independence,* 2011, https://sites.google.com/site/breivikmanifesto/2083; and Michiko Kakutani, *The Death of Truth: Notes on Falsehood in the Age of Trump* (New York: Penguin Random House, 2018), 160–61.

12 Slavoj Žižek, *Less Than Nothing: Hegel and the Shadow of Dialectical Materialism* (New York: Verso, 2013), 744.

13 Jacques Lacan, *The Four Fundamental Concepts of Psychoanalysis: The Seminar of Jacques Lacan, Book XI,* ed. Jacques-Alain Miller, trans. Alan Sheridan (New York: W. W. Norton, 1998), 25.

14 Lacan, *Four Fundamental Concepts of Psychoanalysis,* 26.

15 Lacan, *Four Fundamental Concepts of Psychoanalysis,* 29.

16 Lacan, *Four Fundamental Concepts of Psychoanalysis,* 30, 31.

17 One could think about polysemy here as the mere multiplication of closed ones, much in the way that arguments for the multiplication of differences (social, political, cultural) presuppose the integrity of the elements thus differentiated from and added to each other.

18 As one example among many, consider a passage from Kathleen Collins's short story "Whatever Happened to Interracial Love?" The father of the central character, Cheryl, whom the author characterizes, within ironizing quotation marks, as "negro," visits his daughter's New York apartment to have dinner with her; her white roommate, Charlotte (who had been, like Cheryl, a student at Sarah Lawrence); and Charlotte's Black boyfriend, Henry. Cheryl herself has a white boyfriend in prison in Georgia for his activities as a freedom rider. In the aftermath of the dinner, Collins writes, "When Cheryl accompanied him to their car, he was still crying. He asked her to come home; he realized now that he had made a terrible mistake sending her to that exclusive school to be the first and only one. It had made her queer. It had made her want a queer life among queer, unnatural people. It was not what he had in mind at all. He had simply wanted her to have a good education with a solid, respected ('white') name behind it. That was all he wanted. Then he had expected her to come home again and teach and get married and live in the apartment on their third floor. He did not want her to lead this queer integrated life with some pasty freedom rider who liked to flagellate himself for ('negroes'). It was unhealthy. It was wrong. He should go home, too. They should all go home. Henry should go back to his ghetto. Charlotte should return to her well-bred country-life. She, Cheryl, should come home and get a job teaching school. Everything else was too queer, too unspeakably queer, and made him cry." Kathleen Collins, *Whatever Happened to Interracial Love?* (New York: HarperCollins, 2016), Kindle loc. 640 of 1790.

19 Jacques Derrida, "Différance," in *Margins of Philosophy,* trans. Alan Bass (Chicago: University of Chicago Press, 1986), 12. I am very grateful to Elizabeth Wilson for reminding me about Derrida's phrase and for being so incisive a reader and interlocutor.

20 For a detailed engagement with the concept of the unbearable and its relation to the Real, see Lauren Berlant and Lee Edelman, *Sex, or the Unbearable* (Durham, NC: Duke University Press, 2014).

21 Guy Le Gaufey, "Le plus atopique des deux . . . ," in *Lacan avec les philosophes* (Paris: Albin Michel, 1991), 168. "Signifie son incapacité à recevoir une quelconque imposition d'unité, ce qui est à soi seul lourd de conséquences quant à son être, ne serait-ce que d'un point de vue leibnizien où un *être* est d'abord *un* être."

22 See Berlant and Edelman, *Sex, or the Unbearable*.

23 Jacques Lacan, *L'Étourdit*, in *Autres écrits* (Paris: Seuil, 2001), 454–55.

24 Lacan, *L'Étourdit*, 452. "Freud nous met sur la voie de ce que l'ab-sens désigne le sexe: c'est à la gonfle de ce sens-absexe qu'une topologie se déploie où c'est le mot qui tranche."

25 *Designates* (*désigne*) may condense this double gesture by suggesting an act of designification (*de-signe*) as well.

26 Alenka Zupančič, "Sexual Difference and Ontology," *e-flux Journal*, no. 32 (February 2012), http://www.e-flux.com/journal/sexual-difference-and-ontology/. More recently, in *What Is Sex?*, a brilliant book that came out as my own was being finished, Zupančič broaches this question of sex and meaning in similar terms, though from a somewhat different direction. As she puts it concisely near the outset: "It is as if sexual meaning, so generously produced by the unconscious, were here to mask the reality of a more fundamental negativity at work in sexuality, to separate us from it by a screen that derives its efficacy from the fact that it is itself a means of satisfaction—satisfaction through meaning, satisfaction in the production of sexual meaning, and (as the obverse of this) in the production of meaning of the sexual. Paradoxical as this may sound, one of the primary tasks of psychoanalysis is to slowly but thoroughly deactivate the path of this satisfaction, to render it useless. To produce sex as absolutely and intrinsically meaningless, not as the ultimate horizon of all humanly produced meaning. That is to say to restore sex in its dimension of the Real." Alenka Zupančič, *What Is Sex?* (Cambridge, MA: MIT Press, 2017), 8.

27 Ellie Ragland, "The Discourse of the Master," in *Lacan, Politics, Aesthetics*, ed. Willy Apollon and Richard Feldstein (Albany: State University of New York Press, 1996), 142.

28 As we will see, this putting askew bears a crucial relation to the etymology of *queer*.

29 "C'est à partir de là qu'il nous faut obtenir deux universels, deux *tous* suffisamment consistants pour nous séparer chez des parlants—, qui, d'être des, se croient des êtres—, deux moitiés telles qu'elles ne s'embrouillent pas trop dans la coïtération quant ils y arrivent." Lacan, *L'Étourdit*, 456.

30 In this context one should note that the Lacanian position would not assert that there are multiple sexes instead of two but rather would insist that every reification of sex into some sort of knowledge or identity is a fantasy.

31 Kenneth Reinhard, "Introduction to Alain Badiou and Barbara Cassin," draft shared with author (2015).

32　Alain Badiou, "Formulas of 'L'Étourdit,'" in *There's No Such Thing as a Sexual Relationship: Two Lessons on Lacan*, by Alain Badiou and Barbara Cassin, trans. Susan Spitzer and Kenneth Reinhard (New York: Columbia University Press, 2017), 50.

33　No list could be inclusive or make the chosen examples less selective and less partial. The point, indeed, is that any set will include the null set that signifies what cannot be signified or added to the count. In making the case for queer theory as a theory of this libidinized relation to ab-sens, I have no interest in discrediting or superseding other possible nominations. Every nomination will be a catachresis that attempts to pass as literal. Queerness, in its openness to anything stigmatized as unusual, deviant, foreign, or strange, and hence to anything that disturbs the coherence on which an aesthetic community relies, seems particularly well suited as a catachrestic nomination for this unnameable alterity to the meaning of any social order.

34　Justin Clemens, *Psychoanalysis Is an Antiphilosophy* (Edinburgh: Edinburgh University Press, 2013), 53.

35　Zupančič, "Sexual Difference and Ontology."

36　Joan Copjec, "The Sexual Compact," *Angelaki: Journal of the Theoretical Humanities* 17, no. 2 (2012): 46.

37　In Žižek's words, jouissance "is never fully achieved, always missed, but, simultaneously, we never can get rid of it." Žižek, *Less Than Nothing*, 308.

38　See, for instance, Lacan, *Séminaire 2*, 157, where Lacan offers the following account of a moment in Sigmund Freud's interpretation of the dream of Irma's injection: "Ce n'est pas simplement pour lui qu'il trouve le *Nemo*, ou *l'alpha et l'oméga* du sujet acéphale, comme représentant son inconscient, c'est au contraire lui qui parle, par l'intermédiaire de ce rêve, qui s'aperçoit qu'il nous dit, sans l'avoir voulu, sans l'avoir reconnu d'abord, et le reconnaissant uniquement dans son analyse du rêve, c'est-à-dire pendant qu'il nous parle, il nous dit quelque chose qui est à la fois lui et pas lui, qui a parlé dans les dernières parties du rêve, qui nous dit: *Je suis celui qui veut être pardonné d'avoir osé commencer a guérir ces malades, que jusqu'à présent on ne voulait pas comprendre, donc que l'on s'interdisait de guérir. Je suis celui qui veut être pardonné de cela. Je suis celui qui veut n'en être pas coupable, car c'est toujours être coupable que de transgresser une limite jusque-là imposée à l'activité humaine. Je veux n'être pas cela. À la place de moi, il y a tous les autres. Je ne suis là que le représentant de ce vaste mouvement assez vague qui est cette recherche de la vérité dans ce sens où moi je m'efface. Je ne suis plus rien. Mon ambition a été plus grande que moi. La seringue était sale, sans doute. Et c'est justement dans la mesure où je l'ai trop désiré, où j'ai participé à cette action, où j'ai voulu être moi, le créateur. Je ne suis pas le créateur. Le créateur est quelqu'un de plus grand que moi. C'est mon inconscient, c'est cette parole qui parle en moi, au-delà de moi.*" Sylvana Tomaselli translates as follows: "It isn't just for himself that he finds the *Nemo* or the alpha and omega of the acephalic subject, which represents his unconcious. On the contrary, by means of this dream it's him who speaks, and who realises that he is telling us—without having wanted to, without having recognised it at first, and only recognising it in his analysis of the dream, that is to say, while speaking to us—something which is both him and no longer him—*I am he who wants to be forgiven for having dared to begin to cure these patients, who until now no one wanted to understand and whose cure was forbidden. I am he who wants not to be guilty of it, for to transgress any limit imposed up to now on human activity is always to be guilty. I want to not be (born) that. Instead of me, there are all the others. Here I am only the representative of that vast, vague movement, the quest for truth, in which I efface myself. I am no longer anything. My ambition was greater than I. No doubt the syringe was dirty. And precisely to that extent that I desired it too much, that I partook in this action, that I wanted to be, myself, the creator, I am not the creator. The creator is someone greater than I. It is my unconscious, it is this voice which speaks in me. Beyond me."* Jacques Lacan, *The Seminar of Jacques Lacan: Book 2, The Ego in Freud's Theory and in the Technique of Psychoanalysis 1954–1955*, ed. Jacques-Alain Miller, trans. Sylvana Tomaselli (New York: W. W. Norton, 1991), 170–71.

39 Judith Butler, *The Psychic Life of Power: Theories in Subjection* (Stanford, CA: Stanford University Press, 1997), 35.

40 Alenka Zupančič, "Encountering Lacan in the Next Generation: An Interview with Alenka Zupančič," in *Žižek and His Contemporaries: On the Emergence of the Slovenian Lacan*, ed. Jones Irwin and Helena Motoh (London: Bloomsbury Academic, 2014), 163.

41 Jacques Lacan, *Four Fundamental Concepts of Psychoanalysis*, 43.

42 Lacan, *Four Fundamental Concepts of Psychoanalysis*, 204.

43 Malabou, *Changing Difference*, 140.

44 Catherine Malabou, "A Conversation with Catherine Malabou," interview by Noëlle Vahanian, *Journal for Cultural and Religious Theory* 9, no. 1 (2008): 3, https://jcrt.org/archives/09.1/Malabou.pdf.

45 Malabou, "Conversation with Catherine Malabou," 4.

46 Jacques Lacan, *Encore: 1972–1973*, ed. Jacques-Alain Miller (Paris: Seuil, 1975), 93. "Il n'y a pas *La* femme, article défini pour désigner l'universel."

47 Lacan, *L'Étourdit*, 466. "Ainsi à se fonder de cette moitié, 'elles' ne sont pastoutes, avec pour suite et du même fait, qu'aucune non plus n'est toute."

48 Catherine Malabou, *The Heidegger Change: On the Fantastic in Philosophy*, trans. Peter Skafish (Albany: State University of New York Press, 2011), 270.

49 Malabou, *Heidegger Change*, 283. This "strange" or "queer" economy might be thought in terms of the meanings of *atopia* discussed later in this chapter.

50 Malabou, *Heidegger Change*, 270.

51 Malabou, *Heidegger Change*, 274.

52 Malabou, *Changing Difference*, 39.

53 Catherine Malabou and Judith Butler, "You Be My Body for Me: Body, Shape, and Plasticity in Hegel's *Phenomenology of Spirit*," in *A Companion to Hegel*, ed. Stephen Houlgate and Michael Baur (Malden, MA: Blackwell, 2011), 623, 624.

54 Malabou, *Changing Difference*, 135.

55 Malabou, *Changing Difference*, 140, 139.

56 Malabou, *Changing Difference*, 108.

57 Luce Irigaray, *Marine Lover: Of Friedrich Nietzsche*, trans. Gillian G. Gill (New York: Columbia University Press, 1991); Jacques Derrida, *Spurs: Nietzsche's Styles*, trans. Barbara Harlow (Chicago: University of Chicago Press, 1979), 50. "Il n'y a pas d'essence de la femme parce que la femme écarte et s'écarte d'elle même." The phrase might better be translated as "There is no essence of woman because woman parts and strays from herself."

58 Jacques Derrida and Christie V. McDonald, "Interview: Choreographies," *diacritics* 12, no. 2 (1982): 76; Malabou, *Changing Difference*, 108.

59 Malabou, *Changing Difference*, 14.

60 Malabou, *Changing Difference*, 98.

61 Henry Louis Gates Jr., introduction to *The Slave's Narrative*, ed. Charles T. Davis and Henry Louis Gates Jr. (New York: Oxford University Press, 1985), xxiii; Ronald Judy, *(Dis)Forming the American Canon: African-Arabic Slave Narratives and the Vernacular* (Minneapolis: University of Minnesota Press, 1993), 84.

62 Judy, *(Dis)Forming the American Canon*, 84.

63 Judy, *(Dis)Forming the American Canon*, 84.

64 Olaudah Equiano, "The Interesting Narrative of the Life of Olaudah Equiano, or Gustavas Vassa, the African. Written by Himself," in Olaudah Equiano, *The Interesting Narrative and Other Writings*, ed. Vincent Carretta (New York: Penguin Books, 2003); Judy, *(Dis)Forming the American Canon*, 91, 88.

65 Judy, *(Dis)Forming the American Canon*, 88–89.

66 Judy, *(Dis)Forming the American Canon*, 92.

67 Judy, *(Dis)Forming the American Canon*, 96, 97.

68 Frank B. Wilderson III, *Red, White, and Black: Cinema and the Structure of U.S. Antagonisms* (Durham, NC: Duke University Press, 2010), 40.

69 Judy, *(Dis)Forming the American Canon*, 88.

70 Wilderson, *Red, White, and Black*, 43, 42.

71 Wilderson, *Red, White, and Black*, 43.

72 Frank B. Wilderson III, *"We're Trying to Destroy the World": Anti-Blackness and Police Violence after Ferguson; An Interview with Frank B. Wilderson III*, interview by Jared Ball, Todd Steven Burroughs, and Dr. Hate (n.p.: Ill Will Editions, 2014), 8, https://illwilleditions.noblogs.org/files/2015/09/Wilderson-We-Are-Trying-to-Destroy-the-World-READ.pdf.

73 Frantz Fanon, *Black Skin, White Masks*, trans. Charles Lam Markmann (New York: Grove Press, 1967), 110; Wilderson, *Red, White, and Black*, 57.

74 Wilderson, *Red, White, and Black*, 56.

75 Wilderson, *Red, White, and Black*, 56.

76 Wilderson, *Red, White, and Black*, 54.

77 Wilderson, *Red, White, and Black*, 54, 15.

78 Wilderson, *Red, White, and Black*, 56.

79 For Wilderson, the violability of woman is not essential but contingent, at least as he describes it in the context of whiteness: "To be precise, violence as it pertains to and structures gender relations between White men and White women (and it

does!) is of a contingent nature: White women who 'transgress' their position in the symbolic order run the risk of attack." Wilderson, *Red, White, and Black*, 88. Malabou, among others, would argue that such violability requires no "transgression" of one's Symbolic position but inheres in that position itself.

80 David Marriott, "Black Cultural Studies," *Year's Work in Critical and Cultural Theory* 20, no. 1 (2012): 47; and Judith Butler, *Bodies That Matter: On the Discursive Limits of Sex* (New York: Routledge, 2011), 15–16.

81 Judy, *(Dis)Forming the American Canon*, 94.

82 Judy, *(Dis)Forming the American Canon*, 94.

83 Wilderson, *"We're Trying to Destroy the World,"* 12; emphasis mine.

84 Each, of course, does so differently, in response to particular cultural and historical conditions. My purpose here is to chart the catachrestic logic underlying these identities and their relation to sex as the unthinkable negativity of ab-sens as the primal cut.

85 Lee Edelman, *No Future: Queer Theory and the Death Drive* (Durham, NC: Duke University Press, 2004).

86 Annamarie Jagose, *Queer Theory: An Introduction* (New York: New York University Press, 1996), 2.

87 Michel Foucault, *The History of Sexuality*, vol. 1, *An Introduction*, trans. Robert Hurley (New York: Vintage Books, 1990), 122.

88 Jonathan Goldberg, *Sodometries: Renaissance Texts, Modern Sexualities* (New York: Fordham University Press, 2010), 18.

89 Jared Sexton, "Afro-Pessimism: The Unclear Word," *Rhizomes: Cultural Studies in Emerging Knowledge*, no. 29 (2016): 3, https://doi.org/10.20415/rhiz/029.e02; and Edelman, *No Future*, 17.

90 Amber Jamilla Musser, *Sensational Flesh: Race, Power, and Masochism* (New York: New York University Press, 2014), 18.

91 Chandan Reddy, *Freedom with Violence: Race, Sexuality, and the U.S. State* (Durham, NC: Duke University Press, 2011), 17.

92 Žižek, *Less Than Nothing*, 745.

93 Jean-Claude Milner, "The Doctrine of Science," in *Jacques Lacan: Critical Evaluations in Cultural Theory*, ed. Slavoj Žižek (New York: Routledge, 2002), 1:288.

94 Reddy, *Freedom with Violence*, 174.

95 Reddy, *Freedom with Violence*, 174.

96 Reddy, *Freedom with Violence*, 174.

97 Reddy, *Freedom with Violence*, 175.

98 Wilderson, *Red, White, and Black*, 311.

99 Barbara Johnson, *The Wake of Deconstruction* (Cambridge, MA: Basil Blackwell, 1994), 98.

100 Calvin Warren, "Onticide: Afropessimism, Queer Theory, and Ethics," Ill Will, November 18, 2014, 6, 11, https://illwill.com/onticide-afropessimism-queer-theory-and-ethics. I put quotation marks around the phrase "Black queer" and around "Black" and "queer" when used to indicate specific types of persons in order to recall their catachrestic function as placeholders for ontological exclusion.

101 Stefano Harney and Fred Moten, *The Undercommons: Fugitive Planning and Black Study* (New York: Minor Composition, 2013), 93; and Warren, "Onticide," 14. Note that Harney and Moten on page 93 produce a neologism, *exsense*, that comes strikingly close to Lacan's: "Present and unmade in presence, blackness is an instrument in the making. *Quasi una fantasia* in its paralegal swerve, its mad-worked braid, the imagination produces nothing but exsense in the hold."

102 Warren, "Onticide," 14–15.

103 Unlike Judy's attention to "the catachresis at work in the biological misnomer of race," Warren's essay reads only the "black queer" as "a catachresis." "Blacks" and "queers" are otherwise ontologized as if they were not also catachreses.

104 Warren, "Onticide," 20.

105 Neither the absence of the father nor the destruction of the family that frequently followed from chattel slavery would disrupt this process of subjectivization through the image of the other. Hortense Spillers rightly observes that "legal enslavement removed the African-American male not so much from sight as from *mimetic* view as a partner in the prevailing social fiction of the father's name, the father's law." But the children born in slavery were not thereby removed from the logic of subjectivization through that fiction or that law. Hortense Spillers, "Mama's Baby, Papa's Maybe: An American Grammar Book," in *Black, White, and in Color* (Chicago: University of Chicago Press, 2003), 228.

106 Jacques Lacan, "The Mirror Stage as Formative of the *I* Function as Revealed in Psychoanalytic Experience," in *Écrits: The First Complete Edition in English*, trans. Bruce Fink (New York: W. W. Norton, 2002), 76.

107 In his account of onticide as "overkill," Warren describes the brutal murder of Steen Keith Fenrich as "the literal projection of the unconscious fantasy of fragmentation—the 'body in bits and pieces.'" Warren, "Onticide," 25n13. To recognize this violence as a *projection* of fragmentation is already to acknowledge the anxiety, born with the subject as such, of a movement between subject and object. It would be interesting to juxtapose Warren's conclusion from Fenrich's murder that "the queer" but not "the black" is popularly grievable with David Marriott's discussion of the "media melodrama" surrounding the death of Stephen Lawrence in England (the year after the murder of Matthew Shepard). See David Marriott, *On Black Men* (New York: Columbia University Press, 2000), 117–24.

108 Lacan, "Mirror Stage," 79.

109 Wilderson, *"We're Trying to Destroy the World,"* 7.

110 Wilderson, *Afropessimism*, 17.

111 Warren, "Onticide," 18.

112 As one example from Wilderson's book, consider the following collocation of Fanon and Lacan: "There is an uncanny connection between Fanon's absolute violence and Lacan's real. Thus, by extension, the grammar of suffering of the Black itself is on the level of the real." Wilderson, *Red, White, and Black*, 75.

113 This does not, of course, mean that obtrusions of queerness eradicate world-making, but queerness's obtrusion of "nothing" compels new figures of meaning

whose defensive structure (insofar as they defend a given world) contributes to undoing that world as known and to ushering in another. In this sense we might take issue with Shakespeare's Lear: something (new) *only* comes of nothing. In the context of this discussion of the agrammatical and anacoluthic structure of queerness, I would call attention to Christina Sharpe's brilliant account of the "anagrammatical blackness" and "dysgraphia" that bespeak "the inability of language to cohere around the bodies and suffering of those . . . Black people who live and die in the wake." Christina Sharpe, *In the Wake: On Blackness and Being* (Durham, NC: Duke University Press, 2016), 75, 96.

114 Warren, "Onticide," 20.

115 Cited by Warren, in "Onticide," 14. See Eric Stanley, "Near Life, Queer Death: Overkill and Ontological Capture," *Social Text* 29, no. 2 (107) (Summer 2011): 9.

116 Warren, "Onticide," 14.

117 Warren, "Onticide," 15.

118 Warren, "Onticide," 10.

119 Warren, "Onticide," 9.

120 Warren, "Onticide," 14.

121 Warren, "Onticide," 7, 19.

122 Warren, "Onticide," 20, 21, 19.

123 Alternatively, Warren could be read as insisting on the historicity of ontology and as focusing on a specific moment of ontological determination within the context of Western discourse. But that raises the question of ontological exclusion (which "preconditions" the Symbolic, as Warren acknowledges) anterior to the regime of ontology determined by anti-Blackness and whether or not that anterior logic is bound to the Symbolic ontologically.

124 Zakiyyah Iman Jackson, "Waking Nightmares—on David Marriott," *GLQ* 17, no. 2–3 (June 2011): 357–63.

125 Warren, "Onticide," 19.

126 Warren, "Onticide," 9.

127 Warren, "Onticide," 19.

128 As a wager, of course, this involves some risk. Many, after all, continue to positivize queer as an identity, linking it, variously, to same-sex relations, to nonheteronormative sexualities, to radical forms of sexual experimentation, to nonbinaristic experiences of embodiment, and to countless other forms of minoritized, abjected, or unrecognized "being." That variety, though, is precisely the point. Queerness, originating in the stigmatization of categorical disturbance, can never name a particular group without opening itself to challenge by those who disturb such categorization (Are pedophiles queer? Are children? Are racial fetishists, rapists, or serial killers?). As the legal and social normalization of gay and lesbian citizens accelerates (for the time being, at any rate) in many Western democracies (stratified though that normalization is by vectors of race, class, and gender expression), queerness no longer maps onto sexual orientation as tightly as it did. For some the experience of queerness today may thus be gone tomorrow. But the very mobility of the term makes the wager on

queerness seem all the more cogent insofar as it signals the term's negativity beyond a specific content.

129 David Marriott, "Judging Fanon," *Rhizomes: Cultural Studies in Emerging Knowledges,* no. 29 (2016): 7, https://doi.org/10.20415/rhiz/029.e03.

130 Jackson, "Waking Nightmares," 360.

131 Jackson, "Waking Nightmares," 361.

132 Warren, "Onticide," 18–19.

133 Jackson, "Waking Nightmares," 361.

134 At a certain moment in Warren's text, he seems to open onto the alignment of Blackness and queerness as radical categories without ontological content, writing, "What we call 'heterosexism' or anti-gay violence might be a particular *form* of anti-black violence." Warren, "Onticide," 10. But, in context, he seems to be referring to "heterosexism" or "anti-gay violence" directed toward what he defines as "black-objects," making some such "objects" "more vulnerable to forms of violence not easily recognized as anti-blackness" (10).

135 Warren, "Onticide," 19–20.

136 This is not to dismiss ethics as mere disavowal or to denigrate the importance of ethical projects that conceptualize the possibilities and consequences of living with an awareness of this structuring antagonism. Alenka Zupančič, Lynne Huffer, Fred Moten, and Lauren Berlant, for example, all, in their different ways, attempt just that.

137 Warren, "Onticide," 19.

138 Warren, "Onticide," 13.

139 With regard to the fungibility of queerness, it is important to note that the term does not necessarily carry a politically "progressive" force. In a given social formation, queerness may express itself through racism, sexism, homophobia, monoculturalism, xenophobia, or religious fundamentalism. The relation of those ideological value systems to queerness will always depend on their relation to power in the dominant social and political order, and a gauge of their "queerness" may be found in the degree to which their institutional suppression takes place in the name of the greater good. This requires us to ask if we are willing to accept queerness as a value in itself rather than continuing our adherence to the dominant values we think should be extended to a subclass of "queers." Socratic irony, in my view, compels us to risk such a "valuing" of queerness as such, even as it necessitates a constant questioning of the grounds of our values.

140 Houston Baker, *Blues, Ideology, and Afro-American Literature: A Vernacular Theory* (Chicago: University of Chicago Press, 1987), 5; Moten, "Blackness and Nothingness," 751; and Rebecka Rutledge Fisher, *Habitations of the Veil: Metaphor and the Poetics of Black Being in African American Literature* (Albany: State University of New York Press, 2014), 336.

141 Julia Kristeva, *Powers of Horror: An Essay on Abjection*, trans. Leon S. Roudiez (New York: Columbia University Press, 1982), 22; Moira Gatens, "Polysemy, Atopia, and Feminist Thought," in *Michèle Le Doeuff: Operative Philosophy and Imaginary Practice*, ed. Max Deutscher (Amherst, NY: Humanity Books,

2000), 57; and Adriana Cavarero, "Dire la nascita," quoted in Cristina Mazzoni, *Maternal Impressions: Pregnancy and Childbirth in Literature and Theory* (Ithaca, NY: Cornell University Press, 2000), 191.

142   Gregory Vlastos, *Socrates: Ironist and Moral Philosopher* (Ithaca, NY: Cornell University Press, 1991), 1n1.

143   Joel Alden Schlosser, *What Would Socrates Do? Self-Examination, Civic Engagement, and the Politics of Philosophy* (New York: Cambridge University Press, 2014), 12.

144   Roland Barthes, *A Lover's Discourse: Fragments*, trans. Richard Howard (New York: Hill and Wang, 1977), 34; and Sarah Kofman, *Socrates: Fictions of a Philosopher*, trans. Catherine Porter (Ithaca, NY: Cornell University Press, 1989), 8.

145   Pierre Hadot, *Philosophy as a Way of Life: Spiritual Exercise from Socrates to Foucault*, trans. Michael Chase (Malden, MA: Blackwell, 2003), 156.

146   Søren Kierkegaard, *The Concept of Irony with Continual Reference to Socrates*, ed. and trans. Howard V. Hong and Edna H. Hong (Princeton, NJ: Princeton University Press, 1992), 196.

147   Kierkegaard, *Concept of Irony with Continual Reference to Socrates*, 228.

148   Kierkegaard, *Concept of Irony with Continual Reference to Socrates*, 198.

149   Kierkegaard, *Concept of Irony with Continual Reference to Socrates*, 228.

150   Kierkegaard, *Concept of Irony with Continual Reference to Socrates*, 228.

151   Wilderson, *"We're Trying to Destroy the World,"* 18, 19, 20.

152   Kierkegaard, *Concept of Irony with Continual Reference to Socrates*, 264. For Benjamin's discussion of "divine violence," see Walter Benjamin, "Critique of Violence," in *Reflections: Essays, Aphorisms, Autobiographical Writings*, trans. by Edmund Jephcott (New York: Harcourt Brace Jovanovich, 1978).

153   Kierkegaard, *Concept of Irony with Continual Reference to Socrates*, 261.

154   See Jacques Lacan, *The Other Side of Psychoanalysis: The Seminar of Jacques Lacan, Book XVII*, ed. Jacques-Alain Miller, trans. Russell Grigg (New York: W. W. Norton, 2007), 18–24.

155   Claire Colebrook, *Irony* (New York: Routledge, 2004), 29, 30.

156   Alain Badiou, *Images du temps présent, 2001–2004* (Paris: Fayard, 2014), 68. "De ce point de vue, je pense que nous sommes obligés d'accepter pour part, et au moins transitoirement, le verdict antiphilosophique de la psychanalyse selon lequel la philosophie ne veut rien avoir à connaitre de la jouissance. En tout cas, le philosophie, dans l'épreuve, que je lui propose ici, de penser le contemporain, ne partira pas de la jouissance. Elle s'en detournera méthodiquement, avec toutefois l'espérance de pouvoir y revenir."

157   Badiou, *Images du temps présent*, 61.

158   Alain Badiou, *Plato's Republic: A Dialogue in 16 Chapters*, trans. Susan Spitzer (New York: Columbia University, 2012), 284.

159   Jonathan Lear, *A Case for Irony* (Cambridge, MA: Harvard University Press, 2011), 20.

160   Badiou, *Plato's Republic*, 203.

161   Kierkegaard, *Concept of Irony with Continual Reference to Socrates*, 196.

162 Kierkegaard, *Concept of Irony with Continual Reference to Socrates*, 198. Badiou writes, "La philosophie fait comme si pouvait exister un amour de la vérité comme plenitude" (Philosophy proceeds as if there could be a love of truth as fullness or plenitude). Alain Badiou, *Lacan: L'antiphilosophie 3; 1994–1995* (Paris: Fayard, 2013), 213.

163 Badiou, *Lacan*, 129, 142: "la tentation de l'Un"; "une tentation de recollection du sens"; and "une pensée du vrai comme étranger au sens."

164 Badiou, *Lacan*, 143. "Où la vérité est résorbée dans l'espace du sens"; and "vous pouvez bien dire que la religion insiste dans la philosophie, mais à condition d'ajouter que la philosophie est constitutivement un certain régime d'interruption de cette insistence."

165 "Je conclurai donc sur le rapport de la philosophie à la politique un peu de la même manière que sur celui qu'elle soutient à la mathématique: même au comble de sa volonté fondatrice—et Dieu sait que c'est le cas dans le *République* de Platon—, la philosophie identifie, dans la politique, quelque chose qui ne se laisse pas suture, mais qui reste soumis à une sort de béance contingente que la pensée fondatrice même ne peut pas réduire" (I will end with the relation of philosophy to politics a bit in the same fashion as its relation to mathematics: even at the height of its founding will—and God knows that it's the case with Plato's *Republic*—philosophy identifies something in politics that can't be sutured, something that remains subject to a kind of contingent gap that even philosophy's foundational thought can't reduce.) Badiou, *Lacan*, 150.

166 Badiou, *Lacan*, 230, 231.

167 Badiou, *Lacan*, 219.

168 Badiou, *Lacan*, 213, 214. "La pensée ultime de Lacan est qu'il n'y a pas de légitimité intrinsèque à la durée d'un collectif quell qu'il soit"; and "'Collez-vous ensemble, le temps qu'il faut pour faire quelque chose, et puis, dissolvez-vous après, pour faire autre chose.'"

169 Badiou, *Lacan*, 152, 131.

170 Badiou, *Lacan*, 232, 231.

171 Badiou, *Lacan*, 224. "Socrate n'a aucunement l'intention de rallier les sophistes. Il veut seulement montrer aux jeunes qu'on peut leur clouer le bec et passer aux choses sérieuses."

172 Kofman, *Socrates*, 4.

173 Badiou, *Lacan*, 220.

174 Jacques Lacan, "D'Écolage," March 11, 1980, http://staferla.free.fr/S27/S27.htm. Lacan here describes an apparatus for moving forward after the dissolution of his school in order to prevent the repetition of "*l'effet de colle*." Whether or not this constitutes a new foundation in Badiou's terms, it speaks to the effort to assure the constancy of interruption in the psychoanalytic field.

175 "Interview de Jean Allouch," September 6, 2001, 7, 8, http://www.jeanallouch .com/pdf/193. "Le psychanalyste, à mon sens, n'a rien à faire du côté du pouvoir, du côté de ceux qui décident de comment doit fonctionner la société, de quelles règles elle se donne, de comment elle traite ses membres"; and "Marguerite Duras

en a donné la meilleure formule lorsqu'elle exprimait ce voeu, qu'elle inscrivait, elle, comme la maxime même du politique : 'Que le monde aille à sa perte !' Si vous ne campez pas sur cette radicalité-là, celle du 'décharite' de Lacan, celle d'un grand Autre barré, inexistant, il n'y a aucune chance de pouvoir être du côté de ceux dont les symptômes ne cessent de hurler ça."

176 Badiou, *Lacan*, 211–12. "Le propos lacanien, même s'il se présente sous le signe de discours, est précisément distant, bien entendu, du discours de l'université, mais plus profondement distant de toute visée educative. Et c'est d'ailleurs une donée antiphilosophique. Car on pourrait établir que la conviction de Lacan— conviction qu'on peut aisément partager—, c'est qu'il y a dans la philosophie une pulsion educative. Après tout, le dispositif platonicien, considéré comme fonda-teur, peut être perçu comme un dispositif éducatif. À cette visée educative de la philosophie, même en prenant 'education' en un sens aussi noble que possible, s'oppose ceci que la psychanalyse, fût-ce dans son discours, est rupture au regard de toute visée educative. Lacan le dit, avec la plus grande fermeté, dans un texte qui est la cloture du Congrès de 1970. Il dit: Ce qui me sauve de l'enseignement, c'est l'acte."

177 Jacques Lacan, "Allocution sur l'enseignment," in *Autres écrits*, 297.

178 Lacan, "Allocution sur l'enseignment," 302.

179 Bruce Fink, *The Lacanian Subject: Between Language and Jouissance* (Princeton, NJ: Princeton University Press, 1997), 134.

180 Kofman, *Socrates*, 245.

181 Lacan, "Allocution sur l'enseignment," 302. "Cette production la plus folle pour n'être pas enseignable comme nous ne l'éprouvons que trop, ne nous libère pas pour autant de l'hypothèque du savoir."

182 Lacan, "Allocution sur l'enseignment," 302, 305. "L'antagonisme que je souligne ici entre l'enseignmenet et le savoir" and "le savoir passe en acte."

183 Jean-François Balaudé, "Socrates's Demon," in *Dictionary of Untranslatables: A Philosophical Lexicon*, ed. Barbara Cassin, trans. Steven Rendall, Christian Hubbert, Jeffrey Mehlman, Nathanael Stein, and Michael Syrotinski, translation ed. Emily Apter, Jacques Lezra, and Michael Wood (Princeton, NJ: Princeton University Press, 2014), 194.

184 Lacan, *Four Fundamental Concepts of Psychoanalysis*, 268.

185 Slavoj Žižek, *The Parallax View* (Cambridge, MA: MIT Press, 2006), 18.

186 While conventions for proper names vary, in cultures that use the patronymic, one's name is always "borrowed," and the same holds true for one's "given name," as the speaker in Elizabeth Bishop's "In the Waiting Room" understands when she cries, "You are an *Elizabeth*, / you are one of *them. / Why* should you be one, too?" Elizabeth Bishop, "In the Waiting Room," in *Geography III* (New York: Farrar, Straus and Giroux, 1976), 3–8.

187 Žižek, *Less Than Nothing*, 589.

188 Slavoj Žižek, *Looking Awry: An Introduction to Jacques Lacan through Popular Culture* (Cambridge, MA: MIT Press, 1991), 33.

189 Žižek, *Parallax View*, 62.

190 Jacques Lacan, "Dissolution," March 18, 1980, http://espace.freud.pagesperso
-orange.fr/topos/psycha/psysem/dissolu9.htm.

191 Lacan, "Dissolution." "Voyez comme je pose ça par petites touches. Je vous laisse
votre temps pour comprendre. Comprendre quoi ? Je ne me targue pas de faire
sens. Pas du contraire non plus. Car le réel est ce qui s'oppose à ça. J'ai rendu
hommage à Marx comme à l'inventeur du symptôme. Ce Marx est pourtant
le restaurateur de l'ordre, du seul fait qu'il a réinsufflé dans le prolétariat la dit-
mension du sens. Il a suffi pour ça que le prolétariat, il le dise tel.

"L'Église en a pris de la graine, c'est ce que je vous ai dit le 5 janvier. Sachez
que le sens religieux va faire un boom dont vous n'avez aucune espèce d'idée.
Parce que la religion, c'est le gîte originel du sens. C'est une évidence qui s'impose. A ceux qui sont responsables dans la hiérarchie plus qu'aux autres.

"J'essaye d'aller là contre, pour que la psychanalyse ne soit pas une religion,.
comme elle y tend, irrésistiblement, dès lors qu'on s'imagine que *l'interprétation*
n'opère que du sens. J'enseigne que *son ressort est ailleurs, nommément dans le
signifiant comme tel.*

"A quoi résistent ceux que la dissolution panique.

"La hiérarchie ne se soutient que de gérer le sens."

192 Colette Soler, "Lacan en Antiphilosophe," *Filozofski vestnik* 24, no. 2 (2006): 127.

193 Soler, "Lacan en Antiphilosophe," 128.

194 Although it is not possible to discuss the question adequately in passing and the
present book does not permit me to address it at length, the relation between
this notion of queerness and the logic of capitalism cannot be left wholly
unremarked. Let me merely sketch the framework in which one might try to
approach it. Certainly, insofar as it manifests the repetitions of the death drive
and undermines logics of meaning, capitalism could be said to "queer" the
structures of social order. But it does so by presenting the expansion of capital as
meaningful in itself, indeed as the quasi-theological corollary of subjective self-
realization. To that extent it operates, like the social order, as a vector of jouissance
that refuses the queerness of the death drive it projects onto its others (the "idle"
poor, the "lazy" worker, the "pampered" communist, the welfare "queen," etc.).
In this context it is surely worth asking if, as some psychoanalytic critics suggest,
capitalism really encourages us to "enjoy" in the Lacanian sense. It is true that the
double logic of capitalism promises, by way of the commodity, the jouissance we
otherwise lack, but it does so while promoting wage labor as the means of gaining
access to commodities. Even when it seems to be encouraging us to "enjoy," it
is actually commanding us to "submit"—not to enjoyment or to the drive but
to the law the keeps the subject enchained to the logic of desire. As laborers
we may enjoy our submission to desire, and as capitalists we may enjoy the
surplus value the submission of wage laborers accords us, but the system itself
constrains that "enjoyment" to operate (with rare exceptions) within the limits
of the law of desire.

Chapter One: Learning Nothing

1 As de Man maintains, "It is better to fail in teaching what should not be taught than to succeed in teaching what is not true." Paul de Man, *The Resistance to Theory* (Minneapolis: University of Minnesota Press, 1993), 4. But Bersani's sentence implicitly asks the question: Better for whom?

2 The proponents of bad education are condemned, as this chapter suggests, to be implicated in a "good" education—that is, an education in the good—to the extent that their "lessons" remain committed to the transmission of ideas rather than to the radicality of what Jacques Lacan describes as an "act." But as Socrates, de Man, and Lacan, among others, had occasion to find out, the teacher whose words come to figure the negation of (recognizable) meaning, the teacher who threatens, like "the queer," to make visible the incompletion of the world, will become, like "the queer," a figure for ontological negation.

3 Jacques Derrida, "Structure, Sign, and Play in the Discourse of the Human Sciences," in *Writing and Difference*, trans. Alan Bass (Chicago: University of Chicago Press, 1978), 293.

4 Since the publication of *No Future*, several critics have written about the presumed "whiteness" of the Child in Western culture. While the figure of meaning and cultural promise in a racist and anti-Black order will disproportionately find representation in images of the dominant racial class, the Child itself has no intrinsic or invariable relation to whiteness. It can just as easily, where ideologically useful, be embodied, within that racist order, in (the image of) a Black child or child of color. Antiabortion activists, for example, use photographs of Black and Hispanic children to demonize abortion as racist genocide in the hope of enlisting BIPOC persons to conservative social causes. These children are raised to the level of the Child not because the organizations deploying their images have any investment in those young Black lives but because the Child can exert a disciplinary force over Black adults. At the same time, many of these activists promulgate the myth of the "welfare queen," a woman whose class and color are aligned with excessive reproductivity (made possible by "handouts" from the state), and in this case her very fecundity threatens the future that belongs to the Child of the dominant, white social order. Similar antireproductive arguments against the excessive fertility of immigrants remain tied to the (racial) ideal of the Child as imagined from within a given community. Antivaccination movements in Pakistan that see a Western plot to destroy their children, and antigay rhetoric in Kenya that sees same-sex intimacy as a threat to the survival of indigenous traditions, make clear that the Child has no racial qualities in itself but assumes those qualities as needed to figure survival as such. The question often posed against *No Future* by those who positivize "queer" as an identity—"What about assuring the future for those actual children who happen to be queer?"—reappropriates those children as figures of futurity to oppose *No Future*'s argument as one more threat to the Child. In this context it may be worth noting, as well, the increasing controversies over Pride celebrations as voices from within the "queer community," for the most part homonormative subjects embracing the "respectability" that comes with increasing legal recognition, excoriate

the public display of sex toys, provocative clothing, or kink by insisting that Pride be a "safe space" for "queer" parents, and others, to take their children.

5 "For poetry makes nothing happen." W. H. Auden, "In Memory of W. B. Yeats (d. Jan. 1939)" in *W. H. Auden: Collected Poems*, ed. Edward Mendelson (New York: Random House, 1991). Lauren Berlant has rightly observed that for many human subjects the world does not seem coherent, stable, or comprehensible. But such experiences of the world's precarity do not exclude such subjects from an investment in meaning or from clinging to their faith in the coherence of reality, although it seems incoherent *to them*. Even the theorizing of the world as incoherent attempts a coherent account of the world. See Berlant and Edelman, *Sex, or the Unbearable*, 5–15.

6 See Jonathan Swift, *Gulliver's Travels: An Authoritative Text*, ed. Robert A. Greenberg, 2nd ed. (New York: W. W. Norton, 1970), 214.

7 Jacques Lacan, *The Ethics of Psychoanalysis, 1959–1960: The Seminar of Jacques Lacan, Book VII*, ed. Jacques-Alain Miller, trans. Dennis Porter (New York: W. W. Norton, 1997), 54, 139.

8 Lacan, *Ethics of Psychoanalysis*, 112.

9 Lacan, *Ethics of Psychoanalysis*, 99.

10 Slavoj Žižek remarks, "With regard to this relation between drive and desire, we could perhaps risk a small rectification of the Lacanian maxim of the psychoanalytic ethic 'not to cede one's desire': is not desire as such already a certain yielding, a kind of compromise formation, a metonymic displacement, retreat, a defense against intractable drive?" Žižek, *Looking Awry*, 172n1.

11 Lacan, for example, discusses the formulation "that sublimation is the satisfaction of the drive with a change of object, that is, without repression." Noting that "if the drive allows the change of object, it is because it is already deeply marked by the articulation of the signifier," he then goes on to add, "I emphasize the following: the properly metonymic relation between one signifier and another that we call desire is not a new object or a previous object, but the change of object in itself." Lacan, *Ethics of Psychoanalysis*, 293.

12 Lacan, *Ethics of Psychoanalysis*, 67, 66.

13 For Lacan on the sublimation of the father, see *Ethics of Psychoanalysis*, 181. For Lacan on courtly love, see *Ethics of Psychoanalysis*, 139–54.

14 Pedophilo-phobia refers to the obsessive fixation on pedophilia, not to opposition to acts of pedocriminality. In pedophilo-phobia, the phobic structure masks (however imperfectly) a libidinal investment that makes protecting the Child an excuse for ceaselessly imagining its violation. The results can be seen in many of the conspiracy theories promulgated by right-wing extremists.

15 See, for instance, Lacan's comments on the vase, which he uses to explore the relation between the always veiled Thing and the construction of an object that represents it. "Now if you consider the vase from the point of view I first proposed, as an object made to represent the emptiness at the center of the real that is called the Thing, this emptiness as represented in the representation presents itself as a *nihil*, as nothing. And that is why the potter, just like you to whom I am

speaking, creates the vase with his hand around an emptiness, creates it, just like the mythical creator, *ex nihilo*, starting with a hole." And later: "I referred last time to the schematic example of the vase, so as to allow you to grasp where the Thing is situated in the relationship that places man in the mediating function between the real and the signifier. This Thing, all forms of which created by man belong to the sphere of sublimation, this Thing will always be represented by emptiness, precisely because it cannot be represented by anything else—or, more exactly, because it can only be represented by something else. But in every form of sublimation, emptiness is determinative." Lacan, *Ethics of Psychoanalysis*, 121, 129–30.

16 See Kevin Ohi's *Innocence and Rapture: The Erotic Child in Pater, Wilde, James, and Nabokov* (New York: Palgrave Macmillan, 2005) for a brilliant reading of our ideological construction of childhood sexuality in relation to questions of "purity, guilt, and predation" (6).

17 Jean-Jacques Rousseau, *Émile, or On Education*, trans. Allan Bloom (New York: Basic Books, 1979), 37.

18 "Dès cette époque interviennent de façon extérieure des interdictions qui empechent le nourrisson de se masturber, de sucer son puce, de pisser partout quand il a envie." Lucien Israël, *Pulsions de mort: Séminaire 1977–1978* (Strasbourg: Arcanes, 1998), 86.

19 Rousseau, *Émile*, 34.

20 Jacques Derrida, ". . . That Dangerous Supplement . . . ," in *Acts of Literature*, ed. Derek Attridge (New York: Routledge, 1992), 84.

21 Derrida, ". . . That Dangerous Supplement . . . ," 85–86.

22 Sylvia Plath, "The Munich Mannequins," in *The Collected Poems of Sylvia Plath*, ed. Ted Hughes (New York: Harper Collins, 2008), 262.

23 Rousseau, *Émile*, 217.

24 Rousseau, *Émile*, 217.

25 Israël, *Pulsions de mort*, 87. "L'éducation, c'est l'éducation contre la pulsion. Faire sortir hors de . . . , c'est que veut dire éduquer, faire sortir hors de l'univers pulsionnel."

26 Lacan, *Ethics of Psychoanalysis*, 144.

27 Israël, *Pulsions de mort*, 87. "On ne sait plus rien de l'univers pulsionnel parce que le seul petit moyen d'en sauvegarder quelque chose est de n'en rien savoir. Il n'est plus accessible qu'à travers tout ce détour d'une boucle remplacée par une parole sans fin"; and "éducation comme antipulsion."

28 The Child, as an allegory of this dialectic, which is to say, as an allegory of sublimation, thus allegorizes allegorization. The piling up of these synonymies in relation to the Child points to the insistence on the production of knowledge as social positivity, as social reproduction—an insistence that marks, as *repetition*, the structurally determining negativity internal to reproduction itself.

29 Friedrich Schiller, *On the Aesthetic Education of Man*, trans. Reginald Snell (Mineola, NY: Dover, 2004), 31.

30 Schiller, *On the Aesthetic Education of Man*, 55.

31 Schiller, *On the Aesthetic Education of Man*, 29–30.

32 Schiller, *On the Aesthetic Education of Man*, 115.

33 Paul de Man, "Kant and Schiller," in *Aesthetic Ideology*, ed. Andrzej Warminski (Minneapolis: University of Minnesota Press, 1996), 150.

34 Andrzej Warminski quotes this phrase in "Introduction: Allegories of Reference," in de Man, *Aesthetic Ideology*, 7. A very similar assertion appears in de Man's "Kant and Schiller": "Whatever writing we do, whatever way we have of talking about art, whatever way we have of teaching, whatever justification we give ourselves for teaching, whatever the standards and the values by means of which we teach, they are more than ever and profoundly Schillerian." De Man, "Kant and Schiller," 142.

35 For de Man, of course, Schiller's aesthetic ideology retreats from, by misreading, Immanuel Kant, who, as de Man declares in "Kant and Schiller," "disarticulated the project of articulation which the aesthetic—which he had undertaken and which he found himself, by the rigor of his own discourse to break down under the power of his own critical epistemological discourse." De Man, "Kant and Schiller," 134.

36 Schiller, *On the Aesthetic Education of Man*, 61.

37 Blaise Pascal, "De l'esprit géométrique," in *Oeuvres completes*, ed. Michel Le Guern (Paris: Gallimard, 2000), 2:162.

38 Pascal, "De l'esprit géométrique," in *Oeuvres completes*, 2:154.

39 Pascal, "De l'esprit géométrique," in *Oeuvres completes*, 2:167. "La seule raison pour laquelle l'unité n'est pas au rang des nombres, est qu'Euclide et les premiers auteurs qui ont traité de l'arithmétique, ayant plusiers propriétés à donner, qui convenoient à tous les nombres, hormis à l'unité, pour éviter de dire souvent qu'en tout nombre hors l'unité, telle condition se rencontre; ils ont exclu l'unité de la signification du mot de nombre."

40 Paul de Man, "Pascal's Allegory of Persuasion," in *Aesthetic Ideology*, 59.

41 Pascal, "De l'esprit géométrique," in *Oeuvres completes*, 2:169. "Mais si l'on veut prendre parmi les nombres une comparaison qui représente avec justesse ce que nous considérons dans l'étendue, il faut que ce soit le rapport du zéro aux nombres. Car le zéro n'est pas du même genre que les nombres, . . . c'est un véritable indivisible de nombre, comme l'indivisible est un véritable zéro d'étendue."

42 Ernesto Laclau, "Identity and Hegemony: The Role of Universality in the Constitution of Political Logics," in *Contingency, Hegemony, Universality: Contemporary Dialogues on the Left*, by Judith Butler, Ernesto Laclau, and Slavoj Žižek (New York: Verso, 2000), 68, 67.

43 De Man, "Kant and Schiller," 151; "Pascal's Allegory of Persuasion," 59.

44 Pascal, "De l'esprit géométrique," in *Oeuvres completes*, 2:163. "Tout ces vérités ne peuvent se démontrer; et cependant ce sont les fondements et les principes de la géométrie."

45 De Man, "Pascal's Allegory of Persuasion," 59.

46 This reading of Pascal can be understood better in relation to Brian Rotman's excellent account of zero as "the meta-sign which both initiates the linguistic system and participates within it as a constituent sign." Brian Rotman, *Signifying Nothing: The Semiotics of Zero* (Stanford, CA: Stanford University Press, 1987),

27. Rotman goes on to describe the consequences of this in terms that correlate closely with de Man's account of "rudderless" signification: "To make the zero the origin of number is to claim for all numbers, including the unit, the status of free, unreferenced signs. Not signs of *something*, not *arithmoi*, certainly not real collections, and not abstractions of 'units' considered somehow as external and prior to numbers, but signs produced by and within arithmetical notation" (29). These discussions would allow us roughly to map the order of units, number, and the zero onto the three orders of the Lacanian system, collocating the substantiality of the unit with the Imaginary, the abstraction of number with the Symbolic, and the negativity of the zero with the Real.

47 The metaphor of the "marriage" of "mind and world" is quoted from Terry Eagleton's *Ideology* (London: Verso, 1991) by Andrzej Warminski in his "Introduction: Allegories of Reference," 8.

48 Laclau, in his reading of de Man, arrives at a similar understanding, though by means of a different path: "If the zero as moment of closure is impossible as an object but also necessary, it will have to have access to the field of representation. But the means of representation will be constitutively inadequate. It will give to the 'innommable' a body, a name, but this can be done only at the price of betraying its true 'nonbeing'; thus the tropological movement that prolongs sine die the non-resolvable dialectics between the zero and the one." Ernesto Laclau, "The Politics of Rhetoric," in *Material Events: Paul de Man and the Afterlife of Theory*, ed. Tom Cohen, Barbara Cohen, J. Hillis Miller, and Andrzej Warminski (Minneapolis: University of Minnesota Press, 2001), 234.

49 Rotman, *Signifying Nothing*, 29.

50 Warminski, "Introduction," 31; and de Man, "Hegel on the Sublime," in *Aesthetic Ideology*, 116.

51 *Bad Education* (2004), directed by Pedro Almodóvar; screenplay by Pedro Almodóvar, Sony Pictures Classics, DVD.

52 Lacan, *Four Fundamental Concepts of Psychoanalysis*, 256.

53 J. Hillis Miller, "Three Literary Theorists in Search of O," in *Provocations to Reading: J. Hillis Miller and the Democracy to Come*, ed. Barbara Cohen and Dragan Kuzundžič (New York: Fordham University Press, 2005), 214.

54 Of course, the allegory that installs the human as value necessarily reduces the human to an instance of allegory itself since allegorization introduces a distance or division within the ostensible unity of the signifier's referential function. In this sense the very allegory that attempts to rise beyond the permanent disruption of irony merely refigures that disruption, recalling what de Man affirms in "Pascal's Allegory of Persuasion": "Allegory (as sequential narration) is the trope of irony (as one is the trope of zero)." De Man, "Pascal's Allegory of Persuasion," 61.

55 De Man, "Kant and Schiller," 150.

56 Pedro Almodóvar, *La mauvaise éducation: Scénario bilingue* (Paris: Petites Bibliothèque des Cahiers du cinema, 2004), 130. "Pienso que acabo de perder la fe en este momento y, al no tener fe, ya no creo en Dios ni en el infierno. Y si no creo en el infierno, ya no tengo miedo. Y sin miedo, soy capaz de cualquier cosa."

57 *Psycho* (1960, Paramount), directed by Alfred Hitchcock, screenplay by Joseph Stefano; *Vertigo* (1958, Paramount), directed by Alfred Hitchcock, screenplay by Alec Coppel and Samuel A. Taylor; *Rope* (1948, Warner Brothers), directed by Alfred Hitchcock, screenplay by Arthur Laurents, adaptation by Hume Cronyn.

58 D. A. Miller, "Anal *Rope*," in *Inside/Out: Lesbian Theories, Gay Theories*, ed. Diana Fuss (New York: Routledge, 1991), 133.

59 This is not to say that Ignacio takes any *pleasure* in the encounter; the film, quite literally, leaves us in the dark about his affective response, offering, in its place, his pained reaction to Enrique's expulsion.

60 Almodóvar, *La mauvaise éducation*, 132. "La pantalla permanece negra dos o tres segundos. Lentamente, dentro de la negrura del fotograma empieza a definirse un grupo de alumnos (los compañeros del curso de Ignacio, unos 20 ó 30) haciendo gymnasia sueca en el campo de fútbol."

61 Almodóvar repeats this trope of pederastic enticement later in the film when he shows us, through Father Manolo's eyes—or rather (since by then he has left the priesthood) through the eyes of the publisher Berenguer—the seductively undulating body of Juan (he has not yet become Angel) as he performs, wearing only a pair of shorts and a look of studied indifference, a series of push-ups that awaken the excitement of the former priest.

62 De Man, "Kant and Schiller," 150.

63 Alenka Zupančič, *Ethics of the Real: Kant, Lacan* (New York: Verso, 2000), 95.

64 As work in progress by Carla Freccero suggests, this reduction of the human allows us to begin to think queerness in relation to animality as well—or, at any rate, in relation to the figural logics by which the categories of "human" and "animal" have been variously constructed and reinforced at different moments and in different places.

65 Lacan, "Dissolution."

66 See my discussion of (be)hindsight in "Seeing Things: Representation, the Scene of Surveillance, and the Spectacle of Gay Male Sex," in *Homographesis: Essays in Gay Literary and Cultural Theory* (New York: Routledge, 1994), 173–91.

67 Almodóvar, *La mauvaise éducation*, 90.

68 Almodóvar, *La mauvaise éducation*, 134.

69 Almodóvar, *La mauvaise éducation*, 134; emphasis mine.

70 The Spanish version of the lyrics, written by Almodóvar, changes the sense of the song dramatically, describing the river itself as muddy and touching on matters involving memory, God, good and evil, and concealment.

71 Almodóvar, *La mauvaise éducation*, 96. "Hay algo hipnótico y perverso en el hecho que sea un niño quien la cante."

72 Almodóvar, *La mauvaise éducation*, 98.

73 Almodóvar, *La mauvaise éducation*, 100. "Un hilo de sangre dividía mi frente en dos. Tuve el presentimiento de que con mi vida ocurriría los mismo; siempre estaría dividida y no podría hacer nada para evitarlo." Although the English subtitles translate the last phrase as "I couldn't help it," one might more render it more accurately as "I couldn't do anything to avoid it."

74 "Su adorado victima." Almodóvar, *La mauvaise éducation*, 100.

75 See Catherine Malabou, *La plasticité au soir de l'écriture: Dialectique, destruction, deconstruction* (Clamecy: Leo Scheer, 2005), 13–16.

76 Tad Leckman gives a useful overview of some films that have made changes in aspect ratio play a role in their narrative construction, citing, among others, Abel Gance's *Napoléon*, Frank Tashlin's *The Girl Can't Help It*, and Doug Trumbull's *Brainstorm*. See Tad Leckman, "Shapeshifting Films," *Sanctuary Moon: Back on the Forest Homeworld*, October 29, 2012, https://tadleckman.wordpress.com/2012/10/29/shapeshifting-films/.

77 Almodóvar uses one other aspect ratio in the film to indicate shots taken by the video camera Sr. Berenguer gives Juan.

78 I say "subsequently" despite the fact that in historical time the shot of the cinema frames it some years after that experience took place. For the viewer of *Bad Education*, however, as for the viewer of Enrique's *La Visita* (and, indeed, for Enrique as he reads Ignacio's story, *La Visita*, at this moment in the film), that experience has not yet occurred.

79 The insistence on framing is heightened by the camera's glimpse of Enrique framed within a window as the film fades in on the shot of the cinema.

80 To be as precise as possible: the text that Father Manolo reads is the one given him, in the diegesis of Enrique's *La Visita*, by Zahara, while the text Enrique is reading is the one given him by Juan/Angel. Enrique will later receive, from the hands of Ignacio's mother, an envelope containing another typescript of Ignacio's story. Insofar as the scene of Father Manolo reading *La Visita* in Enrique's film of *La Visita* is shot after Enrique has received this second manuscript, it is quite possible that either one could *literally* be the prop that the actor playing Father Manolo is reading in Enrique's film. But the change in aspect ratio from Father Manolo's face to the manuscript makes clear that Father Manolo has now melted, like the Child Ignacio, back into the signifier of which his visual manifestation is the imaginary effect.

81 Shakespeare, *Hamlet*, 2.2.529, 534, in *The Norton Shakespeare*, ed. Stephen Greenblatt et al., 2nd ed. (New York: W. W. Norton, 2008).

82 Slavoj Žižek, *Tarrying with the Negative: Kant, Hegel, and the Critique of Ideology* (Durham, NC: Duke University Press, 1993), 26.

83 Although it is Father José who actually kills Ignacio/Zahara, his action responds to Father Manolo's request that he get rid of the problem caused by Ignacio/Zahara's "visit."

84 This belief is reinforced by our having seen Juan/Angel as Zahara, the woman Ignacio becomes, in the visualization of Ignacio's narrative that, as we later discover, is actually a sequence in Enrique's film.

85 "En persona está mucho más deteriorado. Es alto, extremadamente delgado, el pelo largo y desordenado, dentadura en pésimo estado y más femenino que masculino." Almodóvar, *La mauvaise éducation*, 208. Unlike Zahara, who is given a female pronoun, Ignacio Adulto is referred to in the screenplay as male. In the absence of

any indication that Ignacio Adulto prefers female pronouns, I take my cue from the screenplay and use male pronouns in what follows.

86 "Ser mona cuesta muchismo dinero." Almodóvar, *La mauvaise éducation*, 210. The film suggests that the surgeries Ignacio seeks are aesthetic rather than gender-confirming. Complaining about Berenguer's many delays in getting him the money he demands, Ignacio Adulto, as he leaves to pay a visit to his mother, exclaims: "I hate that she has to see me with this mug and it's all your fault" (¡Odio que me vea con este careto y Vd. tiene la culpa!). Almodóvar, *La mauvaise éducation*, 220.

87 Almodóvar, *La mauvaise éducation*, 242.

88 "Por si acaso he escrito dos cartas, una para la editorial y otra para tu mujer." Almodóvar, *La mauvaise éducation*, 242.

89 Almodóvar, *La mauvaise éducation*, 244.

90 That shot of the typewriter's mechanism as a figure for cinematic inscription recalls an equally surprising shot from earlier in the film when the camera observes the interior workings of the cinematic camera itself just after we have seen Enrique fucking Juan/Angel (who is still pretending to be Ignacio) and just before they discuss the revisions Enrique has made to the end of *La Visita*. This should remind us that the only sex scenes we see in *Bad Education* recurrently play out in relation to film. The scene in which Zahara has sex with an intoxicated Enrique takes place only in the film of *La Visita* and represents a fantasy Ignacio never realizes. His only actual encounter with Enrique, which also takes place in *La Visita*, is when they jerk each other off while watching Sara Montiel onscreen; later Juan and Manolo/Berenguer will begin a sexual encounter while Juan excitedly records it on a video camera he has received as a gift. Sexual encounters take place as the division between the body, its signification, and the signifying mechanism itself.

91 Jacques Lacan, "The Signification of the Phallus," in *Écrits: The First Complete Edition in English*, trans. Bruce Fink (New York: W. W. Norton, 2006), 578.

92 Almodóvar, *La mauvaise éducation*, 284. The freezing of the image should be considered in relation to the beginning of the film, where Enrique, seeking inspiration for a screenplay, clips a newspaper article about a motorcyclist found frozen to death while his motorcycle drives on. This anticipates the questions of mechanicity, desire, and the death drive that loom so large in the film.

93 Parveen Adams, *The Emptiness of the Image: Psychoanalysis and Sexual Difference* (New York: Routledge, 1966), 131.

94 Jonathan Lear, *Happiness, Death, and the Remainder of Life* (Cambridge, MA: Harvard University Press, 2000), 109.

95 Lear, *Happiness, Death, and the Remainder of Life*, 111–12.

96 It might be useful, in this context, to consider Theodor Adorno's take on the excess that constitutes negativity and its attempted capture by the law: "Contradiction is nonidentity under the aspect of identity; the dialectical primary of the principle of contradiction makes the thought of unity the measure of heterogeneity. As the heterogeneous collides with its limit it exceeds itself. . . . [C]ontradictoriness itself has

an inescapably and fatefully legal character. Identity and contradiction of thought are welded together. Total contradiction is nothing but the manifested untruth of total identification. Contradiction is nonidentity under the rule of a law that affects the nonidentical as well." Theodor Adorno, *Negative Dialectics*, trans. E. B. Ashton (New York: Continuum, 1994), 5–6.

97 Slavoj Žižek, *The Ticklish Subject: The Absent Centre of Political Ontology* (New York: Verso, 2000), 160.

98 Eric Santner, *On the Psychotheology of Everyday Life: Reflections on Freud and Rosenzweig* (Chicago: University of Chicago Press, 2001), 33.

99 Santner, *On the Psychotheology of Everyday Life*, 64.

100 Paul de Man, *Blindness and Insight: Essays in the Rhetoric of Contemporary Criticism*, 2nd ed., rev. (Minneapolis: University of Minnesota Press, 1983), 224.

101 Perhaps that explains an unremarked aspect of the opening credits. Along with scabrous sexual graffiti, religious images, and cinematic signifiers, the credits depict, on three separate occasions, a passage from Marcel Duchamp's "The Green Box," the notes in which he comments on one of his masterworks, *Large Glass* (*Grande Verre*), also known as *The Bride Stripped Bare by Her Bachelors, Even*. Specifically depicting the notes that discuss "The Illuminating Gas," these citations from Duchamp bring to the fore the questions of sublimation, desire, and the image as they figure in his investigation of sexual division and the alternatives to "retinal" art. In this context the following remarks by Jacques-Alain Miller may be relevant to its relation to the film as I have discussed it: "Can the subject align himself with the drive and with its surefootedness? The problematic of removing fantasy, of traversing the screen it represents, aims at a laying bare of jouissance. It is, as Duchamp says, 'The Bride Stripped Bare by Her Bachelors, Even.' The bride is jouissance. Can one marry her? . . . The bride is stripped bare by her bachelors, even. Who wants her to be laid bare? Who wants to lay bare jouissance? Who wants to discover it underneath the [fundamental] fantasy? . . . There are two bachelors: the analysand and the analyst. Lacan completes his 'On Freud's Trieb' with 'and the Psychoanalyst's Desire' by saying that the one who wants to lay bare jouissance is the analyst bachelor: his desire is to lay bare the subject's jouissance, whereas the subject's desire is sustained only by the misrecognition of the drive known as fantasy." Jacques-Alain Miller, "Commenting on Lacan's Text," in *Reading Seminars I and II: Lacan's Return to Freud*, ed. Richard Feldman, Bruce Fink, and Maire Jaanus (Albany: State University of New York Press, 1996), 426.

Chapter Two: Against Survival

1 Jacques Derrida, "Marx & Sons," in *Ghostly Demarcations: A Symposium on Jacques Derrida's "Specters of Marx,"* ed. Michael Sprinker (New York: Verso, 2008), 231.

2 Julia Reinhard Lupton and Kenneth Reinhard, *After Oedipus: Shakespeare in Psychoanalysis* (Ithaca, NY: Cornell University Press, 1993), 15.

3 Citations from *Hamlet*, unless otherwise noted, are from *The Norton Shakespeare*, cited in the text by act, scene, and line.

4 "As we know, an autoimmunitary process is that strange behavior where a living being, in quasi-*suicidal* fashion, 'itself' works to destroy its own protection, to immunize itself *against* its 'own' immunity." Jacques Derrida, "Autoimmunity: Real and Symbolic Suicides; A Dialogue with Jacques Derrida," in *Philosophy in a Time of Terror: Dialogues with Jürgen Habermas and Jacques Derrida*, by Giovanna Borradori (Chicago: University of Chicago Press, 2003), 94.

5 "The essence of politics is dissensus." Jacques Rancière, *Dissensus: On Politics and Aesthetics*, ed. and trans. Stephen Corcoran (New York: Continuum Books, 2010), 38. Note, too, how this question of dissensus gets articulated, for Rancière, in relation to ontological inclusion and exclusion that centers precisely on the way in which one construes articulation as such: "Whoever is in the presence of an animal that possesses the ability to articulate language and its power of demonstration, knows that he is dealing with a human—and therefore political—animal. The only difficulty lies in knowing in which sign this sign can be recognized; that is, how you can be sure that the human animal mouthing a noise in front of you is articulating a discourse[.] . . . If there is someone you do not wish to recognize as a political being, you begin by not seeing him as the bearer of signs of politicity" (37–38).

6 Carla Freccero, *Queer/Early/Modern* (Durham, NC: Duke University Press, 2006), 80.

7 Jacques Lacan, "Seminar on the Purloined Letter," in *The Purloined Poe: Lacan, Derrida, and Psychoanalytic Reading*, ed. John Muller and William Richardson (Baltimore, MD: Johns Hopkins University Press, 1988), 39, 40, 39, 39.

8 *Supra-cognitive* is the term Alain Badiou applies to antiphilosophy in his account of Gilles Deleuze and is cited in Peter Hallward, *Badiou: A Subject to Truth* (Minneapolis: University of Minnesota Press, 2003), 20. Describing Badiou's concept of antiphilosophy through the example of Lacan, Hallward writes, "Unlike Badiou, Lacan holds that 'the dimension of truth is mysterious, inexplicable' (S3, 214/214), that desire is constitutively elusive (S20, 71), that the real is essentially ambivalence and loss, that analysis is steeped in the *tragic* and *horrific* dimensions of experience. Lacanian insight, in other words, is not so much a function of clarity and hope as it is an endurance of radical abjection" (21).

9 I am grateful to Jeffrey Masten who called this to my attention following an early presentation of this material at Cornell University in 2008.

10 Instead of *the world* here, perhaps one should say *the globe*, especially, as William Shakespeare, referring to his theater, tropes on it as "this wooden O" (*Henry V*, prologue, 13).

11 Roland Barthes, *Writing Degree Zero*, trans. Annette Lavers and Colin Smith (New York: Hill and Wang, 1970), 75, 75–76.

12 Barthes, *Writing Degree Zero*, 75.

13 Jacques Derrida, *Apprendre à vivre enfin: Entretien avec Jean Birnbaum* (Paris: Galilée, 2005), 26. "Je me suis toujours intéressé à cette thématique de la survie,

dont le sens *ne s'ajoute pas* au vivre et au mourir. Elle est originaire: la vie *est* la survie. Survivre au sens courant veut dire continuer à vivre, mais aussi vivre après la mort. À propos de la traduction, Benjamin souligne la distinction entre *überleben,* d'une part, survivre à la mort, comme un livre peut survivre à la mort de l'auteur, ou un enfant à la mort des parent, et, d'autre part, *fortleben, living on,* continuer à vivre. Tous les concepts qui m'ont aide à travailler, notamment celui de la trace ou du spectral, étaient lies au 'survivre' comme dimension structurale et rigoureuse-ment originaire. Elle ne dérive ni du vivre ni du morir."

14 Elsewhere Derrida notes that "one can sign neither a child nor a work." See Jacques Derrida and Maurizio Ferraris, *A Taste for the Secret*, ed. Giacomo Donis and David Webb, trans. Giacomo Donis (Malden, MA: Polity, 2001), 29.

15 For a compelling reading of literary and genetic codes, see Henry Turner, *Shake-speare's Double Helix* (New York: Continuum, 2007).

16 Hamlet's evocation of memory here as simultaneously the inscription of a pressure and the surface material that can be wiped away might be usefully considered in relation to Derrida's reading of Freud's "A Note upon the 'Mystic Writing Pad.'" See Derrida, "Freud and the Scene of Writing," in *Writing and Difference*, 196–231.

17 Jonathan Goldberg, *Shakespeare's Hand* (Minneapolis: University of Minnesota Press, 2003), 45; emphasis mine.

18 Goldberg, *Shakespeare's Hand*, 45.

19 Jacques Lacan, "Desire and the Interpretation of Desire in *Hamlet*," trans. James Hulbert, *Yale French Studies*, nos. 55–56 (1977): 12.

20 Sigmund Freud, *Civilization and Its Discontents*, in *The Standard Edition of the Complete Psychological Works of Sigmund Freud*, ed. James Strachey (London: Hogarth, 1991), 21:93.

21 Jacques Derrida, "I Have a Taste for the Secret," in Derrida and Ferraris, *Taste for the Secret*, 88.

22 Jacques Derrida, *Specters of Marx: The State of the Debt, the Work of Mourning, and the New International*, trans. Peggy Kamuf (New York: Routledge, 2006), xvi, xvii.

23 Derrida, *Specters of Marx*, xvii.

24 Derrida, *Specters of Marx*, xviii.

25 Derrida, *Specters of Marx*, xviii.

26 "If it is possible and if one must take it seriously, the possibility of the question, which is perhaps no longer a question and which we are calling here *justice*, must carry beyond *present* life, life as *my* life or *our* life. *In general*. For it will be the same thing for 'my life' or 'our life' 'tomorrow,' that is, for the life of others, as it was yesterday for other others: *beyond therefore the living present in general*." Derrida, *Specters of Marx*, xx.

27 Jacques Derrida, *Archive Fever: A Freudian Impression*, trans. Eric Prenowitz (Chicago: University of Chicago Press, 1996), 3.

28 Derrida, *Archive Fever*, 11.

29 Emily Bartels underscores the importance of the fact that this declaration takes place at Ophelia's interment. In her discussion on the gendered associations of

nation and "race" in *Hamlet*, Bartels writes, "Had Gertrude's dream come true, Ophelia might have become not only wife but mother to 'the Dane,' and the play might have worked itself out of the binding past, moving forward—via the female body—from father to son to son, rather than backward from son to father." Emily Bartels, "Identifying 'the Dane': Gender and Race in *Hamlet*," in *The Oxford Handbook of Shakespeare and Embodiment: Gender, Sexuality, and Race*, ed. Valerie Traub (Oxford: Oxford University Press, 2016), 204. As I argued in *No Future*, the logic of futurism that presents itself as the movement "forward" (toward the promise of the Child) cannot be distinguished from the movement backward (toward the preservation of the father). Hamlet himself, by embodying the archive, assumes that bidirectionality and at the same time suggests the imperfect sublimation of the death drive in misreadings of the archive as survival.

30   Derrida, "I Have a Taste for the Secret," 91; and Derrida, *Specters of Marx*, xx.

31   Yosef Hayim Yerushalmi, *Freud's Moses: Judaism Terminable and Interminable* (New Haven, CT: Yale University Press, 1991).

32   Derrida, *Archive Fever*, 23 (quoting the inscription in Freud's Bible), 51.

33   Derrida, *Archive Fever*, 44; emphasis mine.

34   As in *No Future*, I distinguish here between the Child as an ideological fantasy and the child that exists as a historical and biological entity. Though that division is never stable, since the latter is constantly subject to cultural articulation as the former, it provides an important basis for trying to recognize the distinction between an ideological construct and the substrate on which it rests.

35   Derrida, *Archive Fever*, 7, 79, 78.

36   Derrida, *Archive Fever*, 79.

37   "The One, as self-repetition, can only repeat and recall this instituting violence." Derrida, *Archive Fever*, 79.

38   Hamlet's "Yes, yes" might be read as an index of his willingness to fill the lack in the Other with himself, to accede to the futurist imperative of a repetition that effectively keeps the *a-venir* from arriving. He plugs the hole in the Other that also opens a hole in the Real, as Lacan describes it in his seminar on Hamlet. See Lacan, "Desire and the Interpretation of Desire in *Hamlet*," esp. 37–40.

39   Derrida, *Archive Fever*, 11.

40   Jacques Lacan, *The Ethics of Psychoanalysis, 1959–1960: Seminar VII*, ed. Jacques-Alain Miller, trans. Dennis Porter (New York: W. W. Norton, 1997), 211.

41   Lacan, *Ethics of Psychoanalysis*, 212.

42   Lacan, *Ethics of Psychoanalysis*, 212.

43   Lacan, *Ethics of Psychoanalysis*, 214.

44   Lacan, "Desire and the Interpretation of Desire in *Hamlet*," 28.

45   Lacan, "Desire and the Interpretation of Desire in *Hamlet*," 29.

46   Lacan, "Desire and the Interpretation of Desire in *Hamlet*," 28.

47   Lacan, "Desire and the Interpretation of Desire in *Hamlet*," 29.

48   Jacques Lacan, "The Subversion of the Subject and the Dialectic of Desire," in *Écrits*, 697.

49 Lacan, "Subversion of the Subject and the Dialectic of Desire," 694.

50 Lacan, "Subversion of the Subject and the Dialectic of Desire," 695.

51 Slavoj Žižek, "Neighbors and Other Monsters: A Plea for Ethical Violence," in *The Neighbor: Three Inquiries in Political Theology*, by Slavoj Žižek, Eric L. Santner, and Kenneth Reinhard (Chicago: University of Chicago Press, 2005), 172.

52 Derrida, *Archive Fever*, 79.

53 Derrida, *Archive Fever*, 21.

54 Derrida, *Specters of Marx*, 10.

55 On the concept of (be)hindsight, see Lee Edelman, "Seeing Things: Representation, the Scene of Surveillance, and the Spectacle of Gay Male Sex," in *Homographesis*, 173–91.

56 Derrida, *Archive Fever*, 68.

57 Derrida, *Archive Fever*, 74.

58 Derrida, "Marx & Sons," 250.

59 Derrida, *Apprendre à vivre enfin*, 54–55. "Je ne voudrait pas laisser cours a l'interprétation selon laquelle la survivance est plutot du coté de la mort, du passé, que de la vie et de l'avenir. Non, tout le temps, la déconstruction est du coté du *oui*, de l'affirmation de la vie. Tout ce que je dis . . . de la survie comme complication de l'opposition vie/mort, procède chez moi d'une affirmation inconditionelle de la vie. . . . [C]'est l'affirmation d'un vivant qui préfere le vivre et donc le survivre a la mort."

60 Derrida, *Apprendre à vivre enfin*, 30.

61 Derrida, "Autoimmunity," 113.

62 W. J. T. Mitchell, "Picturing Terrorism: Derrida's Autoimmunity," *Critical Inquiry* 33, no. 2 (Winter 2007): 288.

63 Derrida, "Autoimmunity," 115.

64 Derrida, *Archive Fever*, 14.

65 Derrida, "Différance," 19.

66 Derrida, "Structure, Sign, and Play," 283–84.

67 Lacan, *L'Étourdit*, 452.

68 Lacan, "Desire and the Interpretation of Desire in *Hamlet*," 34.

69 *Oxford English Dictionary Online*, s.v. "out of joint," "joint, n.1," accessed February 21, 2022, https://www-oed-com.ezproxy.library.tufts.edu/view/Entry/101544?rskey=RjleIm&result=1&isAdvanced=false.

70 Hamlet's disgust at the interimplication of matter, sexuality, and decay anticipates that of another figure linked to incestuous maternal investments: Uncle Charlie as written by Thornton Wilder and as played by Joseph Cotten in Alfred Hitchcock's *Shadow of a Doubt* (1943, Universal Pictures). Hamlet's speech lies somewhere in the background of Uncle Charlie's most rancid depictions of the world to his niece, "young Charlie": "Do you know the world is a foul sty? Do you know if you rip the fronts off houses you'd find swine? The world's a hell. What does it matter what happens in it? Wake up, Charlie! Use your wits. Learn something." *Shadow of a Doubt* (1943), directed by Alfred Hitchcock, screenplay by Thronton Wilder, Sally Benson, and Alma Reville. Uncle Charlie here aims at

a bad education, as his final phrase suggests. But his actions throughout the film reveal his attachment to a fantasy of purity (the lost world of his childhood as represented by the waltzing dancers and the portraits of his parents) that keeps him from encountering the zero at stake in any such bad education.

71　The use of "sallied" in the Second Quarto (1604), instead of the First Folio's "solid," would underscore the repugnance inspired by the body that impels Hamlet's wish for sublimation.

72　The phrase "shall live behind me" appears in the First Folio of 1623; the Second Quarto (1604) has "shall I leave behind me," and the First Quarto (1603) has Hamlet reproaching Horatio: "O fie Horatio, and if thou shouldst die, / What a scandal thou wouldst leave behind." The shuttle in these versions between *live* and *leave* brings out the unresolved relation between life and survival in the play, between living being and its archivization by way of what it leaves.

73　Derrida, *Archive Fever*, 12.

74　Derrida, *Archive Fever*, 19 (translation modified).

75　Lacan, *Ethics of Psychoanalysis*, 80, 81.

76　Lacan, *Ethics of Psychoanalysis*, 81.

77　Lacan, *Ethics of Psychoanalysis*, 83.

78　Lacan, *Ethics of Psychoanalysis*, 63. Note that earlier, in discussing the *Vorstellung* as "that around which Western philosophy since Aristotle and φαντασία has always revolved," Lacan goes on to describe the "radical sense" in which Freud understood it: "He assigned to it an extreme form that philosophers themselves have been unable to reduce it to, namely, that of an empty body, a ghost, a pale incubus of the relation to the world." Lacan, *Ethics of Psychoanalysis*, 60, 61.

79　Lacan, *Ethics of Psychoanalysis*, 83.

80　Lacan, *Ethics of Psychoanalysis*, 112.

81　Slavoj Žižek, *The Sublime Object of Ideology* (New York: Verso, 1989), 18.

82　Žižek, *Sublime Object of Ideology*, 18–19.

83　Simon Ryle, "Moles, Spots, Stains, and Tincts: Marks of Futurity in Shakespeare and Kurosawa," *Textual Practice* 28, no. 5 (2014): 825.

84　Rodolphe Gasché, *The Wild Card of Reading: On Paul de Man* (Cambridge, MA: Harvard University Press, 1998), 176.

85　Lacan, *Ethics of Psychoanalysis*, 83.

86　That affirmation might be formulated in the following way as a corollary to "Look! A Negro!," Frantz Fanon's famous words from *Black Skin, White Masks*: "Look, I really *am* a (Woman, Queer, Black, etc.)," where looking, the logic of the imaginary, sustains the assumption of the Symbolic name to affirm the ontological status of what thereby becomes reality. Fanon, *Black Skin, White Masks*, 105.

87　Saidiya V. Hartman and Frank Wilderson III, "The Position of the Unthought: An Interview with Saidiya V. Hartman, Conducted by Frank B. Wilderson III," *Qui Parle* 13, no. 2 (Spring/Summer 2003): 185. In *Red, White, and Black*, Wilderson also insists on politics as the attempt to fill the void in being, which he registers as Blackness: "Politics, for the Black, has as its prerequisite some discursive move which replaces the Black void with a positive, Human, value" (141–42).

88 Jean Allouch, "Nécrologie d'une 'science juive': Pour saluer Mal d'Archive de Jacques Derrida," *L'Unebévue*, no. 6 (1995): 144.

89 If Hamlet's name suggests "[I] am let," then it is all the more telling that near the end of the play he responds to this constraint that determines his identity by proposing its inversion: "Let be" (5.2.208). Dismissing investments in futurity and efforts to shape or control events, he performs what Alain Badiou would call a "subtraction" from the temporal politics informing his situation. This subtraction reiterates the negativity of the death drive played out in reproductive futurism even as it withdraws from the political order in which futurism defines what is.

Chapter Three: Funny/Peculiar/Queer

1 Paul de Man, "The Resistance to Theory," in *The Resistance to Theory* (Minneapolis: University of Minnesota Press, 1993), 3. Subsequent page references to this essay in this chapter will be given in parentheses in the text.

2 See the discussion of Pascal and the zero in chapter 1. Paul de Man, in his reading of Pascal's mathematical elaboration of Euclid writes, "The question remains, of course, whether the pair figure/reality can or cannot be itself thus reconciled, whether it is a contradiction of the type we encountered when it was said that one is a number and is not a number at the same time, or whether the order of figure and the order of reality are heterogeneous." De Man, "Pascal's Allegory of Persuasion," 62.

3 De Man, "Pascal's Allegory of Persuasion," 59.

4 De Man, "Pascal's Allegory of Persuasion," 69, 69, 59, 59, 69.

5 De Man, "Pascal's Allegory of Persuasion," 59.

6 See Paul de Man, "Kant's Materialism," in *Aesthetic Ideology*, 121.

7 On "facing" and "defacement," see Paul de Man, *The Rhetoric of Romanticism* (New York: Columbia University Press, 1984), esp. "Autobiography as Defacement" (67–81) and "Wordsworth and the Victorians" (83–92).

8 Lacan, *Other Side of Psychoanalysis*, 303.

9 Zupančič, *Ethics of the Real*, 95.

10 See the work of Lauren Berlant, especially *The Female Complaint: The Unfinished Business of Sentimentality in American Culture* (Durham, NC: Duke University Press, 2008).

11 Žižek, *Tarrying with the Negative*, 97.

12 Žižek, *Tarrying with the Negative*, 96.

13 If, as Lacan asserts, something can be missing from its place only in the Symbolic, that is because the Symbolic requires the space or gap that establishes the correlation of things and places—a gap like the empty space in those puzzles that require you to slide tile-like counters up and down across the horizontal and vertical rows of a grid, which contains a single empty space, in order to construct a coherent image or a consecutive sequence from those elements.

14 Freud, *Civilization and Its Discontents*, 21:93.

15 Sigmund Freud, *Beyond the Pleasure Principle*, in *The Standard Edition of the Complete Psychological Works of Sigmund Freud*, ed. by James Strachey (London: Hogarth, 1991), 18:44.

16 "The first signifier is the notch by which it is indicated, for example, that the subject has killed *one* animal. . . . The subject himself is marked off by the single stroke, and first he marks himself as a tattoo, the first of the signifiers. When this signifier, this *one*, is established—the reckoning is *one* one. It is at this level, not of the one, but of the *one* one, at the level of the reckoning, that the subject has to situate himself as such." Lacan, *Four Fundamental Concepts of Psychoanalysis*, 141.

17 Žižek, *Tarrying with the Negative*, 99.

18 Žižek, *Tarrying with the Negative*, 101.

19 Alain Badiou, *Ethics: An Essay on the Understanding of Evil*, trans. Peter Hallward (New York: Verso, 2001), 60. Subsequent page references to this work in this chapter will be given in parentheses in the text.

20 Insofar as truth-procedures pertain to love, art, politics, and science, Paul's conversion does not, as Badiou acknowledges, make him a proper subject of truth. And insofar as the escapee from Plato's cave is the agent of his own liberation, his encounter with truth is not exactly the result of an event in its aspect of gratuitous arrival, which Badiou discusses as grace.

21 Alain Badiou, "On the Truth-Process," lecture, European Graduate School, August 2002, http://www.lacan.com/badeurope.htm.

22 Badiou, "On the Truth-Process."

23 Badiou, "On the Truth-Process."

24 Lacan points the way to such an analysis in his own reading of the incompleteness of logical structures: "[A] logical system is consistent, however 'weak' it is, as they say, only by designating its force of effect of incompleteness, where its limit is marked. To what *jouissance* does this way in which the logical foundation itself proves to be opening up correspond? In other words, what is truth here?" Lacan, *Other Side of Psychoanalysis*, 67.

25 Lacan, *Ethics of Psychoanalysis*, 212, 213, 214. Subsequent page references to this work in this chapter will be given in parentheses in the text.

26 Shakespeare, *Hamlet*, 1.2.73–74, in *The Norton Shakespeare*. References are to act, scene, and line.

27 As Jacques-Alain Miller observes, "What's difficult about *jouissance* is that while desire is connected to speech, and to signifiers, *jouissance*, on the contrary, is silence. And Freud spoke mysteriously of the silence of the drives." Jacques-Alain Miller, "The A and the a in Clinical Studies," *Symptom* 6 (Spring 2005), https://www.lacan.com/newspaper6.htm.

28 The drive, I have argued, is the radical of desire just as desire can be understood as a sublimation of the drive.

29 Schiller, *On the Aesthetic Education of Man*, 134, 136–37.

30 Schiller, *On the Aesthetic Education of Man*, 130.

31 Schiller, *On the Aesthetic Education of Man*, 138.

32 Jean Allouch, demonstrating that psychoanalysis, for Lacan, is not founded on a "love of truth," quotes Lacan as follows: "La verité est seduction d'abord, et pour vous couillonner. Pour ne pas s'y laisser prendre, il faut être fort" (Truth is first of all seduction in order to con you. You have to be strong not to let yourself be had). Jean Allouch, *L'amour Lacan* (Paris: Epel, 2009), 237.

33 Lacan, *Other Side of Psychoanalysis*, 52.

34 "*L'amour c'est la vérité*, mais seulement en tant que c'est à partir d'elle, à partir d'une coupure, que commence un autre savoir que le savoir propositionnel, à savoir *le savoir inconscient*, . . . C'est la division irrémédiable." Jacques Lacan, *Séminaire 21: Les non-dupes errent (1973–74)*, January 15, 1974, 44, http://staferla.free.fr/S21 /S21.htm.

35 Lacan, *Other Side of Psychoanalysis*, 66, 66, 67.

36 Lacan, *Four Fundamental Concepts of Psychoanalysis*, 185.

37 Jacques Derrida, *Specters of Marx*, xvii.

38 In his 1966 lecture "Psychoanalysis and Medicine," Lacan writes, "What I call *jouissance* . . . is always of the order of a tension, of a forcing, of an expenditure" (Car ce que j'appelle jouissance . . . est toujours de l'ordre de la tension, du forçage, de la dépense). Jacques Lacan, "Psychanalyse et médecine," *Lettres de l'École freudienne de Paris* 1 (February–March 1967): 46, http://ecole-lacanienne.net/wp-content /uploads/2016/04/EFP-N1-1967.pdf.

39 Dany Nobus, *Jacques Lacan and the Freudian Practice of Psychoanalysis* (Philadelphia: Routledge, 2000), 44.

40 Jacques Lacan, "Kant with Sade," trans. James B. Swenson Jr., *October*, no. 51 (Winter 1989): 58.

41 Both "good" and "desire" become words that carry antithetical meanings here. On the one hand, *good* designates the good of the community and the subject in its relation to the ego ideal, and, on the other, it bespeaks the good of the unconscious subject of the drive; similarly, *desire* names both the Symbolic exchange, the signifying economy of reserve for which jouissance must be renounced, *and* the radical desire that knows no reserve and enacts jouissance as aneconomy. Hence, Lacan, who explicitly names jouissance as "the pound of flesh" we pay for sublimation, goes on to declare, "That good which is sacrificed for desire—and you will note that that means the same thing as that desire which is lost for the good—that pound of flesh is precisely the thing that religion undertakes to recuperate." Lacan, *Ethics of Psychoanalysis*, 322.

42 Translation modified to acknowledge that the French *fantasme* means "fantasy," not "phantasm." Lacan's designation of this fantasy as derisory recalls Walter Benjamin's similar repudiation of such a categorical imperative in "Critique of Violence": "Nor, of course, unless one is prepared to proclaim a quite childish anarchism—is it [the critique of violence as a means to legal ends] achieved by refusing to acknowledge any constraint toward persons and declaring 'What pleases is permitted.' Such a maxim merely excludes reflection on the moral and historical spheres, and thereby on any meaning in action, and beyond this on any mean-

ing in reality itself, which cannot be constituted if 'action' is removed from its sphere." Walter Benjamin, "Critique of Violence," in *Reflections: Essays, Aphorisms, Autobiographical Writings*, trans. Edmund Jephcott (New York: Harcourt Brace Jovanovich, 1978), 284.

43 Although one might more precisely translate the French as "that which is sacrificed of the good for the sake of desire . . . means the same thing as that which is lost of desire for the sake of the good," the English translation as published by Norton, and cited in the text, is correct, so I have used it. I provide the French from the stenotyped transcript here: "C'est que ce qui est sacrificié de *bien* pour le *désir*—et vous observerez que ça veut dire la même chose que ce qui est perdu de *désir* pour le *bien*—c'est justement cette '*livre de chair*' que la religion se fait office et emploi de récupérer." Jacques Lacan, *Séminaire 7: L'éthique (1959–60)*, July 6, 1960, 247, http://staferla.free.fr/S7/S7.htm

44 Many readers of Lacan ignore this insistence on the "good" of jouissance, trying to redeem Lacan for a more conventional moral framework with a *socially recognizable* good. Mari Ruti, for instance, belongs to this camp, as does Élisabeth Roudinesco, who twists what she identifies as the formula of Lacanian ethics ("ne céder pas sur son désir" [don't give ground relative to your desire]) into a rejection of jouissance as a mortification that resists the "good" as determined by reason. She is, of course, right about that resistance, but precisely because jouissance, like the drive, *refuses* the mortification imposed by the Symbolic. Roudinesco's position can be summed up in the following, to my mind utterly misguided, assertion: "La psychanalyse renoue avec toute une tradition philosophique de la maîtrise raisonnable des passions" (Psychoanalysis takes up once more the whole philosophical tradition of the reasonable mastery of the passions). Élisabeth Roudinesco, "On peut tirer de Lacan une pensée progressiste authentique," *L'Humanité*, September 9, 2011, https://www.humanite.fr/societe/elisabeth-roudinesco-%C2%AB -peut-tirer-de-lacan-une-pensee-progressiste-authentique-%C2%BB-479127. Mari Ruti, *The Ethics of Opting Out: Queer Theory's Defiant Subjects* (New York: Columbia University Press, 2017).

45 Alain Badiou, *Saint Paul: The Foundation of Universalism*, trans. Ray Brassier (Stanford, CA: Stanford University Press, 2003), 42.

46 Badiou, *Ethics*, 41; and Badiou, *Saint Paul*, 2.

47 Bruno Bosteels, *Badiou and Politics* (Durham, NC: Duke University Press, 2011), 195.

48 Alain Badiou, "Being and Spatialization: An Interview with Alain Badiou," by Marios Constantinou, *Environment and Planning D: Society and Space* 27, no. 5 (October 2009): 794. What Badiou writes as "unnameable" in the *Ethics* appears as "unnamable" here.

49 Badiou, *Saint Paul*, 79.

50 See, for example, Michel Foucault, *The History of Sexuality*, vol. 1, *An Introduction*, trans. Robert Hurley (New York: Vintage Books, 1990).

51 Badiou, *Saint Paul*, 79.

52 Badiou, *Saint Paul*, 79–81.

53 Žižek, *Ticklish Subject*, 154.

54 Alain Badiou, "Rhapsody for the Theatre: A Short Philosophical Treatise," trans. Bruno Bosteels, *Theatre Survey* 49, no. 2 (November 2008): 187, 190.

55 Jacques Lacan, "The Instance of the Letter in the Unconscious, or Reason since Freud," in *Écrits*, 430.

56 Lacan, "Instance of the Letter," 430–31.

57 Immanuel Kant, *Critique of Judgment*, trans. Werner S. Pluhar (Indianapolis: Hackett, 1987), 129.

58 De Man talks about the imagination's self-sacrifice to make possible the triumph of reason in "Phenomenality and Materiality in Kant" (*Aesthetic Ideology*, esp. 85–87). For instance, he writes, "In the experience of the sublime, the imagination achieves tranquility, it submits to reason, achieves the highest degree of freedom by freely sacrificing its natural freedom to the higher freedom of reason" (86). In "Kant's Materialism," he writes, "What makes the sublime compatible with reason is its independence from sensory experience; it is beyond the senses, übersinnlich" (*Aesthetic Ideology*, 125).

59 J.-A. Miller, "The A and the a in Clinical Studies," 9.

60 This is not to say that the competition, however amicable, in the couple's game is without relation to the "games" to come, any more than the "civilized" game of golf is unrelated to the violent use to which the intruders later put the couple's clubs. But the difference lies in the degree to which one has a coherent set of rules that grant one knowledge of how to play and determine when one has entered the space of a game. The young men's games are "funny" because they ignore both consistency and consent.

61 Schiller, *On the Aesthetic Education of Man*, 138.

62 Christopher Weingarten et al., "The 100 Greatest Metal Albums of All Time: 91) Naked City: 'Torture Garden' (1990)," *Rolling Stone*, June 21, 2017, https://www.rollingstone.com/music/music-lists/the-100-greatest-metal-albums-of-all-time-113614/naked-city-torture-garden-1990-194353/.

63 Since Paul, by the time he pursues young Schorschi, has already signaled an awareness of the extradiegetic *within* the diegesis, one might say that he has "heard" the extradiegetic music and brought it into the film.

64 Michael Haneke, quoted in John Wray, "Minister of Fear," *New York Times Magazine*, September 23, 2007, 47.

65 The absence of that rape, its translation into sexual humiliation by other means, may contribute to the queering of the two intruders and thereby ascribe to their violence a more perverse, less recognizable, genealogy than that displayed in Kubrick's film.

66 Michael Haneke, "Interview: Michael Haneke; The Bearded Prophet of *Code Inconnu* and *The Piano Teacher*," by Scott Foundas, *IndieWire*, December 4, 2001, https://www.indiewire.com/2001/12/interview-michael-haneke-the-bearded-prophet-of-code-inconnu-and-the-piano-teacher-2-80636/.

67   Haneke, "Michael Haneke, *Funny Games U.S.*," by Nick Dawson, *Filmmaker Magazine*, March 14, 2008, https://filmmakermagazine.com/1307-michael-haneke -funny-games-u-s/#.YhlGpZZOlPY.

68   *Oxford English Dictionary Online*, s.v. "rape, v.2," accessed February 25, 2022, https://www-oed-com.ezproxy.library.tufts.edu/view/Entry/158153?rskey =jipF5W&result=10&isAdvanced=false.

69   Quoted in Allouch, *L'amour Lacan*, 237.

70   Michael Haneke, "An Interview with Michael Haneke," by Serge Toubiana, audio commentary on *Funny Games*, directed by Michael Haneke (1997; New York: Kino Video, 2006), DVD.

71   Michael Haneke, "A propos de *Funny Games*," an interview by Laurent Rigoulet included in the press materials for the release of *Funny Games* in France. "Funny Games: Un film de Michael Haneke," January 1998, Pressbook, Les Films du Paradoxe (Paris, France).

72   Haneke, "A propos de *Funny Games*." "Et puisque le cinéma fait partie de ces medias, il a l'obligation de porter une réfléxion sur ses propres moyens, sur la question de la violence et la manière dont elle est representée."

73   Roy Grundmann, "Auteur de Force: Michael Haneke's 'Cinema of Glaciation,'" *Cineaste* 32, no. 2 (Spring 2007): 7.

74   Haneke, "Interview with Michael Haneke."

75   Michael Haneke, "Michael Haneke: Les temps postmodernes," interview by Sebastien Ors, *Reperages*, no. 43 (Autumn 2003), 39. "Car ce n'est pas un film réaliste. Ce sont deux personages drolement artificiels confrontés à une famille qui, elle, est réaliste. Les deux garçons sont comme des robots sur le plan emotionnel, ils n'ont aucune réflexion humaine."

76   Luc Lagier, "*Funny Games*: Jeux de Vilains," *Reperages*, no. 43 (Autumn 2003). "Pour les deux adolescents, abreuvés de jeux videos et de télévision, le monde se résume à un jeu simplifié jusqu'à la caricature, un monde sans consequences où la 'vraie' mort ne peut exister et où les personnes croisées s'apparentent à des personages ou à des silhouettes, comme autant de pantins à manupuler dans sa propre fiction."

77   Haneke, "A propos de *Funny Games*." "Toutes ces explications ne servent à rien: si on veut tuer, on tue."

78   Haneke, "Interview with Michael Haneke."

79   Jonathan Culler makes this point in his discussion of Cleanth Brooks's reading of John Donne's "The Canonization." See Jonathan Culler, *On Deconstruction: Theory and Criticism after Structuralism* (Ithaca, NY: Cornell University Press, 1983), 201–5, esp. 204.

80   This does not mean that film cannot index the illusory nature of its representations. It may do so by way of special effects or changes in lighting, decor, costume, sound, camera angle, etc. But however this difference may be figured, the status of the image as projected representation makes it ontologically identical to the other images that are given to be seen.

81 Barbara Johnson, *Persons and Things* (Cambridge, MA: Harvard University Press, 2008), 49.

82 Plato, *The Republic of Plato*, trans. Benjamin Jowett (Project Gutenberg, 2017), bk. VII, p. 515, C–D, https://www.gutenberg.org/files/55201/55201-h/55201-h.htm.

83 In this he differs from Hamlet, who sees no escape from the patriarchal imperative of pedag-archivilization ("Remember me!") except in the death where, however fully "silence" may mark his rest, he still insists that his name live on, through Horatio, in the Symbolic. Similarly, though Almodóvar's film derealizes both Ignacio as Child and the image of Father Manolo, neither can recognize his status as Imaginary any more than can Haneke's Family.

84 Alain Badiou, *Pour aujourd'hui: Platon! (2): Séminaire d'Alain Badiou (2008–2009)*, transcript by Daniel Fischer, March 4, 2009, http://www.entretemps.asso .fr/Badiou/08-09.htm. "Platon exclut toute forme de desalignment spontane" (Section 16).

85 Badiou, *Pour aujourd'hui: Platon!*, Section 16. "Pour qu'il y ait désalignement, il faut une forme de contrainte, une poussée du dehors, qui désigne, dans mon vocabulaire, son caractère *événementiel*."

86 Badiou, *Saint Paul*, 66.

87 Badiou, *Saint Paul*, 85.

88 Badiou, *Pour aujourd'hui: Platon!*, Section 17. "L'État de la situation est le système des contraintes qui limitent la possibilité des possibles."

89 Badiou, *Pour aujourd'hui: Platon!*, Section 16. "L'idée qu'on ne peut accÉder à un autre mode du visible que sur le mode de la contrainte s'oppose à l'idée pour laquelle ce qui importe c'est l'acquisition d'un savoir nouveau. Or, si on devoilait aux spectateurs la mécanique de la machination des apparances, cela ne changerait pas grand-chose, ils seraient peut-être 'stupéfaits et gênés,' et c'est tout."

90 Alex Ling, *Badiou and Cinema* (Edinburgh: Edinburgh University Press, 2011), 96.

91 Michael Haneke, "Interview," gathered by Louis Guichard, Frederic Strauss, Mathilde Bottiere, and Pierre Murat, *Telerama: Les grands entretiens* (Hors-serie), May 13, 2010, 35, 34. "J'ai déjà entendu ce reproche de sadisme que vous m'ad-dressez, mais il est totalement infondé. C'est le rôle des artistes de gratter la où ça fait mal, de dévoiler ce qu'on ne veut pas voir ou savoir."

92 Shakespeare, *Hamlet*, 2.2.562, in *The Norton Shakespeare*.

93 Interestingly, the moment that most fully distances the viewer from the filmic illusion of "reality" is the moment at which Paul is most caught up in it: the moment when he loses his cool and reacts with genuine fear and rage to the "murder" of his companion.

94 Johnson, *Wake of Deconstruction*, 63.

95 Paul de Man, "The Rhetoric of Temporality," in *Blindness and Insight*, 189.

96 De Man, "Rhetoric of Temporality," 207.

97 Paul de Man, *Allegories of Reading: Figural Language in Rousseau, Nietzsche, Rilke, and Proust* (New Haven, CT: Yale University Press, 1979), 205. Recognizing that allegory undoes the stability of every referent, that it calls into question precisely

what the signifier is a signifier "of," de Man follows this formulation with its necessary deconstruction: "Allegories are always allegories of metaphor, and, as such, are always allegories of the impossibility of reading—a sentence in which the genitive 'of' has itself to be 'read' as a metaphor."

Chapter Four: There Is No Freedom to Enjoy

1 Schiller, *On the Aesthetic Education of Man*, 80, 140.
2 Schiller, *On the Aesthetic Education of Man*, 107, 55, 50.
3 Schiller, *On the Aesthetic Education of Man*, 132.
4 Schiller, *On the Aesthetic Education of Man*, 120.
5 Carolin Duttlinger, "Between Contemplation and Distraction: Configurations of Attention in Walter Benjamin," *German Studies Review* 30, no. 1 (February 2007): 41.
6 Such distracted spectatorship allows the subject to master the violent shock of the urban encounter with modernity—a violence that threatens the contemplative subject of aesthetic education as fully as do the home invaders in Haneke's *Funny Games*.
7 Christopher Castiglia and Russ Castronovo, "A 'Hive of Subtlety': Aesthetics and the End(s) of Cultural Studies," *American Literature* 76, no. 3 (September 2004): 424.
8 Fredric Jameson, "Marx's Purloined Letters," in *Ghostly Demarcations: A Symposium on Jacques Derrida's "Specters of Marx,"* ed. Michael Sprinker (New York: Version, 2008), 52; and Castiglia and Castronovo, "'Hive of Subtlety,'" 427.
9 See Moten, "Blackness and Nothingness," 740.
10 Sylvia Wynter, "The Ceremony Must Be Found: After Humanism," *boundary 2* 12, no. 1, and 13, no. 3 (Spring–Autumn 1984): 36, 44.
11 Simon Gikandi, "Race and the Idea of the Aesthetic," *Michigan Quarterly Review* 40, no. 2 (Spring 2001): 333.
12 Castiglia and Castronovo, "'Hive of Subtlety,'" 433.
13 Rita Felski, *The Limits of Critique* (Chicago: University of Chicago Press, 2015), 175.
14 Christopher Castiglia, "Revolution Is a Fiction: The Way We Read (Early American Literature) Now," *Early American Literature* 51, no. 2 (2016): 397.
15 Castiglia, "Revolution Is a Fiction," 415.
16 Castiglia, "Revolution Is a Fiction," 415.
17 See José Esteban Muñoz, *Cruising Utopia: The Then and There of Queer Futurity* (New York: New York University Press, 2009); Castiglia, "Revolution Is a Fiction," 403, 405.
18 Schiller, *On the Aesthetic Education of Man*, 126.
19 Schiller, *On the Aesthetic Education of Man*, 127.
20 Schiller, *On the Aesthetic Education of Man*, 127.
21 Schiller, *On the Aesthetic Education of Man*, 128.
22 Schiller, *On the Aesthetic Education of Man*, 128.
23 De Man, *Aesthetic Ideology*, 146.

24 Schiller, *On the Aesthetic Education of Man*, 138.

25 As in the case of social politics as already described, that ideal might well be one, like "the people," that finds its embodiment in the most mundane or even vulgar forms of expression, but that very vulgarity thus becomes the element that raises it above its mere materiality to figure an abstract idea.

26 Jacques Rancière, *Aesthetics and Its Discontents*, trans. Steven Corcoran (Malden, MA: Polity, 2009), 43–44. Although Castiglia clearly endorses the becoming-life of art and Schiller is closer to embracing the politics of resistant form, it is important to note, as Rancière will, that Schiller's attention to the inaccessibility, the "celestial self-sufficiency," of a work like the Juno Ludovici (Schiller, *On the Aesthetic Education of Man*, 81) indicates, nonetheless, the aesthetic opening of a space of *human* freedom and, to that extent, enters, despite itself, into the "becoming-life" of art.

27 Castiglia and Castronovo, "'Hive of Subtlety,'" 427.

28 Castiglia, "Revolution Is a Fiction," 403.

29 Elizabeth Maddock Dillon, "Sentimental Aesthetics," *American Literature* 76, no. 3 (September 2004): 518.

30 Castiglia, "Revolution Is a Fiction," 403.

31 Paul Gilmore, "Romantic Electricity, or the Materiality of Aesthetics," *American Literature* 76, no. 3 (September 2004): 472.

32 Rancière, *Aesthetics and Its Discontents*, 37.

33 Castiglia, "Revolution Is a Fiction," 402; and Rancière, *Aesthetics and Its Discontents*, 39.

34 Levi Bryant, *Difference and Givenness: Deleuze's Transcendental Empiricism and the Ontology of Immanence* (Evanston, IL: Northwestern University Press, 2008), 12. Bryant goes on to discuss Gilles Deleuze's concept of the encounter "in a twofold way. On the one hand, . . . it suspends our habitual relations of recognition with being and allows us to call these structures into question. . . . On the other hand, the encounter functions as a sign of the transcendental, announcing an internal difference within intuition whose structure and essence must be unfolded" (13).

35 Kant, *Critique of Judgment*, 188.

36 Felski, *Limits of Critique*, 176.

37 Felski, *Limits of Critique*, 180; emphasis mine.

38 Rancière, *Aesthetics and Its Discontents*, 43–44, 40.

39 Rancière, *Aesthetics and Its Discontents*, 41.

40 Rancière, *Aesthetics and Its Discontents*, 43.

41 Rancière, *Aesthetics and Its Discontents*, 42.

42 Rancière, *Aesthetics and Its Discontents*, 90.

43 Rancière, *Aesthetics and Its Discontents*, 94.

44 See, for example, Jared Sexton, who writes, "Coalitions require a logic of identity and difference, of collective selves modeled on the construct of the modern individual, an entity whose coherence is purchased at the expense of whatever is cast off by definition." Sexton, "Afro-Pessimism," paragraph 6.

45 Lacan, *Ethics of Psychoanalysis*, 54, 139.

46 Rancière, *Aesthetics and Its Discontents*, 128.

47 Wilderson, *"We're Trying to Destroy the World,"* 57, 54.

48 Moten, "Blackness and Nothingness," 739, 740, 741.

49 Moten, "Blackness and Nothingness," 742.

50 Moten, "Blackness and Nothingness," 742; and Jared Sexton, "The Social Life of Social Death: On Afro-Pessimism and Black Optimism," *InTensions Journal*, no. 5 (Fall/Winter 2011): 16.

51 Zupančič, *Ethics of the Real*, 40.

52 Zupančič, *Ethics of the Real*, 39.

53 Jacques Lacan, *Seminar XX: On Feminine Sexuality: The Limits of Love and Knowledge, 1972–73*, ed. Jacques-Alain Miller, trans. Bruce Fink (New York: W. W. Norton, 1998), 126.

54 Lacan, *Seminar XX: On Feminine Sexuality*, 126.

55 Lacan, *Seminar XX: On Feminine Sexuality*, 126.

56 Frantz Fanon, *Peau noire, masques blancs*, in *Oeuvres* (Paris: Le Découverte, 2011), 251; translated as "The Negro is not. Any more than the white man," in Fanon, *Black Skin, White Masks*, 231; Marriott, "Judging Fanon," *Rhizomes: Cultural Studies in Emerging Knowledges*, no. 29 (2016), 8 of 18, https://doi.org/10.20415/rhiz/029.e03.

57 Andrea Long Chu, "Black Infinity: Slavery and Freedom in Hegel's Africa," *Journal of Speculative Philosophy* 32, no. 3 (2018): 417.

58 Slavoj Žižek, "The Abyss of Freedom," in *The Abyss of Freedom/The Ages of the World*, by Slavoj Žižek and F. W. J. Von Schelling (Ann Arbor: University of Michigan Press, 1997), 81.

59 Žižek, "The Abyss of Freedom," 81.

60 Badiou, *Images du temps present*, 66.

61 Schiller, *On the Aesthetic Education of Man*, 80.

62 Schiller, *On the Aesthetic Education of Man*, 79, 81, 81,79.

63 Gikandi, "Race and the Idea of the Aesthetic," 331.

64 Elaine Scarry, *On Beauty and Being Just* (Princeton, NJ: Princeton University Press, 1999), 57; and Gikandi, "Race and the Idea of the Aesthetic," 327.

65 Harriet Jacobs, *Incidents in the Life of a Slave Girl*, ed. Frances Smith Foster and Richard Yarborough, 2nd ed. (New York: W. W. Norton, 2019), 28. Subsequent page references to this work in this chapter will be given in parentheses in the text.

66 Schiller, *On the Aesthetic Education of Man*, 79,

67 Chu, "Black Infinity," 416, 415; and G. W. F. Hegel, *Philosophy of History*, trans. J. Sibree (Mineola, NY: Dover, 2004), 99.

68 Gikandi, "Race and the Idea of the Aesthetic," 347.

69 Saidiya Hartman, *Scenes of Subjection: Terror, Slavery, and Self-Making in Nineteenth-Century America* (New York: Oxford University Press, 1997), 120, 112.

70 See Giorgio Agamben, *Homo Sacer: Sovereign Power and Bare Life*, trans. Daniel Heller-Roazen (Stanford, CA: Stanford University Press, 1998), esp. 71–90.

71 Lauren Berlant, *The Queen of America Goes to Washington City: Essays on Sex and Citizenship* (Durham, NC: Duke University Press, 1997), 15.

72 Rebecca N. Hill, *Men, Mobs, and Law: Anti-lynching and Labor Defense in U.S. Radical History* (Durham, NC: Duke University Press, 2009), 58.

73 Sophocles, *Antigone*, trans. Richard Emil Braun (New York: Oxford University Press, 1973).

74 Lacan, *Ethics of Psychoanalysis*, 278.

75 Lacan, *Ethics of Psychoanalysis*, 277.

76 Lacan, *Ethics of Psychoanalysis*, 277–78.

77 In a passage that turns on its head Hegel's claim for slavery as necessary to the progress of world spirit, Jacobs, after Linda's "freedom" has been purchased by her friend and benefactor, Mrs. Bruce, writes bitterly of the bill of sale, "It may hereafter prove a useful document to antiquaries, who are seeking to measure the progress of civilization in the United States" (163).

78 R. Hill, *Men, Mobs, and Law*, 59.

79 Benjamin, "Critique of Violence," 283.

80 In this regard it is worth noting that Thomas R. Gray, to whom Nat Turner delivered his "Confession," observes in the preface to that document that the account of the rebellion will "demonstrate the policy of our laws in restraint of this class of our population." Thomas R. Gray, "To the Public," in Nat Turner, *The Confessions of Nat Turner, the Leader of the Late Insurrection in Southampton, VA* (Baltimore, MD: Thomas R. Gray, printed by Lucas and Deaver, 1831), 5, https://docsouth .unc.edu/neh/turner/turner.html.

81 Gray, "To the Public," 11.

82 Christina Sharpe, *Monstrous Intimacies: The Making of Post-slavery Subjects* (Durham, NC: Duke University Press, 2010), in particular 2, 190n6.

83 Hartman, *Scenes of Subjection*, 119.

84 Berlant, *Queen of America Goes to Washington City*, 228; and Bruce Burgett, *Sentimental Bodies: Sex, Gender, and Citizenship in the Early Republic* (Princeton, NJ: Princeton University Press, 1998), 139.

85 As Aliyyah Abdur-Rahman writes, "While I will not go so far as to posit that 'peculiar' in this designation connotes all that is meant by 'queer' as it is used in the current academic and activist lexicon to refer to non-heteronormative sexuality and identity, I do think it is important to recognize the synonymity of these two terms to grasp fully what the designation 'peculiar' reveals about the sexual arrangements and, therefore, the larger social infrastructure of the institution." Aliyyah Abdur-Rahman, *Against the Closet: Black Political Longing and the Erotics of Race* (Durham, NC: Duke University Press, 2012), 38.

86 For one useful study of Jacobs's relation to Child, see Albert H. Tricomi, "Harriet Jacobs's Autobiography and the Voice of Lydia Maria Child," *ESQ: A Journal of the American Renaissance* 53, no. 3 (2007): 216–52.

87 Deborah M. Garfield, "Earwitness: Female Abolitionism, Sexuality, and *Incidents in the Life of a Slave Girl*," in *Harriet Jacobs and Incidents in the Life of a Slave Girl: New Critical Essays*, ed. Deborah M. Garfield and Rafia Zafar (New York: Cambridge University Press, 1996), 108.

88 Scott Rose, "Putin Signs Law Banning Gay 'Propaganda' among Children," *Bloomberg*, June 30, 2013, http://www.bloomberg.com/news/2013-06-30/putin -signs-law-banning-gay-propaganda-among-children.html.

89 Katherine Weber, "Russian President Putin Signs Law Outlawing Gay Propaganda," *Christian Post*, July 1, 2013, https://www.christianpost.com/news/russian -president-putin-signs-law-outlawing-gay-propaganda.html.

90 Zack Ford, "Russian Court Upholds 'Gay Propaganda' Law to 'Protect Children,'" *ThinkProgress*, December 4, 2013, https://archive.thinkprogress.org/russian-court -upholds-gay-propaganda-law-to-protect-children-f9412fb6f1ab/.

91 Jessica Chasmin, "Putin: Anti-gay Laws Are to Protect Citizens from 'Aggressive Behavior,'" *Washington Times*, December 19, 2013, https://www.washingtontimes .com/news/2013/dec/19/putin-anti-gay-laws-are-protect-citizens-aggressiv/.

92 Quoted in Case of Bayev and Others v. Russia, European Court of Human Rights, 2017, https://hudoc.echr.coe.int/eng?i=001-174422.

93 Alexandra Topping, "Russian LGBT Activists Describe Victimisation, Repression . . . and Hope," *Guardian*, April 6, 2015, https://www.theguardian.com/world /2015/apr/06/russian-lgbt-activists-describe-victimisation-repression-and-hope.

94 Joseph Bamat, "French Parents Boycott Schools over 'Gender Theory' Scare," *France 24*, January 29, 2014, https://www.france24.com/en/20140129-france-sex -education-gender-discrimination-protest-school.

95 As this book goes to press in 2022 such a law has been passed by the Florida state legislature at the same time that numerous states are prohibiting the teaching of what they broadly designate as "critical race theory" in institutions receiving public funding.

96 Karl Marx and Friedrich Engels, *The German Ideology*, vol. 1, in Karl Marx and Friederich Engels, *Collected Works: Volume 5, Marx and Engels 1845–1847*, trans. Clemens Dutt (New York: International Publishers, 1976), 46.

97 Marx and Engels, *The German Ideology*, 33, 44.

98 I am deeply grateful to Benjamin Kahan for calling to my attention a passage in Ronald Walters's essay "The Erotic South: Civilization and Sexuality in American Abolitionism" that speaks to this point while addressing abolitionism's general concern about relations of power. Walters writes, "Few were so extreme as Abby Kelley Foster, who took her nonresistant principles to the point where, an amazed visitor reported, she was 'very conscientious not to use the least worldly authority over her child.'" Going on to describe this position not only as "extreme" but also as "dogmatic" and "foolhardy," Walters underscores the exceptionalism of Foster's stance even while making clear that abolitionist discourse could theorize a relation between children and those enslaved. This reminds us that the Child is not a biological but an ideological product, one that figures centrally in the ideological investment in discourses of biology, including such disturbing offshoots as eugenics and racial sciences. Ronald G. Walters, "The Erotic South: Civilization and Sexuality in American Abolitionism," *American Quarterly* 25, no. 2 (May 1973): 179.

99 Ford, "Russian Court Upholds 'Gay Propaganda' Law to 'Protect Children.'"

100 Frederick Douglass, *My Bondage and My Freedom* (New York: Dover, 1969), 79–80.

101 Douglass, *My Bondage and My Freedom*, 80.

102 Douglass, *My Bondage and My Freedom*, 85.

103 Sharpe, *Monstrous Intimacies*, 7; and Douglass, *My Bondage and My Freedom*, 87.

104 Douglass, *My Bondage and My Freedom*, 40.

105 Douglass, *My Bondage and My Freedom*, 40–41.

106 Douglass, *My Bondage and My Freedom*, 41.

107 Hartman, *Scenes of Subjection*, 81.

108 Hence, where the child is seen as "naturally" associated with enjoyment, it will need the discipline of education. And where bad education threatens to instill enjoyment in the child, it will proscribed as a queer perversion.

109 Judy, *(Dis)Forming the American Canon*, 147.

110 Badiou, *Lacan*, 223. "La thèse selon laquelle le libertin est malheureux, plus malheureux que le sage, est une thèse fondatrice de la philosophie. C'est exactement la thèse de Platon: le méchant est malheureux. C'est pourquoi, pour Socrate, ça marche, parce qu'il peut dire aux gens qu'ils ont le choix entre devenir des tyrans jouisseurs ou des sages philosophes, il peut leur dire: le bon côté, c'est le mien!"

111 Badiou, *Plato's Republic*, 142.

112 Badiou, *Plato's Republic*, 143.

113 Badiou, *Pour aujourd'hui: Platon! (3)*, November 18, 2009, http://www.entretemps.asso.fr/Badiou/09-10.2.htm. "l'Idée liée à la vraie vie, doit être une Idée universelle[;] . . . elle ne doit comporte *aucun élément* interne qui lui interdise d'être partagée par tous."

114 Étienne Balibar, "On Universalism: In Debate with Alain Badiou," *Translate*, February 2007, http://translate.eipcp.net/transversal/0607/balibar/en.html.

115 Alain Badiou, *"La République" de Platon par Alain Badiou (1989–1990)*, Sixième Cours (Sixth Course), http://www.entretemps.asso.fr/Badiou/89-90.htm. "Sophiste et philosophe veulent tous les 2 corrompre la jeunesse, mais ce sont 2 corruptions contraires. L'objectif fixé pour le sophiste comme pour le philosophe, c'est de mettre fin—ce que signifie corrompre—à une indécision de la pensée consécutive à l'heureuse et agréable indécision propre au jeune âge. Au fond, cette figure de la jeunesse se réfère à cette irresponsabilité de la pensée, au moment où son indécision fait toute sa vigueur face à tout ce qui est établi. Cette irresponsabilité première de la pensée suspend l'établissement des corps sociaux tels qu'ils légifèrent."

116 "Le philosophe veut faire de l'irresponsabilité elle-même une responsabilité." Alain Badiou, *"La République" de Platon par Alain Badiou (1989–1990)*.

117 "[L]a pensée suive le double régime du pas encore, *ie* expérimente à vide, pour ainsi dire, le fait qu'une situation est infinie, *ie* chargée de possibles." (Thought follows a double regime of not yet, i.e. an empty test, so to speak, of the fact that

a situation is infinite, i.e., full of possibilities); Badiou, *"La République" de Platon par Alain Badiou (1989–1990)*.

118 "[Elle] tient en sa garde l'irresponsabilité primordial d'une jeunesse qu'il s'agit de transmuer dans la pensée en une responsabilité autre, disjointe du service des biens." (It takes charge of the primordial irresponsibility of youth, which it transmutes through thought into another responsibility, separated from the service of goods.) Badiou, *"La République" de Platon par Alain Badiou (1989–1990)*.

119 Mladen Dolar, "Hegel as the Other Side of Psychoanalysis," in *Jacques Lacan and the Other Side of Psychoanalysis*, ed. Justin Clemens and Russell Grigg (Durham, NC: Duke University Press, 2006), 132.

120 Lacan, *Ethics of Psychoanalysis*, 79 (translation modified).

121 Lacan, *Ethics of Psychoanalysis*, 79.

122 Spillers, "Mama's Baby, Papa's Maybe," 223.

123 See Clementine Autain, "Féminismes et sexualité: 'Jouissons Sans Entraves!," *Mouvements* 2, no. 20 (March–April 2002): 30–36.

124 Guy Hocquenghem, *L'apres-mai des faunes* (Paris: Barnard Grasset, 1974), 142. "En revindiquant l'assignation du sexe à la personne libre et consciente, on perpétue la vielle tromperie. Notre corps, nous appartenir—quelle tristesse! Le corps de chacun 'appartient à tous ceux qui veulent en jouir' serait déjà une formulation plus satisfaisante."

125 Lacan, *Ethics of Psychoanalysis*, 80.

126 Ed Pluth, *Signifiers and Acts: Freedom in Lacan's Theory of the Subject* (Albany, NY: State University of New York Press, 2007), 161.

127 Lacan, *Other Side of Psychoanalysis*, 21, 35.

128 Tom Fisher, "Making Sense: Jacques Rancière and the Language Poets," *Journal of Modern Literature* 36, no. 2 (Winter 2013): 165.

129 T. Fisher, "Making Sense," 164, 165.

130 Rancière, quoted in T. Fisher, "Making Sense," 165.

131 T. Fisher, "Making Sense," 165.

132 Rancière, *Aesthetics and Its Discontents*, 25.

133 Judy, *(Dis)Forming the American Canon*, 92, 88–89.

134 Turner, *The Confessions of Nat Turner*, 12.

135 Hegel, *Philosophy of History*, 99.

136 Judy, *(Dis)Forming the American Canon*, 84.

137 Lacan, *Ethics of Psychoanalysis*, 187.

138 Moten, "Blackness and Nothingness," 740.

139 Jacques Lacan, "Dissolution," March 18, 1980, http://espace.freud.pagesperso -orange.fr/topos/psycha/psysem/dissolu9.htm.

140 Françoise Wolff, director, *Jacques Lacan parle*, RTBF (Radio Télévision Belge Fancophone), 1982, DVD.

141 Jared Sexton, "On Black Negativity, or The Affirmation of Nothing: Jared Sexton Interviewed by Daniel Colucciello Barber," *Society + Space*, September 18, 2017, https://www.societyandspace.org/articles/on-black-negativity-or-the -affirmation-of-nothing.

Coda

1 Judy, *(Dis)Forming the American Canon*, 88–89.

2 Spillers, "Mama's Baby, Papa's Maybe," 222.

3 Douglass, *My Bondage and My Freedom*, 41. In a letter that predates the American translation of G. W. F. Hegel's *The Philosophy of History*, Robert E. Lee, himself a slave-owning white supremacist, expressed remarkably similar views on the educational function of slavery: "In this enlightened age, there are few I believe, but will acknowledge, that slavery as an institution is a moral & political evil in any Country. It is useless to expatiate on its disadvantages. I think it however a greater evil to the white than to the black race, & while my feelings are strongly interested in behalf of the latter, my sympathies are more strong for the former. The blacks are immeasurably better off here than in Africa, morally, socially, & physically. The painful discipline they are undergoing, is necessary for their instruction as a race, & I hope will prepare & lead them to better things. How long their subjugation may be necessary is Known & ordered by a wise & merciful Providence. Their emancipation will sooner result from the mild & melting influence of Christianity, than the storms & tempests of fiery Controversy." He goes on to make clear that Christianity is the mechanism of this educational transformation, and in a passage that anticipates the current protection of the right to discriminate against LGBTQ-identified persons on the ground of religious faith, Lee makes a similar argument on behalf of slaveowners. "While we see the Course of the final abolition of human slavery is onward, & we give it the aid of our prayers & all justifiable means in our power we must leave the progress as well as the result in his hands who Sees the end; who Chooses to work by slow influences; & with whom two thousand years are but a single day. Although the abolitionist must Know this; & must see that he has neither the right or power of operating except by moral means & suasion, & if he means well to the slave, he must not create angry feelings in the master; that although he may not approve the mode by which it pleases Providence to accomplish its purposes, the result will nevertheless be the same: that the reasons he gives for interference in what he has no Concern, holds good for every Kind of interference with our neighbors when we disapprove their Conduct; Still I fear he will persevere in his evil Course. Is it not strange that the descendants of those pilgrim fathers who crossed the Atlantic to preserve their own freedom of opinion, have always proved themselves intolerant of the spiritual liberty of others?" Robert E. Lee to Mary Randolph Custis Lee, December 27, 1856, in *Encyclopedia Virginia*, https://www.encyclopediavirginia.org/Letter_from_Robert_E_Lee_to_Mary _Randolph_Custis_Lee_December_27_1856.

4 Jacobs, *Incidents in the Life of a Slave Girl*, 107, 167.

5 Jacques Lacan, *Séminaire 13: L'objet (1965–66)*, March 23, 1966, 153, http:// staferla.free.fr/S13/S13.htm. "Car loin que le désir soit désir de jouissance, il est précisément la barrière qui vous maintient à la distance plus ou moins justement calculée de ce foyer brûlant, de ce qui est essentiellement à éviter pour le sujet pensant, qui s'appelle la jouissance."

6 Jacobs, *Incidents in the Life of a Slave Girl*, 167.

7 By externalizing the zero of enjoyment as a one, we disavow our own division and so imagine ourselves as one too.

8 Rancière, quoted in T. Fisher, "Making Sense," 165.

9 Merrill Cole, "The Queer Repression of Jacques Lacan," in *After Lacan*, ed. Ankhi Mukherjee (Cambridge: Cambridge University Press, 2018), 102–3. Tim Dean, *Beyond Sexuality* (Chicago: University of Chicago Press, 2000).

10 Jacques Lacan, *Séminaire 17: L'envers de la psychanalyse (1969–70)*, March 18, 1970, http://staferla.free.fr/S17/S17.htm. "Le fantasme domine toute la réalité du désir, c'est-à-dire la Loi."

11 Jacques Lacan, "Intervention sur l'exposé de M. Ritter," October 12, 1968, https://ecole-lacanienne.net/wp-content/uploads/2016/04/1968-10-12b.pdf. "Le fantasme donne son cadre à la réalité."

12 Lacan, *Séminaire 17: L'envers de la psychanalyse*, March 18, 1970, 16. "C'est une idée . . . que le savoir puisse faire totalité . . . Qui si je puis dire est *immanente, immanente* au politique en tant que tel. On le sait depuis longtemps. L'idée imaginaire du tout, telle qu'elle est donnée par le corps, fait partie de la prêcherie politique comme s'appuyant sur *la bonne forme* de la satisfaction, *ce qui fait sphère*, à la limite quoi de plus beau, mais aussi quoi de moins ouvert, quoi qui ressemble plus à la clôture de la satisfaction? La collusion de cette image avec l'idée de la satisfaction: c'est le quelque chose contre quoi nous abordons, chaque fois que nous rencontrons quelque chose qui fait nœud, dans ce travail dont il s'agit, de la mise au jour de quelque chose par les voies de l'inconscient."

13 Compare Lacan's remarks here on the "good form" of satisfaction, the sphere that politics promises, to the following commentary offered by Piera Aulagnier and included in Lacan's Seminar X. Reporting on the effect of Margaret Little's introduction of the function of the cut (in the form of the threat to terminate the analysis) when faced with an analysand who refused her every interpretation, Aulagnier reports, "The subject finally told the analyst . . . her fundamental fantasy, that of the round capsule—spherical, perfect—that she constructed precisely because of her inability to accept a castration, a lack, that no one had ever been able to symbolize for her" (Le sujet dit finalement . . . à l'analyste ce qu'est le fantasme fundamental, celui de la capsule ronde, sphérique, parfait, qu'elle a construite, justement parce qu'incapable d'accepter une castration, un manque, que personne n'avait jamais pu symboliser pour elle). Jacques Lacan, *Séminaire 10: L'angoisse (1963–63)*, February 27, 1963, 98, http://staferla.free.fr/S10/S10 .htm.

14 Beyond his misreading of the relation between politics and fantasy in Lacan, Cole also misreads *No Future*, which maintains that the framing of politics, however radical its attempts to "change people's lives for the better," as Cole would have it, remains fixed to a social order predicated on the "good" of a subject figured in the image of the Child. Far from holding queerness "aloof," *No Future* proposes that queerness remain the site of nonidentity, negativity, and abjection precisely in order to keep it from becoming an identitarian position invested in politi-

cal closure (satisfaction within the social order) at the expense of other abjected populations, who would then become "the queer."

15 Cole, "Queer Repression of Jacques Lacan," 103. See Chris Coffman, "The Unpredictable Future of Fantasy's Traversal," *Angelaki: Journal of the Theoretical Humanities* 18, no. 4 (2013): 43–61.

16 One may well endorse such a notion of "making people's lives better" at the level of what Lacan would call "sentiment," while still recognizing its fantasmatic nature, its implication in our narcissistic imposition of an imaginary altruism, and its perpetuation, as we will see, of the exclusionary logic it assails. Lacan, however, never uses the phrase *traversing the fantasy*. On a single occasion, in Seminar XI, he asks, "How can it be lived, by a subject who has traversed the radical fantasy, how, from that point on, is the drive lived?" (Comment peut être vécue, par un sujet qui a traversé le fantasme radical, comment dès lors peut être vécue la pulsion?). Jacques Lacan, *Séminaire 11: Fondements*, June 24, 1964, 149, http://staferla.free .fr/S11/S11.htm. There is no other elaboration of "traversing the fantasy" as such, though Lacan describes the end of the analysis in various ways in a number of texts. For a valuable insight into the way this concept was developed by others in the aftermath of Lacan's career, see Jean Allouch, *Érotologie analytique (1): La psychanalyse, une érotologie de passage* (Paris: EPEL/L'unebévue, 1998).

17 Jacques Lacan, *Séminaire 11: Fondements*, June 24, 1964, 149.

18 "Qu'est-ce que devient celui qui a passé par cette expérience concernant ce rapport—opaque à l'origine par excellence—à la pulsion? Comment peut être vécue, par un sujet qui a traversé le fantasme radical, comment dès lors peut être vécue la pulsion?" Lacan, *Séminaire 11: Fondements*, June 24, 1964, 149. For a slightly different translation, see Lacan, *Four Fundamental Concepts of Psycho- analysis*, 273: "What, then, does he who has passed through the experience of this opaque relation to the origin, to the drive, become. How can a subject who has traversed the radical fantasy experience the drive?" Here Lacan's twice repeated insistence on "vécue" (from *vivre*, "to live") gets translated as "experienced."

19 Lacan, *Séminaire 11: Fondements*, June 24, 1964, 149. "Ceci est *l'au-delà de l'analyse* et n'a jamais été abordé. Ce n'est jusqu'au present abordable qu'au niveau de l'an- alyste, pour autant qu'il serait exigé de l'analyste d'avoir précisément *traversé dans sa totalité le cycle de l'expérience analytique*." Sheridan translates this as "This is the beyond of analysis, and has never been approached. Up to now, it has only been approachable at the level of the analyst, in as much as it would be required of him to have specifically traversed the cycle of the analytic experience in its totality." Lacan, *Four Fundamental Concepts of Psychoanalysis*, 273–74.

20 Jacques Lacan, "Première version de la Proposition du 9 Octobre 1967 sur le psy- chanalyste de l'École," October 9, 1967, http://ecole-lacanienne.net/wp-content /uploads/2016/04/1967-10-09a.pdf.

21 "La logique de l'analyste est l'αγαλμα, qui s'intègre au fantasme radical que construit le psychanalysant." Lacan, "Première version de la Proposition du 9 Octobre 1967."

22 "N'est ce pas là assez pour semer la panique, l'horreur, la malédiction, voire l'atten-
tat?" Lacan, "Première version de la Proposition du 9 Octobre 1967."

23 "S'enracine dans ce qui s'oppose le plus radicalement à tout ce à quoi il faut et
il suffit d'être reconnu pour être: l'honorabilité par exemple." Lacan, "Première
version de la Proposition du 9 Octobre 1967."

24 "C'est la vrai portée de la negation constituante de la signification d'infamie."
Lacan, "Première version de la Proposition du 9 Octobre 1967."

25 "Ce qu'il faut appeler un au-delà de la psychanalyse." Lacan, "Première version de
la Proposition du 9 Octobre 1967."

26 "Connotation qu'il faudrait bien restaurer dans la psychanalyse." Lacan, "Première
version de la Proposition du 9 Octobre 1967."

27 Mari Ruti, "Why There Is Always a Future in the Future," *Angelaki: Journal of the
Theoretical Humanities* 13, no. 1 (2008): 121, 120.

28 Mari Ruti, "Why There Is Always a Future in the Future," 124.

29 Ruti's argument, in large part, rests on Judith Butler's influential suggestion that
practices of resignification can transform the Symbolic, which she assimilates
to "the social." I discuss that position, and thereby respond to Ruti in advance,
in my engagement with Butler's *Antigone's Claim* in *No Future* (102–7). Judith
Butler, *Antigone's Claim: Kinship between Life and Death* (New York: Columbia
University Press, 2000). Against the transformations signaled by Ruti's "ongoing
and endlessly renewed process of becoming," I would also place Christina
Sharpe's trenchant meditations on what she calls "the anagrammatical life of the
word *still* for the enslaved and for all Black people in slavery's wake." Sharpe, *In
the Wake*, 118.

30 Chris Coffman, "Queering Žižek," *Postmodern Culture* 23, no. 1 (September 2012),
https://doi.org/10.1353/pmc.2013.0024.

31 Slavoj Žižek, "Class Struggle or Postmodernism? Yes, Please," in Butler, Laclau,
and Žižek, *Contingency, Hegemony, Universality*, 122.

32 Žižek, "Class Struggle or Postmodernism?," 122.

33 As would be obvious were reading not always already the problem, while disputing
the theoretical ground on which much progressive politics rests I do not in any
way exempt myself from its animating desire.

34 Ruti, "Why There Is Always a Future in the Future," 117.

35 Zupančič, *Ethics of the Real*, 95. For a discussion of this passage, see chapter 1.

36 Zupančič, *Ethics of the Real*, 95.

37 Ruti, "Why There Is Always a Future in the Future," 116.

38 Ruti, "Why There Is Always a Future in the Future," 116. Self-dissolution and suicide, of course, are not the same. Suicide, rather than dissolving the self, attempts
to extend its sovereignty even where death is concerned. Self-dissolution denotes
the loss of agency, the undoing of selfhood, not its enactment.

39 Ruti, "Why There Is Always a Future in the Future," 116.

40 Bobby Benedicto, "Agents and Objects of Death: Gay Murder, Boyfriend Twins,
and Queer of Color Negativity," *GLQ* 25, no. 2 (2019): 277.

41 Benedicto, "Agents and Objects of Death," 278. See also Antonio Viego, *Dead Subjects: Toward a Politics of Loss in Latino Studies* (Durham, NC: Duke University Press, 2007), 4.

42 Benedicto, "Agents and Objects of Death," 275, 276.

43 Benedicto, "Agents and Objects of Death," 273, 286.

44 Benedicto, "Agents and Objects of Death," 286.

45 Ruti, "Why There Is Always a Future in the Future," 116; Edelman, *No Future*, 5; and Coffman, "Queering Žižek."

46 Cole, "Queer Repression of Jacques Lacan," 103.

47 Edelman, *No Future*, 22; emphasis mine.

48 Steven Knapp explores the link between allegory and literalization in *Personification and the Sublime: Milton to Coleridge* (Cambridge, MA: Harvard University Press, 1985), 2: "Allegorical personification . . . was only the most obvious and extravagant instance of what Enlightenment writers perceived, with a mixture of admiration and uneasiness, as the unique ability of poetic genius to give the force of literal reality to figurative 'inventions.'"

49 Judith Butler, "The Question of Social Transformation," in *Undoing Gender* (New York: Routledge, 2004), 215.

50 Walter Benjamin, *The Origin of German Tragic Drama*, trans. John Osborne (New York: Verso, 2009), 184.

51 Benjamin, *Origin of German Tragic Drama*, 185.

52 De Man, "Pascal's Allegory of Persuasion," in *Aesthetic Ideology*, 61.

53 De Man, "The Resistance to Theory," in *The Resistance to Theory*, 4.

54 This framing of the primal catachresis that allegorizes the negativity of the Real can be compared to Žižek's reading of Friedrich Wilhelm Joseph Von Schelling: "Schelling's fundamental move is thus not simply to ground the ontologically structured universe of *logos* in the horrible vortex of the Real; if we read him carefully, there is a premonition in his work that this terrifying vortex of the pre-ontological Real is itself (accessible to us only in the guise of) a fantasmatic narrative, a lure destined to distract us from the true traumatic cut." Žižek, *Less Than Nothing*, 275.

55 See Lacan, *Ethics of Psychoanalysis*, 69: "The prohibition on incest is nothing other than the condition sine qua non of speech."

56 Derrida, "Structure, Sign, and Play," 283–84.

57 Lacan, *L'Étourdit*, 452.

58 Claude Lévi-Strauss, *The Elementary Structures of Kinship*, trans. James Harle Bell et al. (Boston: Beacon Press, 1969), 12. Petar Ramadanovic, "The Non-meaning of Incest or, How Natural Culture Is," *Postmodern Culture* 20, no. 2 (January 2010), https://doi.org/10.1353/pmc.2010.0004.

59 Ramadanovic, "Non-meaning of Incest."

60 Žižek, *Tarrying with the Negative*, 116. It should be clear that Žižek is not denying that incestuous abuses "really" happen. His claim, instead, is that the object of incestuous desire never finds a "literal" expression because the desire for incestuous union is a desire for union with an object of fantasy. Hence, what we prosecute as incest is

always, psychoanalytically speaking, *attempted* incest, though that makes it no less traumatic for those who experience it as *realized* rape, abuse, or sexual violation.

61 Quoted in Sharpe, *Monstrous Intimacies*, 27; Sharpe, *Monstrous Intimacies*, 28.

62 Spillers, "Mama's Baby, Papa's Maybe," 77.

63 Ramadanovic, "Non-meaning of Incest."

64 Judith Butler, "Quandaries of the Incest Taboo," in *Undoing Gender*, 157, 159.

65 Butler, "Quandaries of the Incest Taboo," in *Undoing Gender*, 157.

66 Kara Keeling, *The Witch's Flight: The Cinematic, the Black Femme, and the Image of Common Sense* (Durham, NC: Duke University Press, 2007), 149.

67 *Eve's Bayou*, directed by Kasi Lemmons, from a screenplay by Kasi Lemmons (Santa Monica, CA: Trimark Pictures, 1997), DVD. Quotations from the dialogue are drawn from this DVD. Quotations concerning scenic directions or descriptions refer to the 1994 draft of the screenplay as published in Kasi Lemmons, "*Eve's Bayou*," *Scenario* 4, no. 20 (Summer 1998): 153–91.

68 Lacan, *L'Étourdit*, 452.

69 Lemmons, "*Eve's Bayou*," 154.

70 Lemmons, "*Eve's Bayou*," 154.

71 Eve's father is dressed in white in this shot while Matty Mereaux's dress shows up as black. This cross-racially identifies Louis with General Batiste in the myth of origin, an identification Kelli Weston underscores by noting that "Louis . . . appears to have inherited the sexual appetite of his forefather." Kelli Weston, "*Eve's Bayou*," *Sight and Sound* 27, no. 11 (November 2017): 96. At the same time, Louis's depiction as a successful doctor allies him with the healing powers of his foremother even as his rejection of Mozelle's spiritual healing suggests his investment in the Western rationalism to which his foremother provides an alternative.

72 Marriott, "Judging Fanon," paragraph 13.

73 Sexton, "Social Life of Social Death," 31–32.

74 Derrida, *Archive Fever*, 74, 74, 68, 68.

75 Keeling, *Witch's Flight*, 140.

76 Between the kiss and the slap, the vision includes shots of Eve and Cisely's greatuncle, Tomy, confined to a wheelchair, writhing in horror at the scene before him and repeatedly dropping a glass. Although he can be observed here and in several other isolated shots from the theatrical release, the character of Uncle Tomy, all but incapable of making himself understood through speech, was removed from the film's final cut.

77 Lacan, "Seminar on the Purloined Letter," 39.

78 Writing in defense of Afropessimism, Jared Sexton observes, "Blackness is not the pathogen in afro-pessimism, the world is. Not the earth, but the world, and maybe even the whole possibility of and desire for a world." Sexton, "Social Life of Social Death," 31.

79 William Shakespeare, *The Tempest*, 5:1:57, in *The Norton Shakespeare*.

80 Toni Morrison, *Beloved* (New York: Knopf, 1988), 275.

81 Wallace Stevens, "The Snow Man," in *The Collected Poems of Wallace Stevens* (New York: Random House, 1982), 9–10.

82 Lacan, *L'Étourdit*, 452.

83 Keeling, *Witch's Flight*, 155.

84 Keeling, *Witch's Flight*, 143.

85 Keeling, *Witch's Flight*, 158.

86 For a discussion of "creation ex nihilo," see Lacan, *Ethics of Psychoanalysis*, esp. 121–22 and 212–14.

87 Herman Melville, "Bartleby, the Scrivener," in *Herman Melville: Tales, Poems, and Other Writings*, ed. John Bryant (New York: Random House, 2001), 158. For a fuller account of this process, see Lee Edelman, "Occupy Wall Street: 'Bartleby' against the Humanities," *History of the Present* 3, no. 1 (Spring 2013): 99–118.

88 Leonardo Sbaraglia, the actor who plays Federico in *Pain and Glory*, remarked in an interview, "Almodóvar told me afterward that *Pain and Glory* completed a trilogy formed by *The Law of Desire, Bad Education*, and it" (Almodóvar me dijo después que *Dolor y gloria* cierra un trilogía que se compone de *La ley del deseo, La mala educación* y esta). Emanuel Bremerman, "Leonardo Sbaraglia y el intenso papel que le cumplió el sueño de actual para Almodóvar," *El Observador*, June 17, 2019, https://www.elobservador.com.uy/nota/sbaraglia-y-el-papel-que-le-cumplio-el -sueno-de-actuar-para-almodovar-20196141830.

89 Quim Casas, for example, writes that "this first scene . . . reminds us of the maternal womb and we pass from this aquatic shot to the river and women washing their laundry." (Esa primera escena . . . nos recuerda al útero materno y de esa composicíon acuosa passamos a la del río y los lavanderas.) Quim Casas, "*Dolor y gloria*: Autobiografía y autoficcíon," *SensaCine*, 2019, http://www.sensacine.com /peliculas/pelicula-264147/sensacine. Similarly, Sergi Sánchez describes "Salvador submerged in a swimming pool that has much of the maternal womb about it, as if the whole film elapsed in a liminal space" (Salvador sumergido en una piscina que tiene mucho de útero materno, como si la película entera trancurriera en una espacio límbico). Sergi Sánchez, "'Dolor y gloria': Sálvese quien pueda," *La Razon*, March 22, 2019, https://www.larazon.es/cultura/cine/dolor-y-gloria—salvese -quien-pueda-FH22523655.

90 Pedro Almodóvar, "Pedro Almodóvar: 'Ni en mis peores sueños de juventud imaginé que estaríamos como hoy," interview by Luis Martínez, *El Mundo*, March 18, 2019, https://www.elmundo.es/papel/cultura/2019/03/18 /5c8ba0dffc6c83e1748b45a4.html. "Llegó el verano y durante las vacaciones yo acostumbraba a sumergirme en la piscina para disfrutar de la ingravidez que proporciona el agua. Era el único momento del día en que no me dolía nada. Toda tensión desaparece bajo el agua. Decidí que aquella era una buena imagen para empezar mi relato y eso es lo que hice. El agua de la piscina me llevó a la corriente del río donde lavan las mujeres, la madre de Salvador; un ritual lleno de vida que Salvador contempla a los cuatro años. Cuando lo recuerda en la piscina, comprende que probablemente aquél fue el día más feliz de su vida. Sin duda es el mejor recuerdo que tiene de su madre, desbordante de belleza y alegría, cantando coplas con las otras lavanderas mientras él jugaba con los pececillos jaboneros. Esta

segunda secuencia, la del río, estableció la alternancia que yo necesitaba para mi relato, para no sentirme atrapado por la negrura que dominaba las primeras notas."

91 Lacan, *Four Fundamental Concepts of Psychoanalysis*, 43.

92 The fact that we see, in the final sequence, the woman and child who appear in his "flashbacks" as actors in *El primer deseo* (The first desire) means that, at best, the "flashbacks" are always mediated by that film; but we have no way of fully knowing the scope of that film. Are Salvador's flashbacks to his mother's last years (where Julieta Serrano plays the part of his mother) also scenes from *El primer deseo* (in which case Salvador would be portraying himself in *El primer deseo*)? Or, alternatively, is the final sequence evoking the making of the film merely a wish-fulfilling fantasy induced by the anesthesia we see him succumb to before his surgery—a fantasy in which, like Federico Fellini at the end of *8 ½* (CineRiz, Francinex, 1963), he directs his "real" mother and childhood self? Movements into sleep or reverie, after all, sometimes induced by drugs, often cued his earlier visions of the past. The ambiguity about the "reality" of the final sequence reinforces the film's generic evocation of late romance, lending the sublimity of self-overcoming to the final return to filmmaking.

93 Pedro Almodóvar, *Dolor y gloria* (Barcelona: Reservoir Books, 2019), EPUB, 16. All subsequent references will be to this edition, English translations of the script are taken from the subtitles of the following DVD with my modifications where indicated: *Pain and Glory*, dir. Pedro Almodóvar (Sony Pictures Home Entertainment, 2020). Almodóvar suggests the importance of the reference to thirty-two years in the first sentence of the essay he includes as "Memoria de las historias" in the published version of the screenplay: "Without having intended it, *Pain and Glory* is the third part of a trilogy of spontaneous creation that it has taken me thirty-two years to complete" (Sin haberlo pretendido *Dolor y gloria* es la tercera parte de una trilogía de creación espontánea que ha tardado treinta y dos años en completarse). Pedro Almodóvar, "Memoria de las historias," in *Dolor y gloria*, 131.

94 To make amends to Alberto after embarrassing him at the screening of *Sabor*, Salvador allows him to perform a theatrical monologue, *La adicción* (Addiction), based on his own relationship with Federico. As it happens, Federico, on his first trip to Madrid since he and Salvador broke up, passes the theater where Alberto is appearing. Recalling the actor's association with Salvador (who has refused credit as the monologue's author), he decides to see the show. Alberto's words overwhelm him with emotion when he recognizes himself as the text's "Marcelo" and realizes that the author of *La adicción* could only be Salvador. He goes backstage when the show is over and, explaining everything to Alberto, gets Salvador's telephone number and address.

95 The English subtitles translate this as a question, "Have I failed you just by being the way I am?" The Spanish text of the script, however, punctuates it as a statement, which is how I have translated it here.

96 Almodóvar, *Dolor y gloria*, 107. "La madre no responde, guarda un silencio digno y cruel. No da su brazo a torcer."

97 Pedro Almodóvar, "Entrevista: Pedro Almodóvar; 'En mi universo hay dos señores mayores que se besan con pasión y lo impongo con orgullo,'" by Mónica Zas Marcos, *El Diario*, March 3, 2019, https://www.eldiario.es/cultura/cine/Almodovar-universo-senores-besan-orgullo_0_877712465.html. "Es en la única parte que me emocioné tanto que me costaba dirigirlos, se me saltaban las lágrimas."

98 Almodóvar, "Entrevista: Pedro Almodóvar." "Es curioso tener que haber rodado la película entera para arañar un sentimiento del que nunca he hablado, primeramente porque es muy desagradable y doloroso. Hay cosas de mi infancia que he borrado deliberadamente para que no tuvieran peso en mi vida, y una de esas fue ese modo de mirarte como alguien distinto y peyorativo que está incluida en la película. Es una sensación muy fea para recordar y la eliminé en cuanto vine a Madrid." Almodóvar's locution, "to scratch at an emotion," recalls Michael Haneke's reference to "scratch[ing] where it hurts" and suggests not only the distance between them but also their shared understanding of the compulsory element in aesthetic creation. Haneke, "Interview," 34.

99 Pedro Almodóvar, "Pedro Almodóvar nos habla de 'Dolor y Gloria,' su película más íntima," by Alicia Montano, *Fotogramas*, March 22, 2019, https://www.fotogramas.es/noticias-cine/a26905764/dolor-y-gloria-pedro-almodovar-entrevista/. "Yo fui un niño distinto y no solo para mis padres: era un niño distinto para el pueblo, para el colegio, incluso para mi familia."

100 Almodóvar, *Dolor y gloria*, 109. "Salvador, yo te he traído a este mundo y me he desvivido por sacarte adelante. . . . Llévame al pueblo. Es mi único y ultimo deseo."

101 Almodóvar, *Dolor y gloria*, 5. "*Dolor y gloria* no es autoficción."

102 Almodóvar, *Dolor y gloria*, 6. "No busco que en las escenas con Julieta Serrano piense que yo tuve problemas con mi madre, sino que se vea a sí mismo frente a su propia madre."

103 Almodóvar, *Dolor y gloria*, 145. "Así que durante el rodaje le escribí, improvisé realmente, varias sequencias nuevas, que brotaron inspiradas por el placer de verlas interpretadas por la actriz, pero que de algún modo estaban escondidas en alguna parte inconsciente de mí mismo."

104 Almodóvar, "Entrevista: Pedro Almodóvar." "Recuerdo mis primeras pulsiones sexuales a los 9 años. Y recuerdo cómo y en qué circunstancia. La sexualidad empieza a esa edad, no eres consciente porque tampoco lo eres de tu cuerpo ni sabes qué tienes que hacer. Pero el deseo existe dentro de ti."

105 Almodóvar, *Dolor y gloria*, 11, 15. "Todo es perfecto, el agua del río, los peces en los manos, las sábanas blanquísimas sobre juncos y poleo, su madre sonriente, y las mujeres cantando 'A tu vera.'"

106 Lacan, *Ethics of Psychoanalysis*, 216; and Slavoj Žižek, *The Fragile Absolute: Or, Why Is the Christian Legacy Worth Fighting For?* (New York: Verso, 2000), 37.

107 The logic of the *après-coup* pervades *Pain and Glory*, complicating the attempt to indicate temporal relations. The scene by the river takes place years before young Salvador sees Eduardo bathing; but it is re-created in *El primer deseo* fifty years *after* the boy's blacking out. The retroactive identification (as a scene from that

film) of every episode from Salvador's youth merely underscores the centrality of *Nachträglichkeit* in Almodóvar's thinking here.

108 This suggests its link to the Foucauldian interpretation of sodomy as an "utterly confused category" and, as discussed in the introduction, to Jonathan Goldberg's extension of that notion when he characterizes sodomy as "incapable of exact definition." Foucault, *History of Sexuality*, 1:122; Goldberg, *Sodometries*, 18.

109 Almodóvar, *Dolor y gloria*, 11. "Me gustaría ser un hombre para poder bañarme en el río desnuda."

110 Such worlds need not be "desirable" to be seen as the loci of our desire, nor is their production limited to those who are privileged; all subjects, insofar as they are subjects of desire, which is also to say, subjects of meaning, perform the aesthetic sublimations by which worlds (and possible worlds) appear. Those sublimations are not aesthetic because we experience them as beautiful but rather because they conform to the aesthetic logic of totalized form.

111 Israël, *Pulsions de mort*, 87.

112 Žižek, *Tarrying with the Negative*, 101.

113 James Baldwin, *The Fire Next Time*, in *Collected Essays*, by James Baldwin, ed. Toni Morrison (New York: Library of America, 1998), 345–46.

114 Denise Ferreira da Silva, "1 (Life) ÷ 0 (Blackness) = ∞ − ∞ or ∞ / ∞: On Matter beyond the Equation of Value," *e-flux Journal*, no. 79 (February 2017), https://www.e-flux.com/journal/79/94686/1-life-o-blackness-or-on-matter-beyond-the-equation-of-value/. Though I would not agree with the designation of Blackness—or the Thing—as matter (except within the figural discourse of a given community), this strikes me as an enormously perceptive and helpful formulation.

115 To refer to those "literalized" as Black or queer is not to suggest that such literalizations are inhabited by way of false consciousness; to the contrary, such literalizations are the condition of consciousness as such, which attaches us to reality as the literalization of the catachreses produced ex nihilo by the cut that absents ab-sens and, with it, incest, the Thing, and the Real.

116 De Man, "Pascal's Allegory of Persuasion," in *Aesthetic Ideology*, 61.

117 De Man, "Kant and Schiller," in *Aesthetic Ideology*, 142.

118 G. W. F. Hegel, *On Art, Religion, Philosophy: Introductory Lectures to the Realm of Absolute Spirit*, ed. J. Glenn Gray (New York: Harper and Row, 1970), 67.

119 Hegel, *On Art, Religion, Philosophy*, 66.

120 Hegel, *On Art, Religion, Philosophy*, 111.

121 Hegel, *On Art, Religion, Philosophy*, 115.

122 Hegel, *On Art, Religion, Philosophy*, 196.

123 Hegel, *On Art, Religion, Philosophy*, 193.

124 Hegel, *On Art, Religion, Philosophy*, 197.

125 Hegel, *On Art, Religion, Philosophy*, 197.

126 Schiller, *On the Aesthetic Education of Man*, 31.

127 Lacan, *Séminaire 17: L'envers de la psychanalyse*, March 18, 1970, 16.

128 Jean-Paul Sartre, *Being and Nothingness*, trans. Hazel E. Barnes (New York: Washington Square, 1984), 47. In *The Science of Logic*, Hegel writes, "Being,

the indeterminate immediate, is in fact *nothing*, and neither more nor less than nothing." G. W. F. Hegel, *The Science of Logic*, trans. A. V. Miller, with additions by Stephen Houlgate, in *The Opening of Hegel's "Logic": From Being to Infinity*, by Stephen Houlgate (West Lafayette, IN: Purdue University Press, 2006), 195.

129 Sartre, *Being and Nothingness*, 49.

130 For a brilliant analysis of the political determinations of irony and literality, see Barbara Johnson's essay "Melville's Fist: The Execution of *Billy Budd*," in *The Critical Difference: Essays in the Contemporary Rhetoric of Reading* (Baltimore, MD: Johns Hopkins University Press, 1985), 79–109.

Bibliography:

Abdur-Rahman, Aliyyah. *Against the Closet: Black Political Longing and the Erotics of Race.* Durham, NC: Duke University Press, 2012.

Adams, Parveen. *The Emptiness of the Image: Psychoanalysis and Sexual Difference.* New York: Routledge, 1966.

Adorno, Theodor. *Negative Dialectics.* Translated by E. B. Ashton. New York: Continuum, 1994.

Agamben, Giorgio. *Homo Sacer: Sovereign Power and Bare Life.* Translated by Daniel Heller-Roazen. Stanford, CA: Stanford University Press, 1998.

Allouch, Jean. *L'amour Lacan.* Paris: Epel, 2009.

Allouch, Jean. *Érotologie analytique (1): La psychanalyse, une érotologie de passage.* Paris: EPEL/L'unebévue, 1998.

Allouch, Jean. "Interview de Jean Allouch." September 6, 2001. http://www.jeanallouch.com/pdf/193.

Allouch, Jean. "Nécrologie d'une 'science juive': Pour saluer Mal d'Archive de Jacques Derrida." *L'Unebévue,* no. 6 (1995): 131–47.

Almodóvar, Pedro. *Dolor y gloria.* Barcelona: Reservoir Books, 2019. EPUB.

Almodóvar, Pedro. "Entrevista: Pedro Almodóvar; 'En mi universo hay dos señores mayores que se besan con pasión y lo impongo con orgullo.'" By Mónica Zas Marcos. *El Diario,* March 3, 2019. https://www.eldiario.es/cultura/cine/Almodovar-universo-senores-besan-orgullo_0_877712465.html.

Almodóvar, Pedro. *La mauvaise éducation: Scénario bilingue.* Paris: Petites Bibliothèque des Cahiers du cinema, 2004.

Almodóvar, Pedro. "Pedro Almodóvar: 'Ni en mis peores sueños de juventud imaginé que estaríamos como hoy.'" By Luis Martínez. *El Mundo,* March 18, 2019. https://www.elmundo.es/papel/cultura/2019/03/18/5c8ba0dffc6c83e1748b45a4.html.

Almodóvar, Pedro. "Pedro Almodóvar nos habla de 'Dolor y Gloria,' su película más íntima." By Alicia Montano. *Fotogramas*, March 22, 2019. https://www.fotogramas
.es/noticias-cine/a26905764/dolor-y-gloria-pedro-almodovar-entrevista/.

Auden, W. H. "In Memory of W. B. Yeats (d. Jan. 1939)." In *W. H. Auden: Collected
Poems*, edited by Edward Mendelson, 247–49. New York: Random House, 1991.

Autain, Clementine. "Féminismes et sexualité: 'Jouissons Sans Entraves!'" *Mouvements*
2, no. 20 (March–April 2002): 30–36.

Badiou, Alain. "Being and Spatialization: An Interview with Alain Badiou." By Marios
Constantinou. *Environment and Planning D: Society and Space* 27, no. 5 (October 2009): 783–95.

Badiou, Alain. *Ethics: An Essay on the Understanding of Evil*. Translated by Peter Hallward. New York: Verso, 2001.

Badiou, Alain. "Formulas of 'L'Étourdit.'" In *There's No Such Thing as a Sexual Relationship: Two Lessons on Lacan*, by Alain Badiou and Barbara Cassin, translated
by Susan Spitzer and Kenneth Reinhard, 45–62. New York: Columbia University Press, 2017.

Badiou, Alain. *Images du temps présent, 2001–2004*. Paris: Fayard, 2014.

Badiou, Alain. *Lacan: L'antiphilosophie 3; 1994–1995*. Paris: Fayard, 2013.

Badiou, Alain. "On the Truth-Process." Lecture. European Graduate School, August 2002.
http://www.lacan.com/badeurope.htm.

Badiou, Alain. *Plato's Republic: A Dialogue in 16 Chapters*. Translated by Susan Spitzer.
New York: Columbia University Press, 2012.

Badiou, Alain. *Pour aujourd'hui: Platon! (2): Séminaire d'Alain Badiou (2008–2009)*.
Transcript by Daniel Fischer. http://www.entretemps.asso.fr/Badiou/08-09.htm.

Badiou, Alain. *Pour aujourd'hui: Platon! (3): Séminaire d'Alain Badiou (2009–2010)*.
Transcription Philippe Goassart.. http://www.entretemps.asso.fr/Ba-
diou/09-102.htm.

Badiou, Alain. *"La République" de Platon par Alain Badiou (1989–1990)* Sixième
Cours (Sixth Course). Notes of Aimé Thiault. Transcription by François Duvert.
http://www.entretemps.asso.fr/Badiou/89-90.htm.

Badiou, Alain. "Rhapsody for the Theatre: A Short Philosophical Treatise." Translated
by Bruno Bosteels. *Theatre Survey* 49, no. 2 (November 2008): 187–238.

Badiou, Alain. *Saint Paul: The Foundation of Universalism*. Translated by Ray Brassier.
Stanford, CA: Stanford University Press, 2003.

Badiou, Alain. *Theory of the Subject*. Translated by Bruno Bosteels. New York: Continuum, 2009.

Baker, Houston A., Jr. *Blues, Ideology, and Afro-American Literature: A Vernacular
Theory*. Chicago: University of Chicago Press, 1987.

Baker, Mike, Jennifer Valentino-DeVries, Manny Fernandez, and Michael LaForgia.
"Three Words. 70 Cases. The Tragic History of 'I Can't Breathe.'" *New York
Times*, June 29, 2020.

Balaudé, Jean-François. "Socrates's Demon." In *Dictionary of Untranslatables: A
Philosophical Lexicon*, edited by Barbara Cassin; translated by Steven Rendall,
Christian Hubbert, Jeffrey Mehlman, Nathanael Stein, and Michael Syro-

tinski; translation edited by Emily Apter, Jacques Lezra, and Michael Wood, 194. Princeton, NJ: Princeton University Press, 2014.

Baldwin, James. *The Fire Next Time*. In *Collected Essays*, by James Baldwin, edited by Toni Morrison, 291–347. New York: Library of America, 1998.

Balibar, Étienne. "On Universalism: In Debate with Alain Badiou." *Translate*, February 2007. http://translate.eipcp.net/transversal/0607/balibar/en.html.

Bamat, Joseph. "French Parents Boycott Schools over 'Gender Theory' Scare." *France 24*, January 29, 2014. https://www.france24.com/en/20140129-france-sex -education-gender-discrimination-protest-school.

Bartels, Emily. "Identifying 'the Dane': Gender and Race in *Hamlet*." In *The Oxford Handbook of Shakespeare and Embodiment: Gender, Sexuality, and Race*, edited by Valerie Traub, 197–210. Oxford: Oxford University Press, 2016.

Barthes, Roland. *A Lover's Discourse: Fragments*. Translated by Richard Howard. New York: Hill and Wang, 1977.

Barthes, Roland. *Writing Degree Zero*. Translated by Annette Lavers and Colin Smith. New York: Hill and Wang, 1970.

Benedicto, Bobby. "Agents and Objects of Death: Gay Murder, Boyfriend Twins, and Queer of Color Negativity." GLQ 25, no. 2 (2019): 273–96.

Benjamin, Walter. "Critique of Violence." In *Reflections: Essays, Aphorisms, Autobiographical Writings*, translated by Edmund Jephcott, 277–300. New York: Harcourt Brace Jovanovich, 1978.

Benjamin, Walter. *The Origin of German Tragic Drama*. Translated by John Osborne. New York: Verso, 2009.

Berlant, Lauren. *The Female Complaint: The Unfinished Business of Sentimentality in American Culture*. Durham, NC: Duke University Press, 2008.

Berlant, Lauren. *The Queen of America Goes to Washington City: Essays on Sex and Citizenship*. Durham, NC: Duke University Press, 1997.

Berlant, Lauren, and Lee Edelman. *Sex, or the Unbearable*. Durham, NC: Duke University Press, 2014.

Bishop, Elizabeth. "In the Waiting Room." In *Geography III*, 3–8. New York: Farrar, Straus and Giroux, 1976.

Bosteels, Bruno. *Badiou and Politics*. Durham, NC: Duke University Press, 2011.

Breivik, Anders Behring. *2083: A European Declaration of Independence*. 2011. https:// sites.google.com/site/breivikmanifesto/2083.

Bremerman, Emanuel. "Leonardo Sbaraglia y el intenso papel que le cumplió el sueño de actual para Almodóvar." *El Observador*, June 17, 2019. https://www .elobservador.com.uy/nota/sbaraglia-y-el-papel-que-le-cumplio-el-sueno-de -actuar-para-almodovar-20196141830.

Bryant, Levi. *Difference and Givenness: Deleuze's Transcendental Empiricism and the Ontology of Immanence*. Evanston, IL: Northwestern University Press, 2008.

Burgett, Bruce. *Sentimental Bodies: Sex, Gender, and Citizenship in the Early Republic*. Princeton, NJ: Princeton University Press, 1998.

Butler, Judith. *Antigone's Claim: Kinship between Life and Death*. New York: Columbia University Press, 2000.

Butler, Judith. *Bodies That Matter: On the Discursive Limits of "Sex."* New York: Routledge, 2011.

Butler, Judith. *The Psychic Life of Power: Theories in Subjection.* Stanford, CA: Stanford University Press, 1997.

Butler, Judith. *Undoing Gender.* New York: Routledge, 2004.

Casas, Quim. "*Dolor y gloria*: Autobiografía y autoficcíon." SensaCine. Accessed April 12, 2022. http://www.sensacine.com/peliculas/pelicula-264147/sensacine.

Castiglia, Christopher. "Revolution Is a Fiction: The Way We Read (Early American Literature) Now." *Early American Literature* 51, no. 2 (2016): 397–418.

Castiglia, Christopher, and Russ Castronovo. "A 'Hive of Subtlety': Aesthetics and the End(s) of Cultural Studies." *American Literature* 76, no. 3 (September 2004): 423–35.

Chasmin, Jessica. "Putin: Anti-gay Laws Are to Protect Citizens from 'Aggressive Behavior.'" *Washington Times*, December 19, 2013. https://www.washingtontimes.com/news/2013/dec/19/putin-anti-gay-laws-are-protect-citizens-aggressiv/.

Chu, Andrea Long. "Black Infinity: Slavery and Freedom in Hegel's Africa." *Journal of Speculative Philosophy* 32, no. 3 (2018): 414–25.

Clemens, Justin. *Psychoanalysis Is an Antiphilosophy.* Edinburgh: Edinburgh University Press, 2013.

Coffman, Chris. "Queering Žižek." *Postmodern Culture* 23, no. 1 (September 2012). https://doi.org/10.1353/pmc.2013.0024.

Coffman, Chris. "The Unpredictable Future of Fantasy's Traversal." *Angelaki: Journal of the Theoretical Humanities* 18, no. 4 (2013): 43–61.

Cole, Merrill. "The Queer Repression of Jacques Lacan." In *After Lacan*, edited by Ankhi Mukherjee, 95–110. Cambridge: Cambridge University Press, 2018.

Colebrook, Claire. *Irony.* New York: Routledge, 2004.

Collins, Kathleen. *Whatever Happened to Interracial Love?* New York: HarperCollins, 2016. Kindle.

Copjec, Joan. "The Sexual Compact." *Angelaki: Journal of the Theoretical Humanities* 17, no. 2 (2012): 31–48.

Culler, Jonathan. *On Deconstruction: Theory and Criticism after Structuralism.* Ithaca, NY: Cornell University Press, 1983.

Davis, Angela Y. *Freedom Is a Constant Struggle: Ferguson, Palestine, and the Foundations of a Movement.* Chicago: Haymarket Books, 2016.

Dean, Tim. *Beyond Sexuality.* Chicago: University of Chicago Press, 2000.

de Man, Paul. *Allegories of Reading: Figural Language in Rousseau, Nietzsche, Rilke, and Proust.* New Haven, CT: Yale University Press, 1979.

de Man, Paul. *Blindness and Insight: Essays in the Rhetoric of Contemporary Criticism.* 2nd ed., rev. Minneapolis: University of Minnesota Press, 1983.

de Man, Paul. "Kant and Schiller." In *Aesthetic Ideology*, edited by Andrzej Warminski, 129–62. Minneapolis: University of Minnesota Press, 1996.

de Man, Paul. "Kant's Materialism." In *Aesthetic Ideology*, edited by Andrzej Warminski, 119–28. Minneapolis: University of Minnesota Press, 1996.

de Man, Paul. "Pascal's Allegory of Persuasion." In *Aesthetic Ideology*, edited by Andrzej Warminski, 51–69. Minneapolis: University of Minnesota Press, 1996.

de Man, Paul. *The Resistance to Theory*. Minneapolis: University of Minnesota Press, 1993.

de Man, Paul. *The Rhetoric of Romanticism*. New York: Columbia University Press, 1984.

de Man, Paul. "The Rhetoric of Temporality." In *Blindness and Insight: Essays in the Rhetoric of Contemporary Criticism*, 2nd ed., rev., 187–228. Minneapolis: University of Minnesota Press, 1983.

Derrida, Jacques. *Apprendre à vivre enfin: Entretien avec Jean Birnbaum*. Paris: Galilée, 2005.

Derrida, Jacques. *Archive Fever: A Freudian Impression*. Translated by Eric Prenowitz. Chicago: University of Chicago Press, 1996.

Derrida, Jacques. "Autoimmunity: Real and Symbolic Suicides; A Dialogue with Jacques Derrida." In *Philosophy in a Time of Terror: Dialogues with Jürgen Habermas and Jacques Derrida*, by Giovanna Borradori, 85–136. Chicago: University of Chicago Press, 2003.

Derrida, Jacques. "Différance." In *Margins of Philosophy*, translated by Alan Bass, 1–28. Chicago: University of Chicago Press, 1986.

Derrida, Jacques. "Freud and the Scene of Writing." In *Writing and Difference*, translated by Alan Bass, 196–231. Chicago: University of Chicago Press, 1978.

Derrida, Jacques. "I Have a Taste for the Secret." In *A Taste for the Secret*, Jacques Derrida and Maurizio Ferraris, edited by Giacomo Donis and David Webb, translated by Giacomo Donis, 1–92. Malden, MA: Polity, 2001.

Derrida, Jacques. "Marx and Sons." In *Ghostly Demarcations: A Symposium on Jacques Derrida's "Specters of Marx,"* edited by Michael Sprinker, 213–69. New York: Verso, 2008.

Derrida, Jacques. *Specters of Marx: The State of the Debt, the Work of Mourning, and the New International*. Translated by Peggy Kamuf. New York: Routledge, 2006.

Derrida, Jacques. *Spurs: Nietzsche's Styles*. Translated by Barbara Harlow. Chicago: University of Chicago Press, 1979.

Derrida, Jacques. "Structure, Sign, and Play in the Discourse of the Human Sciences." In *Writing and Difference*, translated by Alan Bass, 278–93. Chicago: University of Chicago Press, 1978.

Derrida, Jacques. ". . . That Dangerous Supplement . . ." In *Acts of Literature*, by Jacques Derrida, edited by Derek Attridge, 76–109. New York: Routledge, 1992.

Derrida, Jacques, and Maurizio Ferraris. *A Taste for the Secret*. Edited by Giacomo Donis and David Webb. Translated by Giacomo Donis. Malden, MA: Polity, 2001.

Derrida, Jacques, and Christie V. McDonald. "Interview: Choreographies." In *diacritics* 12, no. 2 (1982): 66–76.

Dillon, Elizabeth Maddock. "Sentimental Aesthetics." *American Literature* 76, no. 3 (September 2004): 495–523.

Dolar, Mladen. "Hegel as the Other Side of Psychoanalysis." In *Jacques Lacan and the Other Side of Psychoanalysis*, edited by Justin Clemens and Russell Grigg, 129–54. Durham, NC: Duke University Press, 2006.

Douglass, Frederick. *My Bondage and My Freedom*. New York: Dover, 1969.

Duttlinger, Carolin. "Between Contemplation and Distraction: Configurations of Attention in Walter Benjamin." *German Studies Review* 30, no. 1 (February 2007): 33–54.

Eagleton, Terry. *Ideology*. London: Verso, 1991.

Edelman, Lee. *Homographesis: Essays in Gay Literary and Cultural Theory*. New York: Routledge, 1994.

Edelman, Lee. *No Future: Queer Theory and the Death Drive*. Durham, NC: Duke University Press, 2004.

Edelman, Lee. "Occupy Wall Street: 'Bartleby' against the Humanities." *History of the Present* 3, no. 1 (Spring 2013): 99–118.

Equiano, Olaudah. *The Interesting Narrative and Other Writings*. Edited by Vincent Carretta. New York: Penguin Books, 2003.

Fanon, Frantz. *Black Skin, White Masks*. Translated by Charles Lam Markmann. New York: Grove Press, 1967.

Felski, Rita. *The Limits of Critique*. Chicago: University of Chicago Press, 2015.

Ferreira da Silva, Denise. "1 (life) ÷ 0 (blackness) = ∞ − ∞ or ∞ / ∞: On Matter beyond the Equation of Value." *e-flux Journal*, no. 79 (February 2017). https:// www.e-flux.com/journal/79/94686/1-life-0-blackness-or-on-matter-beyond-the -equation-of-value/.

Fink, Bruce. *The Lacanian Subject: Between Language and Jouissance*. Princeton, NJ: Princeton University Press, 1997.

Fisher, Rebecka Rutledge. *Habitations of the Veil: Metaphor and the Poetics of Black Being in African American Literature*. Albany: State University of New York Press, 2014.

Fisher, Tom. "Making Sense: Jacques Rancière and the Language Poets." *Journal of Modern Literature* 36, no. 2 (Winter 2013): 156–74.

Ford, Zack. "Russian Court Upholds 'Gay Propaganda' Law to 'Protect Children.'" *ThinkProgress*, December 4, 2013. https://archive.thinkprogress.org/russian -court-upholds-gay-propaganda-law-to-protect-children-f9412fb6f1ab/.

Foucault, Michel. *The History of Sexuality*. Vol. 1, *An Introduction*. Translated by Robert Hurley. New York: Vintage Books, 1990.

Freccero, Carla. *Queer/Early/Modern*. Durham, NC: Duke University Press, 2006.

Freud, Sigmund. *Beyond the Pleasure Principle*. In *The Standard Edition of the Complete Psychological Works of Sigmund Freud*, edited by James Strachey, 18:7–64. London: Hogarth, 1991.

Freud, Sigmund. *Civilization and Its Discontents*. In *The Standard Edition of the Complete Psychological Works of Sigmund Freud*, edited by James Strachey, 21:64–145. London: Hogarth, 1991.

Garfield, Deborah M. "Earwitness: Female Abolitionism, Sexuality, and *Incidents in the Life of a Slave Girl*." In *Harriet Jacobs and "Incidents in the Life of a Slave Girl": New Critical Essays*, edited by Deborah M. Garfield and Rafia Zafar, 100–130. New York: Cambridge University Press, 1996.

Gasché, Rodolphe. *The Wild Card of Reading: On Paul de Man*. Cambridge, MA: Harvard University Press, 1998.

Gates, Henry Louis, Jr. Introduction to *The Slave's Narrative*, edited by Charles T. Davis and Henry Louis Gates Jr., xi–xxxiv. New York: Oxford University Press, 1985.

Gatens, Moira. "Polysemy, Atopia, and Feminist Thought." In *Michèle Le Doeuff: Operative Philosophy and Imaginary Practice*, edited by Max Deutscher, 45–59. Amherst, NY: Humanity Books, 2000.

Gikandi, Simon. "Race and the Idea of the Aesthetic." *Michigan Quarterly Review* 40, no. 2 (Spring 2001): 318–51. http://hdl.handle.net/2027/spo.act2080.0040.208.

Gilmore, Paul. "Romantic Electricity, or the Materiality of Aesthetics." *American Literature* 76, no. 3 (September 2004): 467–94.

Goldberg, Jonathan. *Shakespeare's Hand*. Minneapolis: University of Minnesota Press, 2003.

Goldberg, Jonathan. *Sodometries: Renaissance Texts, Modern Sexualities*. New York: Fordham University Press, 2010.

Gray, Thomas R. "To the Public." In *The Confessions of Nat Turner, the Leader of the Late Insurrection in Southampton, VA*. Baltimore, MD: Thomas R. Gray, printed by Lucas and Deaver, 1831. http://docsouth.unc.edu/neh/turner/turner.html.

Grundmann, Roy. "Auteur de Force: Michael Haneke's 'Cinema of Glaciation.'" *Cineaste* 32, no. 2 (Spring 2007): 6–14.

Hadot, Pierre. *Philosophy as a Way of Life: Spiritual Exercise from Socrates to Foucault*. Translated by Michael Chase. Malden, MA: Blackwell, 2003.

Hallward, Peter. *Badiou: A Subject to Truth*. Minneapolis: University of Minnesota Press, 2003.

Haneke, Michael, dir. *Funny Games*. 1997; New York: Kino Video, 2006. DVD.

Haneke, Michael. "Interview." Gathered by Louis Guichard, Frederic Strauss, Mathilde Bottiere, and Pierre Murat. *Telerama: Les Grands Entretiens* (Hors-serie), May 13, 2010.

Haneke, Michael. "Interview: Michael Haneke; The Bearded Prophet of *Code Inconnu* and *The Piano Teacher*." By Scott Foundas. *IndieWire*, December 4, 2001. https://www.indiewire.com/2001/12/interview-michael-haneke-the-bearded-prophet-of-code-inconnu-and-the-piano-teacher-2-80636/.

Haneke, Michael. "Michael Haneke, *Funny Games U.S.*" By Nick Dawson. *Filmmaker Magazine*, March 14, 2008. https://filmmakermagazine.com/1307-michael-haneke-funny-games-u-s/#.YirecZZOlPY.

Haneke, Michael. "Michael Haneke: Les temps postmodernes." Interview by Sebastien Ors. *Reperages*, no. 43 (Autumn 2003).

Harney, Stefano, and Fred Moten. *The Undercommons: Fugitive Planning and Black Study*. New York: Minor Composition, 2013.

Hartman, Saidiya V. *Scenes of Subjection: Terror, Slavery, and Self-Making in Nineteenth-Century America*. New York: Oxford University Press, 1997.

Hartman, Saidiya V, and Frank Wilderson III. "The Position of the Unthought: An Interview with Saidiya V. Hartman Conducted by Frank B. Wilderson III." *Qui Parle: Critical Humanities and Social Sciences* 13, no. 2 (Spring/Summer 2003): 183–201.

Hegel, G. W. F. *On Art, Religion, Philosophy: Introductory Lectures to the Realm of Absolute Spirit*. Edited by J. Glenn Gray. New York: Harper and Row, 1970.

Hegel, G. W. F. *Philosophy of History*. Translated by J. Sibree. Mineola, NY: Dover, 2004.

Hegel, G. W. F. *The Science of Logic*. Translated by A. V. Miller, with additions by Stephen Houlgate. In *The Opening of Hegel's "Logic": From Being to Infinity*, by Stephen Houlgate, 169–262. West Lafayette, IN: Purdue University Press, 2006.

Hill, Evan, Ainara Tiefenthäler, Christiaan Triebert, Drew Jordan, Haley Willis, and Robin Stein. "How George Floyd Was Killed in Police Custody." *New York Times*, May 31, 2020. https://www.nytimes.com/2020/05/31/us/george-floyd -investigation.html.

Hill, Rebecca N. *Men, Mobs, and Law: Anti-lynching and Labor Defense in U.S. Radical History*. Durham, NC: Duke University Press, 2009.

Hocquenghem, Guy. *L'apres-mai des faunes*. Paris: Barnard Grasset, 1974.

Intermountain Catholic. "USCCB President 'Deeply Concerned' about Court's LGBT Ruling." June 19, 2020. http://www.icatholic.org/article/usccb-president-deeply -concerned-about-courts-lgbt-24213922.

Irigaray, Luce. *Marine Lover: Of Friedrich Nietzsche*. Translated by Gillian G. Gill. New York: Columbia University Press, 1991.

Irigaray, Luce. *This Sex Which Is Not One*. Translated by Catherine Porter. Ithaca, NY: Cornell University Press, 1985.

Israël, Lucien. *Pulsions de mort: Séminaire 1977–1978*. Strasbourg: Arcanes, 1998.

Jackson, Zakiyyah Iman. "Waking Nightmares—on David Marriott." *GLQ* 17, no. 2–3 (June 2011): 357–63.

Jacobs, Harriet. *Incidents in the Life of a Slave Girl*. Edited by Frances Smith Foster and Richard Yarborough. 2nd ed. New York: W. W. Norton, 2019.

Jagose, Annamarie. *Queer Theory: An Introduction*. New York: New York University Press, 1996.

Johnson, Barbara. "Melville's Fist: The Execution of *Billy Budd*." In *The Critical Difference: Essays in the Contemporary Rhetoric of Reading*, 79–109. Baltimore, MD: Johns Hopkins University Press, 1985.

Johnson, Barbara. *Persons and Things*. Cambridge, MA: Harvard University Press, 2008.

Johnson, Barbara. *The Wake of Deconstruction*. Cambridge, MA: Basil Blackwell, 1994.

Judy, Ronald. *(Dis)Forming the American Canon: African-Arabic Slave Narratives and the Vernacular*. Minneapolis: University of Minnesota Press, 1993.

Kakutani, Michiko. *The Death of Truth: Notes on Falsehood in the Age of Trump*. New York: Penguin Random House, 2018.

Kant, Immanuel. *Critique of Judgment*. Translated by Werner S. Pluhar. Indianapolis: Hackett, 1987.

Keeling, Kara. *The Witch's Flight: The Cinematic, the Black Femme, and the Image of Common Sense*. Durham, NC: Duke University Press, 2007.

Kendi, Ibram X. *How to Be an Antiracist*. New York: Random House, 2019.

Kierkegaard, Søren. *The Concept of Irony with Continual Reference to Socrates*. Edited and translated by Howard V. Hong and Edna H. Hong. Princeton, NJ: Princeton University Press, 1992.

Knapp, Steven. *Personification and the Sublime: Milton to Coleridge*. Cambridge, MA: Harvard University Press, 1985.

Kofman, Sarah. *Socrates: Fictions of a Philosopher.* Translated by Catherine Porter. Ithaca, NY: Cornell University Press, 1989.

Kristeva, Julia. "La femme, ce n'est jamais ça / Woman Can Never Be Defined." In *New French Feminisms: An Anthology,* edited by Elaine Marks and Isabelle de Courtivron, 137–41. New York: Schocken Books, 1981.

Kristeva, Julia. *Powers of Horror: An Essay on Abjection.* Translated by Leon S. Roudiez. New York: Columbia University Press, 1982.

Lacan, Jacques. "Allocution sur l'enseignment." In *Autres écrits,* 297–305. Paris: Seuil, 2001.

Lacan, Jacques. "D'Écolage." March 11, 1980, http://staferla.free.fr/S27/S27.htm.

Lacan, Jacques. "Desire and the Interpretation of Desire in *Hamlet.*" Translated by James Hulbert. *Yale French Studies,* nos. 55–56 (1977): 11–52.

Lacan, Jacques. "Dissolution." March 18, 1980. http://espace.freud.pagesperso-orange.fr/topos/psycha/psysem/dissolu9.htm.

Lacan, Jacques. *The Ego in Freud's Theory and in the Technique of Psychoanalysis 1954–1955, The Seminar of Jacques Lacan: Book II.* Edited by Jacques-Alain Miller. Translated by Sylvana Tomaselli. New York: W. W. Norton, 1991.

Lacan, Jacques. *Encore: 1972–1973.* Edited by Jacques-Alain Miller. Paris: Seuil, 1975.

Lacan, Jacques. *The Ethics of Psychoanalysis, 1959–1960: The Seminar of Jacques Lacan, Book VII.* Edited by Jacques-Alain Miller. Translated by Dennis Porter. New York: W. W. Norton, 1997.

Lacan, Jacques. *L'Étourdit.* In *Autres écrits,* 449–95. Paris: Seuil, 2001.

Lacan, Jacques. *The Four Fundamental Concepts of Psychoanalysis: The Seminar of Jacques Lacan, Book XI.* Edited by Jacques-Alain Miller. Translated by Alan Sheridan. New York: W. W. Norton, 1998.

Lacan, Jacques. "The Instance of the Letter in the Unconscious, or Reason since Freud." In *Écrits: The First Complete Edition in English.* Translated by Bruce Fink, 412–41. New York: W. W. Norton, 2006.

Lacan, Jacques. "Intervention sur l'exposé de M. Ritter." October 12, 1968. https://ecole-lacanienne.net/wp-content/uploads/2016/04/1968-10-12b.pdf.

Lacan, Jacques. "Kant with Sade." Translated by James B. Swenson Jr. *October,* no. 51 (Winter 1989): 55–75.

Lacan, Jacques. "The Mirror Stage as Formative of the *I* Function as Revealed in Psychoanalytic Experience." In *Écrits: The First Complete Edition in English,* translated by Bruce Fink, 75–81. New York: W. W. Norton, 2006.

Lacan, Jacques. *The Other Side of Psychoanalysis: The Seminar of Jacques Lacan, Book XVII.* Edited by Jacques-Alain Miller. Translated by Russell Grigg. New York: W. W. Norton, 2007.

Lacan, Jacques. "Première version de la Proposition du 9 Octobre 1967 sur le psychanalyste de l'École." October 9, 1967. http://ecole-lacanienne.net/wp-content/uploads/2016/04/1967-10-09a.pdf.

Lacan, Jacques. "Psychanalyse et médecine." *Lettres de l'École freudienne de Paris* 1 (February–March 1967): 34–61. http://ecole-lacanienne.net/wp-content/uploads/2016/04/EFP-N1-1967.pdf.

Lacan, Jacques. *Séminaire 2, 1954–1955: Le moi dans la théorie de Freud et dans la technique de la psychanalyse.* http://staferla.free.fr/S2/S2.htm.

Lacan, Jacques. *Séminaire 7: L'Éthique.* 1959–60. http://staferla.free.fr/S7/S7.htm.

Lacan, Jacques. *Séminaire 10: L'Angoisse.* 1962–63. http://staferla.free.fr/S10/S10.htm.

Lacan, Jacques. *Séminaire 11: Fondements.* 1964. http://staferla.free.fr/S11/S11.htm.

Lacan, Jacques. *Séminaire 13: L'objet.* 1965–66. http://staferla.free.fr/S13/S13.htm.

Lacan, Jacques. *Séminaire 17: L'envers de la psychanalyse.* 1969–70. http://staferla.free .fr/S17/S17.htm.

Lacan, Jacques. *Séminaire 21: Les non-dupes errent.* 1973–74. http://staferla.free.fr/S21 /S21.htm.

Lacan, Jacques. "Seminar on the Purloined Letter." Translated by Jeffrey Mehlman. In *The Purloined Poe: Lacan, Derrida, and Psychoanalytic Reading,* edited by John Muller and William Richardson, 28–54. Baltimore, MD: Johns Hopkins University Press, 1988.

Lacan, Jacques. *Seminar XX: On Feminine Sexuality: The Limits of Love and Knowledge, 1972–73.* Edited by Jacques-Alain Miller. Translated by Bruce Fink. New York: W. W. Norton, 1998.

Lacan, Jacques. "The Signification of the Phallus." In *Écrits: The First Complete Edition in English,* translated by Bruce Fink, 575–84. New York: W. W. Norton, 2006.

Lacan, Jacques. "The Subversion of the Subject and the Dialectic of Desire." In *Écrits: The First Complete Edition in English,* translated by Bruce Fink, 671–702. New York: W. W. Norton, 2006.

Laclau, Ernesto. "Identity and Hegemony: The Role of Universality in the Constitution of Political Logics." In *Contingency, Hegemony, Universality: Contemporary Dialogues on the Left,* by Judith Butler, Ernesto Laclau, and Slavoj Žižek, 44–89. New York: Verso, 2000.

Laclau, Ernesto. "The Politics of Rhetoric." In *Material Events: Paul de Man and the Afterlife of Theory,* edited by Tom Cohen, Barbara Cohen, J. Hillis Miller, and Andrzej Warminski, 229–53. Minneapolis: University of Minnesota Press, 2001.

Lagier, Luc. "*Funny Games*: Jeux de Vilains." *Reperages,* no. 43 (Autumn 2003).

Lear, Jonathan. *A Case for Irony.* Cambridge, MA: Harvard University Press, 2011.

Lear, Jonathan. *Happiness, Death, and the Remainder of Life.* Cambridge, MA: Harvard University Press, 2000.

Leckman, Tad. "Shapeshifting Films." *Sanctuary Moon: Back on the Forest Homeworld,* October 29, 2012. https://tadleckman.wordpress.com/2012/10/29 /shapeshifting-films/.

Lee, Robert E. Letter from Robert E. Lee to Mary Randolph Custis Lee. December 27, 1856. In *Encyclopedia Virginia,* https://www.encyclopediavirginia.org/Letter _from_Robert_E_Lee_to_Mary_Randolph_Custis_Lee_December_27_1856.

Le Gaufey, Guy. "Le plus atopique des deux. . . ." In *Lacan avec les philosophes.* Paris: Albin Michel, 1991.

Lemmons, Kasi, dir. *Eve's Bayou.* Screenplay by Kasi Lemmons. Santa Monica, CA: Trimark Pictures, 1997. DVD.

Lemmons, Kasi. "*Eve's Bayou*." 1994 draft of screenplay. *Scenario* 4, no. 2 (Summer 1998): 153–91.

Ling, Alex. *Badiou and Cinema*. Edinburgh: Edinburgh University Press, 2011.

Lupton, Julia Reinhard, and Kenneth Reinhard. *After Oedipus: Shakespeare in Psychoanalysis*. Ithaca, NY: Cornell University Press, 1993.

Malabou, Catherine. *Changing Difference: The Feminine and the Question of Philosophy*. Translated by Carolyn Shread. Malden, MA: Polity, 2014.

Malabou, Catherine. "A Conversation with Catherine Malabou." Interview by Noëlle Vahanian. *Journal for Cultural and Religious Theory* 9, no. 1 (2008). https://jcrt.org/archives/09.1/Malabou.pdf.

Malabou, Catherine. *The Heidegger Change: On the Fantastic in Philosophy*. Translated by Peter Skafish. Albany: State University of New York Press, 2011.

Malabou, Catherine. *La plasticité au soir de l'écriture: Dialectique, destruction, deconstruction*. Clamecy: Leo Scheer, 2005.

Malabou, Catherine, and Judith Butler. "You Be My Body for Me: Body, Shape, and Plasticity in Hegel's *Phenomenology of Spirit*." In *A Companion to Hegel*, edited by Stephen Houlgate and Michael Baur, 611–40. Malden, MA: Blackwell, 2011.

Marriott, David. "Black Cultural Studies." *The Year's Work in Critical and Cultural Theory* 20, no. 1 (2012): 37–66.

Marriott, David. "Judging Fanon." *Rhizomes: Cultural Studies in Emerging Knowledges*, no. 29 (2016). https://doi.org/10.20415/rhiz/029.e03.

Marriott, David. *On Black Men*. New York: Columbia University Press, 2000.

Marx, Karl, and Friederich Engels. *The German Ideology*, vol. 1. In *Collected Works: Volume 5, Marx and Engels, 1845–1847*, translated by Clemens Dutt. New York: International Publishers, 1976.

Mazzoni, Cristina. *Maternal Impressions: Pregnancy and Childbirth in Literature and Theory*. Ithaca, NY: Cornell University Press, 2000.

Miller, D. A. "Anal Rope." In *Inside/Out: Lesbian Theories, Gay Theories*, edited by Diana Fuss, 119–41. New York: Routledge, 1991.

Miller, Jacques-Alain. "Commentary on Lacan's Text." In *Reading Seminars I and II: Lacan's Return to Freud*, edited by Richard Feldman, Bruce Fink, and Maire Jaanus, 422–27. Albany: State University of New York Press, 1996.

Miller, Jacques-Alain. "The A and the a in Clinical Structures." In *Symptom: Online Journal for Lacan.com*, no. 6 (Spring 2005). https://www.lacan.com/newspaper6.htm.

Miller, J. Hillis. "Three Literary Theorists in Search of O." In *Provocations to Reading: J. Hillis Miller and the Democracy to Come*, edited by Barbara Cohen and Dragan Kuzundžič, 210–27. New York: Fordham University Press, 2005.

Milner, Jean-Claude. "The Doctrine of Science." In *Jacques Lacan: Critical Evaluations in Cultural Theory*, edited by Slavoj Žižek, 1:268–88. New York: Routledge, 2002.

Mitchell, W. J. T. "Picturing Terror: Derrida's Autoimmunity." *Critical Inquiry* 33, no. 2 (Winter 2007): 277–90.

Morrison, Toni. *Beloved*. New York: Knopf, 1988.

Moten, Fred. "Blackness and Nothingness (Mysticism in the Flesh)." *South Atlantic Quarterly* 112, no. 4 (Fall 2013): 737–80.

Muñoz, José Esteban. *Cruising Utopia: The Then and There of Queer Futurity*. New York: New York University Press, 2009.

Musser, Amber Jamilla. *Sensational Flesh: Race, Power, and Masochism*. New York: New York University Press, 2014.

Nagourney, Adam, and Jeremy W. Peters. "A Half-Century On, an Unexpected Milestone for L.G.B.T.Q. Rights." *New York Times*, June 15, 2020, https://www.nytimes.com/2020/06/15/us/politics/supreme-court-lgbtq-rights.html.

Nobus, Dany. *Jacques Lacan and the Freudian Practice of Psychoanalysis*. Philadelphia: Routledge, 2000.

Ohi, Kevin. *Innocence and Rapture: The Erotic Child in Pater, Wilde, James, and Nabokov*. New York: Palgrave Macmillan, 2005.

Parra, Marissa. "Oak Park Black Lives Matter Mural Painted Over to Read, 'All Lives Matter.'" *CBS Chicago*, July 8, 2020. https://chicago.cbslocal.com/2020/07/08/oak-park-black-lives-matter-mural-painted-over-to-read-all-lives-matter/.

Pascal, Blaise. *Oeuvres completes*. Vol. 2. Edited by Michel Le Guern. Paris: Gallimard, 2000.

Plath, Sylvia. "The Munich Mannequins." In *The Collected Poems of Sylvia Plath*, edited by Ted Hughes, 262–63. New York: Harper Collins, 2008.

Plato. *The Republic of Plato*. Translated by Benjamin Jowett. Project Gutenberg, 2017. https://www.gutenberg.org/files/55201/55201-h/55201-h.htm.

Pluth, Ed. *Signifiers and Acts: Freedom in Lacan's Theory of the Subject*. Albany: State University of New York Press, 2007.

Ragland, Ellie. "The Discourse of the Master." In *Lacan, Politics, Aesthetics*, edited by Willy Apollon and Richard Feldstein, 127–49. Albany: State University of New York Press, 1996.

Ramadanovic, Petar. "The Non-meaning of Incest or, How Natural Culture Is." *Postmodern Culture* 20, no. 2 (January 2010). https://doi.org/10.1353/pmc.2010.0004.

Rancière, Jacques. *Aesthetics and Its Discontents*. Malden, MA: Polity, 2009.

Rancière, Jacques. *Dissensus: On Politics and Aesthetics*. Edited and translated by Stephen Corcoran. New York: Continuum Books, 2010.

Reddy, Chandan. *Freedom with Violence: Race, Sexuality, and the U.S. State*. Durham, NC: Duke University Press, 2011.

Reinhard, Kenneth. "Introduction to Alain Badiou and Barbara Cassin." Draft shared with author. 2015.

Rose, Scott. "Putin Signs Law Banning Gay 'Propaganda' among Children." *Bloomberg*, June 30, 2013. http://www.bloomberg.com/news/2013-06-30/putin-signs-law-banning-gay-propaganda-among-children.html.

Rotman, Brian. *Signifying Nothing: The Semiotics of Zero*. Stanford, CA: Stanford University Press, 1987.

Roudinesco, Élisabeth. "On peut tirer de Lacan une pensée progressiste authentique." *L'Humanité*, September 9, 2011. https://www.humanite.fr/societe/elisabeth-roudinesco-%C2%AB-peut-tirer-de-lacan-une-pensee-progressiste-authentique-%C2%BB-479127.

Rousseau, Jean-Jacques. *Émile, or On Education*. Translated by Allan Bloom. New York: Basic Books, 1979.

Ruti, Mari. *The Ethics of Opting Out: Queer Theory's Defiant Subjects*. New York: Columbia University Press. 2017.

Ruti, Mari. "Why There Is Always a Future in the Future." *Angelaki: Journal of the Theoretical Humanities* 13, no. 1 (2008): 113–26.

Ryle, Simon. "Moles, Spots, Stains, and Tincts: Marks of Futurity in Shakespeare and Kurosawa." *Textual Practice* 28, no. 5 (2014): 807–32.

Sánchez, Sergi. "'Dolor y gloria': Sálvese quien pueda." *La Razon*, March 22, 2019. https://www.larazon.es/cultura/cine/dolor-y-gloria--salvese-quien-pueda-FH22523655.

Santner, Eric. *On the Psychotheology of Everyday Life: Reflections on Freud and Rosenzweig*. Chicago: University of Chicago Press, 2001.

Sartre, Jean-Paul. *Being and Nothingness*. Translated by Hazel E. Barnes. New York: Washington Square, 1984.

Scarry, Elaine. *On Beauty and Being Just*. Princeton, NJ: Princeton University Press, 1999.

Schiller, Friedrich. *On the Aesthetic Education of Man*. Translated by Reginald Snell. Mineola, NY: Dover, 2004.

Schlosser, Joel Alden. *What Would Socrates Do? Self-Examination, Civic Engagement, and the Politics of Philosophy*. New York: Cambridge University Press, 2014.

Seale, Bobby. "Interview with Bobby Seale." Conducted by Blackside, November 4, 1988. Eyes on the Prize II Interviews, Washington University Digital Gateway Texts. http://digital.wustl.edu/e/eii/eiiweb/sea5427.0172.147bobbyseale.html.

Sexton, Jared. "Afro-Pessimism: The Unclear Word." *Rhizomes: Cultural Studies in Emerging Knowledge*, no. 29 (2016). https://doi.org/10.20415/rhiz/029.e02.

Sexton, Jared. "On Black Negativity, or The Affirmation of Nothing: Jared Sexton By Daniel Coluccielo Barber." *Society + Space*, September 18, 2017. https://www.societyandspace.org/articles/on-black-negativity-or-the-affirmation-of-nothing.

Sexton, Jared. "The Social Life of Social Death: On Afro-Pessimism and Black Optimism." *InTensions Journal*, no. 5 (Fall/Winter 2011): 1–47. https://www.google.com/url?sa=t&rct=j&q=&esrc=s&source=web&cd=&ved=2ahUKEwi-q-TJvr32AhU3lIkEHRryBNQQFnoECAMQAQ&url=https%3A%2F%2Fwww.yorku.ca%2Fintent%2Fissue5%2Farticles%2Fpdfs%2Fjaredsextonarticle.pdf&usg=AOvVaw2iXyIuRvfGrphda9gZTrIz.

Sexton, Jared. "Unbearable Blackness." *Cultural Critique*, no. 90 (Spring 2015): 159–78.

Shakespeare, William. *The Norton Shakespeare*. Edited by Stephen Greenblatt, Walter Cohen, Jean Howard, and Katharine Maus. 2nd ed. New York: W. W. Norton, 2008.

Sharpe, Christina. *In the Wake: On Blackness and Being*. Durham, NC: Duke University Press, 2016.

Sharpe, Christina. *Monstrous Intimacies: The Making of Post-slavery Subjects*. Durham, NC: Duke University Press, 2010.

Soler, Colette. "Lacan en Antiphilosophe." *Filozofski vestnik* 24, no. 2 (2006): 121–44.

Sophocles. *Antigone*. Translated by Richard Emil Braun. New York: Oxford University Press, 1973.

Spillers, Hortense J. "Mama's Baby, Papa's Maybe: An American Grammar Book." In *Black, White, and in Color*, 203–29. Chicago: University of Chicago Press, 2003.

Stanley, Eric. "Near Life, Queer Death: Overkill and Ontological Capture." *Social Text* 29, no. 2 (107) (Summer 2011): 1–19.

Swift, Jonathan. *Gulliver's Travels: An Authoritative Text*. Edited by Robert A. Greenberg. New York: W. W. Norton, 1970.

Tobias, Manuela, and Anthony Galavi. "Woman Allegedly Attempts to Deface Fresno Black Lives Matter Street Art." *Fresno Bee*, June 19, 2020. https://www.fresnobee.com/news/local/article243672582.html.

Topping, Alexandra. "Russian LGBT Activists Describe Victimisation, Repression . . . and Hope." *Guardian*, April 6, 2015. https://www.theguardian.com/world/2015/apr/06/russian-lgbt-activists-describe-victimisation-repression-and-hope.

Tricomi, Albert H. "Harriet Jacobs's Autobiography and the Voice of Lydia Maria Child." *ESQ: A Journal of the American Renaissance* 53, no. 3 (2007): 216–52.

Turner, Henry. *Shakespeare's Double Helix*. New York: Continuum, 2007.

Viego, Antonio. *Dead Subjects: Toward a Politics of Loss in Latino Studies*. Durham, NC: Duke University Press, 2007.

Vlastos, Gregory. *Socrates: Ironist and Moral Philosopher*. Ithaca, NY: Cornell University Press, 1991.

Walters, Ronald G. "The Erotic South: Civilization and Sexuality in American Abolitionism." *American Quarterly* 25, no. 2 (May 1973): 177–201.

Warminski, Andrzej. "Introduction: Allegories of Reference." In *Aesthetic Ideology*, by Paul de Man, edited by Andrzej Warminski, 1–33. Minneapolis: University of Minnesota Press, 1996.

Warren, Calvin. "The Catastrophe: Black Feminist Poethics, (Anti)Form, and Mathematical Nihilism." *Qui Parle: Critical Humanities and Social Sciences* 28, no. 2 (December 2019): 353–72.

Warren, Calvin. "Onticide: Afropessimism, Queer Theory, and Ethics." Ill Will, November 18, 2014. https://illwill.com/onticide-afropessimism-queer-theory-and-ethics.

Weber, Katherine. "Russian President Putin Signs Law Outlawing Gay Propaganda." *Christian Post*, July 1, 2013. https://www.christianpost.com/news/russian-president-putin-signs-law-outlawing-gay-propaganda.html.

Weingarten, Christopher, Tom Beaujour, Hank Shteamer, Kim Kelly, Steve Smith, Brittany Spanos, Suzy Exposito, et al. "The 100 Greatest Metal Albums of All Time," *Rolling Stone*, June 21, 2017. https://www.rollingstone.com/music/music-lists/the-100-greatest-metal-albums-of-all-time-113614/naked-city-torture-garden-1990-194353/.

Weston, Kelli. "*Eve's Bayou*." *Sight and Sound* 27, no. 11 (November 2017): 96.

Wilderson, Frank B., III. *Afropessimism*. New York: Liveright, 2020.

Wilderson, Frank B., III. *Red, White, and Black: Cinema and the Structure of U.S. Antagonisms*. Durham, NC: Duke University Press, 2010.

Wilderson, Frank B., III. *"We're Trying to Destroy the World": Anti-Blackness and Police Violence after Ferguson; An Interview with Frank B. Wilderson III*. Interview by Jared Ball, Todd Steven Burroughs, and Dr. Hate. N.p.: Ill Will Editions, 2014. https://illwilleditions.noblogs.org/files/2015/09/Wilderson-We-Are-Trying-to -Destroy-the-World-READ.pdf.

Wolff, Francoise. *Jacques Lacan parle*. RTBF (Radio Télévision Belge Fancophone), 1982. DVD.

Wray, John. "Minister of Fear." *New York Times Magazine*, September 23, 2007.

Wynter, Sylvia. "The Ceremony Must Be Found: After Humanism." *boundary 2 12*, no. 1, and 13, no. 3 (Spring–Autumn 1984): 19–70.

Wynter, Sylvia. *"Proud Flesh* Inter/Views: Sylvia Wynter." Interview by Greg Thomas. *ProudFlesh: New Afrikan Journal of Culture, Politics and Consciousness*, no. 4 (2006). https://www.africaknowledgeproject.org/index.php/proudflesh/article/view/202.

Yerushalmi, Josef Hayim. *Freud's Moses: Judaism Terminable and Interminable*. New Haven, CT: Yale University Press, 1991.

Žižek, Slavoj. "The Abyss of Freedom." In *The Abyss of Freedom/Ages of the World*, by Slavoj Žižek and F. W. J. Von Schelling, 1–104. Ann Arbor: University of Michigan Press, 1997.

Žižek, Slavoj. "Class Struggle or Postmodernism? Yes, Please." In *Contingency, Hegemony, Universality: Contemporary Dialogues on the Left*, by Judith Butler, Ernesto Laclau, and Slavoj Žižek, 90–135. New York: Verso, 2000.

Žižek, Slavoj. *The Fragile Absolute: Or, Why Is the Christian Legacy Worth Fighting For?* New York: Verso, 2000.

Žižek, Slavoj. *Less Than Nothing: Hegel and the Shadow of Dialectical Materialism*. New York: Verso, 2013.

Žižek, Slavoj. *Looking Awry: An Introduction to Jacques Lacan through Popular Culture*. Cambridge, MA: MIT Press, 1991.

Žižek, Slavoj. "Neighbors and Other Monsters: A Plea for Ethical Violence." In *The Neighbor: Three Inquiries in Political Theology*, by Slavoj Žižek, Eric L. Santner, and Kenneth Reinhard, 134–90. Chicago: University of Chicago Press, 2005.

Žižek, Slavoj. *The Parallax View*. Cambridge, MA: MIT Press, 2006.

Žižek, Slavoj. *The Sublime Object of Ideology*. New York: Verso, 1989.

Žižek, Slavoj. *Tarrying with the Negative: Kant, Hegel, and the Critique of Ideology*. Durham, NC: Duke University Press, 1993.

Žižek, Slavoj. *The Ticklish Subject: The Absent Centre of Political Ontology*. New York: Verso, 2000.

Zupančič, Alenka. "Encountering Lacan in the Next Generation: An Interview with Alenka Zupančič." In *Žižek and His Contemporaries: On the Emergence of the Slovenian Lacan*, edited by Jones Irwin and Helena Motoh, 158–77. London: Bloomsbury Academic, 2014.

Zupančič, Alenka. *Ethics of the Real: Kant, Lacan*. New York: Verso, 2000.

Zupančič, Alenka. "On Evil: An Interview with Alenka Zupančič." By Christoph Cox. *Cabinet*, no. 5 (Winter 2001–2002). http://www.cabinetmagazine.org/issues/5/alenkazupancic.php.

Zupančič, Alenka. "Sexual Difference and Ontology." *e-flux Journal*, no. 32 (February 2012). http://www.e-flux.com/journal/sexual-difference-and-ontology/.

Zupančič, Alenka. *What Is Sex?* Cambridge, MA: MIT Press, 2017.

Index:

fantasy: the Child and, 91, 93; Cole on, 208–11; politics and, 208–13; traversing, 210, 308n16, 308n18; truth and, 134

Fellini, Federico, 313n92

Felski, Rita, 164–69

Fenrich, Steen Keith, 271n107

Ferreira da Silva, Denise, 254

Fink, Bruce, 40

Fisher, Rebecka Rutledge, 32

Fisher, Tom, 196–97

Floyd, George, x, xi, xiv, xvii–xix

formalism, structural, 22–23

Foster, Abby Kelley, 303n98

Foucault, Michel, 20, 139, 192, 216, 315n108

framing, cinematic, 76–77, 284n79

Freccero, Carla, 95, 102, 283n64

freedom: aesthetic, 162–67, 300n26; Afropessimism, Blackness, aesthetic's ethics of desire, and, 171–74; Andersen's "The Red Shoes," the drive, and, 174–76, 194, 201; Antigone and, 179–80; Beauty and, 176; the Child and, 187–88; Douglass's *My Bondage and My Freedom*, 188–90; dream of, 195; of enjoyment, 188–206; Jacobs's *Incidents in the Life of a Slave Girl* and, 176–88, 197–205; Lacan on philosophy and, 195–96; of the master, 195–96; moral law, shadow of law, and, 179–88, 193–94, 197–98; Rancière's aesthetic politics and, 166–71, 196–97; reason and, 189–93; Sexton's "unfree thing," 206; U.S. court rulings, 188

Freud, Sigmund: on death drive, 105–6; on ego ideal, 198; on *Hamlet*, 93, 104; on helplessness, 90; jouissance and, 135; Lacan on, 6, 267n38; radical sense and, 291n78; on regularization and order, 100, 128; on silence of drives, 293n27; sublimation and, 49

Funny Games (Haneke): aesthetic education and, 147–51, 160–61; the awakening slap, 149–51, 155–57, 159; death drive and repetition compulsion,

144–45, 161; the extradiegetic and breaking the frame, 145–48, 152–53, 296n63; human reflection and self-reflection, 151–53; Imaginary illusion and, 152–58, 160–61; Imaginary sacrifice and, 143; irony and theoretical reflection, 150–51; overview, 143–44; Plato's allegory of the cave and, 156–58; "raping" the audience, 148–49; sadism and, 149, 159–60; sublimation and, 147, 161; Tarkovsky's *Solaris* and, 153–55; violence of the Real and Badiou's event, 157–58

futurism: archive, anamnesis, and, 103; the Child and, 47, 104, 115, 289n29; Derrida and, 109–10; order of meaning and, 211–12; queerness and, 46; reproductive, 45–46, 53, 73, 91–94. See also *No Future* (Edelman)

Garfield, Deborah M., 185

Gasché, Rodolphe, 120

Gatens, Moira, 32

Gates, Henry Louis, Jr., 15–16

Gaufey, Guy Le, 41

Gikandi, Simon, 164, 176–77

Gilmore, Paul, 168, 174

Godard, Jean-Luc, 149

Gödel, Kurt, 131

Goldberg, Jonathan, 20, 33, 99–100, 104, 315n108

Gomez, José H., xvii

good, the: Badiou on, 39, 128–33; death drive and, 161; desire and, 136, 294n41, 295n43; education and, 59, 92, 253, 278n2; *Hamlet* and, 121; Haneke's *Funny Games* and, 161; the Imaginary and, 161, 209; jouissance and, 135, 295n44; law and, 180; radical desire and, 135–37, 294n41; reason and, 191–92; Žižek on, 110, 127–28, 129

Gray, Thomas R., 302n80

Grundmann, Roy, 150–51

Hadot, Pierre, 33

Hallward, Peter, 287n8

Hamlet (Shakespeare): archive, memory, and, 99–109, 117–18, 289n29; bad education and, 120–22; the Child and, 93, 104, 115–16; death as animal destiny and, 132; death drive and, 93–94, 101, 105–8, 117–18; human, concept of, 113; incest and Hamlet's disgust at sex, 112–15; Lemmons's *Eve's Bayou* compared to, 232; *The Matrix* compared to, 298n83; order and, 96–97, 100–101, 107, 113–14, 121; "the rest is silence" and "O, O, O, O!," 96–97; the specter and, 99–104, 116–19; "To be or not to be," 95–96

Haneke, Michael. See *Funny Games*

Harney, Stefano, 24, 271n101

Hartman, Saidiya, 17, 120, 177, 183, 190

Hegel, G. W. F., 33, 174, 176–77, 188–89, 257–58, 302n77

Heidegger, Martin, 12

Hill, Paul, 179

Hill, Rebecca, 179–82

Hitchcock, Alfred: *Psycho*, 60; *Rope*, 60–62, 145; *Shadow of a Doubt*, 290n70; *Stage Fright*, 155; *Vertigo*, 60, 80

Hocquenghem, Guy, 194–95

Huffer, Lynne, 273n136

Hughes, Henry, 218

human, the: allegory and, 282n54; division of, 59, 64–65; *Hamlet* and concept of, 113; Haneke's *Funny Games,* human reflection in, 151–52; learning to be, 1

Hyppolite, Jean, 2

hysteria, 39–40

id-entities, 216, 219

Imaginary, the: the aesthetic and, 155; Almodóvar's *Bad Education* and, 75–79, 86, 91; the Child and, 91, 93; Cole on, 208–9, 215; conservative, 164; de Man on imagination's self-sacrifice, 296n58; desire and, 91; education and, 84; the good and, 161, 209; Haneke's *Funny Games* and Imaginary illusion,

143, 152–58, 160–61, 195; political fantasy and, 209; queerness and, 127; sacrifice, Imaginary, 143, 296n58; the Symbolic and, 2, 65, 109

In and Out (Oz), 212

incest: *ab-sens* and, xiv, 217, 254; in Almodóvar's *Pain and Glory*, 248–54; definition, resistance to, 251; fantasy object and, 310–11n60; indeterminacy of, 221, 228; the Lacanian incestuous Thing, 250; in Lemmons's *Eve's Bayou*, 220–37; as prohibition, 217–19, 228, 253–54, 258–59

Incidents in the Life of a Slave Girl (Jacobs), 176–88, 197–205, 207–8

"In the Waiting Room" (Bishop), 276n186

Irigaray, Luce, 11–12, 14, 18

irony: allegory and, 92, 216–20, 232, 237, 254, 258, 260, 282n54; bad education and, 42, 92, 150; catachresis and, xviii; Haneke's *Funny Games* and, 150–51; incest and, 254; knowledge hystericized by, 40; politics and, 260, 316n130; Schlegel on, 92; Socratic, 33–37, 40–41, 273n139

Israël, Lucien, 50–52, 73, 252–53

Jackson, Zakiyyah Iman, 28–31

Jacobs, Harriet: *Incidents in the Life of a Slave Girl*, 176–88, 197–205, 207–8; tombstone of, 204–5, 207–8, 241

Jagose, Annamarie, 19–20

Jameson, Fredric, 163

Johnson, Barbara, 23, 155, 160, 316n130

jouissance: in Almodóvar's *Bad Education*, 67, 73, 84–91; Badiou on the unnameable and, 131, 134–35; desire, the good, and, 136; desire as barrier, 208; forcing and, 134, 294n38; freedom and, 177, 188–206; the good and, 295n44; Haneke's *Funny Games* and, 145, 150; human helplessness and, 90; Jacobs's *Incidents* and, 178, 182–83; as Kantian imperative, 135–36; logical systems and, 293n24; philosophy and, 35, 38, 42–43;

as radical of desire, 134; reason and, 190–91; *sens-absexe* and, 10–11; as silence, 293n27; sinthomosexuality and, 47; slavery and economy of enjoyment, 178; Socrates and, 41; sublimation and, 294n41; the Thing and, 106, 134; Žižek on, 267n37

Judy, Ronald, xiii, 15–19, 24–25, 190, 200, 202

Kakutani, Michiko, 4, 264n11
Kameny, Frank, xi
Kant, Immanuel, 4, 127–28, 132–36, 143, 168, 173, 180, 193–94, 281n35
Keeling, Kara, 220, 229, 234–36
Kendi, Ibram X., xii–xiii
Kierkegaard, Søren, 33–36, 40
Knapp, Steven, 310n48
Kofman, Sarah, 33, 38, 40
Kristeva, Julia, 3, 9, 11, 32

Lacan, Jacques: "c'est le mot qui tranche," 7, 22, 233, 248, 252; *colle* and *école*, 38–39, 42, 272n174; on commandments, 118–19; on death of the world, 132–33; on discontinuity, 4; on education, 1–2, 38–42; *einziger Zug* ("the single stroke"), 58; on freedom, 205–6; on Freud's *Vorstellung*, 291n78; on *Hamlet*, 100; on limit-experiences, 91; on love of truth, 134, 149, 294n32; on philosophy and psychoanalysis, 35–40; signifier as "symbol only of absence," 95; on sin, 139–40; "there is no sexual relation," 6, 171; on training analysis, 210–11; on truth, 133–34; on the vase, 279n15. *See also specific concepts and topics, such as* ab-sens
Lacan, Jacques, works of: *The Ethics of Psychoanalysis*, 19, 48, 132, 137–40, 179–80, 280n15, 294n41; *Four Fundamental Concepts of Psychoanalysis*, 293n16, 308nn18–19; *L'Étourdit*, xiii–xiv, 4, 6; "The Mirror Stage," 25–26; "On Freud's *Trieb*," 286n101; *The Other Side of Psychoanalysis*, 134,

209, 293n24; "Psychoanalysis and Medicine," 294n38; Seminar VII, 105, 198; Seminar X, 307n13; Seminar XI, 4, 308n16; Seminar XVII, 35; Seminar XX, 12, 173; "The Signification of the Phallus," 86
Laclau, Ernesto, 54–55, 282n48
Lagier, Luc, 152
law: antinomianism, 179, 181, 185, 199, 208; desire and, 140; Foucault on, 151; freedom and moral law, 179–82, 193–94, 197–205; Russian law against "gay propaganda," 185–88, 193; shadow of, 183–85, 188; Symbolic, 211–12
Lear, Jonathan, 35, 90–91
Leckman, Tad, 284n76
Le Doeuff, Michèle, 32
Lee, Robert E., 306n3
Le Gaufey, Guy, 6
Lemmons, Kasi. See *Eve's Bayou*
Lenin, Vladimir, 37
Lévi-Strauss, Claude, 1, 107, 217–18
limit-experiences, 91
Lin, Jun, 215
literalizations: allegory and, 310n48; in Almodóvar's *Bad Education*, 73, 88; the cut and, 259–60; of identities and catachreses, xv, xviii–xix, 214–16, 228, 254, 315n115; incest, Blackness, and, 228; of incest, 218–19; sex confused with, xiv–xv
literary theory, de Man on, 123–26
Little, Margaret, 307n13
Ludovici, Juno, 300n26
Lupton, Julia Reinhard, 93
Lyotard, Jean-François, 170

Magnotta, Luka, 215
Malabou, Catherine, 3, 11–22, 73
Marcus, Sharon, 165
Marriott, David, xvii, 17–18, 28–32, 173, 228, 271n107
Matrix, The (Wachowski and Wachowski), 156–57, 298n83
Mauss, Marcel, 107
Melville, Herman, 237

memory: in Almodóvar's *Pain and Glory*, 240–52; Derrida on, 103, 105; in *Hamlet*, 99–109, 117–18, 289n29. *See also* archive

Miller, D. A., 62

Miller, Jacques-Alain, 144–45, 286n101, 293n27

Miller, J. Hillis, 59, 67, 73

Milner, Jean-Claude, 21

mirror stage, 25–26, 172

Mitchell, W. J. T., 111

More, Thomas, 127

Morrison, Toni, 232

Moten, Fred, 3, 24, 32, 164, 168, 171–72, 204–5, 271n101, 273n136

Muñoz, José Esteban, 21, 165

Musser, Amber Jamilla, 21, 23, 43

My Bondage and My Freedom (Douglass), 188–90

names, proper, 41, 144–45, 276n186

Nietzsche, Friedrich, 12–14

Nobus, Dany, 135

No Future (Edelman), 45–46, 208–16, 278n4, 307–8n14. *See also* futurism

objet a (object a), 6, 40–41, 173

obscenity, 171–78, 182–86, 190–95, 201

onticide, 24–32, 271n107

ontological impossibility. See *ab-sens*

ontology: queerness as limit of, 94; of woman, 11–12; Žižek on, 4, 21, 79

Pain and Glory (*Dolor y gloria*) (Almodóvar): about, 237–38; autofiction and, 242–45; blacking out, memory loss, and desire, 245–52; "flashbacks" and fictionalization of past, 241–45, 255; Lemmons's *Eve's Bayou* compared with, 248–49; opening scenes, 238–41; substrate of the image, 255–56

Pascal, Blaise, 53–55, 292n2

passion of the signifier, 86–90

Paul, St., 140, 157

pedag-archivalization: the drive, desire, and, 252–55; ethical economy and,

254; as imperative, xvi–xvii; Jacobs's *Incidents* and, 200; Lacan on, 211; Lemmons's *Eve's Bayou* and, 232; Rancière's politics of the resistant form and, 197, 208; Sartre on Socrates and, 258–60

pedophilo-phobia, 49, 279n14

phallus, 7, 142

philosophy: Badiou's antiphilosophy, 96, 287n8; freedom of the master and, 195–96; jouissance and, 35, 38, 42–43; reason, the universal, and, 192; slavery, freedom, and, 192–93; as sublimation of irony, 35–39; woman in, 11–12

plasticity, 13–15

Plath, Sylvia, 51

Plato, 32, 35–39, 156–58, 190–92

posthumanist theory, 212–13

Pride celebrations, 278n4

privileged and deprivileged subjects, 213–14

progressive politics: aesthetics and, 163, 167–69, 216, 309n33; becoming and, 211, 258; "community to come" and, 202; exclusion and, xviii–xix, 208, 236, 255; queerness and, 273n139

Psycho (Hitchcock), 60

psychoanalysis and *ab-sens*, 36–40

Putin, Vladimir, 185–86

queerness: as *ab-sens*, xv–xvi, 5, 19–21; abyss of enjoyment and, 195; agrammatical and anacoluthonic structure of, 26–27, 272n113; Almodóvar's *Pain and Glory* and, 252; capitalism and, 277n194; as catachrestic nomination, 267n33; Cole on, 208–10, 215; collectivity and, 93, 126, 171; counterpedagogy and "the Thing which is not" and, 47–48; the cut and, 43; definition, resistance to, 20; evil and, 127; Haneke's *Funny Games* and, 145; ideological value systems, relation to, 273n139; as limit of ontology, 94; mappings of, 272n128; queering as tropological figure, 260; slavery as peculiar institution, 185, 302n85; Warren's "black queer" as onticide, 24–32; zero and, 91–92, 94–95, 107; zero degree of, in Almodóvar's *Bad Education*, 81–82

race: the aesthetic and, 176; Benedicto on Lin murder and, 215; Black Lives Matter, x, xvii–xix; the Child, racial ideal of, 278n4; sexuality and, 21–22; structural, structured, and systemic racism, xi–xiv; trans* and, 27–28. *See also* Blackness
Ragland, Ellie, 8
Ramadanovic, Petar, 217–19, 253
Rancière, Jacques: aesthetic politics of resistant form and of the becoming-life of art, 166–71, 196–97, 208; dissensus, 94, 287n5
Real, the: Almodóvar's *Bad Education* and, 65–66, 75, 80–86; Almodóvar's *Pain and Glory* and, 251; Blackness and, 17; death drive and, 46; education and, 2–6; formal excess and, 90; Haneke's *Funny Games* and violence of, 157; irony and, 92; proper names and, 41; sublimation and, 120; survival and, 95; Žižek on politics of, 212
reason and slavery, 189–93
Reddy, Chandan, 21–23
"Red Shoes, The" (Anderson), 174–75, 194, 201
Reinhard, Kenneth, 8, 93
religion: Christianity, in Jacobs's *Incidents*, 197–205; as "original home of meaning," 205; right to discriminate based on, 188, 306n3
repetition compulsion, 140–42, 144, 172
reproductive futurism, 45–46, 53, 73, 91–94. *See also* futurism
resistant form, politics of, 169–71, 208
Rope (Hitchcock), 60–62, 145
Rotman, Brian, 56, 281n46
Roudinesco, Élisabeth, 295n44
Rousseau, Jean-Jacques, 49–52, 56
Russian law against "gay propaganda," 185–88, 193

Ruti, Mari, 211–16, 255, 258, 295n44, 309n29
Ryle, Simon, 119

sacrifice, Imaginary, 143, 296n58
Sade, Marquis de, 133–36, 149, 159, 174, 193–94
sadism, 149, 159–60
Santner, Eric, 91
Sartre, Jean-Paul, 258–60
Saussurian algorithm, 141–42, 153
Scarry, Elaine, 176
Schelling, Friedrich Wilhelm Joseph Von, 310n54
Schiller, Friedrich: on the aesthetic, 52–53, 55–56, 64, 162–66, 170, 180, 281nn34–35; on Beauty, 133, 166, 176; de Man on, 59; Haneke's *Funny Games* and, 147–48; Hegel on education and, 257–58; on Ludovici, 300n26
Schlegel, Friedrich, 92
Schlosser, Joel Alden, 32
Seal, Bobby, xi–xiii
self-dissolution, 213, 215, 309n38
sens-absexe: about, 6–11; in Almodóvar's *Bad Education*, 73; the Child and, 52; commandments and, 118–19; death of the world and, 132; Equiano and, 16; *Hamlet* and, 113; incest and, 218–19; sexual difference and, xiv–xv, 171; survival and, 98
sex: *ab-sens* and *sens-absexe*, xiv–xv, 6–11, 16, 21–24; *Bostock v. Clayton County*, x–xi, xvii–xix; freedom and, 194; *Hamlet* and, 112–15; Lacan's "there is no sexual relation," 6, 171; sexual privacy and sexualized knowledge, 184–85; subtraction and, xiv, 6–7, 11, 52, 127, 171, 262n14. *See also* incest
Sexton, Jared, 3, 20–21, 171–72, 206, 228, 311n78
sexual difference: *Bostock v. Clayton County* on, xvii; Malabou on, 15; paradigmatic nature of, 262n15; the Real of *ab-sens* and, 8–9; *sens-absexe* and, xiv–xv, 171, 262n14; sex not reducible to, 21

Thing, Lacanian (*das Ding*): about, 48–49; access to, as unbearable, 194–95; the Child and, 49; commandments and, 118–21; incestuous, 250; jouissance and, 106, 134; Lacan's vase and, 279n15; the primal cut of articulation and, 142; Rancière's politics of the resistant form and, 170–71

"Thing which is not," 47–48, 94, 118

torture-porn genre. See *Funny Games*

trans*: always already excluded, xix; as catachresis, 19, 20, 138; law and, x–xi, xviii–xix, 186, 188; race and, 27–28; religious freedom and, 188; transphobia, 236; visibility of, 26

Trump, Donald, x, 188

truth-procedures, 128–32

Turner, Nat, 181–82, 200–201

unbearable, the, 6, 9–10, 137, 194–95

unconscious, Lacanian: the cut and, 142; discontinuity and, 4; jouissance and, 135; as "neither being nor non-being," 33; pulsative function of, 11, 241, 246, 250; sexual meaning and, 266n26

unnameable, the, 130–34, 138–39, 158

Vertigo (Hitchcock), 60, 80

Viego, Antonio, 214

violence: Benjamin's critique of, 294n42; Blackness and, x, xix, 17–18; the Child and, 47; deconstruction as mythic violence, 111; distracted spectatorship and, 299n6; *Hamlet* and, 103; in Haneke's *Funny Games*, 149–52, 156–61, 269n65; in Jacobs's *Incidents*, 177, 180–85, 200–201; law and, 22; in Lemmons's *Eve's Bayou*, 229, 232; as projection of fragmentation, 271n107; queerness and, 26, 43; radical evil and, 65; of repetition compulsion, 144–45; subjectivity and, 26; the unbearable and, 20; the unnameable and, 132; Warren on heterosexism and anti-gay violence, 273n134; Warren's "Black

queer" onticide, 24–31, 43, 271n107; woman and, 14–15, 18, 269n79

Vlastos, Gregory, 32

void: of *ab-sens*, 21–24; *ab-sens* and, 47; allegory and, 92; in Almodóvar's *Bad Education*, 58–64, 70–73, 91, 94; in Almodóvar's *Pain and Glory*, 246–48, 252; Badiou's event and, 140–42; education and, 3, 159; evil and, 128; *Hamlet* and, 97, 105; Haneke's *Funny Games* and, 156, 161; Jacobs's *Incidents* and, 202; Lemmons's *Eve's Bayou* and, 232; *object a* and, 173; the position of the unthought and, 120; queerness and insistence on, 215; Rancière's aesthetics and, 171–72; sinthomosexuality and, 47; survival and, 95; the Thing and, 48–49; truth and, 131–32; as unnameable, 131; Wilderson on Blackness and, 291n87; the zero and, 62–63, 90, 94, 106–7, 118

Walters, Ronald, 303n98

Warminski, Andrzej, 56

Warren, Calvin, xvii–xix, 24–32, 43, 214, 271n107

Weber, Katherine, 185–86

"Whatever Happened to Interracial Love?" (Collins), 265n18

Wilder, Thornton, 290n70

Wilderson, Frank B., III, xii–xiii, 16–26, 28, 30–31, 34, 111, 122, 171, 269n79, 271n112, 291n87

Winter's Tale, The (Shakespeare), 237–38

woman: as *ab-sens*, 3, 11–15; atopia and, 32; violence and, 18, 269n79

Wynter, Sylvia, 3, 164–65, 169

Yerushalmi, Josef Hayim, 104, 108–10, 228

zero, the: allegorical historicization and, 92; death drive, memory, and, 106; Derrida and, 110; of enjoyment, 208, 307n7; Hamlet's "O" as, 97; irrationality of, 106–7; Laclau on, 282n48;

zero, the (continued)
the one and, 54–56, 67; queerness and, 81–82, 91–92, 94–95, 107; Rotman on Pascal and, 281n46; of signification, in Almodóvar's *Bad Education*, 59, 63, 67, 88–92; the void and, 62–63, 90, 94, 106–7, 118

Žižek, Slavoj: on Andersen's "The Red Shoes," 174–75; on the daimonion of Socrates, 41; on death drive and sublimation, 91, 107–8; on drive and desire, 279n10; on evil, 127–28, 253; on incest, 218, 250, 310–11n60; on jouissance, 10, 267n37; on *object a*, 41; "One" and "the good," 110; "ontological crack," 79; "ontological deadlock," 21; "ontological incompleteness of reality itself," 4; politics of the Real, 212; on Schelling, 310n54; on sublime material, 119; on the truth-event, 140–41

Zupančič, Alenka, 2, 7–11, 16, 65, 127–28, 173, 175, 266n26, 273n136